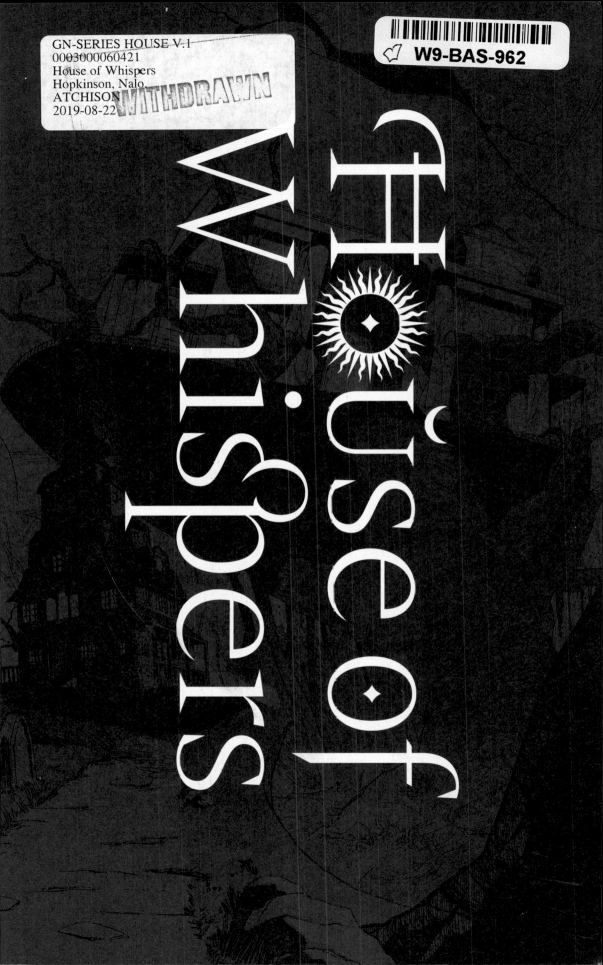

House of Whispers

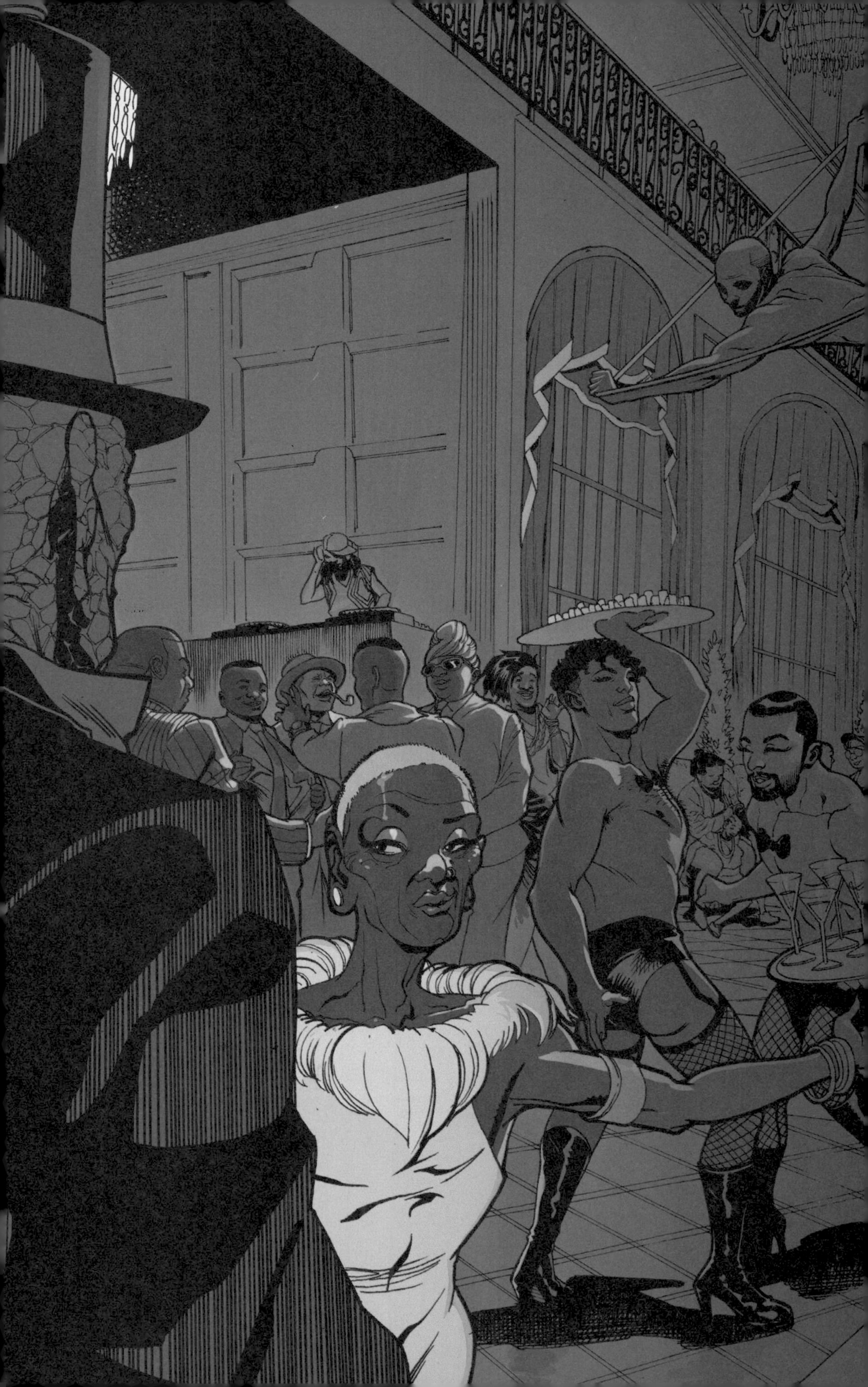

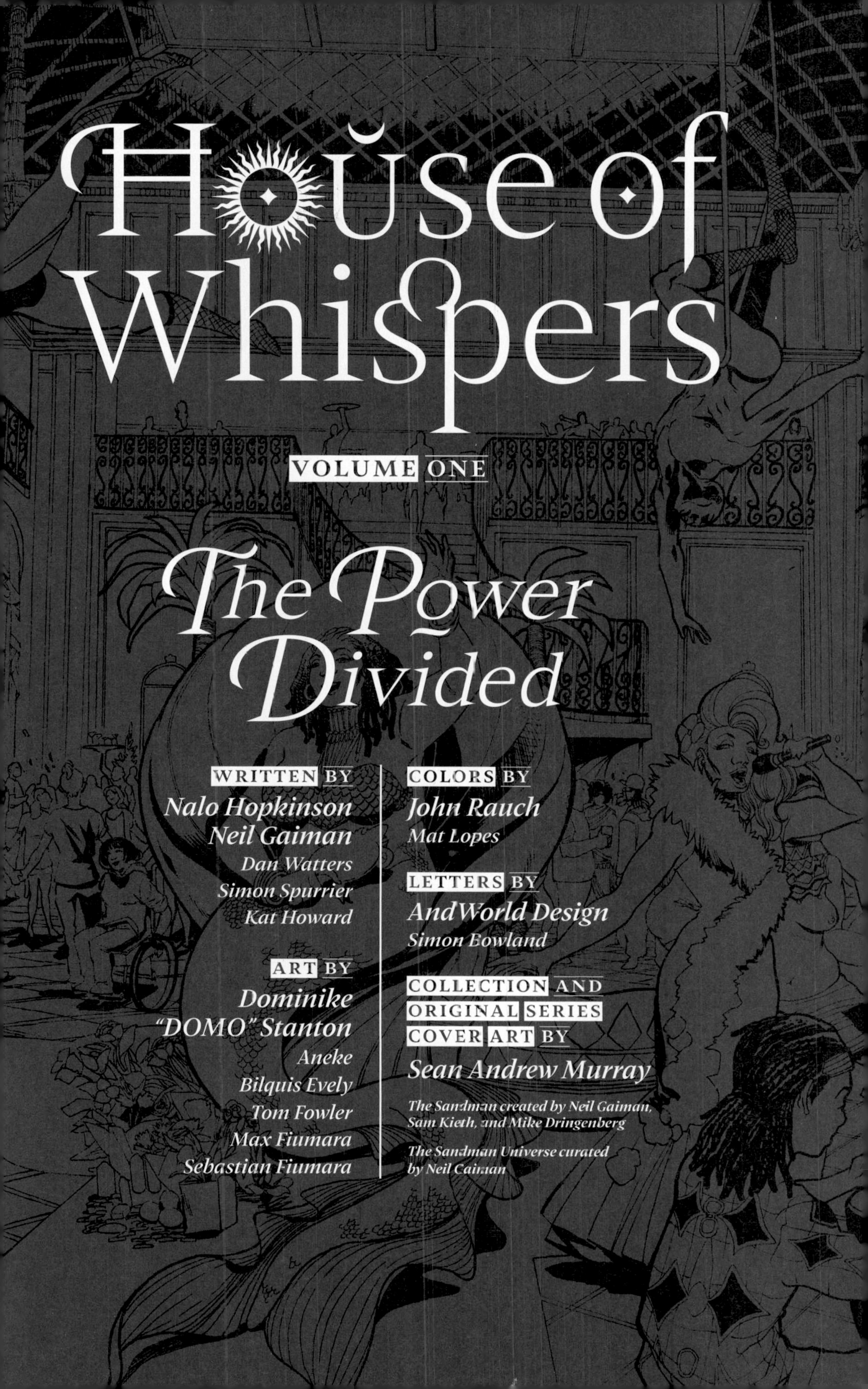

House of Whispers

VOLUME ONE

The Power Divided

WRITTEN BY
Nalo Hopkinson
Neil Gaiman
Dan Watters
Simon Spurrier
Kat Howard

ART BY
Dominike "DOMO" Stanton
Aneke
Bilquis Evely
Tom Fowler
Max Fiumara
Sebastian Fiumara

COLORS BY
John Rauch
Mat Lopes

LETTERS BY
AndWorld Design
Simon Bowland

COLLECTION AND ORIGINAL SERIES COVER ART BY
Sean Andrew Murray

The Sandman created by Neil Gaiman, Sam Kieth, and Mike Dringenberg

The Sandman Universe curated by Neil Gaiman

MOLLY MAHAN   *Editor – Original Series*
AMEDEO TURTURRO   *Associate Editor – Original Series*
MAGGIE HOWELL   *Assistant Editor – Original Series*
JEB WOODARD   *Group Editor – Collected Editions*
ERIKA ROTHBERG   *Editor – Collected Edition*
STEVE COOK   *Design Director – Books
                        and Publication Design*
DANIELLE DIGRADO   *Publication Production*

BOB HARRAS   *Senior VP – Editor-in-Chief, DC Comics*
MARK DOYLE   *Executive Editor, Vertigo & Black Label*

DAN DiDIO   *Publisher*
JIM LEE   *Publisher & Chief Creative Officer*
BOBBIE CHASE   *VP – New Publishing Initiatives & Talent Development*
DON FALLETTI   *VP – Manufacturing Operations & Workflow Management*
LAWRENCE GANEM   *VP – Talent Services*
ALISON GILL   *Senior VP – Manufacturing & Operations*
HANK KANALZ   *Senior VP – Publishing Strategy & Support Services*
DAN MIRON   *VP – Publishing Operations*
NICK J. NAPOLITANO   *VP – Manufacturing Administration & Design*
NANCY SPEARS   *VP – Sales*
MICHELE R. WELLS   *VP & Executive Editor, Young Reader*

HOUSE OF WHISPERS VOL. 1: THE POWER DIVIDED

Published by DC Comics. Compilation and all new material Copyright © 2019 DC Comics. All Rights Reserved.
Originally published in single magazine form in HOUSE OF WHISPERS 1-6, THE SANDMAN UNIVERSE 1. Copyright
© 2018, 2019 DC Comics. All Rights Reserved. All characters, their distinctive likenesses and related elements
featured in this publication are trademarks of DC Comics. The stories, characters and incidents featured in this
publication are entirely fictional. DC Comics does not read or accept unsolicited submissions of ideas, stories or
artwork. DC – a WarnerMedia Company.

DC Comics, 2900 West Alameda Ave., Burbank, CA 91505
Printed by LSC Communications, Owensville, MO, USA. 6/21/19. First Printing.
ISBN: 978-1-4012-9135-8

Library of Congress Cataloging-in-Publication Data is available.

PEFC Certified

This product is from
sustainably managed
forests and controlled
sources

PEFC/29-31-337   www.pefc.org

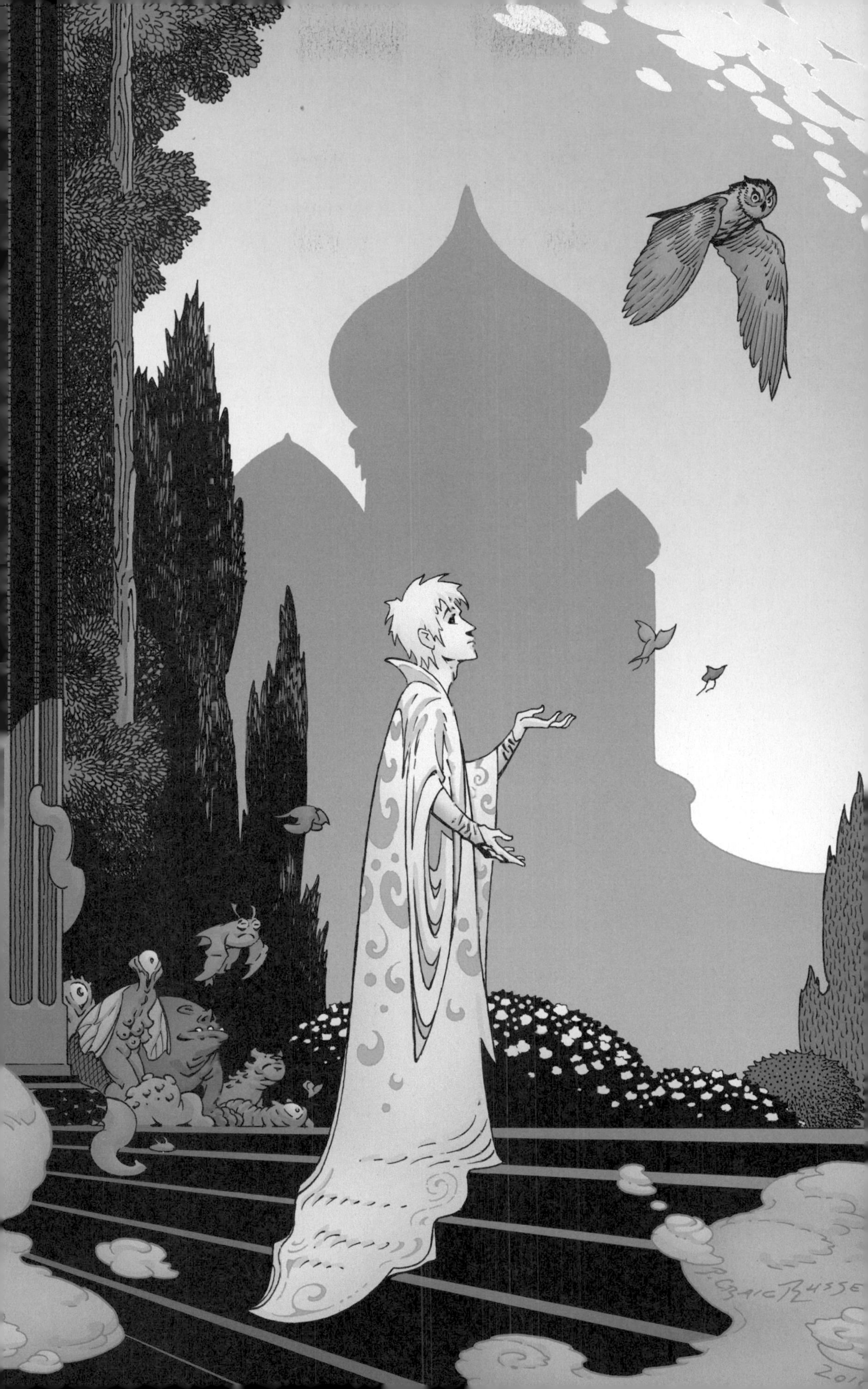
P. CRAIG RUSSE
201

The Sandman Universe

STORY BY
Neil Gaiman

WRITTEN BY
Simon Spurrier
Kat Howard
Nalo Hopkinson
Dan Watters

ILLUSTRATED BY
Bilquis Evely
Tom Fowler
Dominike "DOMO" Stanton
Max Fiumara
Sebastian Fiumara

COLORS BY
Mat Lopes

LETTERS BY
Simon Bowland

COVER ART BY
P. Craig Russell

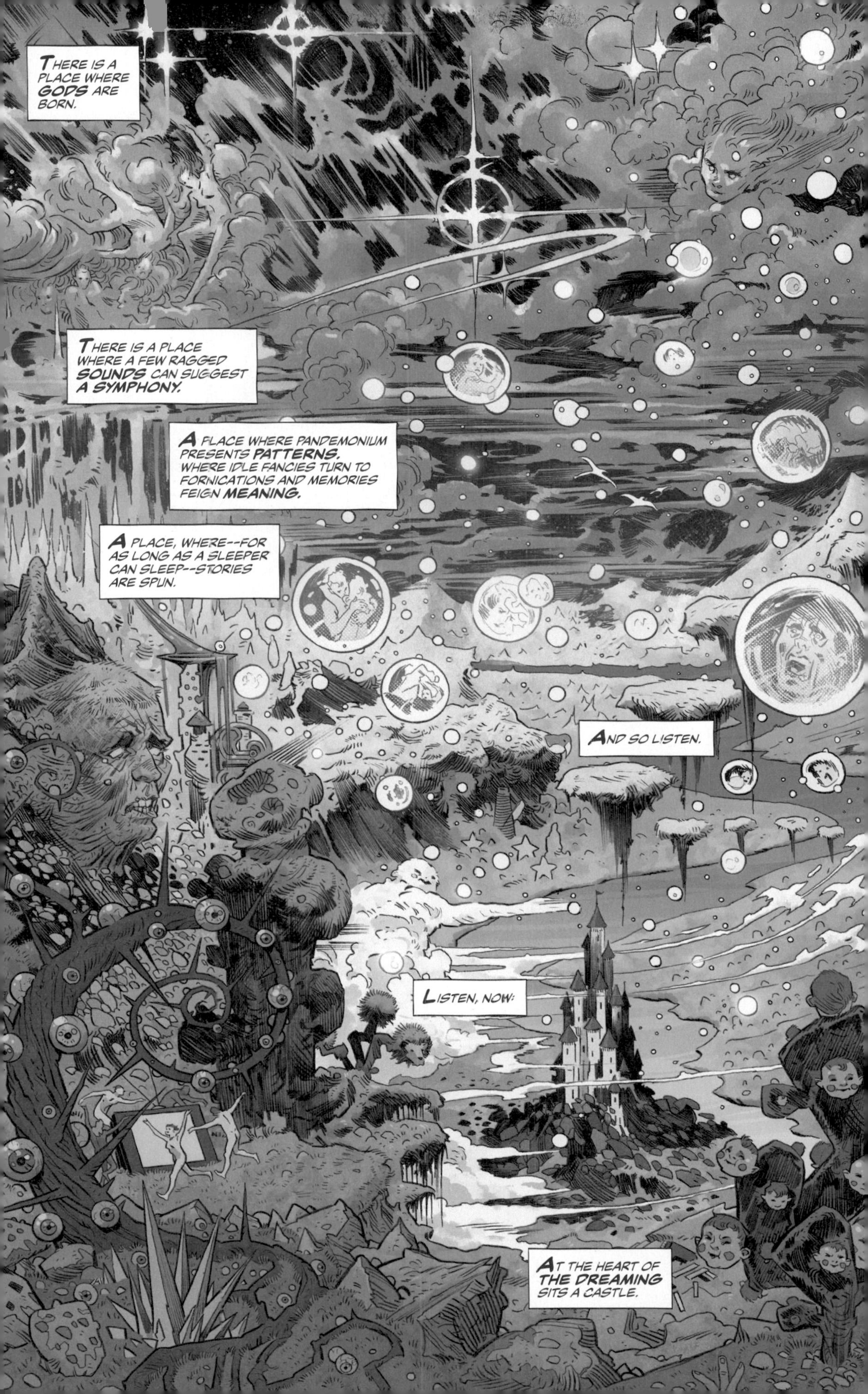
THERE IS A PLACE WHERE GODS ARE BORN.
THERE IS A PLACE WHERE A FEW RAGGED SOUNDS CAN SUGGEST A SYMPHONY.
A PLACE WHERE PANDEMONIUM PRESENTS PATTERNS. WHERE IDLE FANCIES TURN TO FORNICATIONS AND MEMORIES FEIGN MEANING.
A PLACE, WHERE--FOR AS LONG AS A SLEEPER CAN SLEEP--STORIES ARE SPUN.
AND SO LISTEN.
LISTEN, NOW:
AT THE HEART OF THE DREAMING SITS A CASTLE.

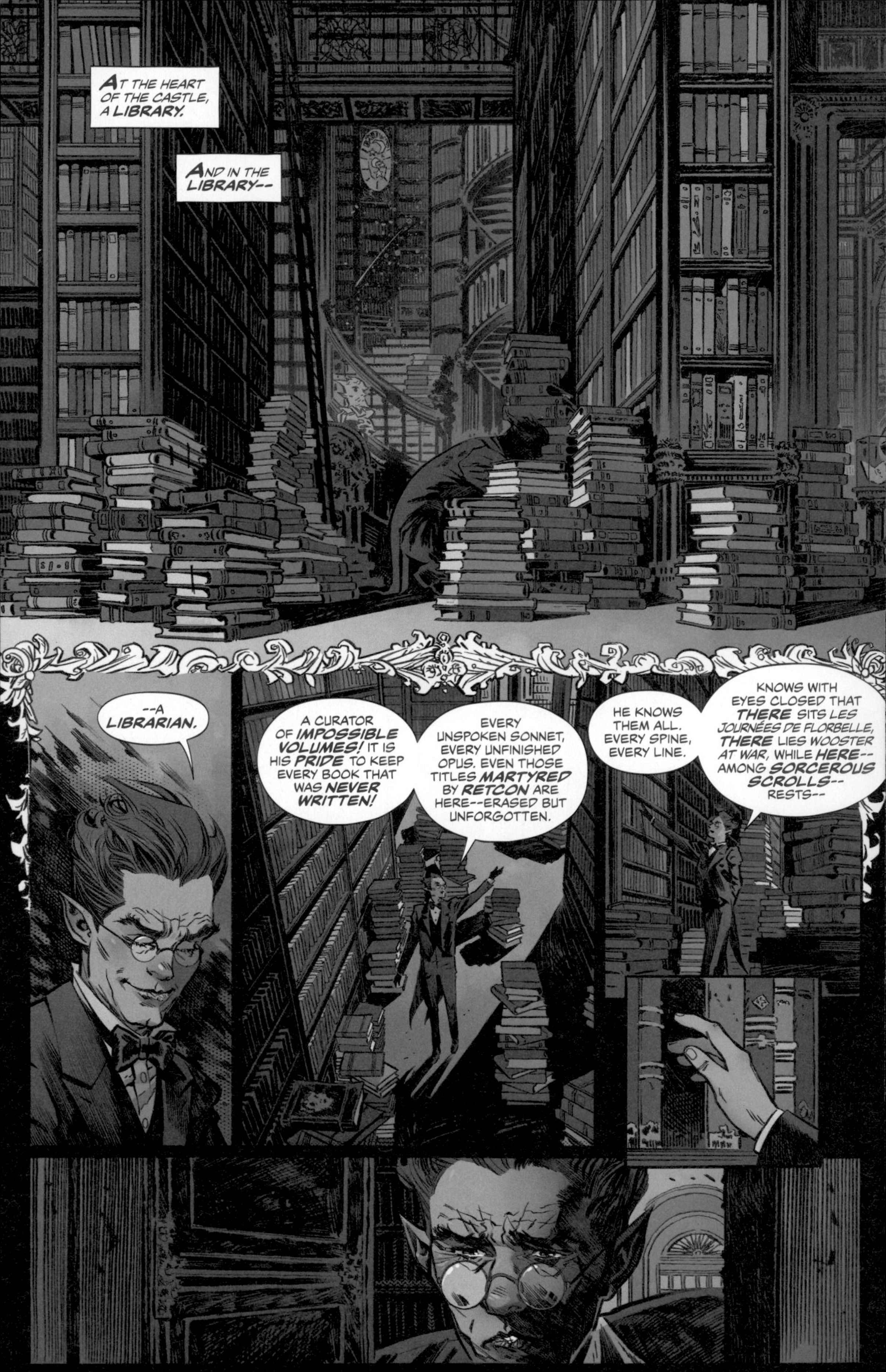
AT THE HEART OF THE CASTLE, A LIBRARY.
AND IN THE LIBRARY--
--A LIBRARIAN.
A CURATOR OF IMPOSSIBLE VOLUMES! IT IS HIS PRIDE TO KEEP EVERY BOOK THAT WAS NEVER WRITTEN!
EVERY UNSPOKEN SONNET, EVERY UNFINISHED OPUS. EVEN THOSE TITLES MARTYRED BY RETCON ARE HERE--ERASED BUT UNFORGOTTEN.
HE KNOWS THEM ALL. EVERY SPINE, EVERY LINE.
KNOWS WITH EYES CLOSED THAT THERE SITS LES JOURNÉES DE FLORBELLE, THERE LIES WOOSTER AT WAR, WHILE HERE--AMONG SORCEROUS SCROLLS--RESTS--

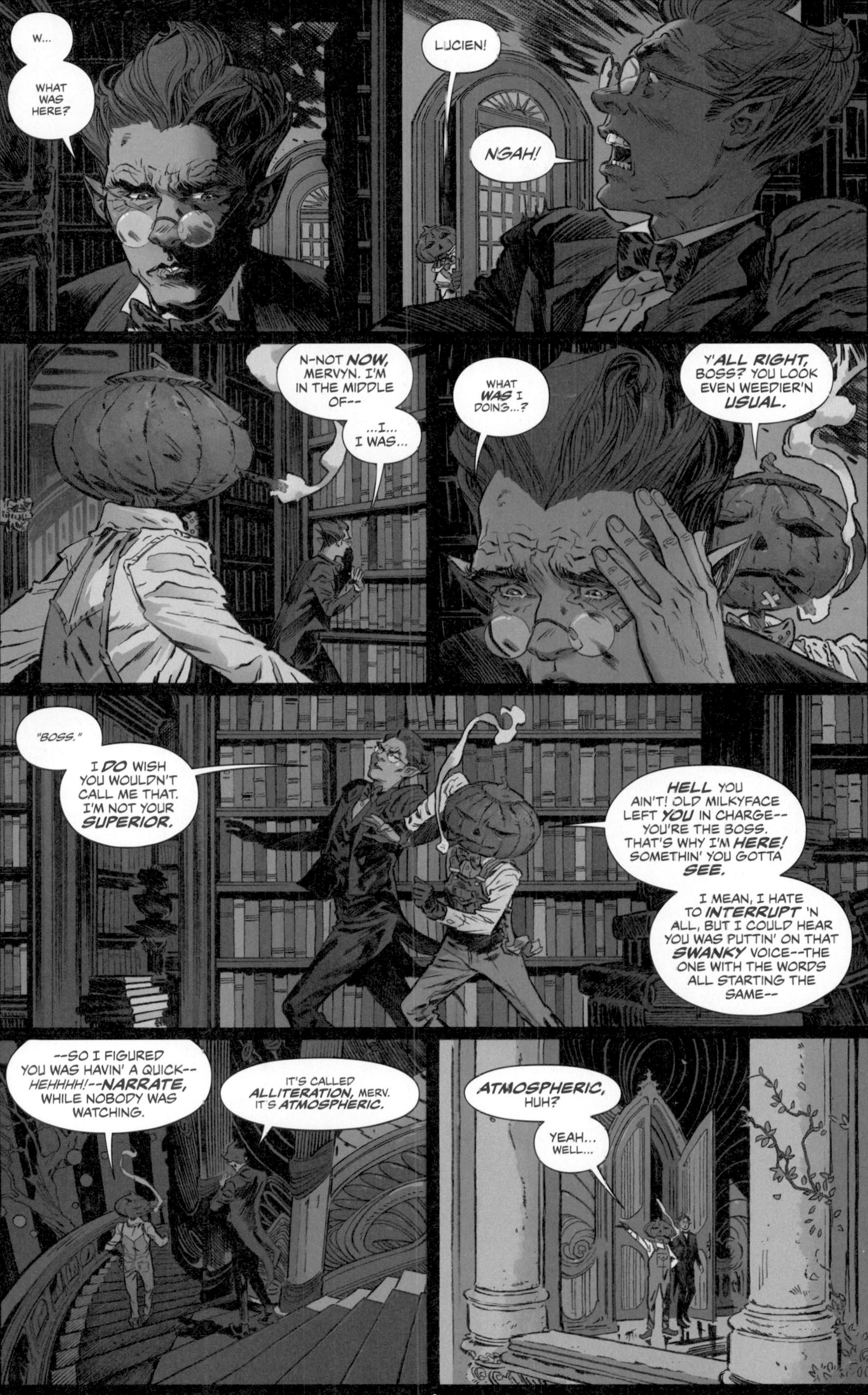
W...
WHAT WAS HERE?
LUCIEN!
NGAH!
N-NOT NOW, MERVYN. I'M IN THE MIDDLE OF--
...I... I WAS...
WHAT WAS I DOING...?
Y'ALL RIGHT, BOSS? YOU LOOK EVEN WEEDIER'N USUAL.
"BOSS."
I DO WISH YOU WOULDN'T CALL ME THAT. I'M NOT YOUR SUPERIOR.
HELL YOU AIN'T! OLD MILKYFACE LEFT YOU IN CHARGE--YOU'RE THE BOSS. THAT'S WHY I'M HERE! SOMETHIN' YOU GOTTA SEE.
I MEAN, I HATE TO INTERRUPT 'N ALL, BUT I COULD HEAR YOU WAS PUTTIN' ON THAT SWANKY VOICE--THE ONE WITH THE WORDS ALL STARTING THE SAME--
--SO I FIGURED YOU WAS HAVIN' A QUICK--HEHHHH!--NARRATE, WHILE NOBODY WAS WATCHING.
IT'S CALLED ALLITERATION, MERV. IT'S ATMOSPHERIC.
ATMOSPHERIC, HUH?
YEAH... WELL...

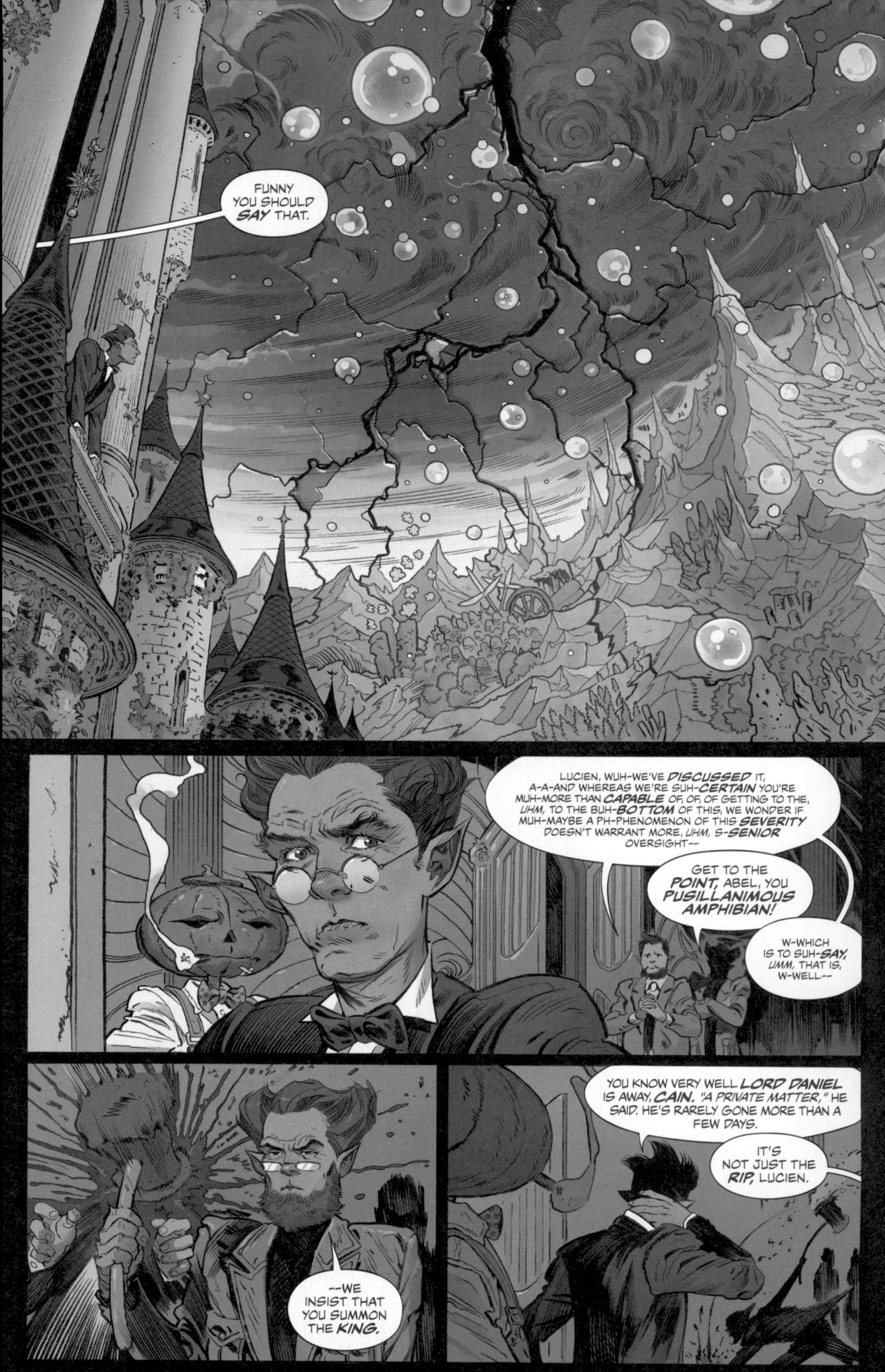
FUNNY YOU SHOULD SAY THAT.
LUCIEN, WUH-WE'VE DISCUSSED IT, A-A-AND WHEREAS WE'RE SUH-CERTAIN YOU'RE MUH-MORE THAN CAPABLE OF, OF, OF GETTING TO THE, UHM, TO THE BUH-BOTTOM OF THIS, WE WONDER IF MUH-MAYBE A PH-PHENOMENON OF THIS SEVERITY DOESN'T WARRANT MORE, UHM, S-SENIOR OVERSIGHT--
GET TO THE POINT, ABEL, YOU PUSILLANIMOUS AMPHIBIAN!
W-WHICH IS TO SUH-SAY, UMM, THAT IS, W-WELL--
--WE INSIST THAT YOU SUMMON THE KING.
YOU KNOW VERY WELL LORD DANIEL IS AWAY, CAIN. "A PRIVATE MATTER," HE SAID. HE'S RARELY GONE MORE THAN A FEW DAYS.
IT'S NOT JUST THE RIP, LUCIEN.

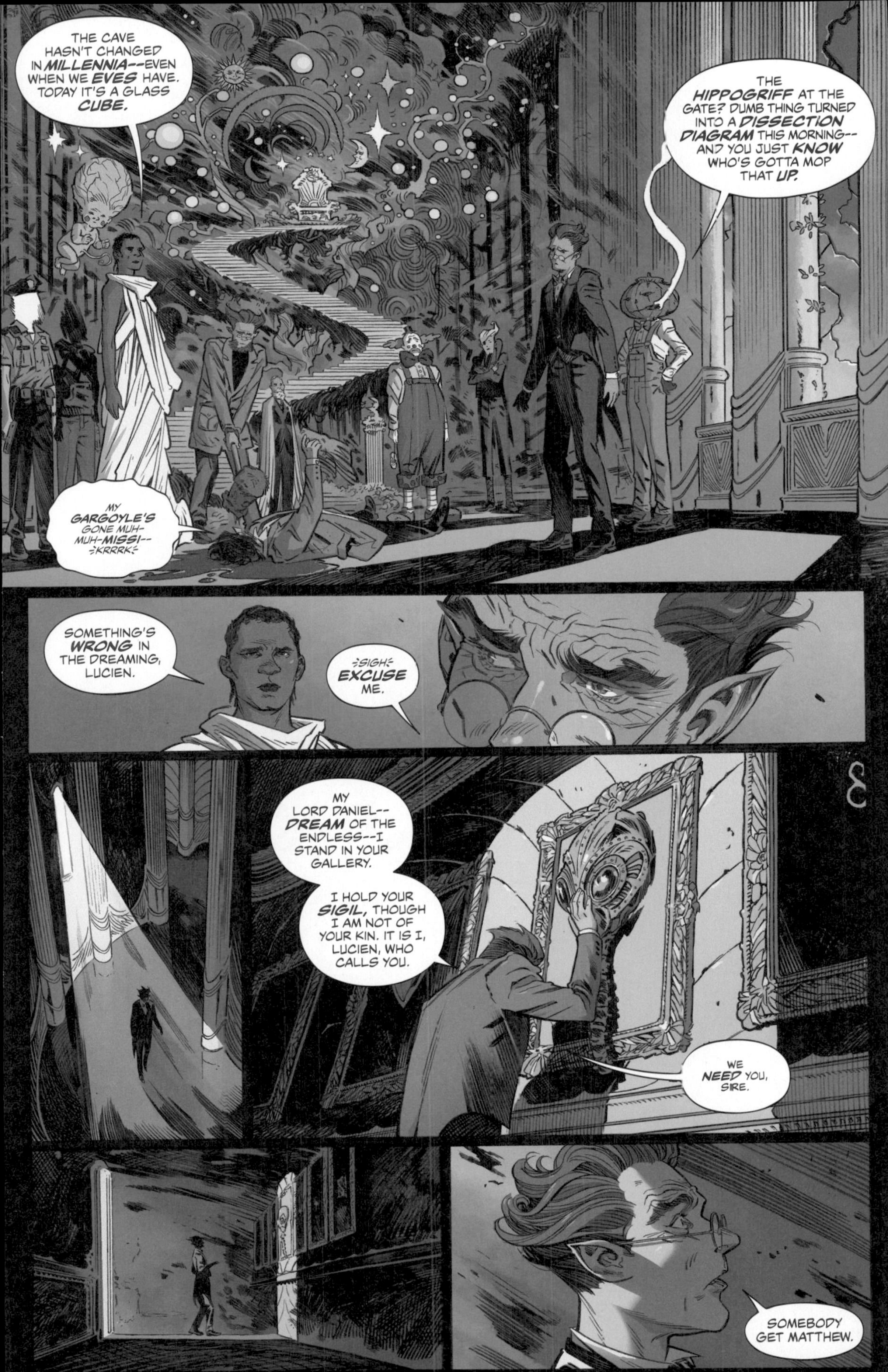

THE CAVE HASN'T CHANGED IN MILLENNIA--EVEN WHEN WE EVES HAVE. TODAY IT'S A GLASS CUBE.
THE HIPPOGRIFF AT THE GATE? DUMB THING TURNED INTO A DISSECTION DIAGRAM THIS MORNING--AND YOU JUST KNOW WHO'S GOTTA MOP THAT UP.
MY GARGOYLE'S GONE MUH-MUH-MISSI--KRRRK
SOMETHING'S WRONG IN THE DREAMING, LUCIEN.
SIGH EXCUSE ME.
MY LORD DANIEL--DREAM OF THE ENDLESS--I STAND IN YOUR GALLERY.
I HOLD YOUR SIGIL, THOUGH I AM NOT OF YOUR KIN. IT IS I, LUCIEN, WHO CALLS YOU.
WE NEED YOU, SIRE.
SOMEBODY GET MATTHEW.

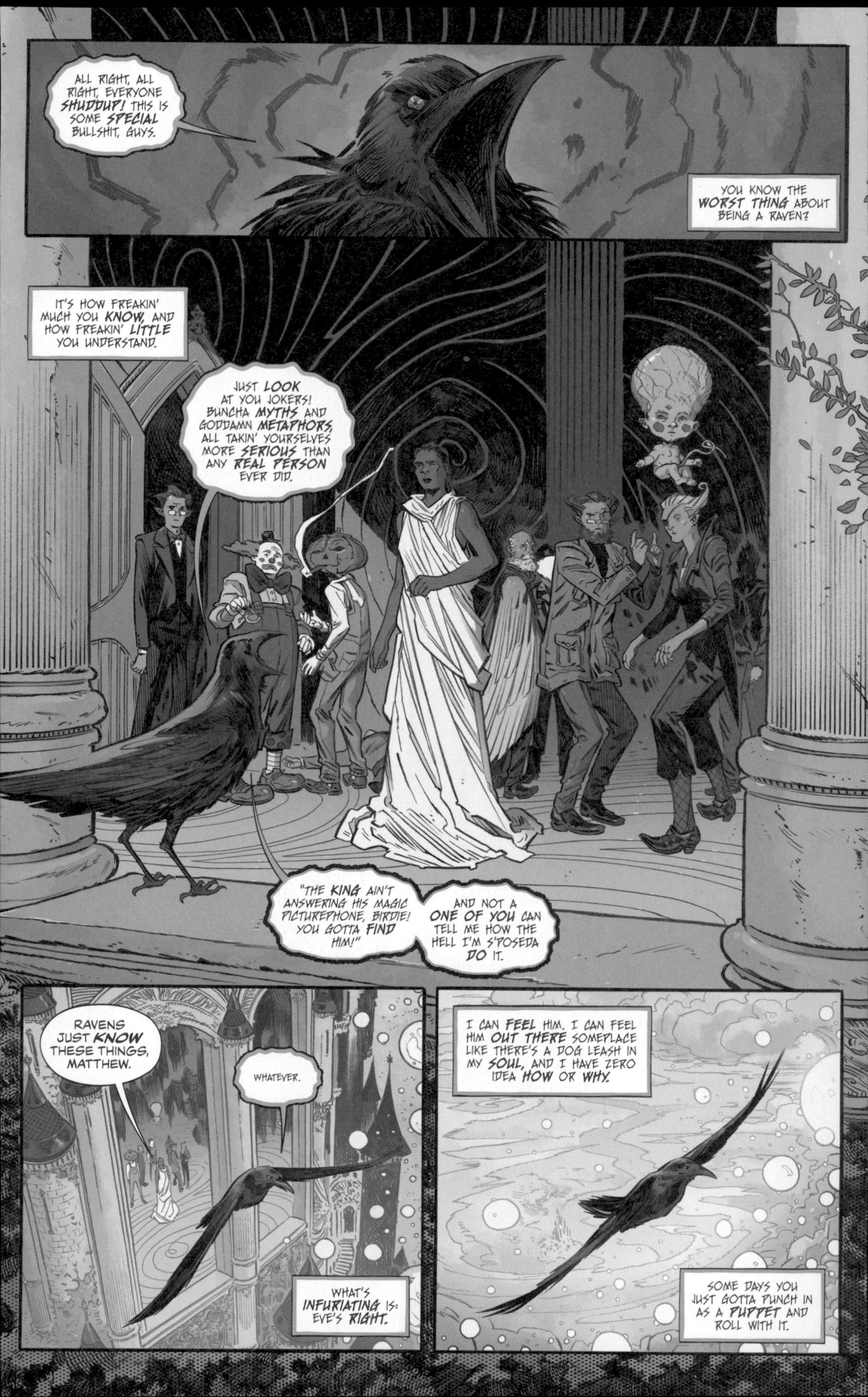

ALL RIGHT, ALL RIGHT, EVERYONE SHUDDUP! THIS IS SOME SPECIAL BULLSHIT, GUYS.
YOU KNOW THE WORST THING ABOUT BEING A RAVEN?
IT'S HOW FREAKIN' MUCH YOU KNOW, AND HOW FREAKIN' LITTLE YOU UNDERSTAND.
JUST LOOK AT YOU JOKERS! BUNCHA MYTHS AND GODDAMN METAPHORS, ALL TAKIN' YOURSELVES MORE SERIOUS THAN ANY REAL PERSON EVER DID.
"THE KING AIN'T ANSWERING HIS MAGIC PICTUREPHONE, BIRDIE! YOU GOTTA FIND HIM!"
AND NOT A ONE OF YOU CAN TELL ME HOW THE HELL I'M S'POSEDA DO IT.
RAVENS JUST KNOW THESE THINGS, MATTHEW.
WHATEVER.
WHAT'S INFURIATING IS: EVE'S RIGHT.
I CAN FEEL HIM. I CAN FEEL HIM OUT THERE SOMEPLACE LIKE THERE'S A DOG LEASH IN MY SOUL, AND I HAVE ZERO IDEA HOW OR WHY.
SOME DAYS YOU JUST GOTTA PUNCH IN AS A PUPPET AND ROLL WITH IT.

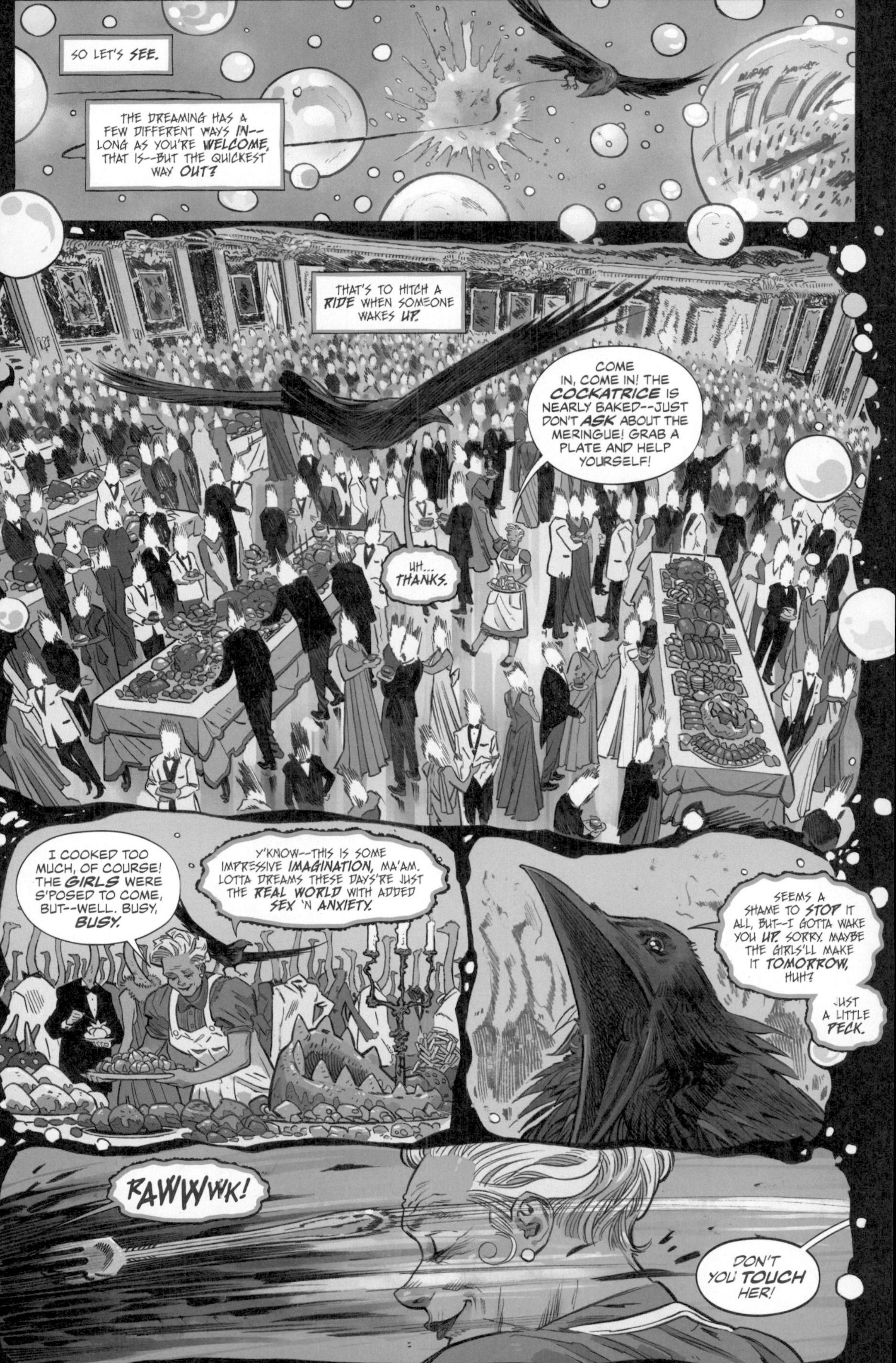
SO LET'S SEE.
THE DREAMING HAS A FEW DIFFERENT WAYS IN--LONG AS YOU'RE WELCOME, THAT IS--BUT THE QUICKEST WAY OUT?
THAT'S TO HITCH A RIDE WHEN SOMEONE WAKES UP.
COME IN, COME IN! THE COCKATRICE IS NEARLY BAKED--JUST DON'T ASK ABOUT THE MERINGUE! GRAB A PLATE AND HELP YOURSELF!
UH... THANKS.
I COOKED TOO MUCH, OF COURSE! THE GIRLS WERE S'POSED TO COME, BUT--WELL. BUSY, BUSY.
Y'KNOW--THIS IS SOME IMPRESSIVE IMAGINATION, MA'AM. LOTTA DREAMS THESE DAYS'RE JUST THE REAL WORLD WITH ADDED SEX 'N ANXIETY.
SEEMS A SHAME TO STOP IT ALL, BUT--I GOTTA WAKE YOU UP. SORRY. MAYBE THE GIRLS'LL MAKE IT TOMORROW, HUH?
JUST A LITTLE PECK.
RAWWWK!
DON'T YOU TOUCH HER!

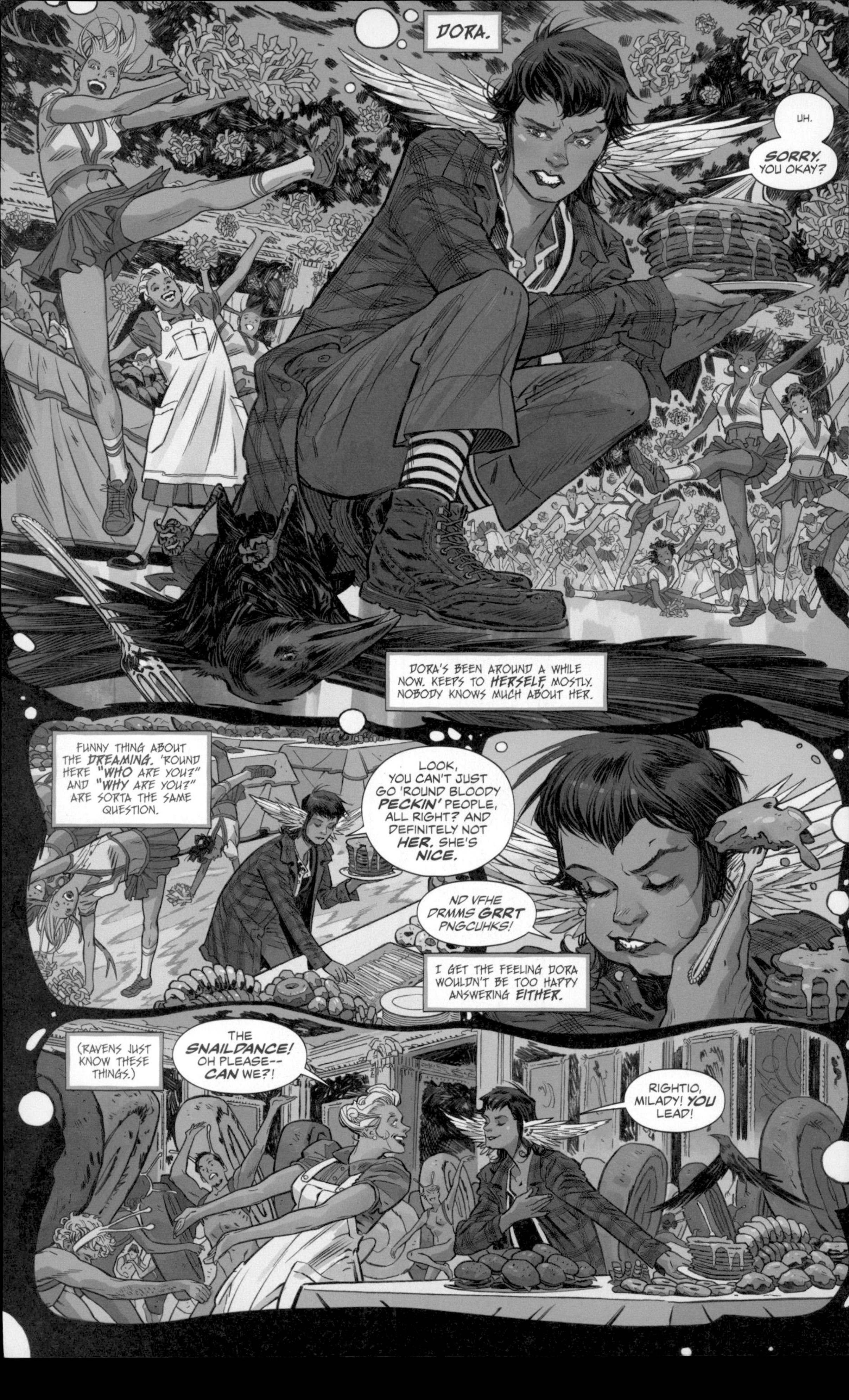
DORA.
UH.
SORRY. YOU OKAY?
DORA'S BEEN AROUND A WHILE NOW. KEEPS TO HERSELF, MOSTLY. NOBODY KNOWS MUCH ABOUT HER.
FUNNY THING ABOUT THE DREAMING. 'ROUND HERE "WHO ARE YOU?" AND "WHY ARE YOU?" ARE SORTA THE SAME QUESTION.
LOOK, YOU CAN'T JUST GO 'ROUND BLOODY PECKIN' PEOPLE, ALL RIGHT? AND DEFINITELY NOT HER. SHE'S NICE.
ND VFHE DRMMS GRRT PNGCUHKS!
I GET THE FEELING DORA WOULDN'T BE TOO HAPPY ANSWERING EITHER.
(RAVENS JUST KNOW THESE THINGS.)
THE SNAILDANCE! OH PLEASE--CAN WE?!
RIGHTIO, MILADY! YOU LEAD!

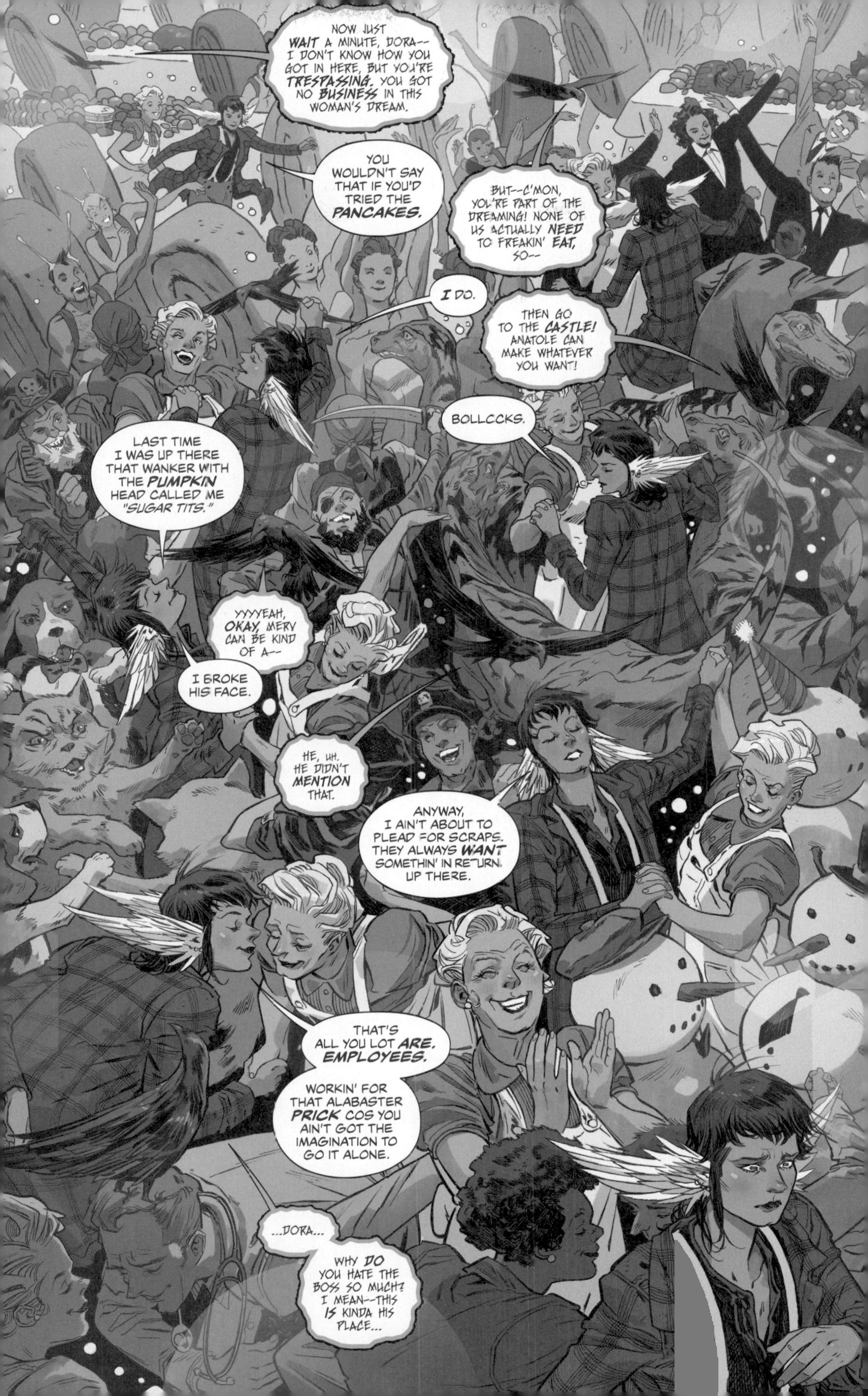
NOW JUST WAIT A MINUTE, DORA-- I DON'T KNOW HOW YOU GOT IN HERE, BUT YOU'RE TRESPASSING. YOU GOT NO BUSINESS IN THIS WOMAN'S DREAM.
YOU WOULDN'T SAY THAT IF YOU'D TRIED THE PANCAKES.
BUT--C'MON, YOU'RE PART OF THE DREAMING! NONE OF US ACTUALLY NEED TO FREAKIN' EAT, SO--
I DO.
THEN GO TO THE CASTLE! ANATOLE CAN MAKE WHATEVER YOU WANT!
BOLLOCKS.
LAST TIME I WAS UP THERE THAT WANKER WITH THE PUMPKIN HEAD CALLED ME "SUGAR TITS."
YYYYEAH, OKAY, MERV CAN BE KIND OF A--
I BROKE HIS FACE.
HE, UH. HE DIDN'T MENTION THAT.
ANYWAY, I AIN'T ABOUT TO PLEAD FOR SCRAPS. THEY ALWAYS WANT SOMETHIN' IN RETURN UP THERE.
THAT'S ALL YOU LOT ARE. EMPLOYEES.
WORKIN' FOR THAT ALABASTER PRICK COS YOU AIN'T GOT THE IMAGINATION TO GO IT ALONE.
...DORA...
WHY DO YOU HATE THE BOSS SO MUCH? I MEAN--THIS IS KINDA HIS PLACE...

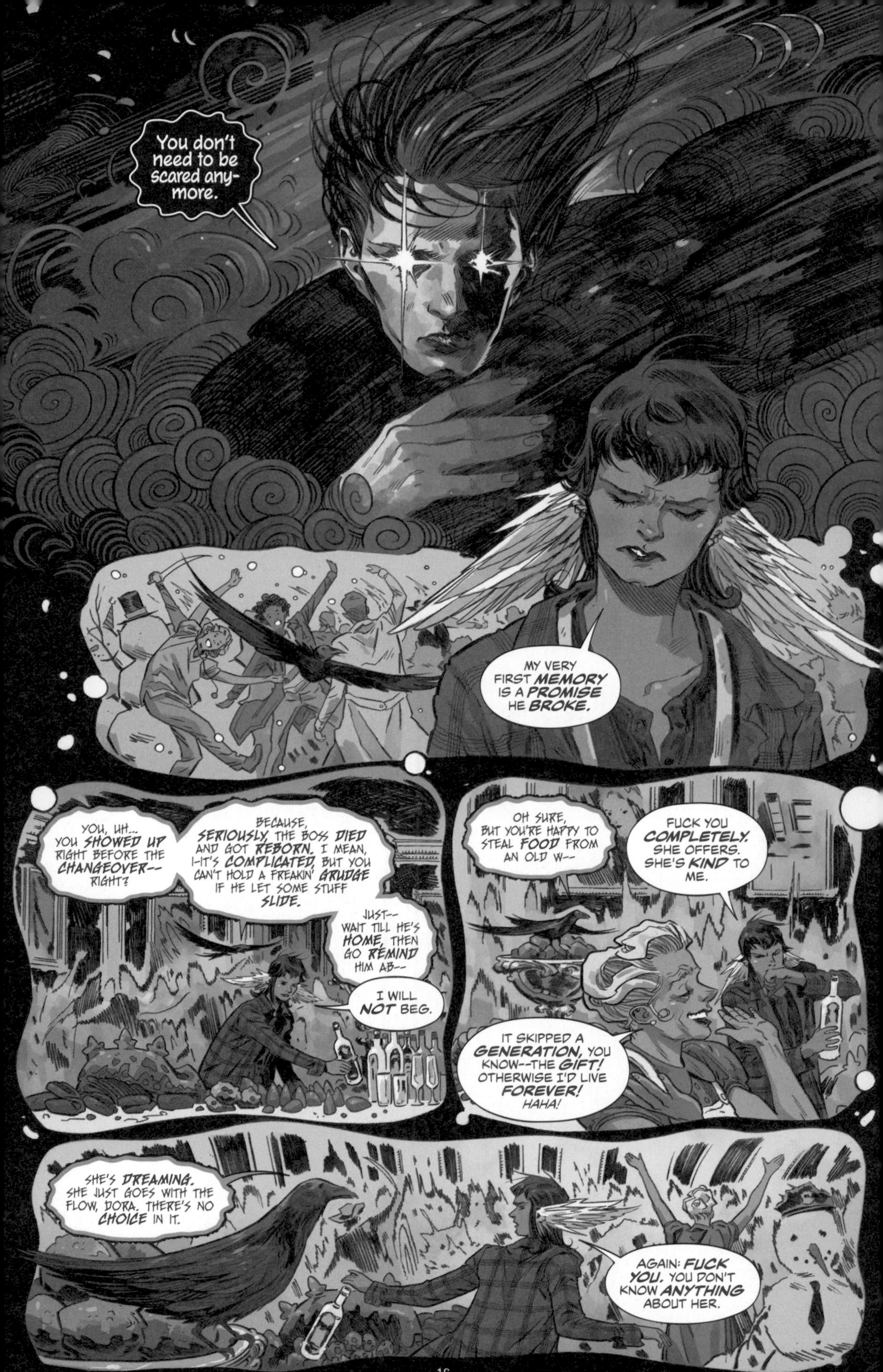
You don't need to be scared anymore.
MY VERY FIRST MEMORY IS A PROMISE HE BROKE.
YOU, UH... YOU SHOWED UP RIGHT BEFORE THE CHANGEOVER--RIGHT?
BECAUSE, SERIOUSLY, THE BOSS DIED AND GOT REBORN. I MEAN, I-IT'S COMPLICATED, BUT YOU CAN'T HOLD A FREAKIN' GRUDGE IF HE LET SOME STUFF SLIDE.
JUST-- WAIT TILL HE'S HOME, THEN GO REMIND HIM AB--
I WILL NOT BEG.
OH SURE, BUT YOU'RE HAPPY TO STEAL FOOD FROM AN OLD W--
FUCK YOU COMPLETELY. SHE OFFERS. SHE'S KIND TO ME.
IT SKIPPED A GENERATION, YOU KNOW--THE GIFT! OTHERWISE I'D LIVE FOREVER! HAHA!
SHE'S DREAMING. SHE JUST GOES WITH THE FLOW, DORA. THERE'S NO CHOICE IN IT.
AGAIN: FUCK YOU. YOU DON'T KNOW ANYTHING ABOUT HER.

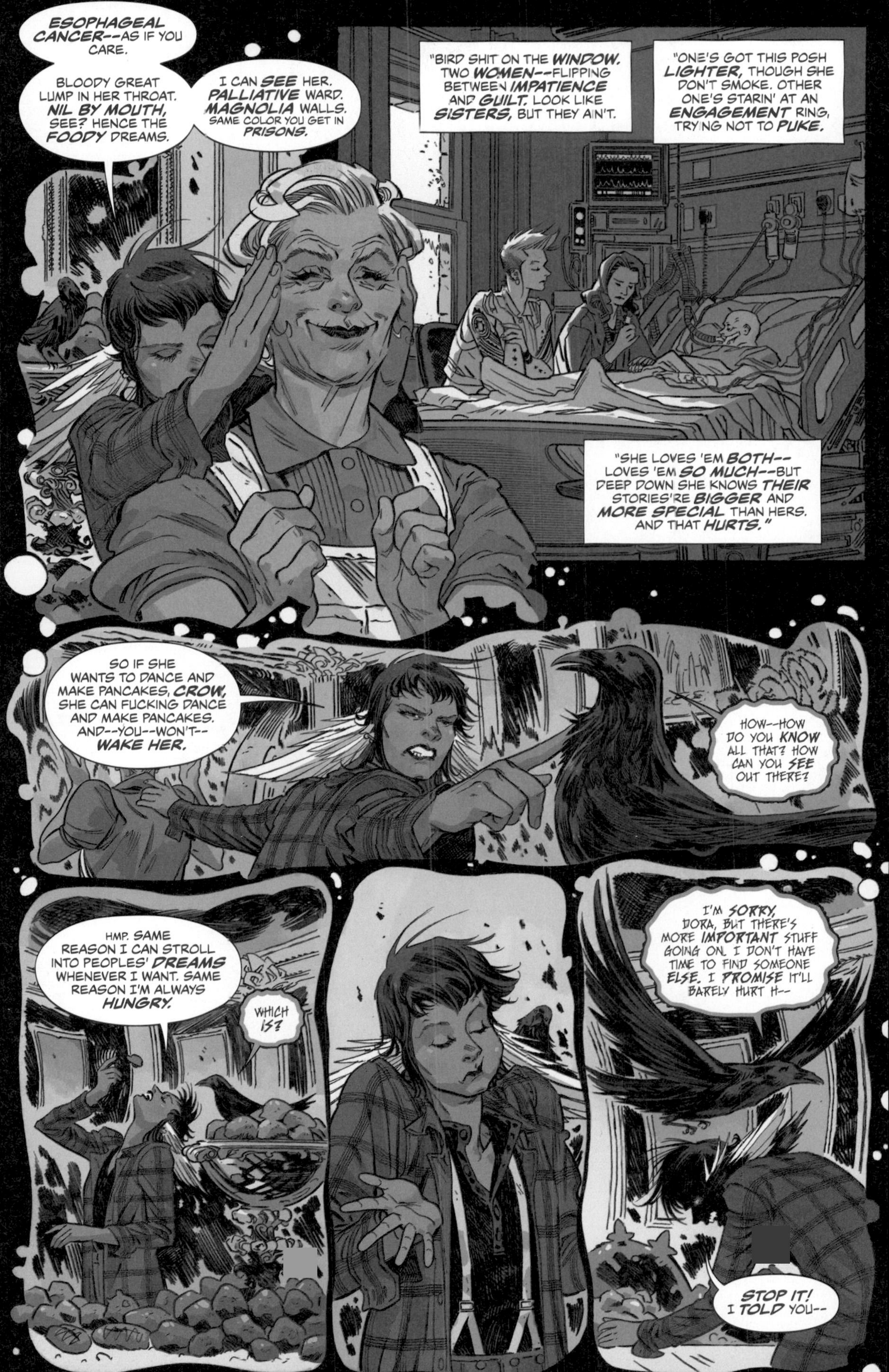
ESOPHAGEAL CANCER--AS IF YOU CARE.
BLOODY GREAT LUMP IN HER THROAT. NIL BY MOUTH, SEE? HENCE THE FOODY DREAMS.
I CAN SEE HER. PALLIATIVE WARD. MAGNOLIA WALLS. SAME COLOR YOU GET IN PRISONS.
"BIRD SHIT ON THE WINDOW. TWO WOMEN--FLIPPING BETWEEN IMPATIENCE AND GUILT. LOOK LIKE SISTERS, BUT THEY AIN'T.
"ONE'S GOT THIS POSH LIGHTER, THOUGH SHE DON'T SMOKE. OTHER ONE'S STARIN' AT AN ENGAGEMENT RING, TRYING NOT TO PUKE.
"SHE LOVES 'EM BOTH--LOVES 'EM SO MUCH--BUT DEEP DOWN SHE KNOWS THEIR STORIES'RE BIGGER AND MORE SPECIAL THAN HERS. AND THAT HURTS."
SO IF SHE WANTS TO DANCE AND MAKE PANCAKES, CROW, SHE CAN FUCKING DANCE AND MAKE PANCAKES. AND--YOU--WON'T--WAKE HER.
HOW--HOW DO YOU KNOW ALL THAT? HOW CAN YOU SEE OUT THERE?
HMP. SAME REASON I CAN STROLL INTO PEOPLES' DREAMS WHENEVER I WANT. SAME REASON I'M ALWAYS HUNGRY.
WHICH IS?
I'M SORRY, DORA, BUT THERE'S MORE IMPORTANT STUFF GOING ON. I DON'T HAVE TIME TO FIND SOMEONE ELSE. I PROMISE IT'LL BARELY HURT H--
STOP IT! I TOLD YOU--

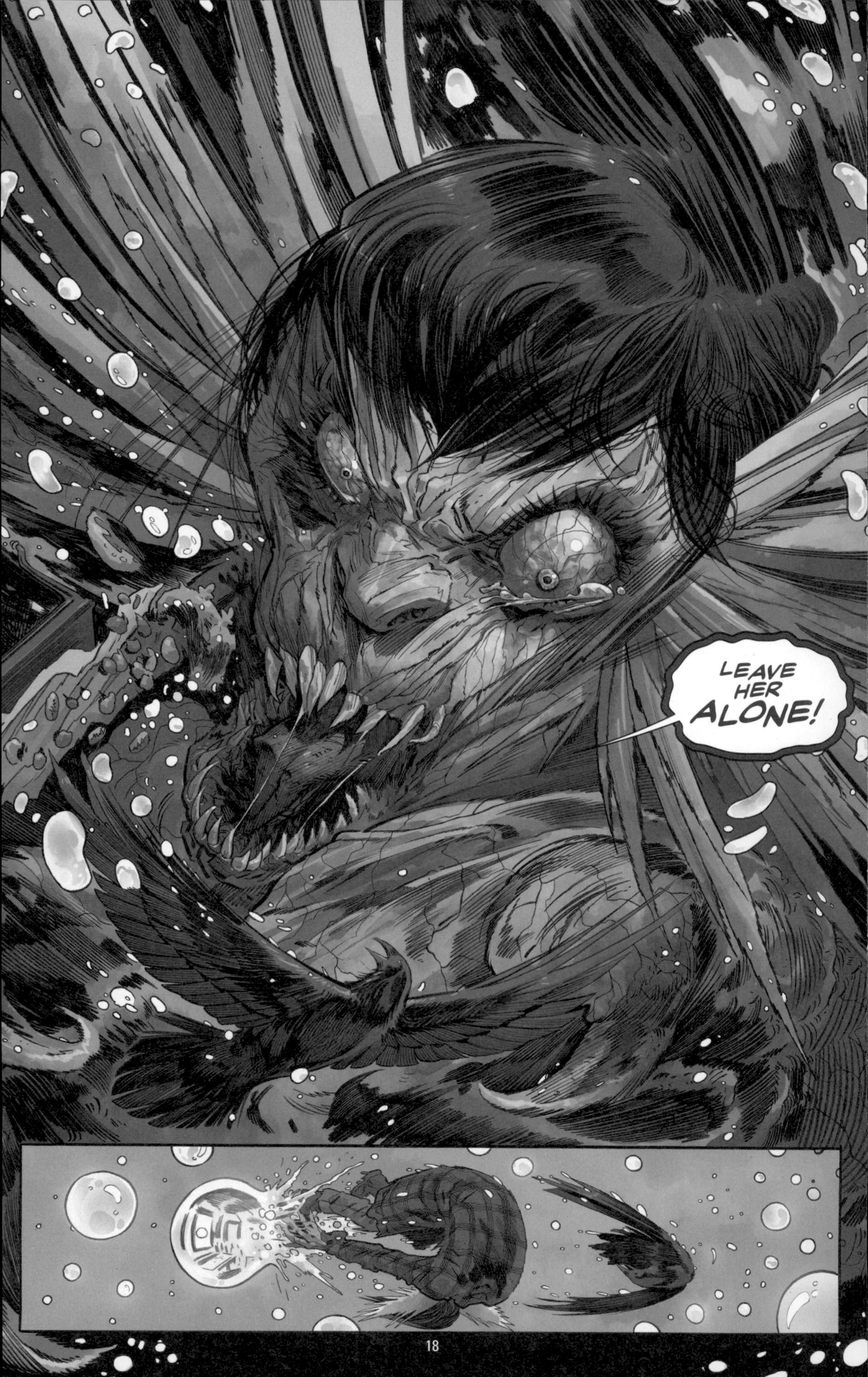
LEAVE HER ALONE!

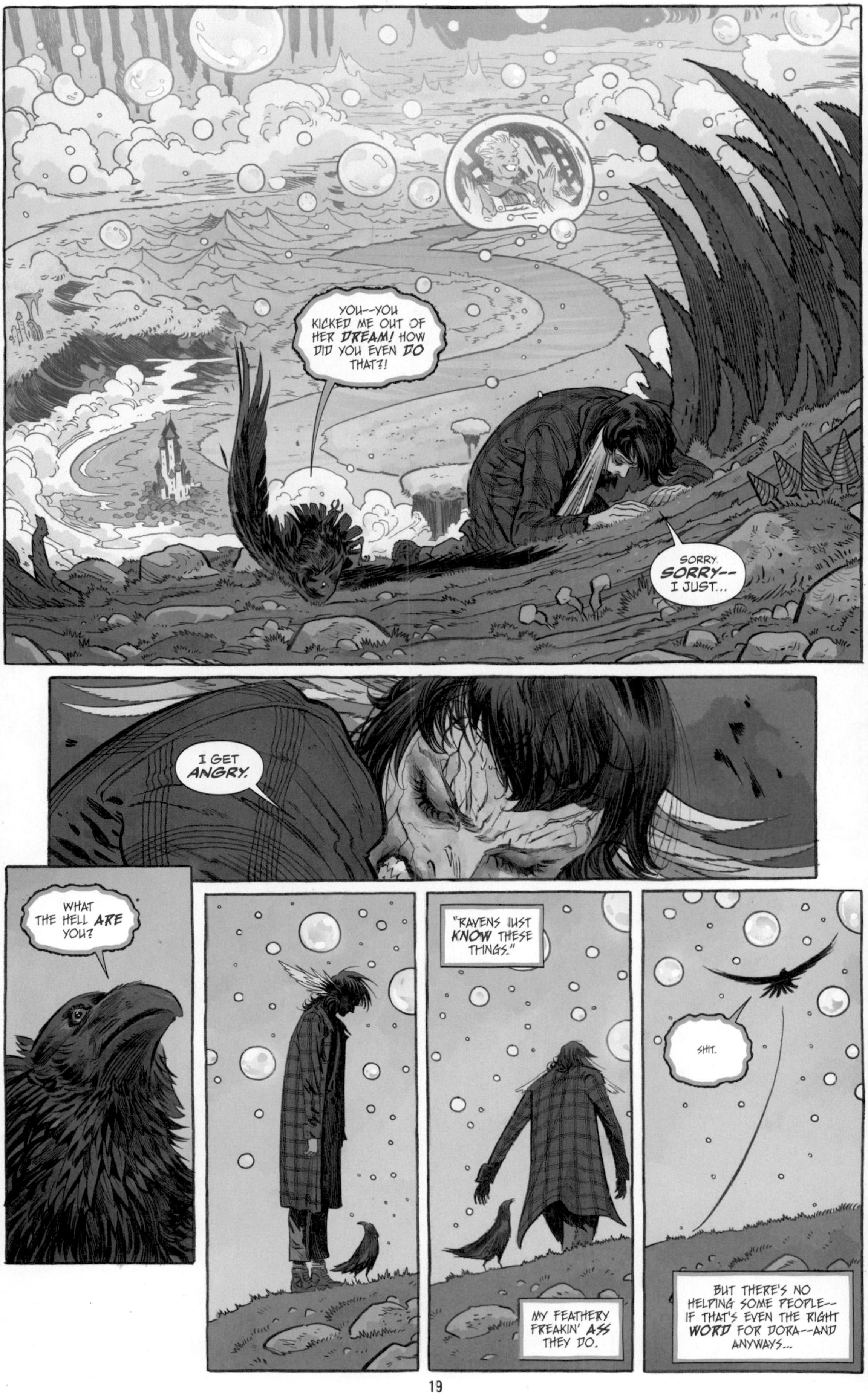
YOU--YOU KICKED ME OUT OF HER DREAM! HOW DID YOU EVEN DO THAT?!
SORRY. SORRY-- I JUST...
I GET ANGRY.
WHAT THE HELL ARE YOU?
"RAVENS JUST KNOW THESE THINGS."
MY FEATHERY FREAKIN' ASS THEY DO.
SHIT.
BUT THERE'S NO HELPING SOME PEOPLE-- IF THAT'S EVEN THE RIGHT WORD FOR DORA--AND ANYWAYS...

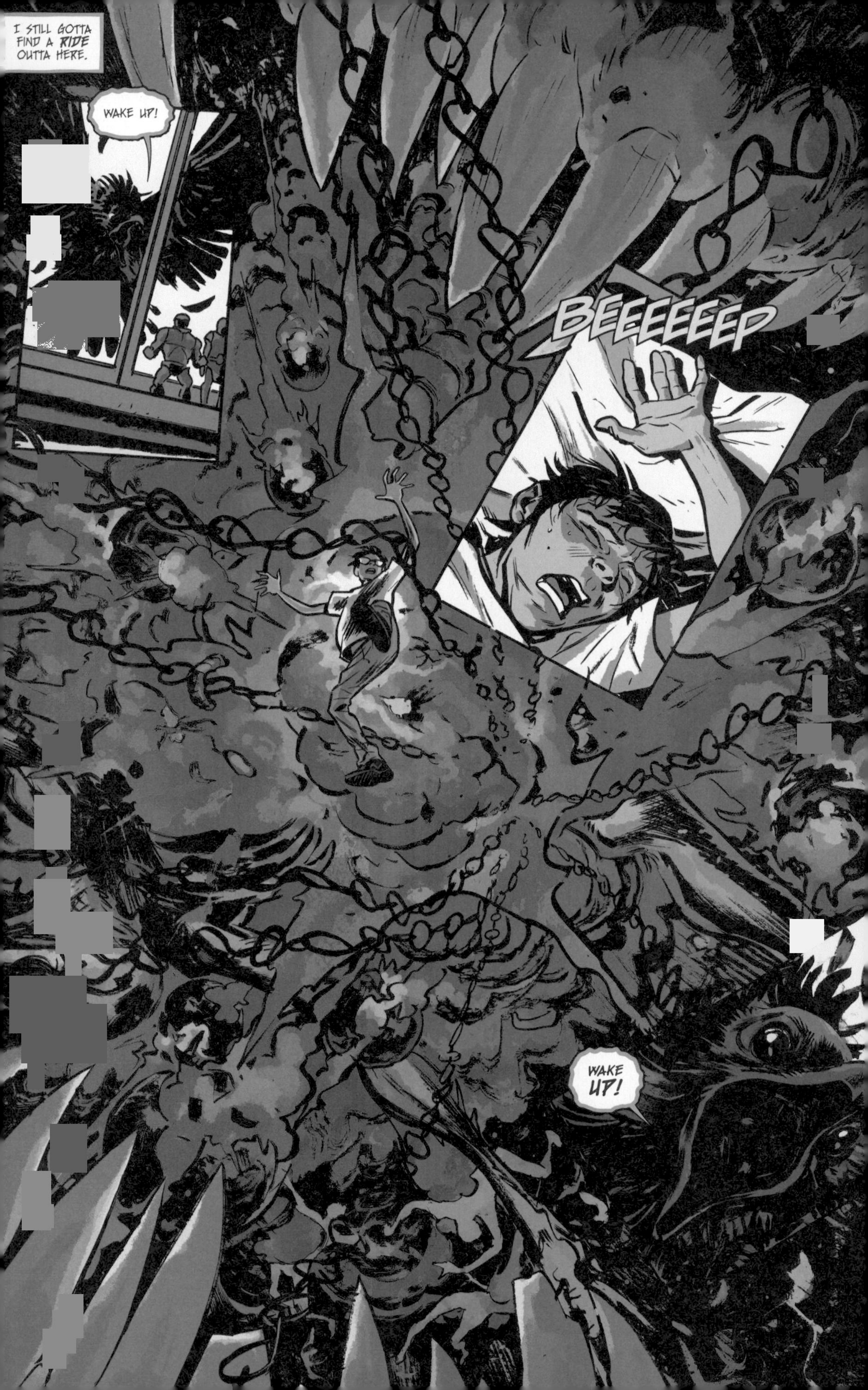
I STILL GOTTA FIND A RIDE OUTTA HERE.
WAKE UP!
BEEEEEEEP
WAKE UP!

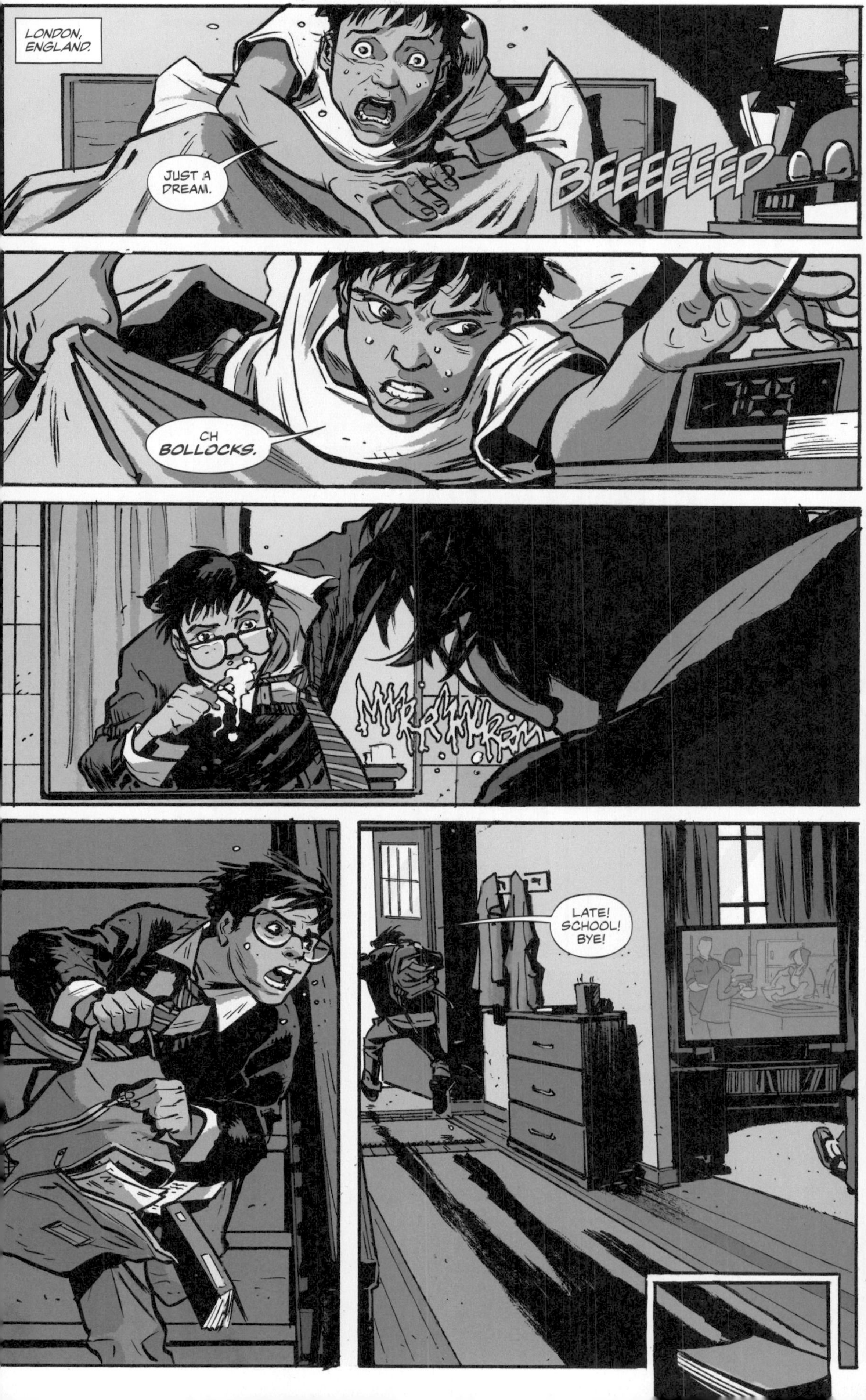
LONDON, ENGLAND.
JUST A DREAM.
BEEEEEEEP
CH BOLLOCKS.
MMRMMRM
LATE! SCHOOL! BYE!

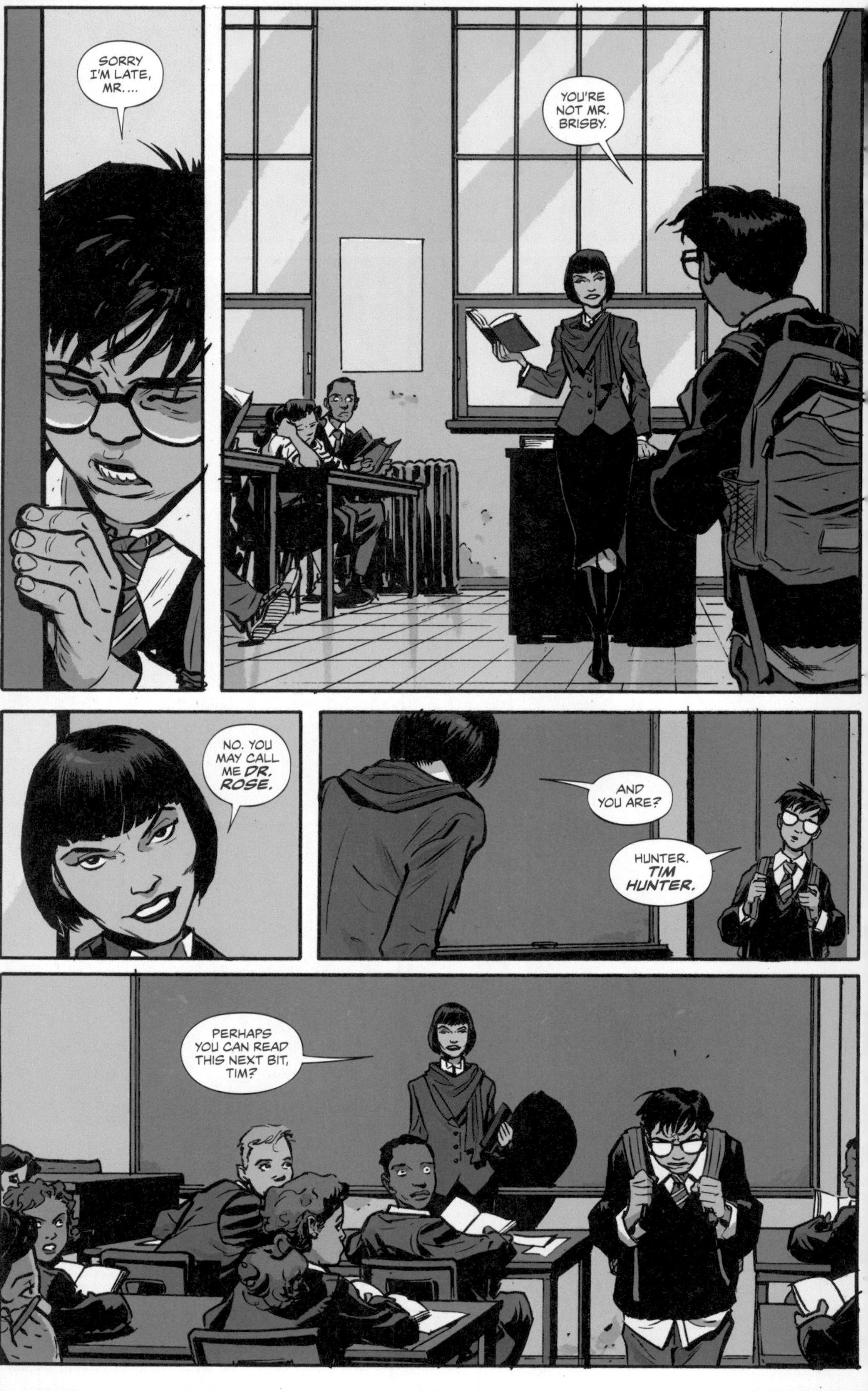
SORRY I'M LATE, MR....
YOU'RE NOT MR. BRISBY.
NO. YOU MAY CALL ME **DR. ROSE.**
AND YOU ARE?
HUNTER. **TIM HUNTER.**
PERHAPS YOU CAN READ THIS NEXT BIT, TIM?

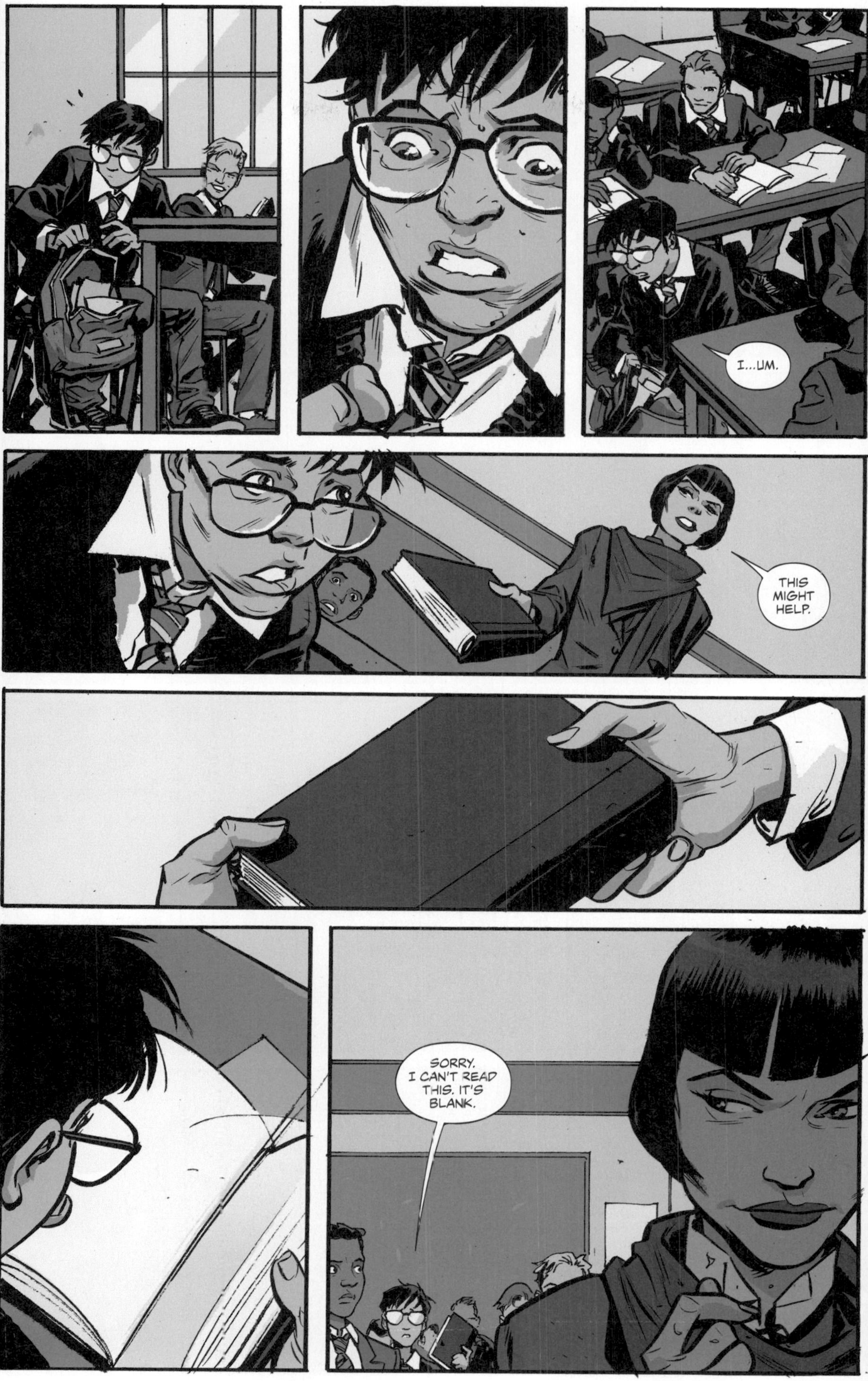
I...UM.
THIS MIGHT HELP.
SORRY. I CAN'T READ THIS. IT'S BLANK.

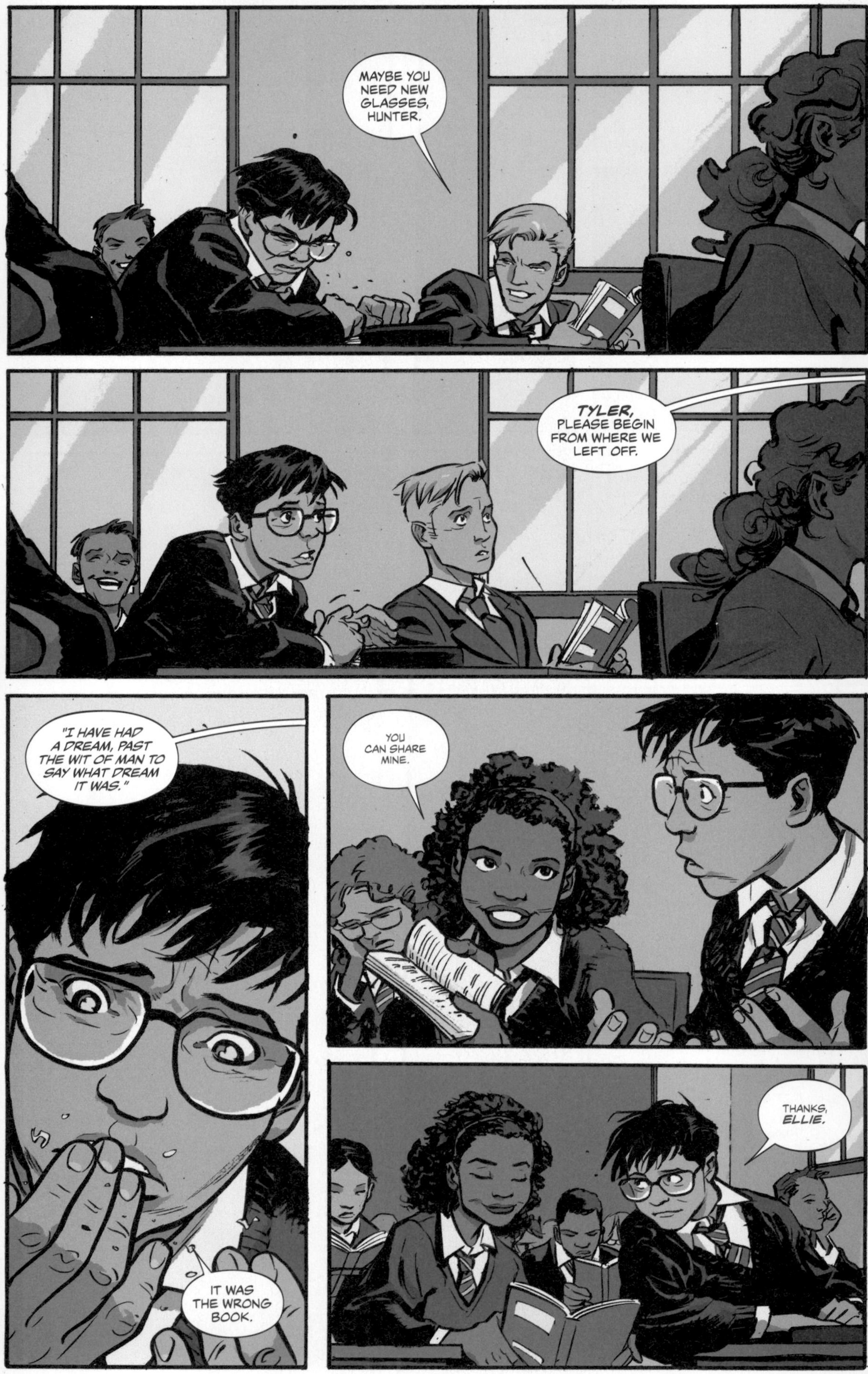
MAYBE YOU NEED NEW GLASSES, HUNTER.
TYLER, PLEASE BEGIN FROM WHERE WE LEFT OFF.
"I HAVE HAD A DREAM, PAST THE WIT OF MAN TO SAY WHAT DREAM IT WAS."
IT WAS THE WRONG BOOK.
YOU CAN SHARE MINE.
THANKS, ELLIE.

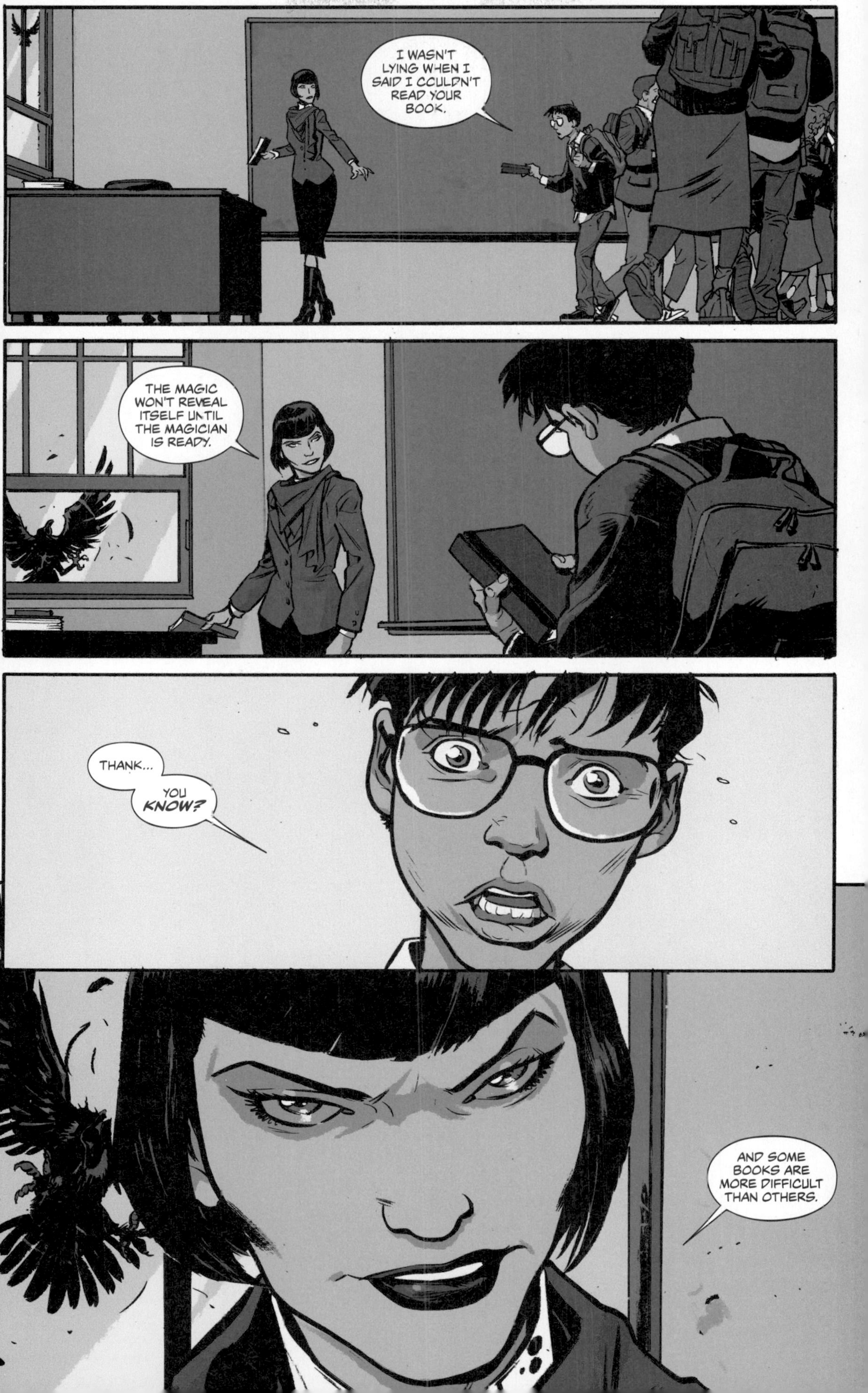
I WASN'T LYING WHEN I SAID I COULDN'T READ YOUR BOOK.
THE MAGIC WON'T REVEAL ITSELF UNTIL THE MAGICIAN IS READY.
THANK...
YOU *KNOW?*
AND SOME BOOKS ARE MORE DIFFICULT THAN OTHERS.

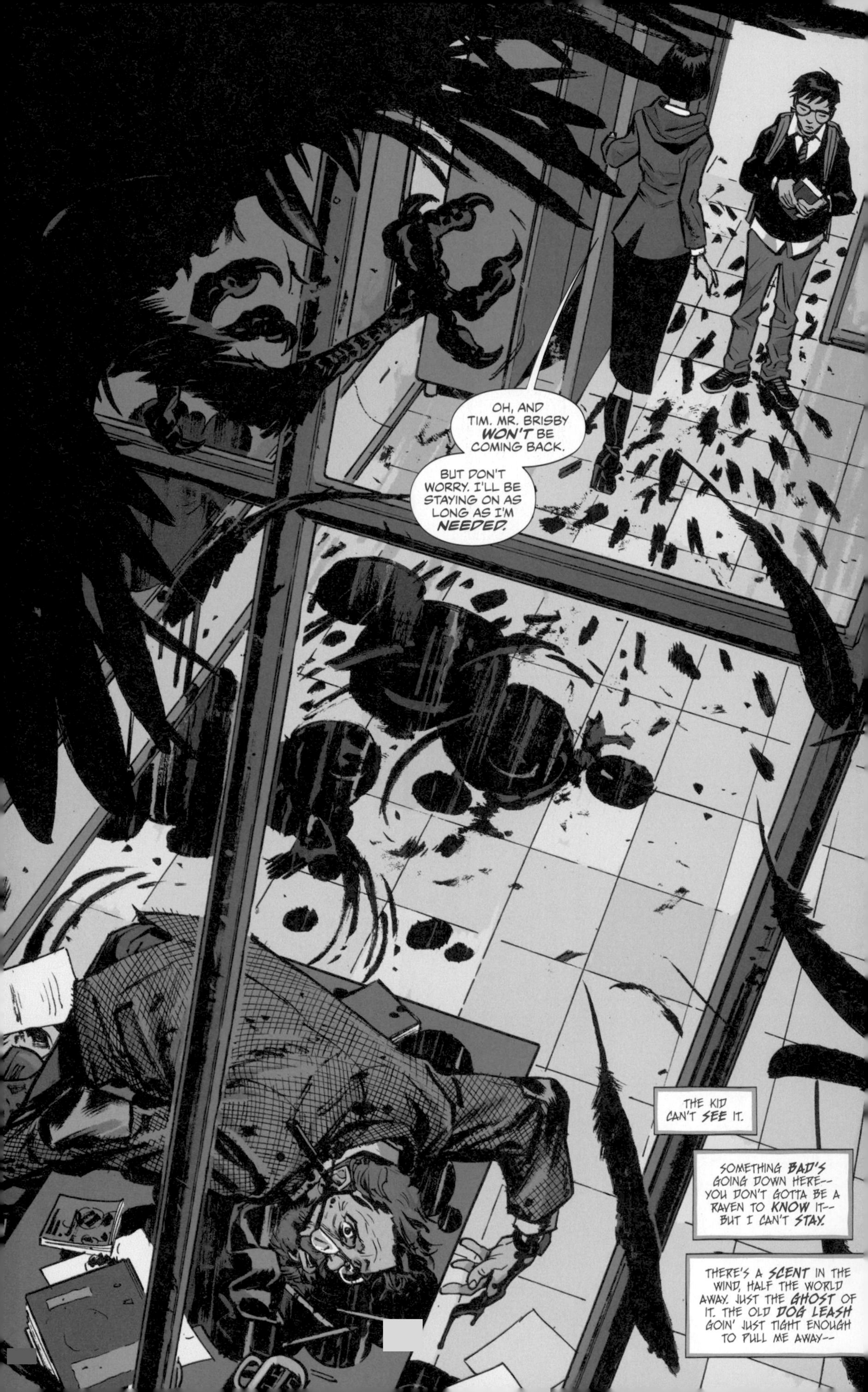
OH, AND TIM. MR. BRISBY WON'T BE COMING BACK.
BUT DON'T WORRY. I'LL BE STAYING ON AS LONG AS I'M NEEDED.
THE KID CAN'T SEE IT.
SOMETHING BAD'S GOING DOWN HERE-- YOU DON'T GOTTA BE A RAVEN TO KNOW IT-- BUT I CAN'T STAY.
THERE'S A SCENT IN THE WIND, HALF THE WORLD AWAY. JUST THE GHOST OF IT. THE OLD DOG LEASH GOIN' JUST TIGHT ENOUGH TO PULL ME AWAY--

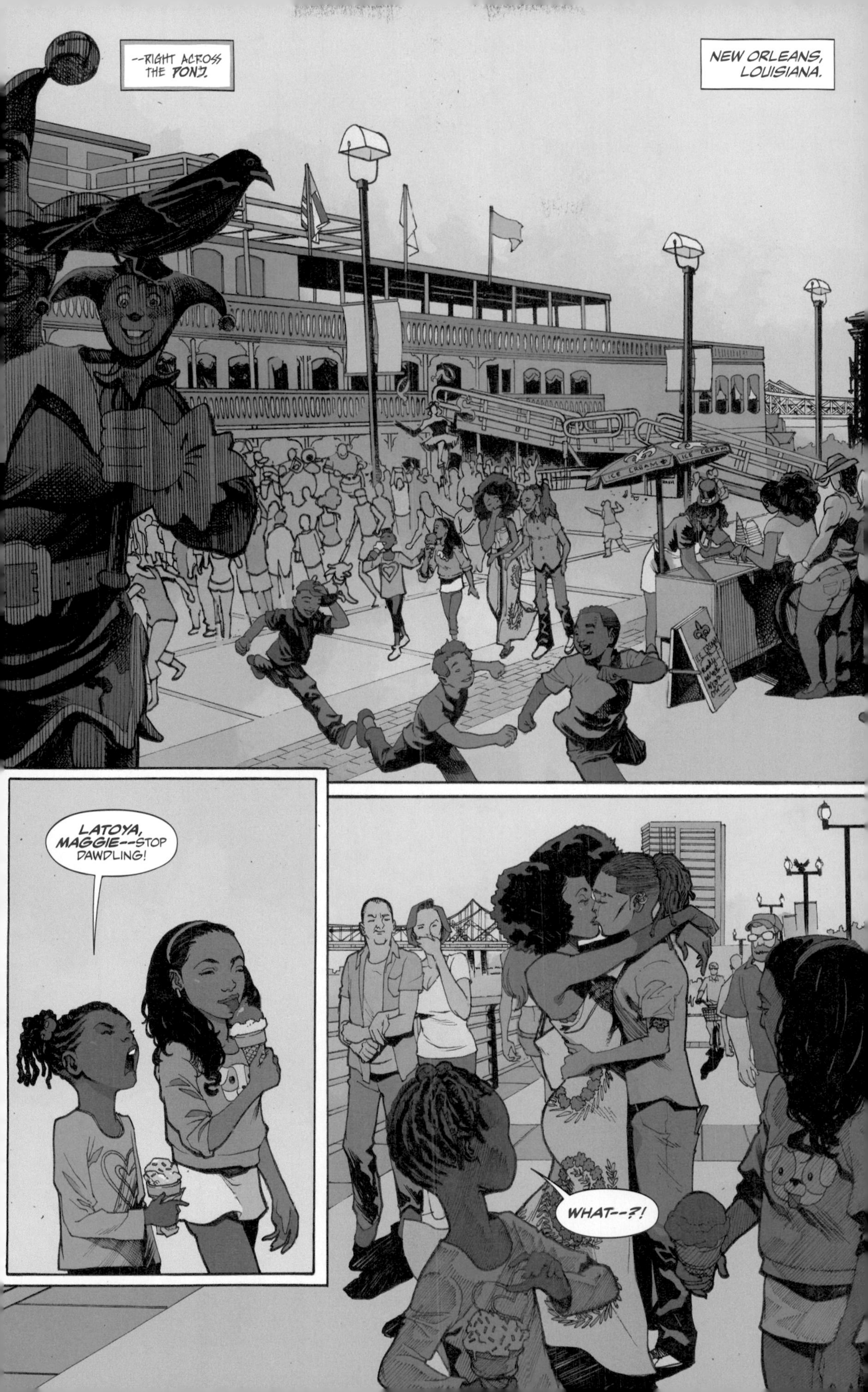
--RIGHT ACROSS THE POND.
NEW ORLEANS, LOUISIANA.
ICE CREAM
LATOYA, MAGGIE--STOP DAWDLING!
WHAT--?!

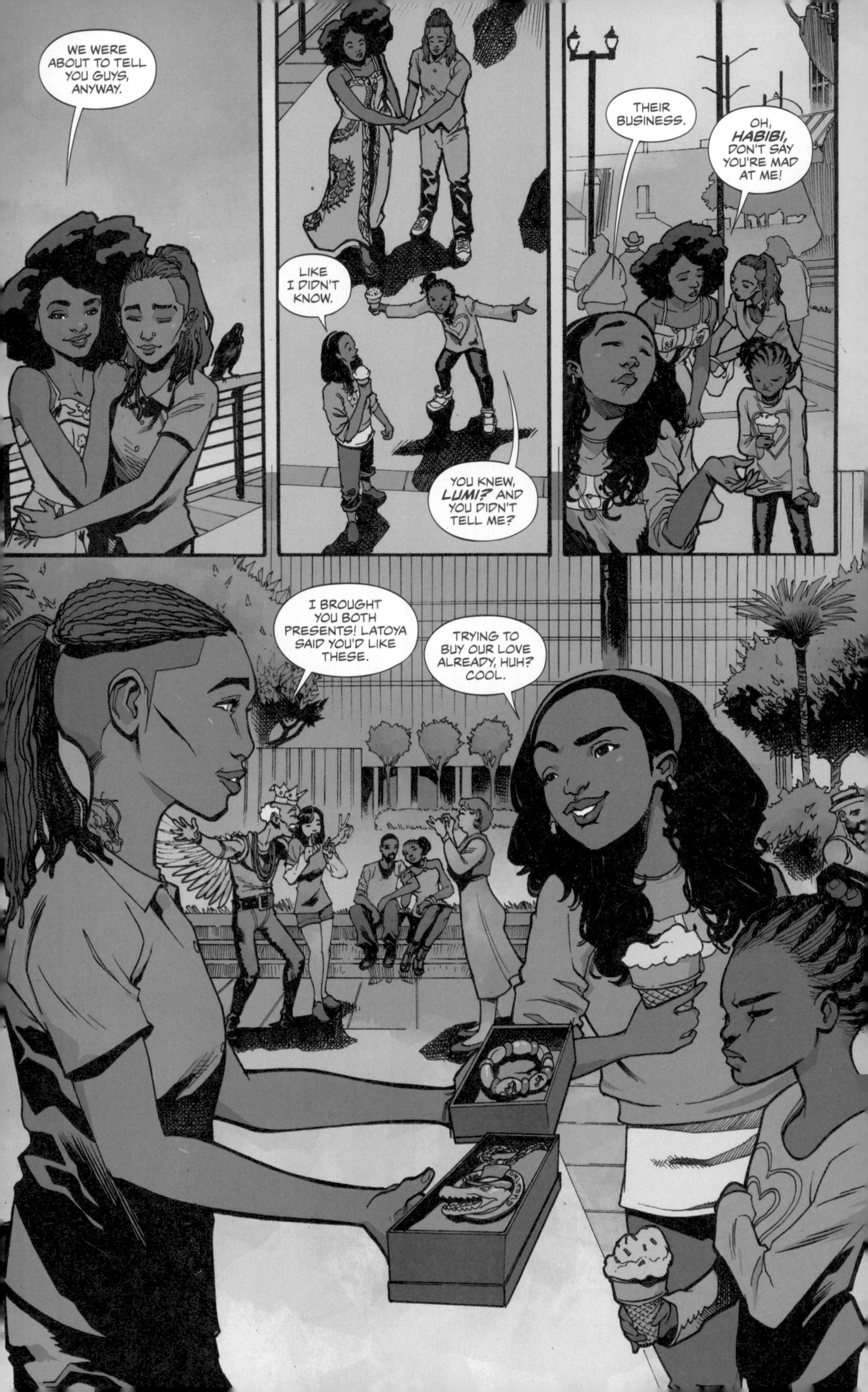
WE WERE ABOUT TO TELL YOU GUYS, ANYWAY.
LIKE I DIDN'T KNOW.
YOU KNEW, LUMI? AND YOU DIDN'T TELL ME?
THEIR BUSINESS.
OH, HABIBI, DON'T SAY YOU'RE MAD AT ME!
I BROUGHT YOU BOTH PRESENTS! LATOYA SAID YOU'D LIKE THESE.
TRYING TO BUY OUR LOVE ALREADY, HUH? COOL.

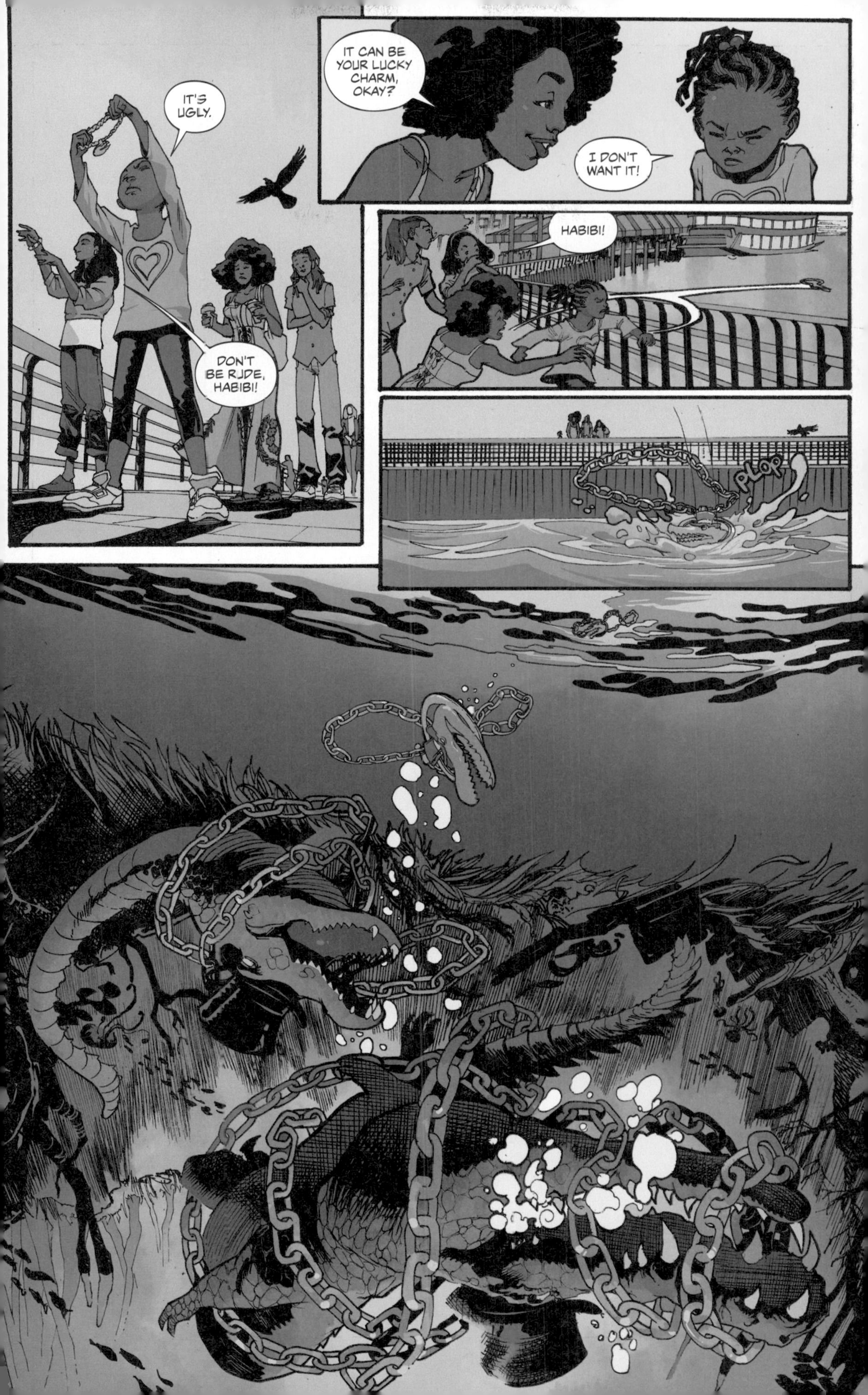
IT'S UGLY.
DON'T BE RUDE, HABIBI!
IT CAN BE YOUR LUCKY CHARM, OKAY?
I DON'T WANT IT!
HABIBI!
PLOP

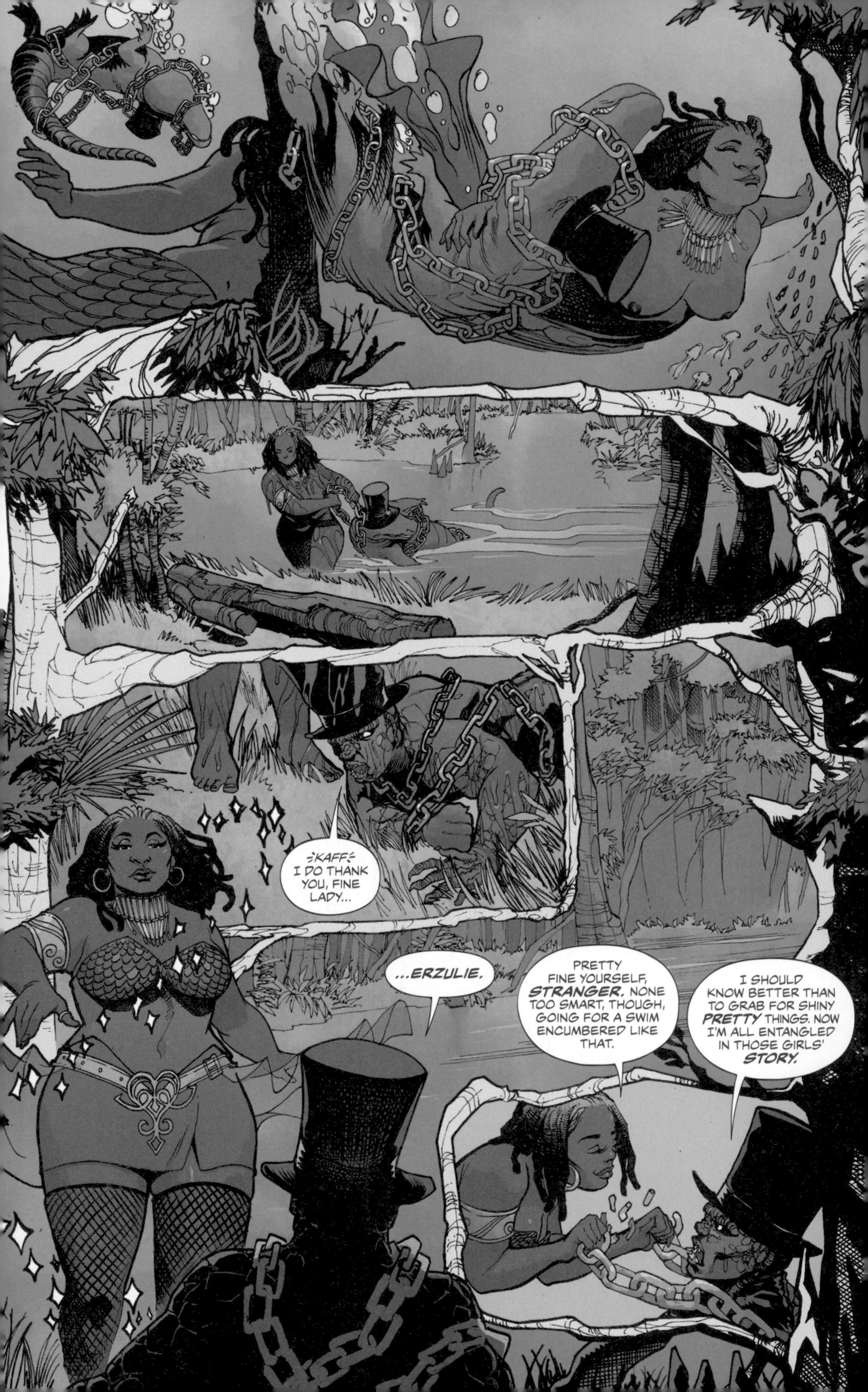

KAFF I DO THANK YOU, FINE LADY...
...ERZULIE.
PRETTY FINE YOURSELF, STRANGER. NONE TOO SMART, THOUGH, GOING FOR A SWIM ENCUMBERED LIKE THAT.
I SHOULD KNOW BETTER THAN TO GRAB FOR SHINY PRETTY THINGS. NOW I'M ALL ENTANGLED IN THOSE GIRLS' STORY.

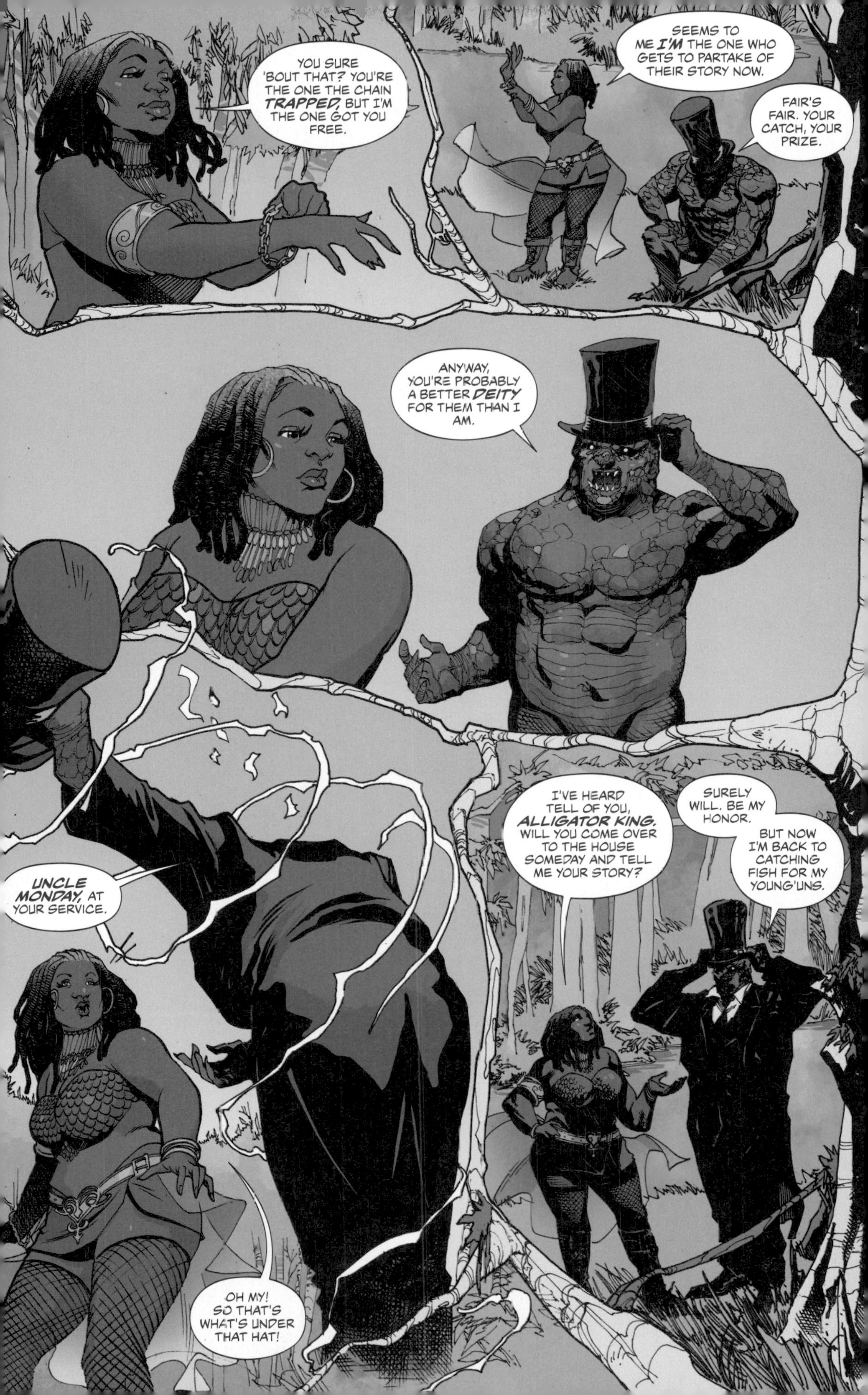
YOU SURE 'BOUT THAT? YOU'RE THE ONE THE CHAIN TRAPPED, BUT I'M THE ONE GOT YOU FREE.
SEEMS TO ME I'M THE ONE WHO GETS TO PARTAKE OF THEIR STORY NOW.
FAIR'S FAIR. YOUR CATCH, YOUR PRIZE.
ANYWAY, YOU'RE PROBABLY A BETTER DEITY FOR THEM THAN I AM.
UNCLE MONDAY, AT YOUR SERVICE.
OH MY! SO THAT'S WHAT'S UNDER THAT HAT!
I'VE HEARD TELL OF YOU, ALLIGATOR KING. WILL YOU COME OVER TO THE HOUSE SOMEDAY AND TELL ME YOUR STORY?
SURELY WILL. BE MY HONOR.
BUT NOW I'M BACK TO CATCHING FISH FOR MY YOUNG'UNS.

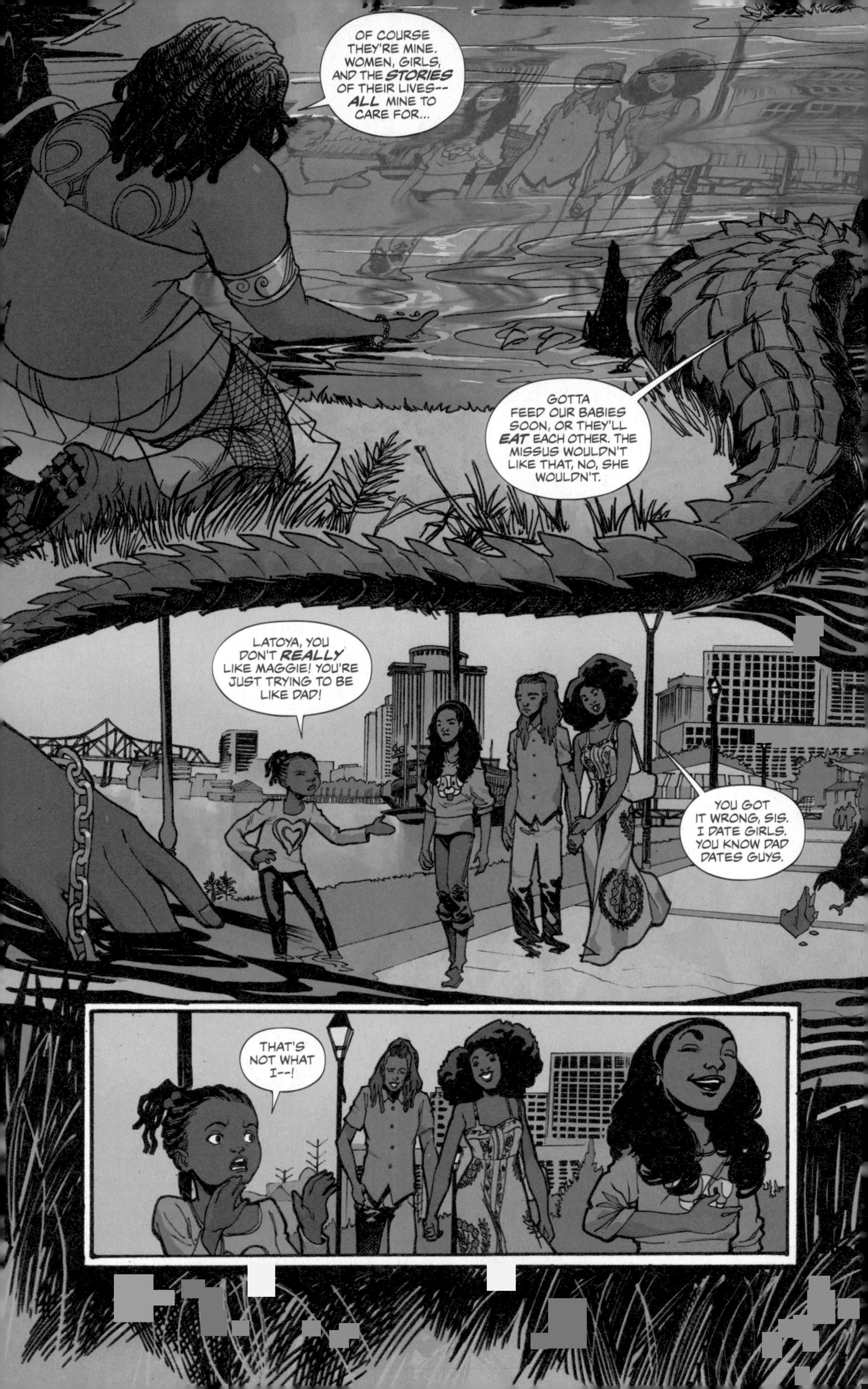
OF COURSE THEY'RE MINE. WOMEN, GIRLS, AND THE STORIES OF THEIR LIVES-- ALL MINE TO CARE FOR...
GOTTA FEED OUR BABIES SOON, OR THEY'LL EAT EACH OTHER. THE MISSUS WOULDN'T LIKE THAT, NO, SHE WOULDN'T.
LATOYA, YOU DON'T REALLY LIKE MAGGIE! YOU'RE JUST TRYING TO BE LIKE DAD!
YOU GOT IT WRONG, SIS. I DATE GIRLS. YOU KNOW DAD DATES GUYS.
THAT'S NOT WHAT I--!

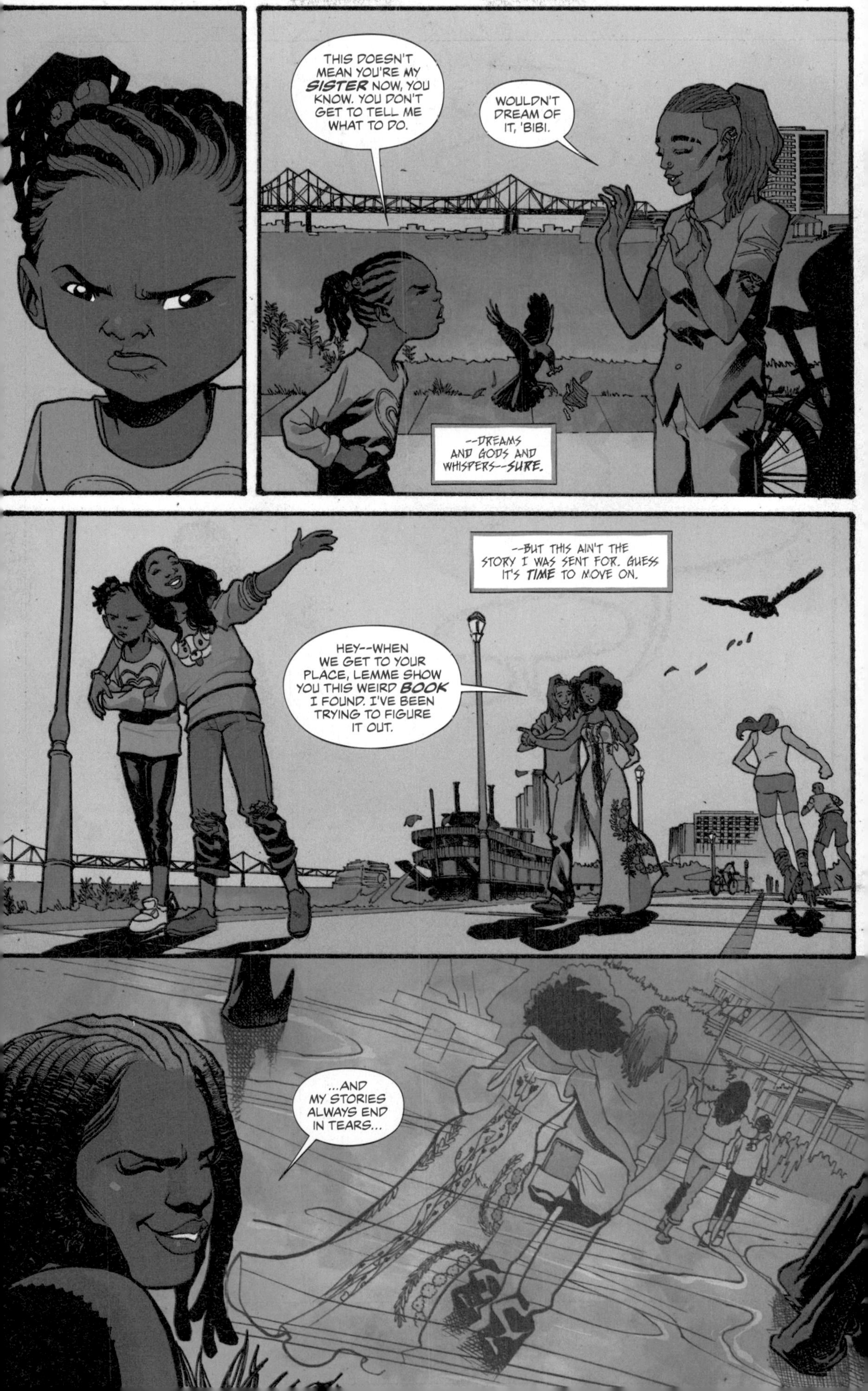
THIS DOESN'T MEAN YOU'RE MY SISTER NOW, YOU KNOW. YOU DON'T GET TO TELL ME WHAT TO DO.
WOULDN'T DREAM OF IT, 'BIBI.
--DREAMS AND GODS AND WHISPERS--SURE.
--BUT THIS AIN'T THE STORY I WAS SENT FOR. GUESS IT'S TIME TO MOVE ON.
HEY--WHEN WE GET TO YOUR PLACE, LEMME SHOW YOU THIS WEIRD BOOK I FOUND. I'VE BEEN TRYING TO FIGURE IT OUT.
...AND MY STORIES ALWAYS END IN TEARS...

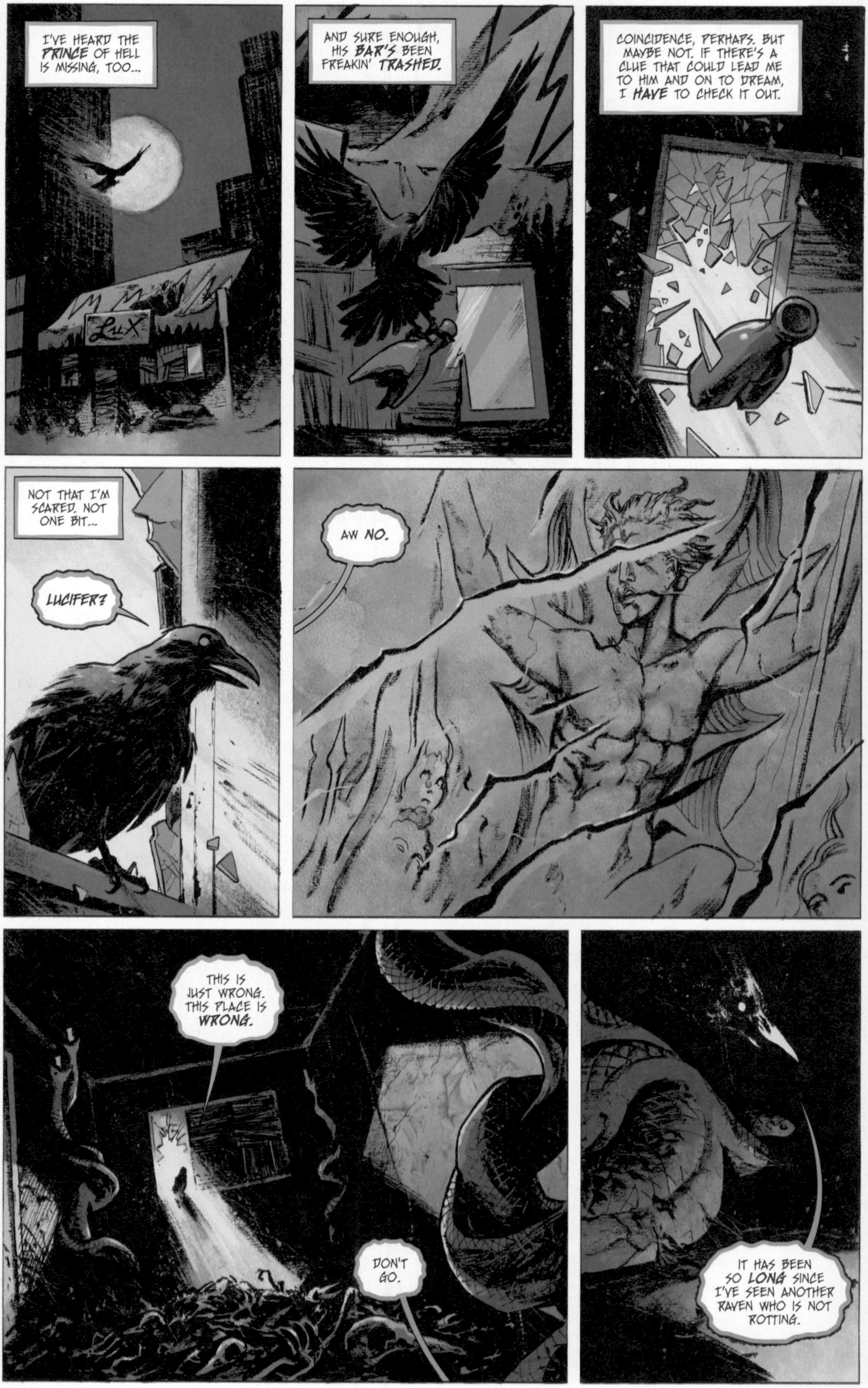
I'VE HEARD THE PRINCE OF HELL IS MISSING, TOO...
AND SURE ENOUGH, HIS BAR'S BEEN FREAKIN' TRASHED.
COINCIDENCE, PERHAPS. BUT MAYBE NOT. IF THERE'S A CLUE THAT COULD LEAD ME TO HIM AND ON TO DREAM, I HAVE TO CHECK IT OUT.
NOT THAT I'M SCARED. NOT ONE BIT...
LUCIFER?
AW NO.
THIS IS JUST WRONG. THIS PLACE IS WRONG.
DON'T GO.
IT HAS BEEN SO LONG SINCE I'VE SEEN ANOTHER RAVEN WHO IS NOT ROTTING.

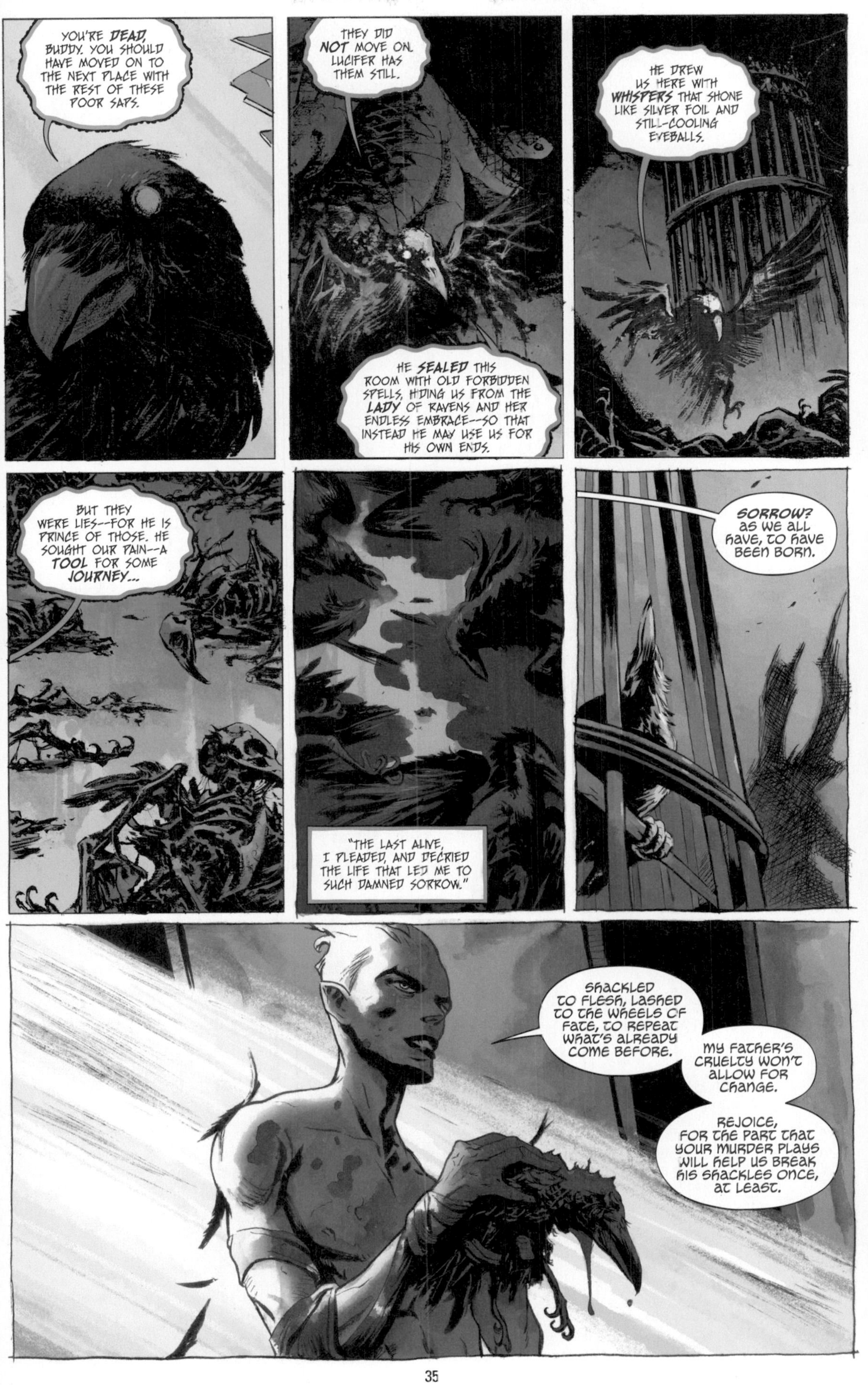

YOU'RE DEAD, BUDDY. YOU SHOULD HAVE MOVED ON TO THE NEXT PLACE WITH THE REST OF THESE POOR SAPS.
THEY DID NOT MOVE ON. LUCIFER HAS THEM STILL.
HE SEALED THIS ROOM WITH OLD FORBIDDEN SPELLS, HIDING US FROM THE LADY OF RAVENS AND HER ENDLESS EMBRACE--SO THAT INSTEAD HE MAY USE US FOR HIS OWN ENDS.
HE DREW US HERE WITH WHISPERS THAT SHONE LIKE SILVER FOIL AND STILL-COOLING EYEBALLS.
BUT THEY WERE LIES--FOR HE IS PRINCE OF THOSE. HE SOUGHT OUR PAIN--A TOOL FOR SOME JOURNEY...
"THE LAST ALIVE, I PLEADED, AND DECRIED THE LIFE THAT LED ME TO SUCH DAMNED SORROW."
SORROW? AS WE ALL HAVE, TO HAVE BEEN BORN.
SHACKLED TO FLESH, LASHED TO THE WHEELS OF FATE, TO REPEAT WHAT'S ALREADY COME BEFORE.
MY FATHER'S CRUELTY WON'T ALLOW FOR CHANGE.
REJOICE, FOR THE PART THAT YOUR MURDER PLAYS WILL HELP US BREAK HIS SHACKLES ONCE, AT LEAST.

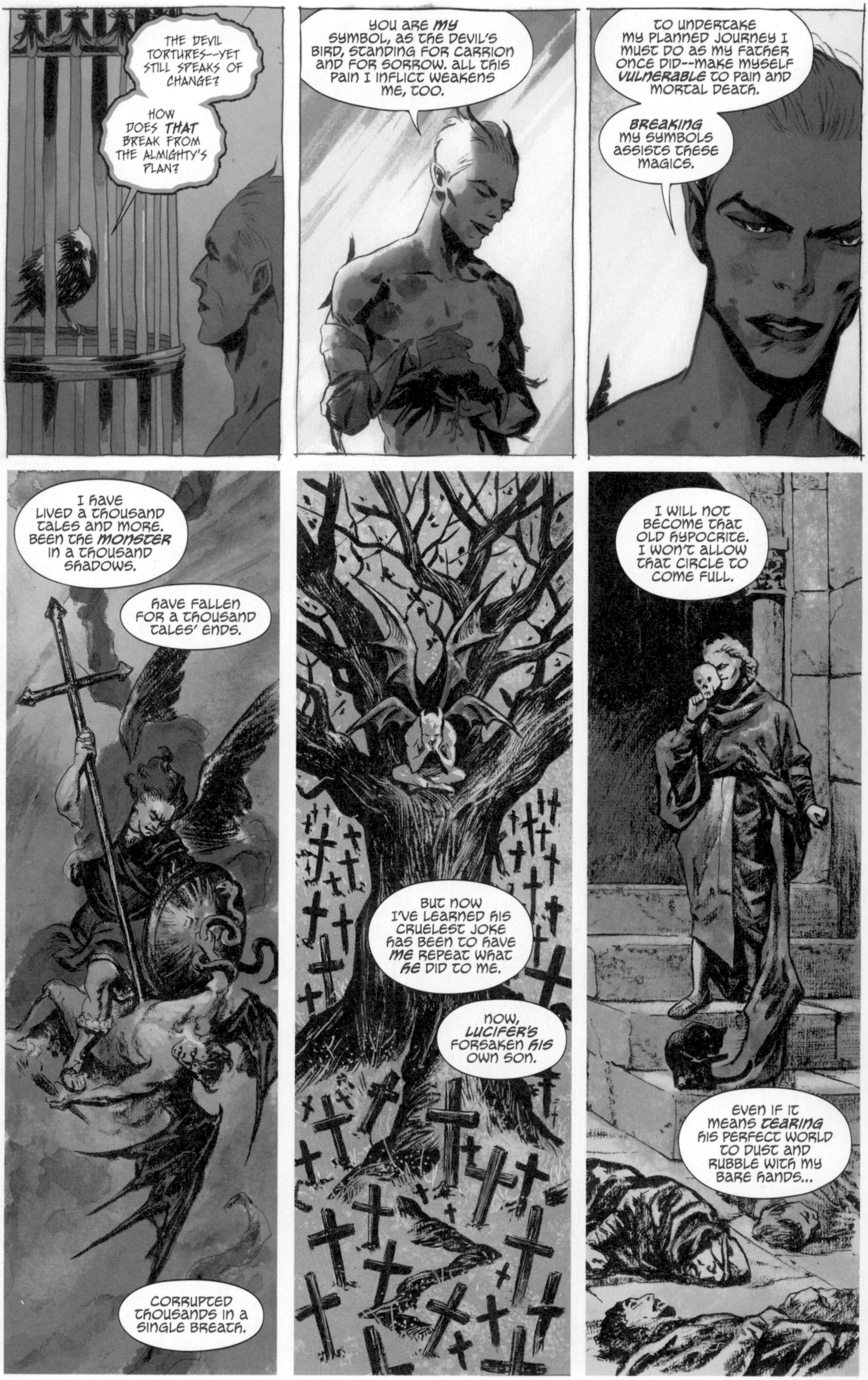
THE DEVIL TORTURES--YET STILL SPEAKS OF CHANGE?
HOW DOES THAT BREAK FROM THE ALMIGHTY'S PLAN?
YOU ARE MY SYMBOL, AS THE DEVIL'S BIRD, STANDING FOR CARRION AND FOR SORROW. ALL THIS PAIN I INFLICT WEAKENS ME, TOO.
TO UNDERTAKE MY PLANNED JOURNEY I MUST DO AS MY FATHER ONCE DID--MAKE MYSELF VULNERABLE TO PAIN AND MORTAL DEATH.
BREAKING MY SYMBOLS ASSISTS THESE MAGICS.
I HAVE LIVED A THOUSAND TALES AND MORE. BEEN THE MONSTER IN A THOUSAND SHADOWS.
HAVE FALLEN FOR A THOUSAND TALES' ENDS.
CORRUPTED THOUSANDS IN A SINGLE BREATH.
BUT NOW I'VE LEARNED HIS CRUELEST JOKE HAS BEEN TO HAVE ME REPEAT WHAT HE DID TO ME.
NOW, LUCIFER'S FORSAKEN HIS OWN SON.
I WILL NOT BECOME THAT OLD HYPOCRITE. I WON'T ALLOW THAT CIRCLE TO COME FULL.
EVEN IF IT MEANS TEARING HIS PERFECT WORLD TO DUST AND RUBBLE WITH MY BARE HANDS...

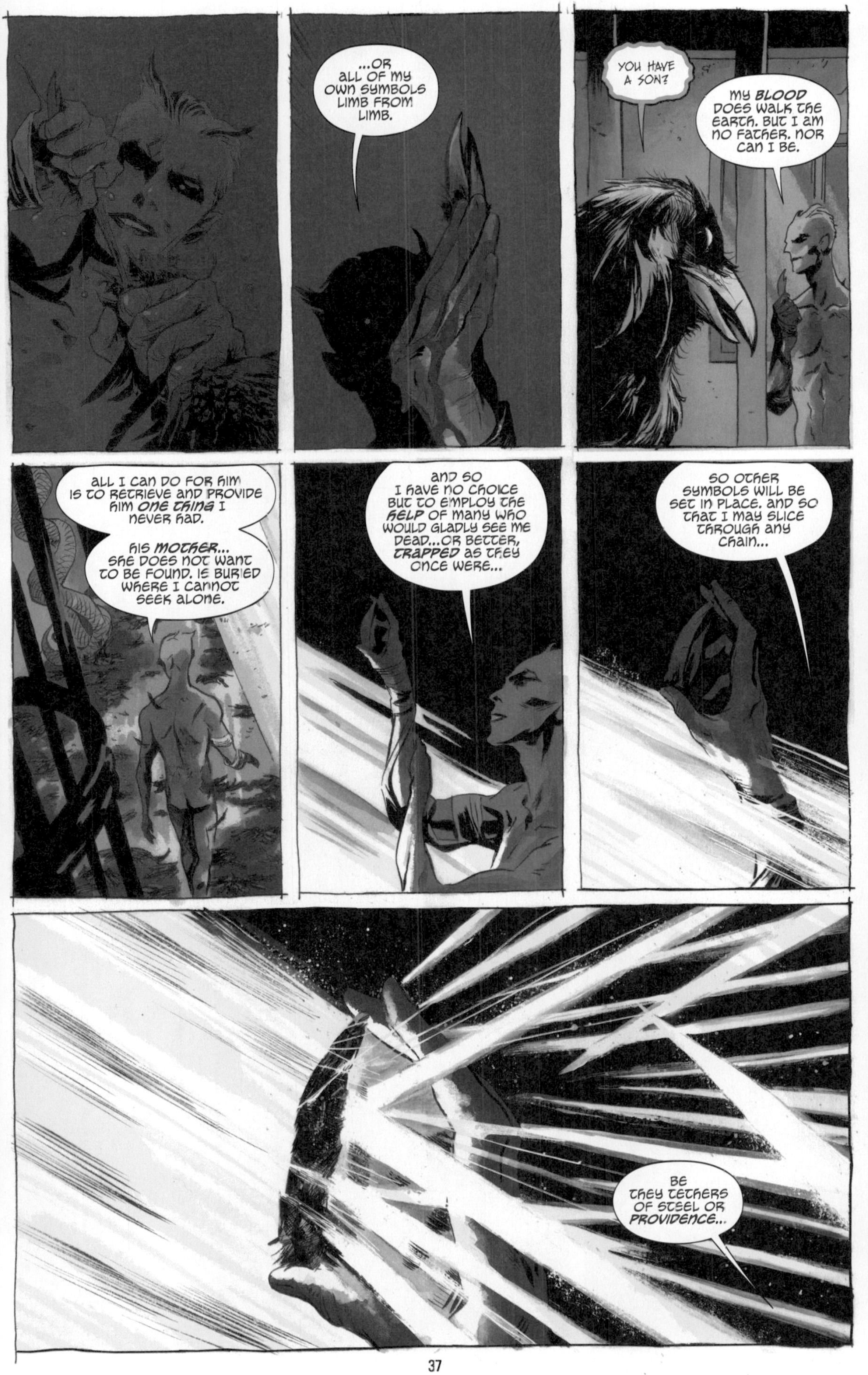
...OR ALL OF MY OWN SYMBOLS LIMB FROM LIMB.
YOU HAVE A SON?
MY BLOOD DOES WALK THE EARTH. BUT I AM NO FATHER. NOR CAN I BE.
ALL I CAN DO FOR HIM IS TO RETRIEVE AND PROVIDE HIM ONE THING I NEVER HAD.
HIS MOTHER... SHE DOES NOT WANT TO BE FOUND. IS BURIED WHERE I CANNOT SEEK ALONE.
AND SO I HAVE NO CHOICE BUT TO EMPLOY THE HELP OF MANY WHO WOULD GLADLY SEE ME DEAD...OR BETTER, TRAPPED AS THEY ONCE WERE...
SO OTHER SYMBOLS WILL BE SET IN PLACE. AND SO THAT I MAY SLICE THROUGH ANY CHAIN...
BE THEY TETHERS OF STEEL OR PROVIDENCE...

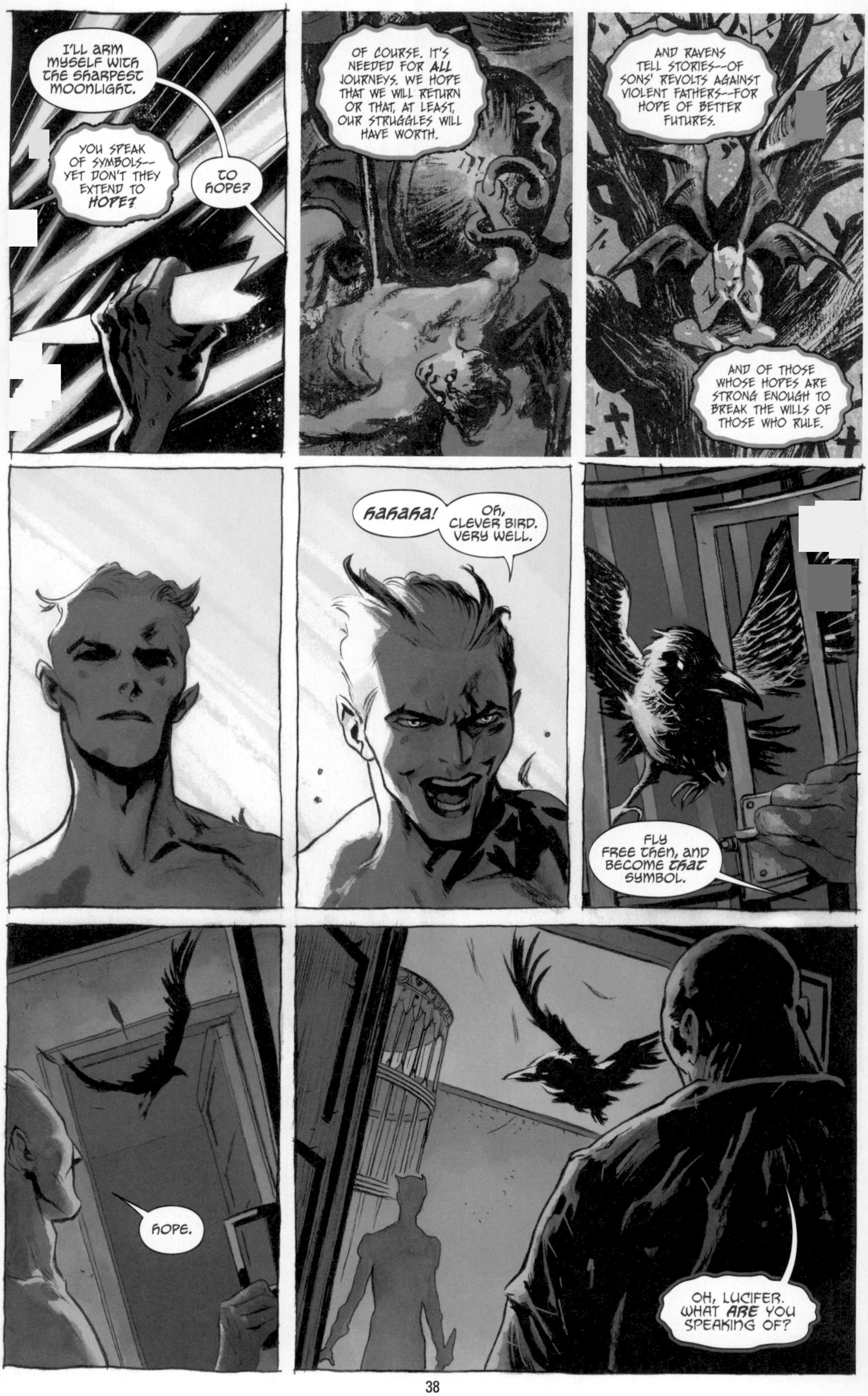
I'LL ARM MYSELF WITH THE SHARPEST MOONLIGHT.
YOU SPEAK OF SYMBOLS--YET DON'T THEY EXTEND TO HOPE?
TO HOPE?
OF COURSE. IT'S NEEDED FOR ALL JOURNEYS. WE HOPE THAT WE WILL RETURN OR THAT, AT LEAST, OUR STRUGGLES WILL HAVE WORTH.
AND RAVENS TELL STORIES--OF SONS' REVOLTS AGAINST VIOLENT FATHERS--FOR HOPE OF BETTER FUTURES.
AND OF THOSE WHOSE HOPES ARE STRONG ENOUGH TO BREAK THE WILLS OF THOSE WHO RULE.
HAHAHA!
OH, CLEVER BIRD. VERY WELL.
FLY FREE THEN, AND BECOME THAT SYMBOL.
HOPE.
OH, LUCIFER. WHAT ARE YOU SPEAKING OF?

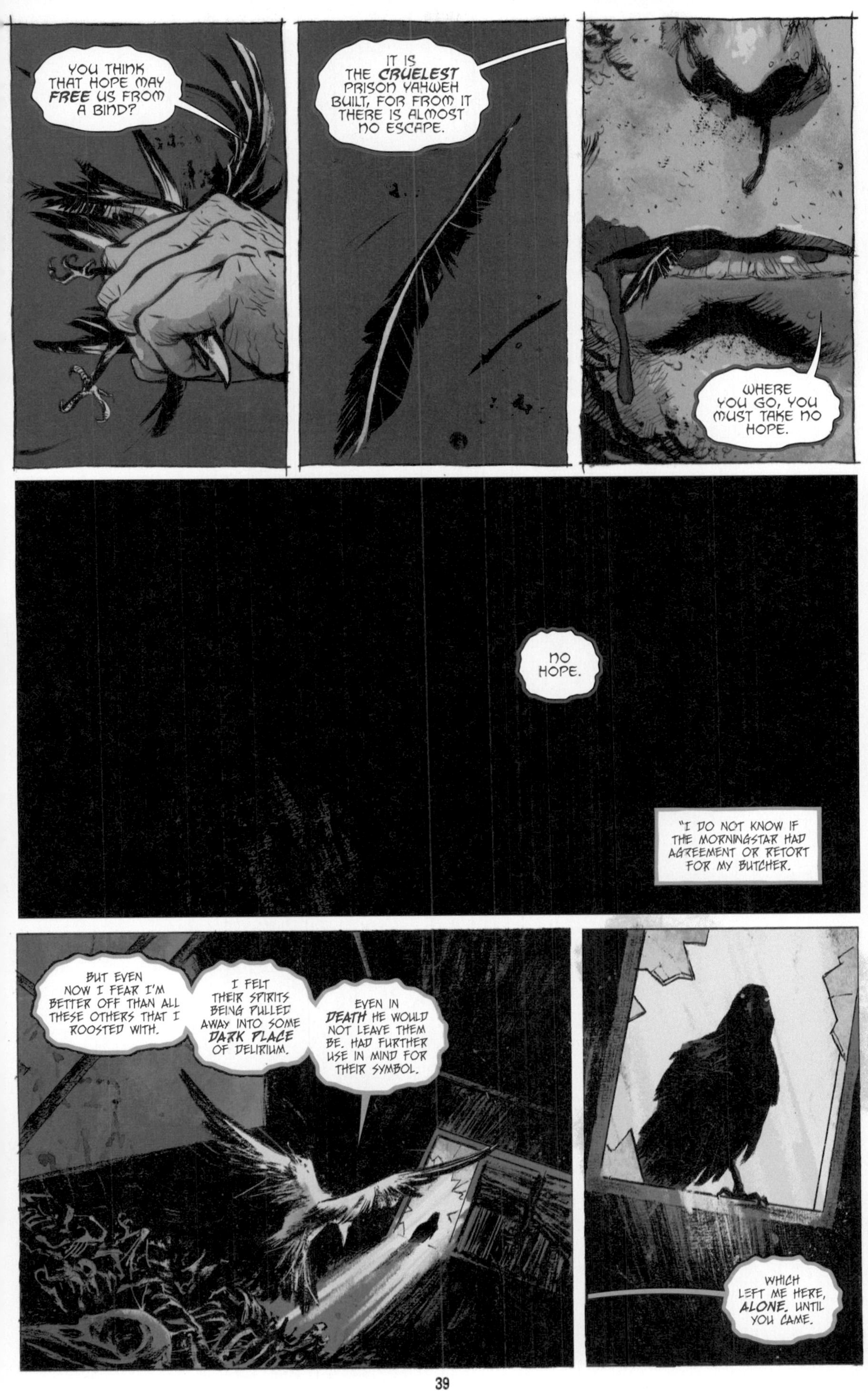
YOU THINK THAT HOPE MAY FREE US FROM A BIND?
IT IS THE CRUELEST PRISON YAHWEH BUILT, FOR FROM IT THERE IS ALMOST NO ESCAPE.
WHERE YOU GO, YOU MUST TAKE NO HOPE.
NO HOPE.
"I DO NOT KNOW IF THE MORNINGSTAR HAD AGREEMENT OR RETORT FOR MY BUTCHER.
BUT EVEN NOW I FEAR I'M BETTER OFF THAN ALL THESE OTHERS THAT I ROOSTED WITH.
I FELT THEIR SPIRITS BEING PULLED AWAY INTO SOME DARK PLACE OF DELIRIUM.
EVEN IN DEATH HE WOULD NOT LEAVE THEM BE. HAD FURTHER USE IN MIND FOR THEIR SYMBOL.
WHICH LEFT ME HERE, ALONE. UNTIL YOU CAME.

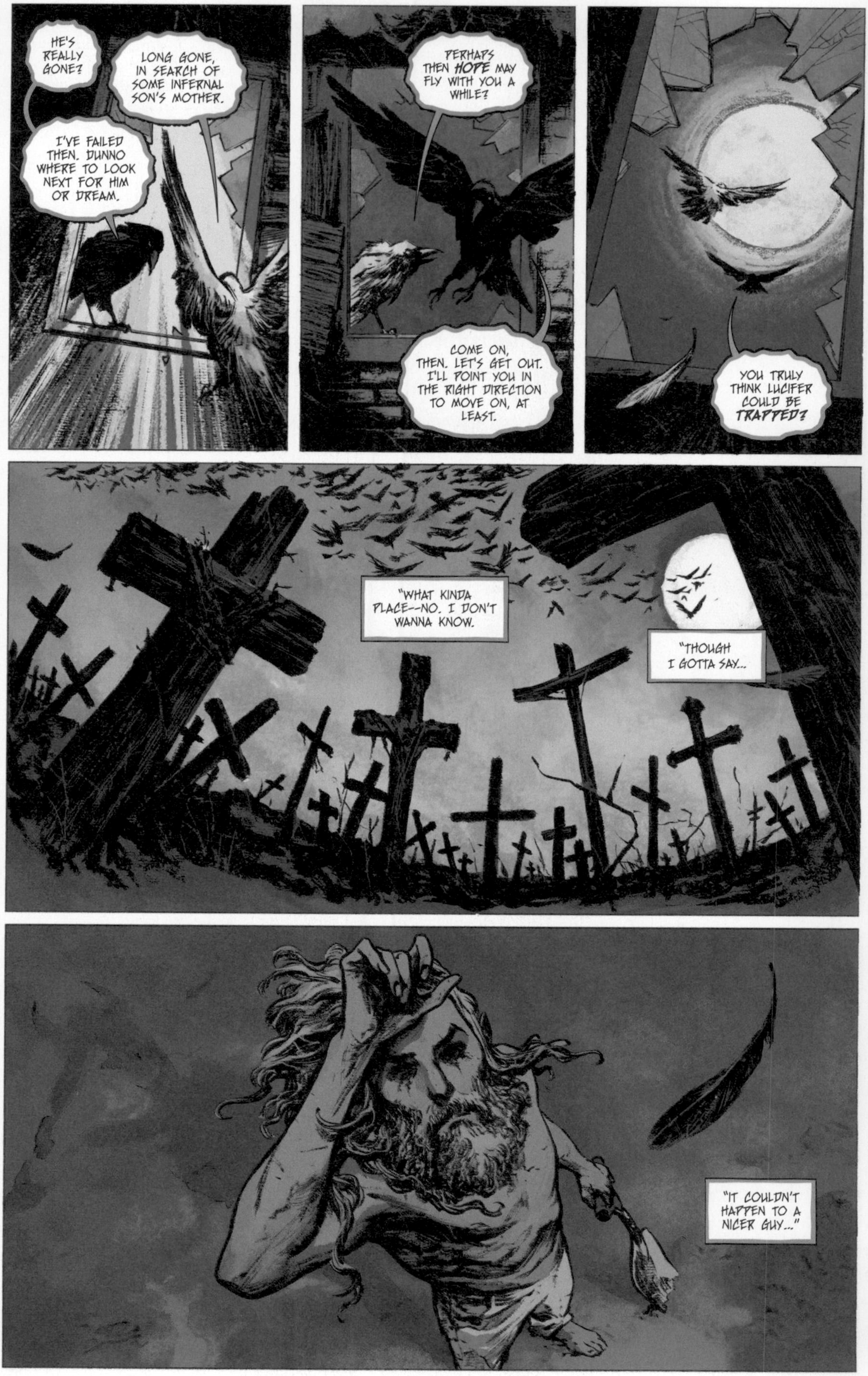
HE'S REALLY GONE?
LONG GONE, IN SEARCH OF SOME INFERNAL SON'S MOTHER.
I'VE FAILED THEN. DUNNO WHERE TO LOOK NEXT FOR HIM OR DREAM.
PERHAPS THEN HOPE MAY FLY WITH YOU A WHILE?
COME ON, THEN. LET'S GET OUT. I'LL POINT YOU IN THE RIGHT DIRECTION TO MOVE ON, AT LEAST.
YOU TRULY THINK LUCIFER COULD BE TRAPPED?
"WHAT KINDA PLACE--NO. I DON'T WANNA KNOW.
"THOUGH I GOTTA SAY...
"IT COULDN'T HAPPEN TO A NICER GUY..."

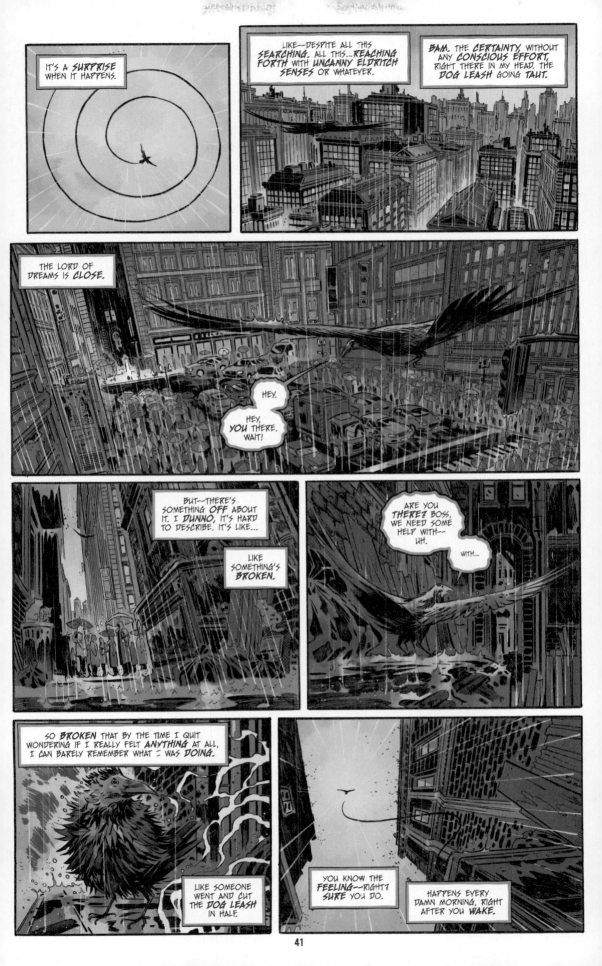

IT'S A *SURPRISE* WHEN IT HAPPENS.

LIKE--DESPITE ALL THIS *SEARCHING.* ALL THIS...*REACHING FORTH* WITH *UNCANNY ELDRITCH SENSES* OR WHATEVER.

BAM. THE *CERTAINTY* WITHOUT ANY *CONSCIOUS EFFORT,* RIGHT THERE IN MY HEAD. THE *DOG LEASH* GOING *TAUT.*

THE *LORD OF DREAMS* IS *CLOSE.*

HEY.

HEY, *YOU* THERE. *WAIT!*

BUT--THERE'S SOMETHING *OFF* ABOUT IT. I *DUNNO,* IT'S HARD TO DESCRIBE. IT'S LIKE...

LIKE SOMETHING'S *BROKEN.*

ARE YOU *THERE?* BOSS, WE NEED SOME HELP WITH--UH.

WITH...

SO *BROKEN* THAT BY THE TIME I QUIT WONDERING IF I REALLY FELT *ANYTHING* AT ALL, I CAN BARELY REMEMBER WHAT Ɪ WAS *DOING.*

LIKE SOMEONE WENT AND CUT THE *DOG LEASH* IN HALF.

YOU KNOW THE *FEELING--RIGHT?* *SURE* YOU DO.

HAPPENS EVERY DAMN MORNING, RIGHT AFTER YOU *WAKE.*

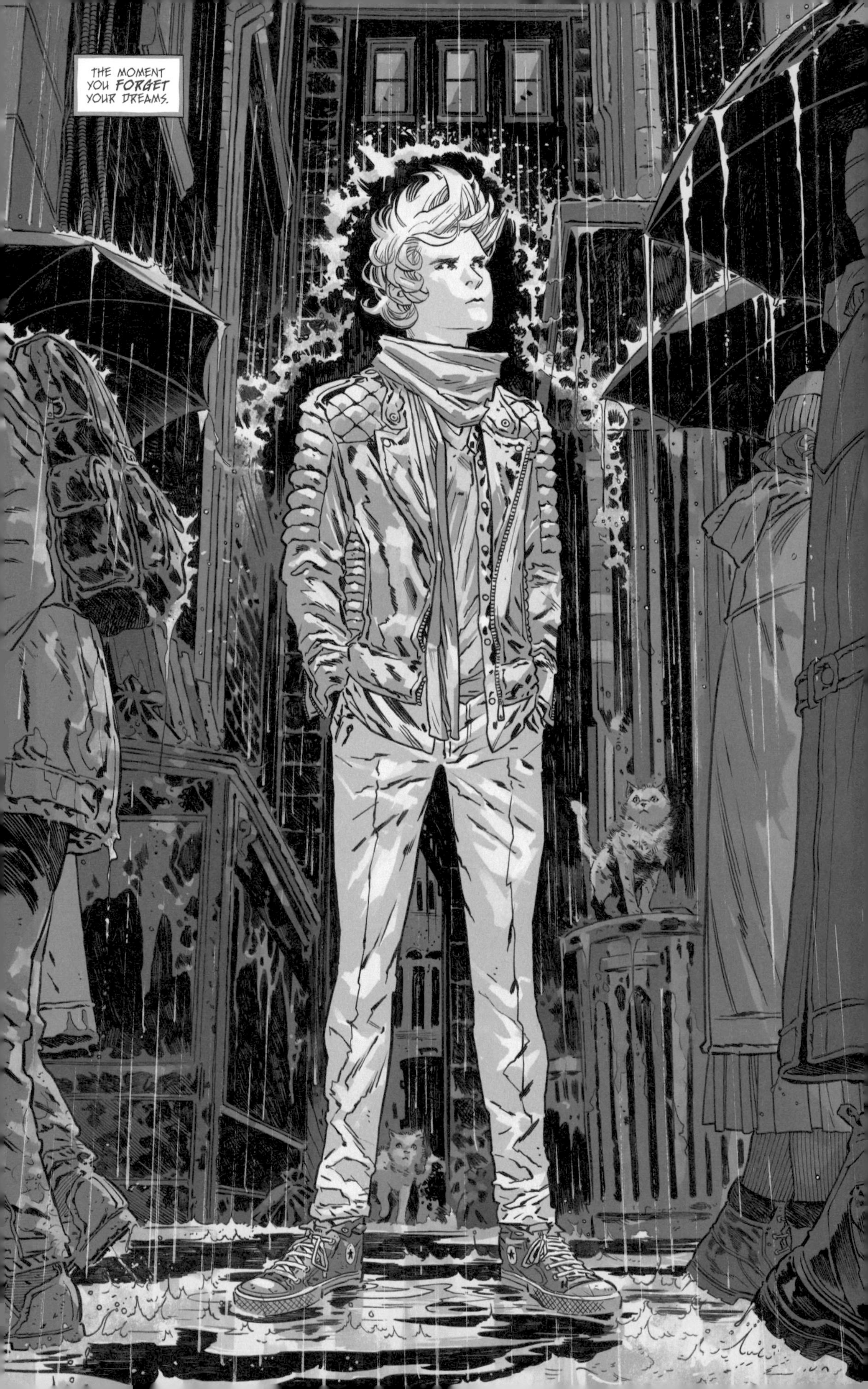
THE MOMENT YOU **FORGET** YOUR DREAMS.

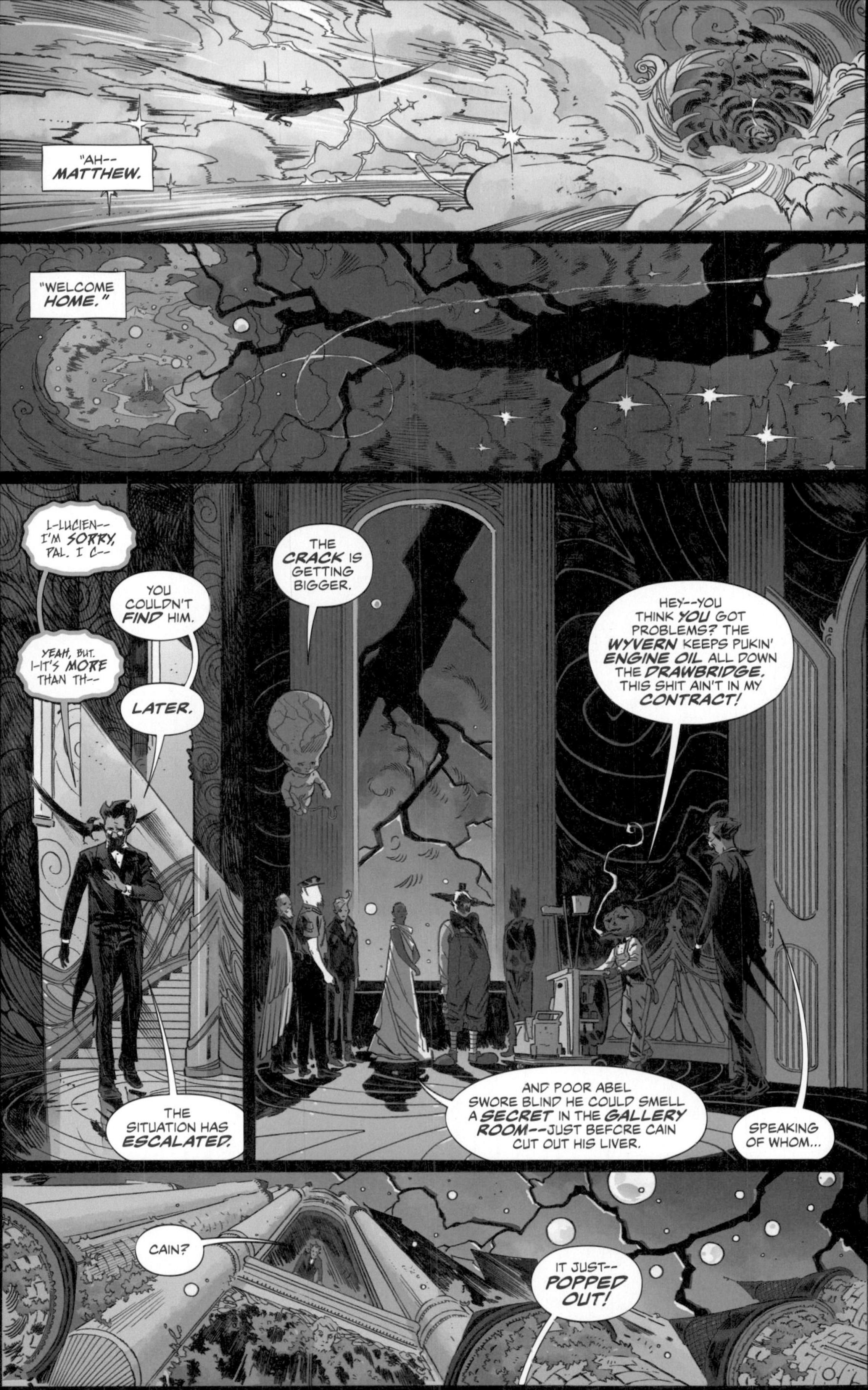

"AH--
MATTHEW.
"WELCOME
HOME."
L-LUCIEN-- I'M SORRY, PAL. I C--
YOU COULDN'T FIND HIM.
YEAH, BUT. I-IT'S MORE THAN TH--
LATER.
THE SITUATION HAS ESCALATED.
THE CRACK IS GETTING BIGGER.
HEY--YOU THINK YOU GOT PROBLEMS? THE WYVERN KEEPS PUKIN' ENGINE OIL ALL DOWN THE DRAWBRIDGE. THIS SHIT AIN'T IN MY CONTRACT!
AND POOR ABEL SWORE BLIND HE COULD SMELL A SECRET IN THE GALLERY ROOM--JUST BEFORE CAIN CUT OUT HIS LIVER.
SPEAKING OF WHOM...
CAIN?
IT JUST-- POPPED OUT!

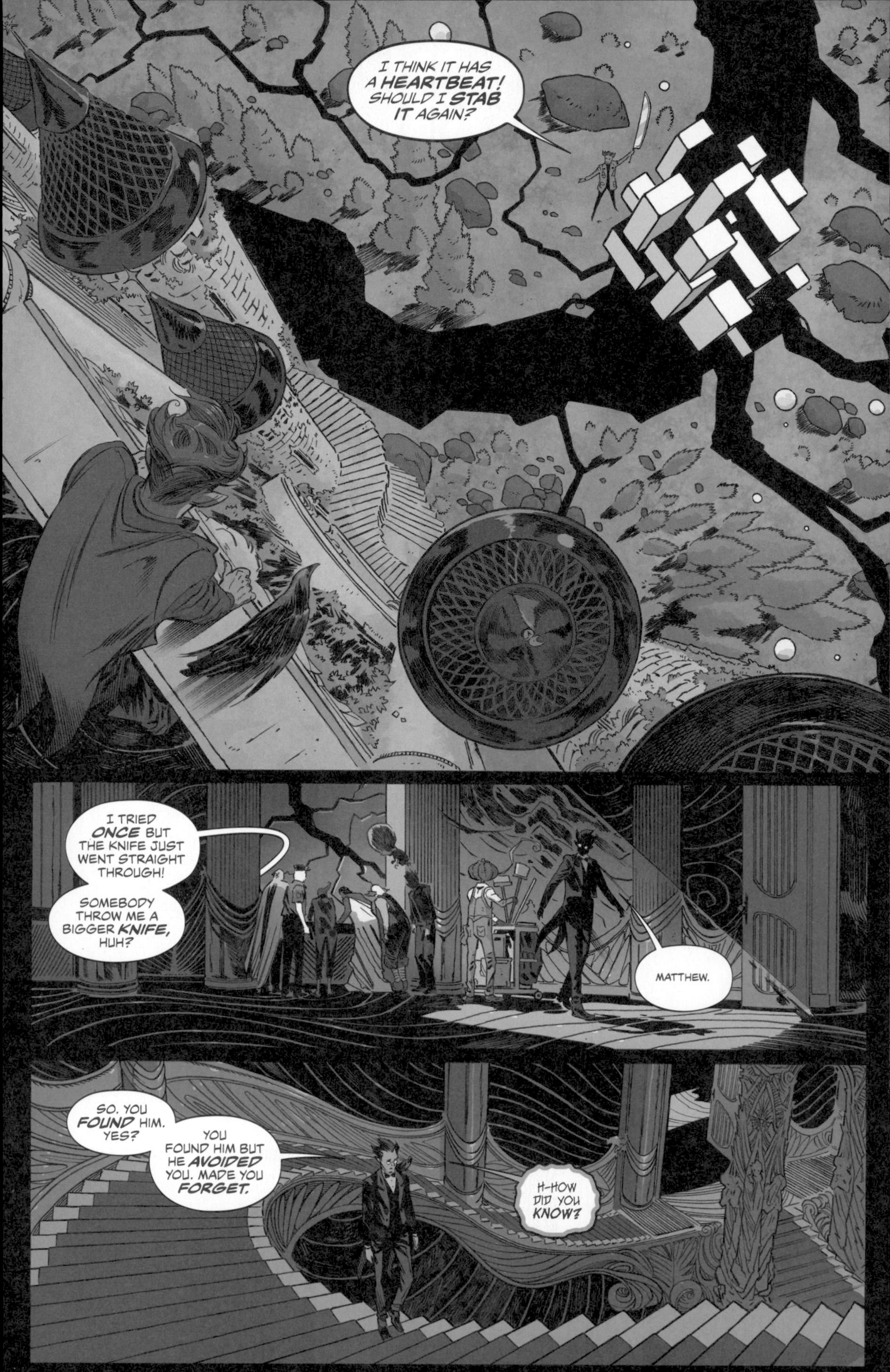
I THINK IT HAS A HEARTBEAT! SHOULD I STAB IT AGAIN?
I TRIED ONCE BUT THE KNIFE JUST WENT STRAIGHT THROUGH!
SOMEBODY THROW ME A BIGGER KNIFE, HUH?
MATTHEW.
SO. YOU FOUND HIM. YES?
YOU FOUND HIM BUT HE AVOIDED YOU. MADE YOU FORGET.
H-HOW DID YOU KNOW?

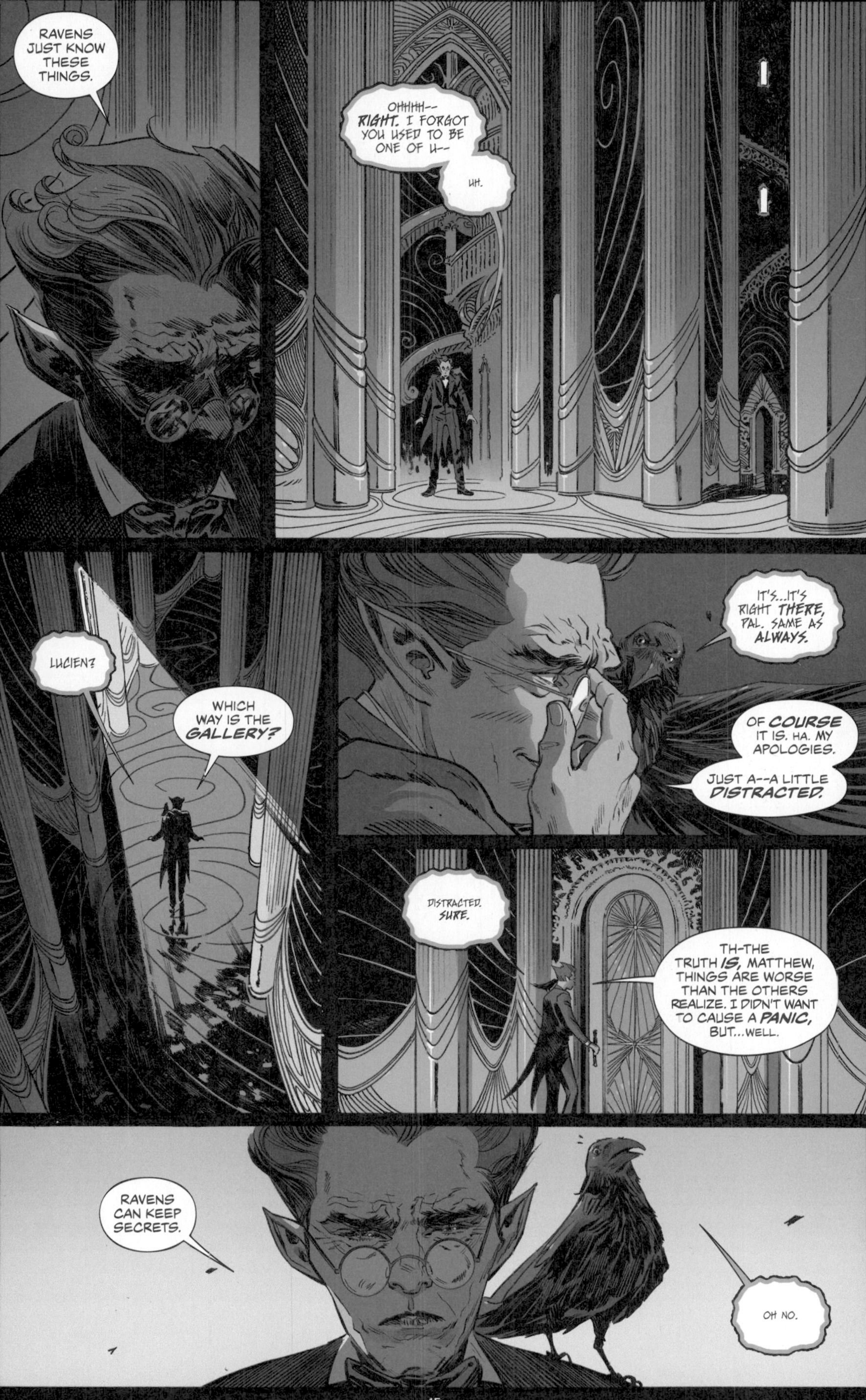
RAVENS JUST KNOW THESE THINGS.
OHHHH-- RIGHT. I FORGOT YOU USED TO BE ONE OF U--
UH.
LUCIEN?
WHICH WAY IS THE GALLERY?
IT'S...IT'S RIGHT THERE, PAL. SAME AS ALWAYS.
OF COURSE IT IS. HA. MY APOLOGIES.
JUST A--A LITTLE DISTRACTED.
DISTRACTED. SURE.
TH-THE TRUTH IS, MATTHEW, THINGS ARE WORSE THAN THE OTHERS REALIZE. I DIDN'T WANT TO CAUSE A PANIC, BUT...WELL.
RAVENS CAN KEEP SECRETS.
OH NO.

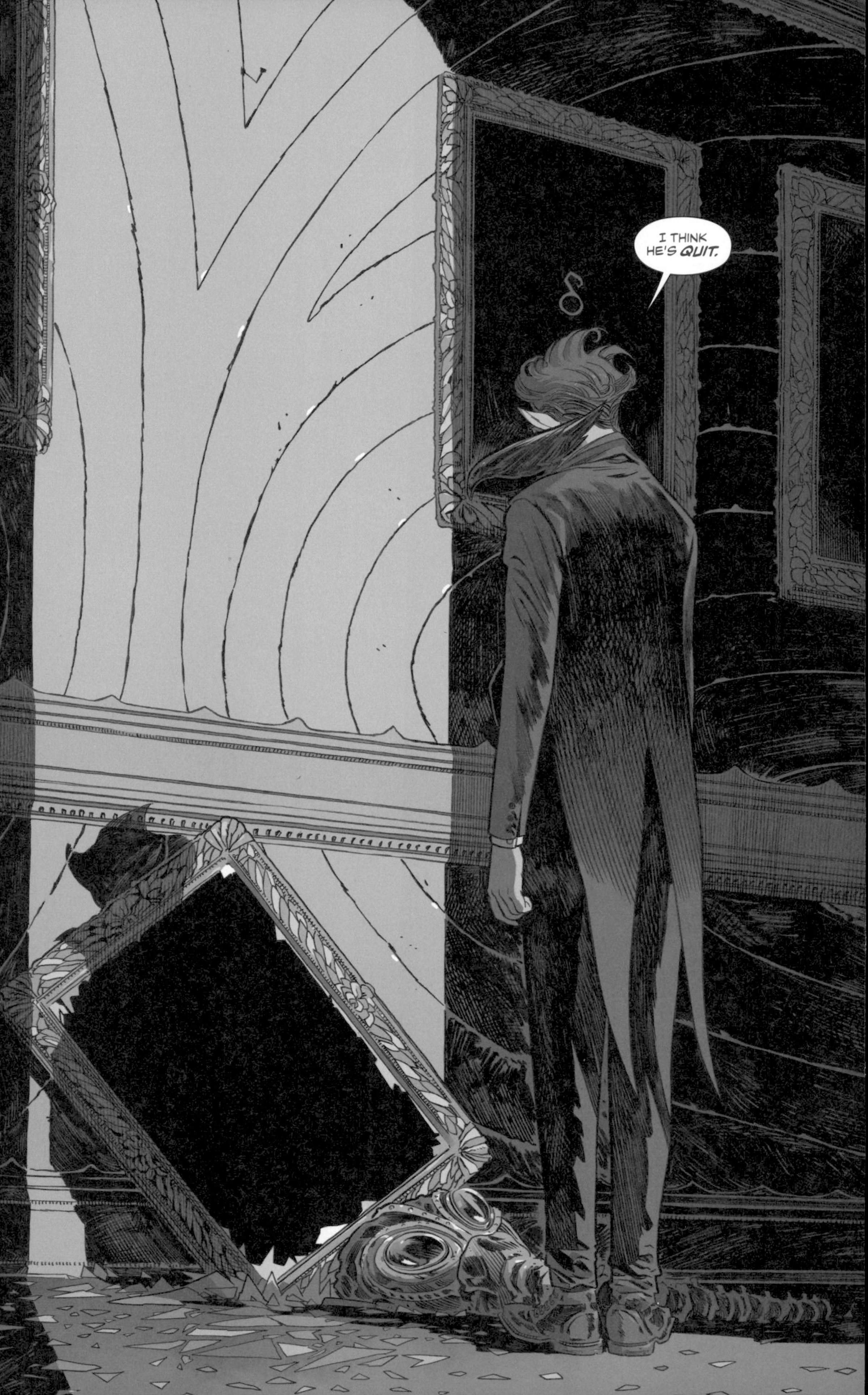
I THINK HE'S QUIT.

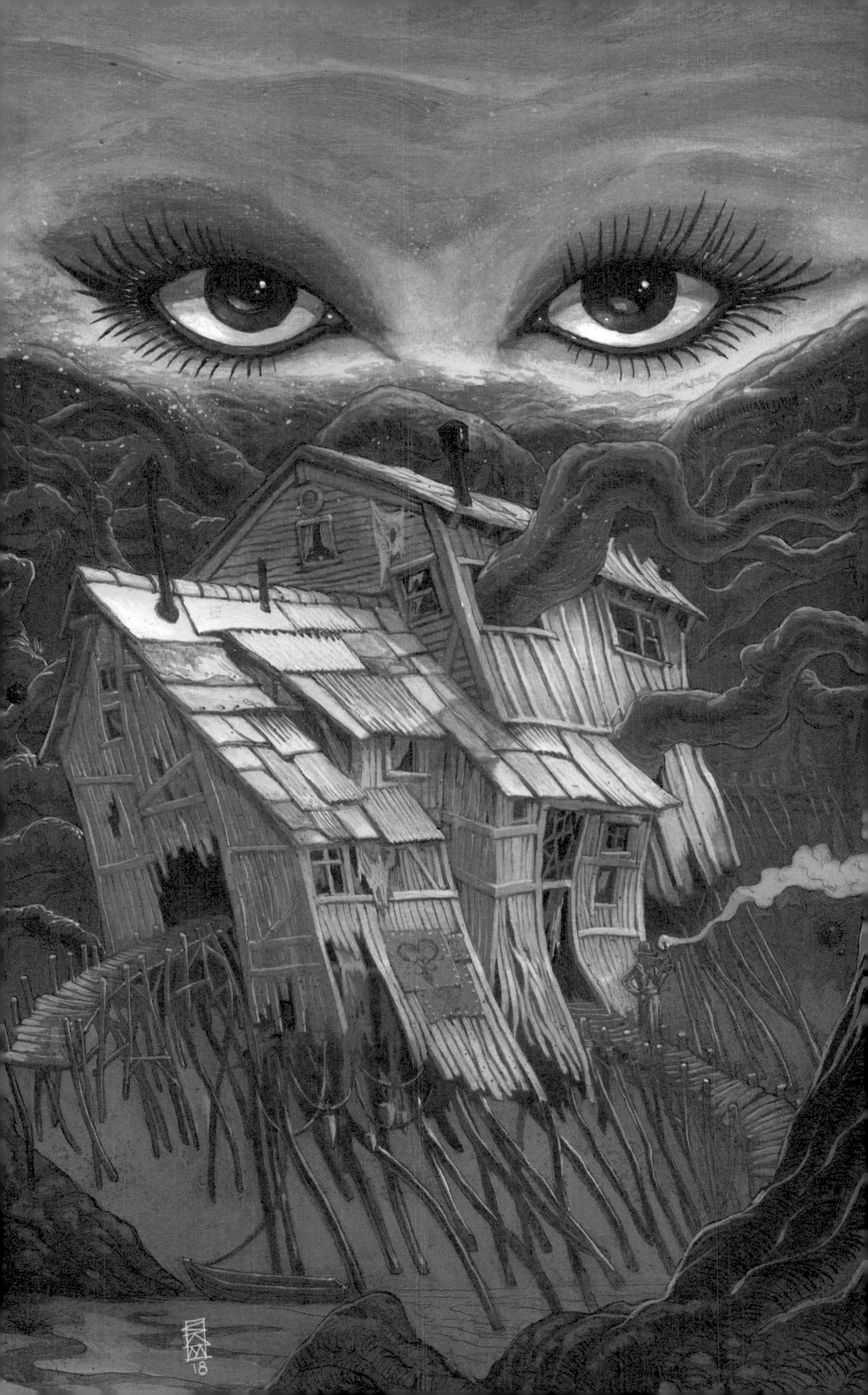

HOUSE OF WHISPERS

Broken Telephone

WRITTEN BY
Nalo Hopkinson

ILLUSTRATED BY
Dominike "DOMO" Stanton

COLORS BY
John Rauch

LETTERS BY
AndWorld Design

COVER ART BY
Sean Andrew Murray

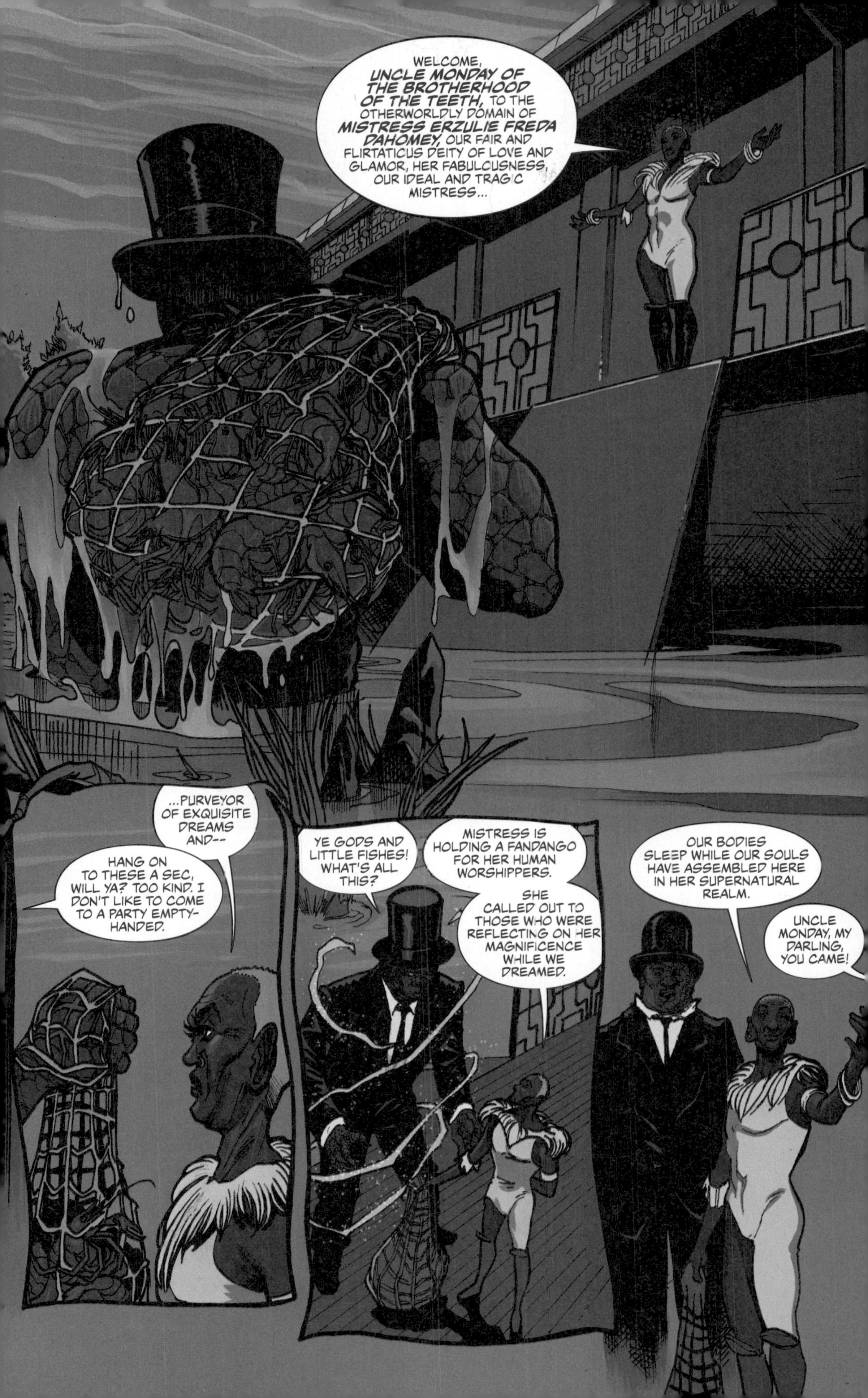
WELCOME, ***UNCLE MONDAY OF THE BROTHERHOOD OF THE TEETH,*** TO THE OTHERWORLDLY DOMAIN OF ***MISTRESS ERZULIE FREDA DAHOMEY,*** OUR FAIR AND FLIRTATIOUS DEITY OF LOVE AND GLAMOR, HER FABULOUSNESS, OUR IDEAL AND TRAGIC MISTRESS...
...PURVEYOR OF EXQUISITE DREAMS AND--
HANG ON TO THESE A SEC, WILL YA? TOO KIND. I DON'T LIKE TO COME TO A PARTY EMPTY-HANDED.
YE GODS AND LITTLE FISHES! WHAT'S ALL THIS?
MISTRESS IS HOLDING A FANDANGO FOR HER HUMAN WORSHIPPERS.
SHE CALLED OUT TO THOSE WHO WERE REFLECTING ON HER MAGNIFICENCE WHILE WE DREAMED.
OUR BODIES SLEEP WHILE OUR SOULS HAVE ASSEMBLED HERE IN HER SUPERNATURAL REALM.
UNCLE MONDAY, MY DARLING, YOU CAME!

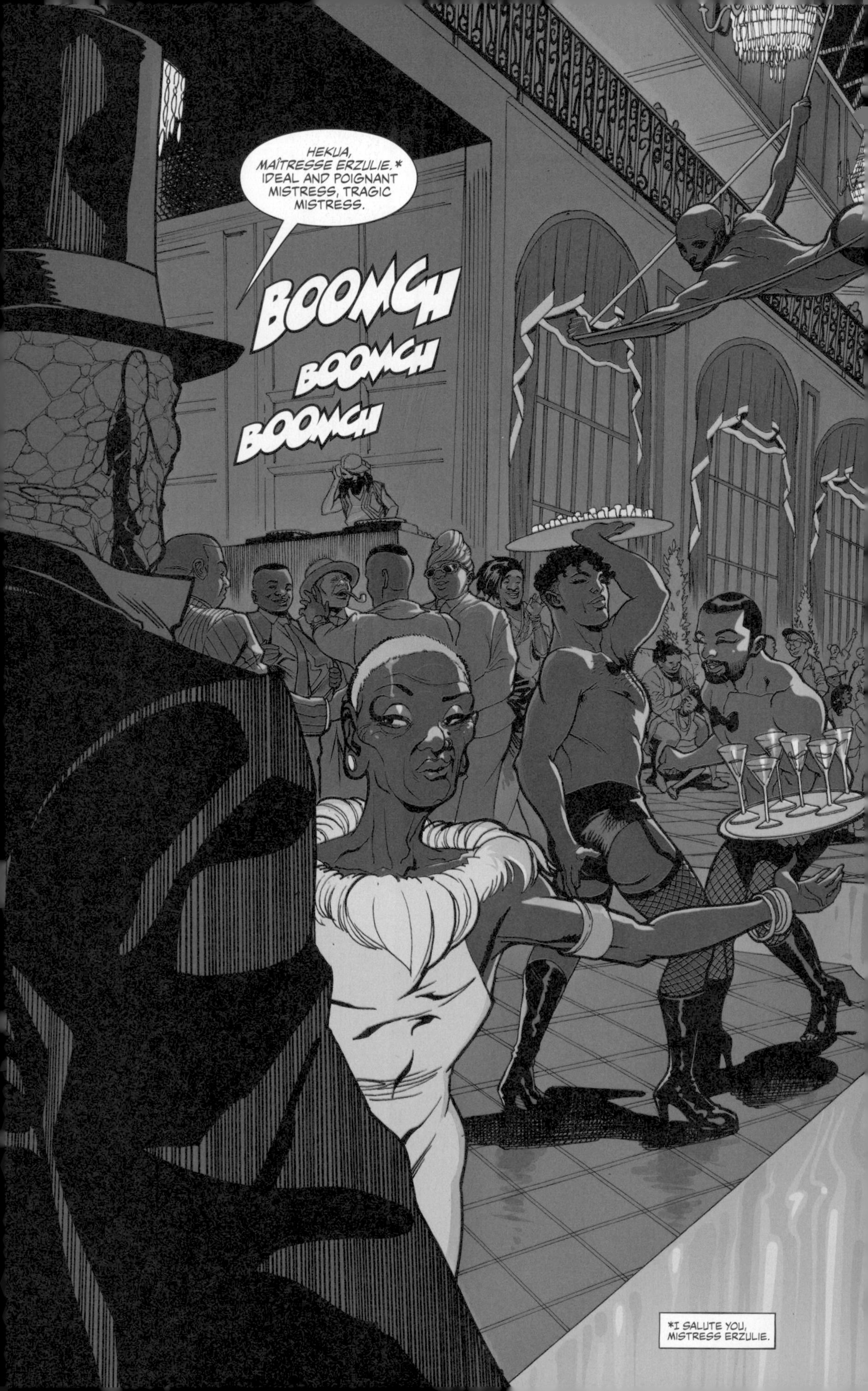
HEKUA, MAÎTRESSE ERZULIE.* IDEAL AND POIGNANT MISTRESS, TRAGIC MISTRESS.
BOOMCH
BOOMCH
BOOMCH
*I SALUTE YOU, MISTRESS ERZULIE.

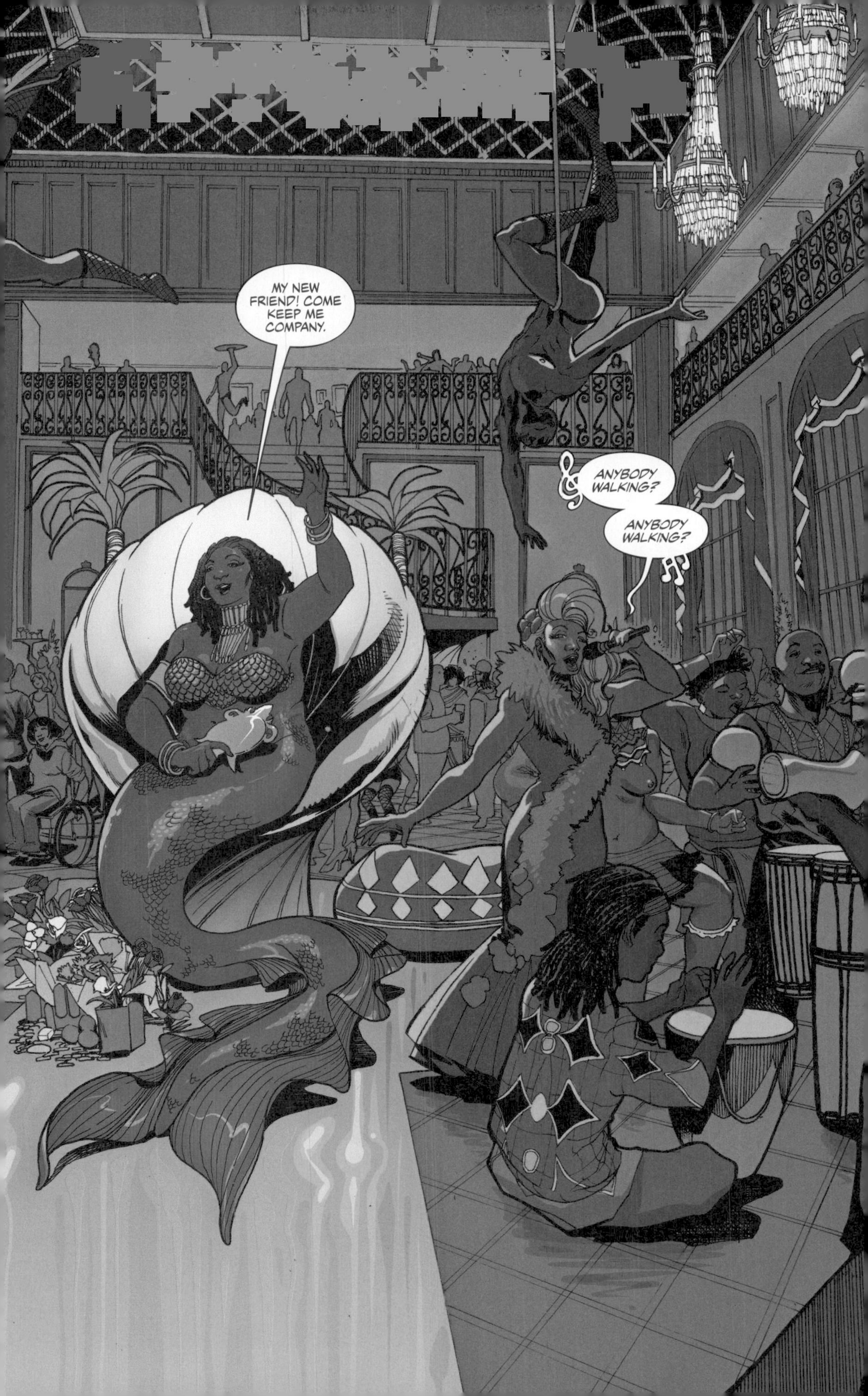
MY NEW FRIEND! COME KEEP ME COMPANY.
ANYBODY WALKING?
ANYBODY WALKING?

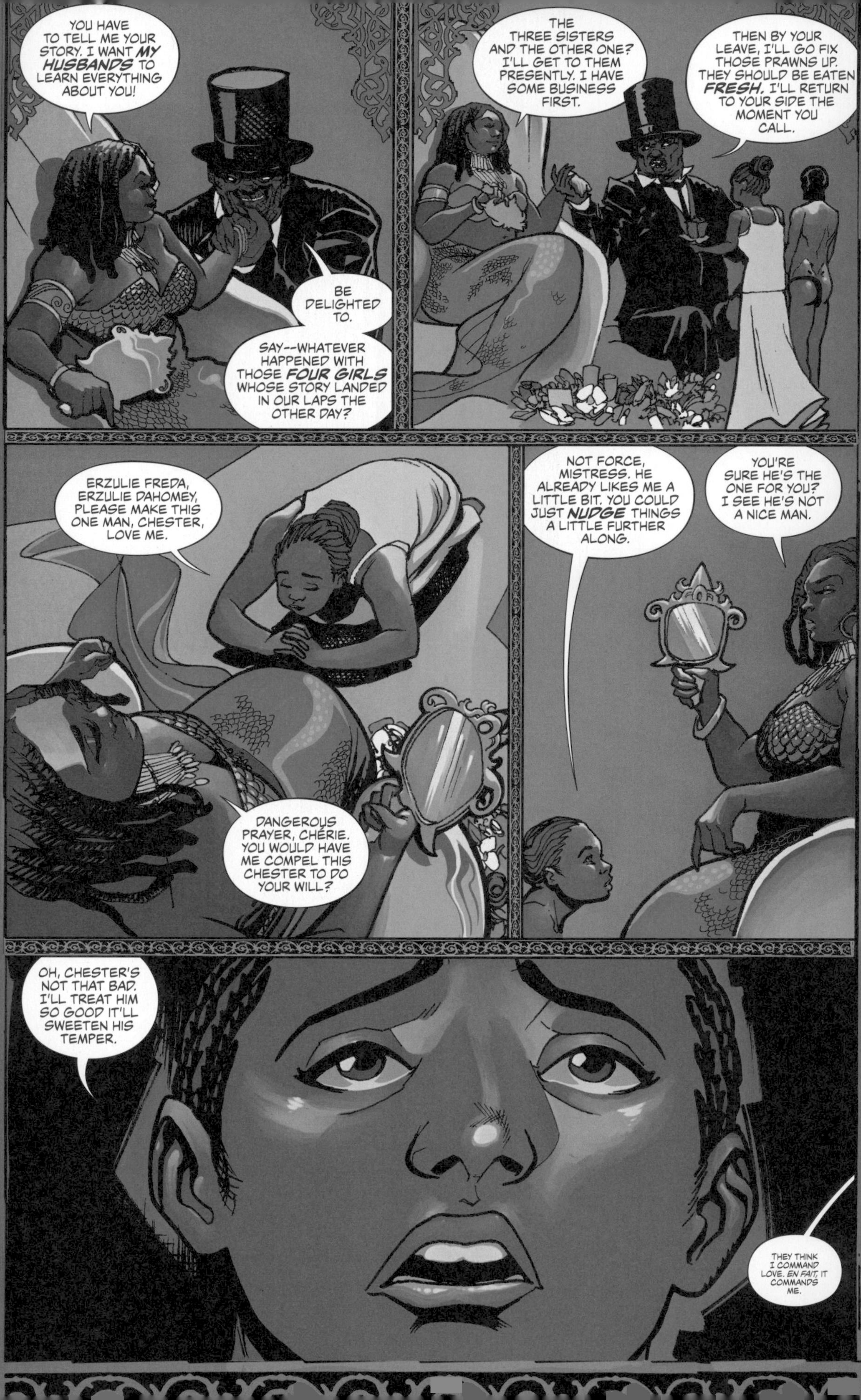

YOU HAVE TO TELL ME YOUR STORY. I WANT MY HUSBANDS TO LEARN EVERYTHING ABOUT YOU!
BE DELIGHTED TO.
SAY--WHATEVER HAPPENED WITH THOSE FOUR GIRLS WHOSE STORY LANDED IN OUR LAPS THE OTHER DAY?
THE THREE SISTERS AND THE OTHER ONE? I'LL GET TO THEM PRESENTLY. I HAVE SOME BUSINESS FIRST.
THEN BY YOUR LEAVE, I'LL GO FIX THOSE PRAWNS UP. THEY SHOULD BE EATEN FRESH. I'LL RETURN TO YOUR SIDE THE MOMENT YOU CALL.
ERZULIE FREDA, ERZULIE DAHOMEY, PLEASE MAKE THIS ONE MAN, CHESTER, LOVE ME.
DANGEROUS PRAYER, CHÉRIE. YOU WOULD HAVE ME COMPEL THIS CHESTER TO DO YOUR WILL?
NOT FORCE, MISTRESS. HE ALREADY LIKES ME A LITTLE BIT. YOU COULD JUST NUDGE THINGS A LITTLE FURTHER ALONG.
YOU'RE SURE HE'S THE ONE FOR YOU? I SEE HE'S NOT A NICE MAN.
OH, CHESTER'S NOT THAT BAD. I'LL TREAT HIM SO GOOD IT'LL SWEETEN HIS TEMPER.
THEY THINK I COMMAND LOVE. EN FAIT, IT COMMANDS ME.

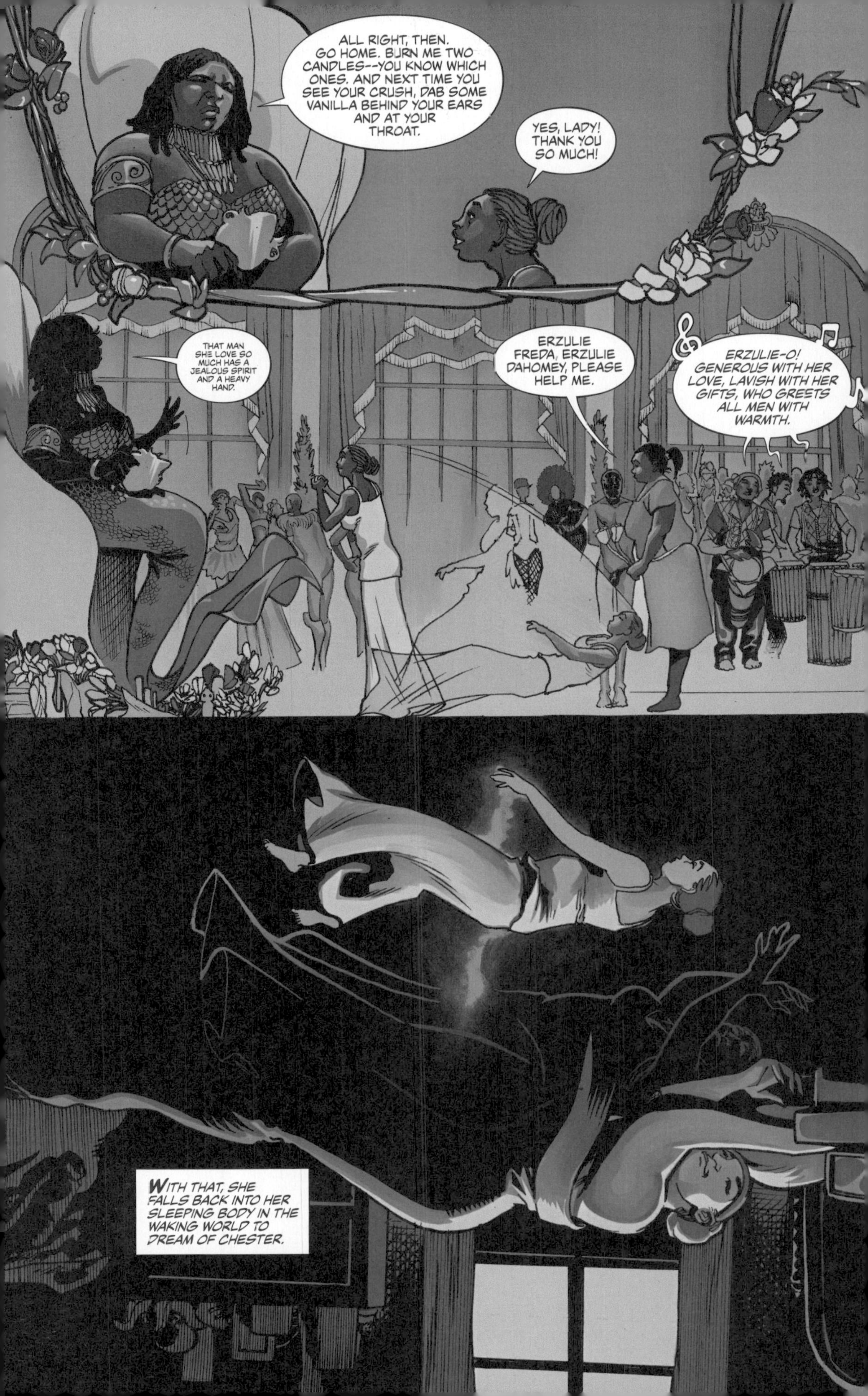
ALL RIGHT, THEN. GO HOME. BURN ME TWO CANDLES--YOU KNOW WHICH ONES. AND NEXT TIME YOU SEE YOUR CRUSH, DAB SOME VANILLA BEHIND YOUR EARS AND AT YOUR THROAT.
YES, LADY! THANK YOU SO MUCH!
THAT MAN SHE LOVE SO MUCH HAS A JEALOUS SPIRIT AND A HEAVY HAND.
ERZULIE FREDA, ERZULIE DAHOMEY, PLEASE HELP ME.
ERZULIE-O! GENEROUS WITH HER LOVE, LAVISH WITH HER GIFTS, WHO GREETS ALL MEN WITH WARMTH.
WITH THAT, SHE FALLS BACK INTO HER SLEEPING BODY IN THE WAKING WORLD TO DREAM OF CHESTER.

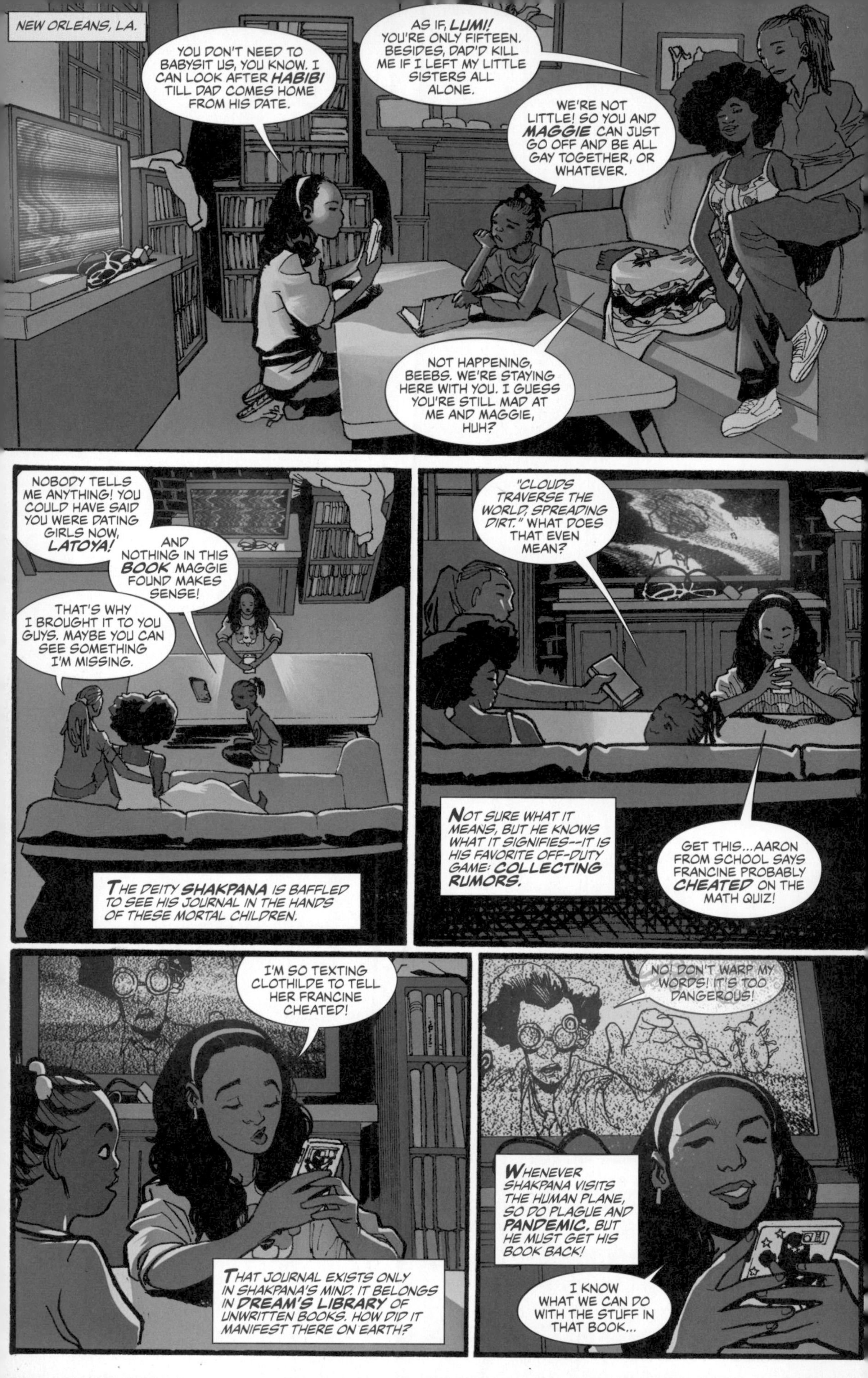
NEW ORLEANS, LA.
YOU DON'T NEED TO BABYSIT US, YOU KNOW. I CAN LOOK AFTER HABIBI TILL DAD COMES HOME FROM HIS DATE.
AS IF, LUMI! YOU'RE ONLY FIFTEEN. BESIDES, DAD'D KILL ME IF I LEFT MY LITTLE SISTERS ALL ALONE.
WE'RE NOT LITTLE! SO YOU AND MAGGIE CAN JUST GO OFF AND BE ALL GAY TOGETHER, OR WHATEVER.
NOT HAPPENING, BEEBS. WE'RE STAYING HERE WITH YOU. I GUESS YOU'RE STILL MAD AT ME AND MAGGIE, HUH?
NOBODY TELLS ME ANYTHING! YOU COULD HAVE SAID YOU WERE DATING GIRLS NOW, LATOYA!
AND NOTHING IN THIS BOOK MAGGIE FOUND MAKES SENSE!
THAT'S WHY I BROUGHT IT TO YOU GUYS. MAYBE YOU CAN SEE SOMETHING I'M MISSING.
THE DEITY SHAKPANA IS BAFFLED TO SEE HIS JOURNAL IN THE HANDS OF THESE MORTAL CHILDREN.
"CLOUDS TRAVERSE THE WORLD, SPREADING DIRT." WHAT DOES THAT EVEN MEAN?
NOT SURE WHAT IT MEANS, BUT HE KNOWS WHAT IT SIGNIFIES--IT IS HIS FAVORITE OFF-DUTY GAME: COLLECTING RUMORS.
GET THIS...AARON FROM SCHOOL SAYS FRANCINE PROBABLY CHEATED ON THE MATH QUIZ!
I'M SO TEXTING CLOTHILDE TO TELL HER FRANCINE CHEATED!
THAT JOURNAL EXISTS ONLY IN SHAKPANA'S MIND. IT BELONGS IN DREAM'S LIBRARY OF UNWRITTEN BOOKS. HOW DID IT MANIFEST THERE ON EARTH?
NO! DON'T WARP MY WORDS! IT'S TOO DANGEROUS!
WHENEVER SHAKPANA VISITS THE HUMAN PLANE, SO DO PLAGUE AND PANDEMIC. BUT HE MUST GET HIS BOOK BACK!
I KNOW WHAT WE CAN DO WITH THE STUFF IN THAT BOOK...

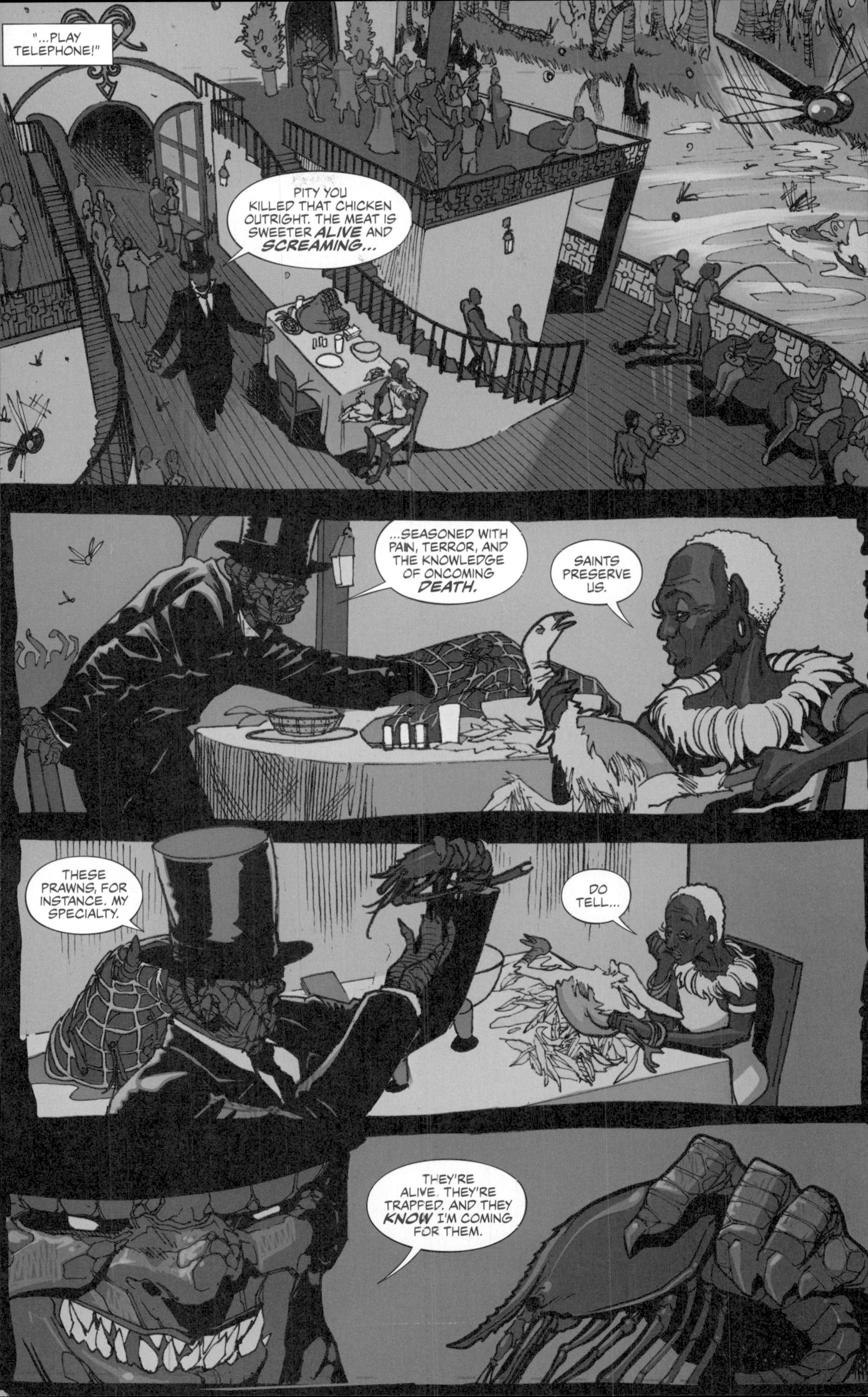
"...PLAY TELEPHONE!"
PITY YOU KILLED THAT CHICKEN OUTRIGHT. THE MEAT IS SWEETER ALIVE AND SCREAMING...
...SEASONED WITH PAIN, TERROR, AND THE KNOWLEDGE OF ONCOMING DEATH.
SAINTS PRESERVE US.
THESE PRAWNS, FOR INSTANCE. MY SPECIALTY.
DO TELL...
THEY'RE ALIVE. THEY'RE TRAPPED. AND THEY KNOW I'M COMING FOR THEM.

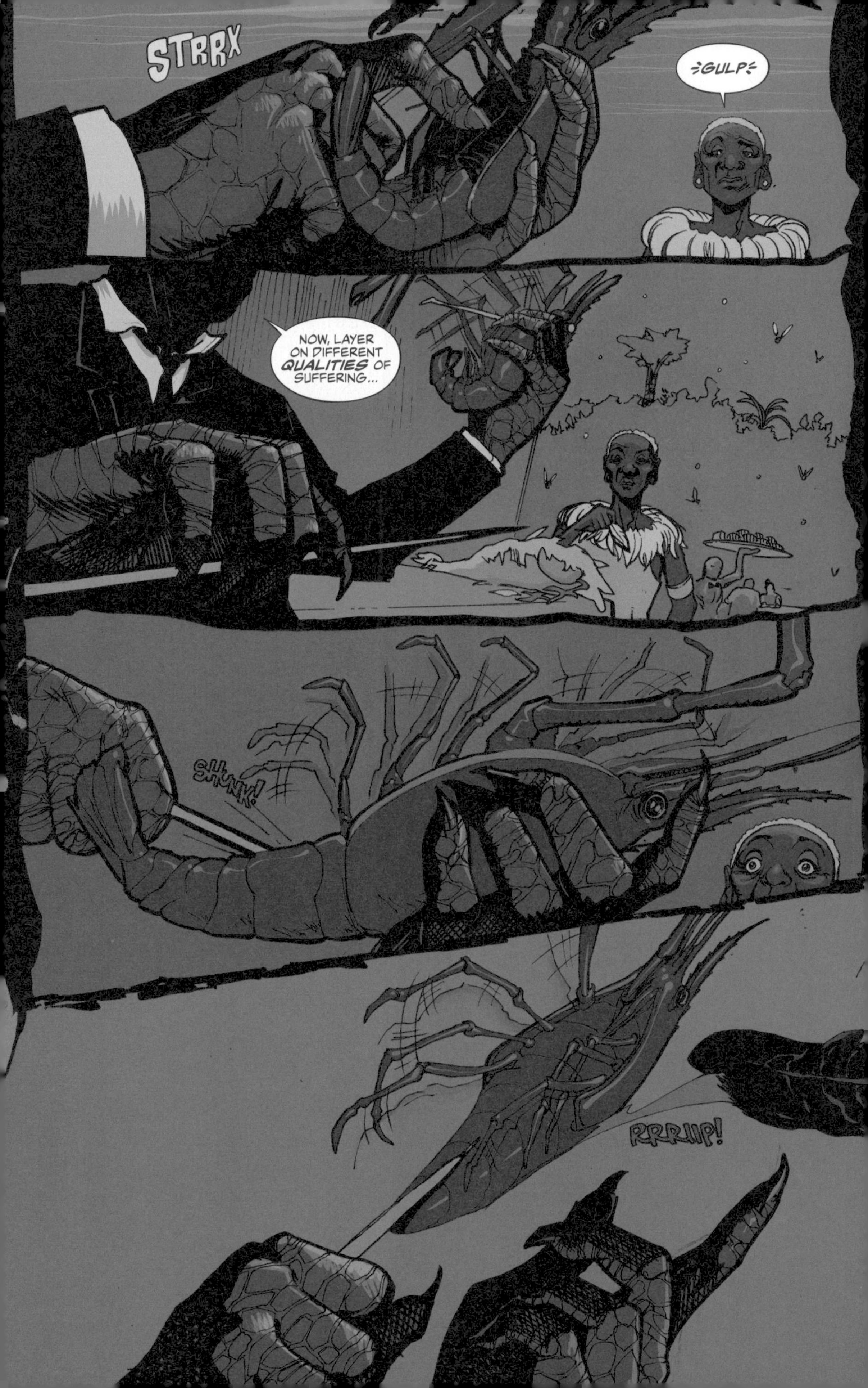
STRRX
GULP
NOW, LAYER ON DIFFERENT QUALITIES OF SUFFERING...
SHUNK!
RRRIIP!

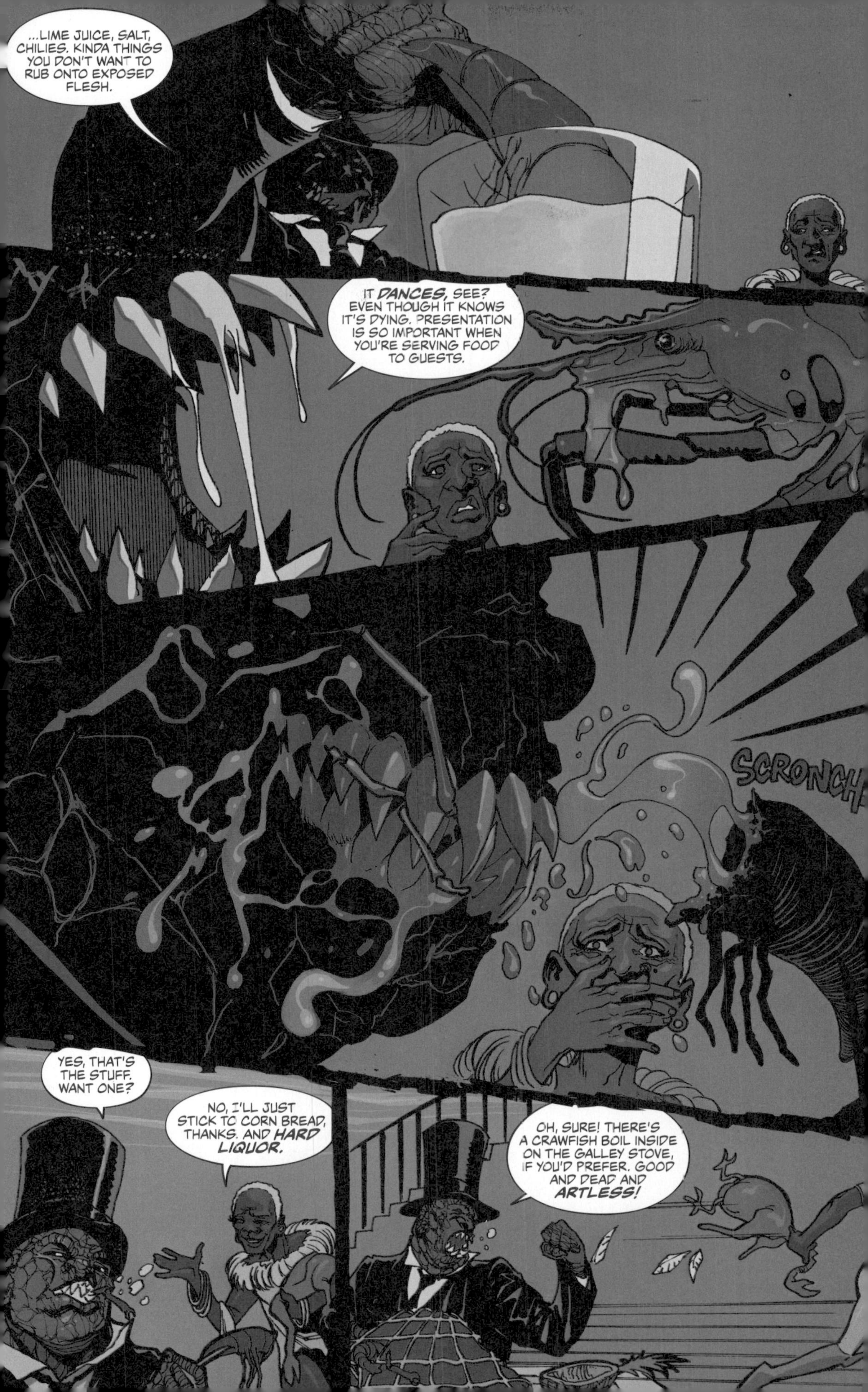

...LIME JUICE, SALT, CHILIES. KINDA THINGS YOU DON'T WANT TO RUB ONTO EXPOSED FLESH.
IT DANCES, SEE? EVEN THOUGH IT KNOWS IT'S DYING. PRESENTATION IS SO IMPORTANT WHEN YOU'RE SERVING FOOD TO GUESTS.
SCRONCH
YES, THAT'S THE STUFF. WANT ONE?
NO, I'LL JUST STICK TO CORN BREAD, THANKS. AND HARD LIQUOR.
OH, SURE! THERE'S A CRAWFISH BOIL INSIDE ON THE GALLEY STOVE, IF YOU'D PREFER. GOOD AND DEAD AND ARTLESS!

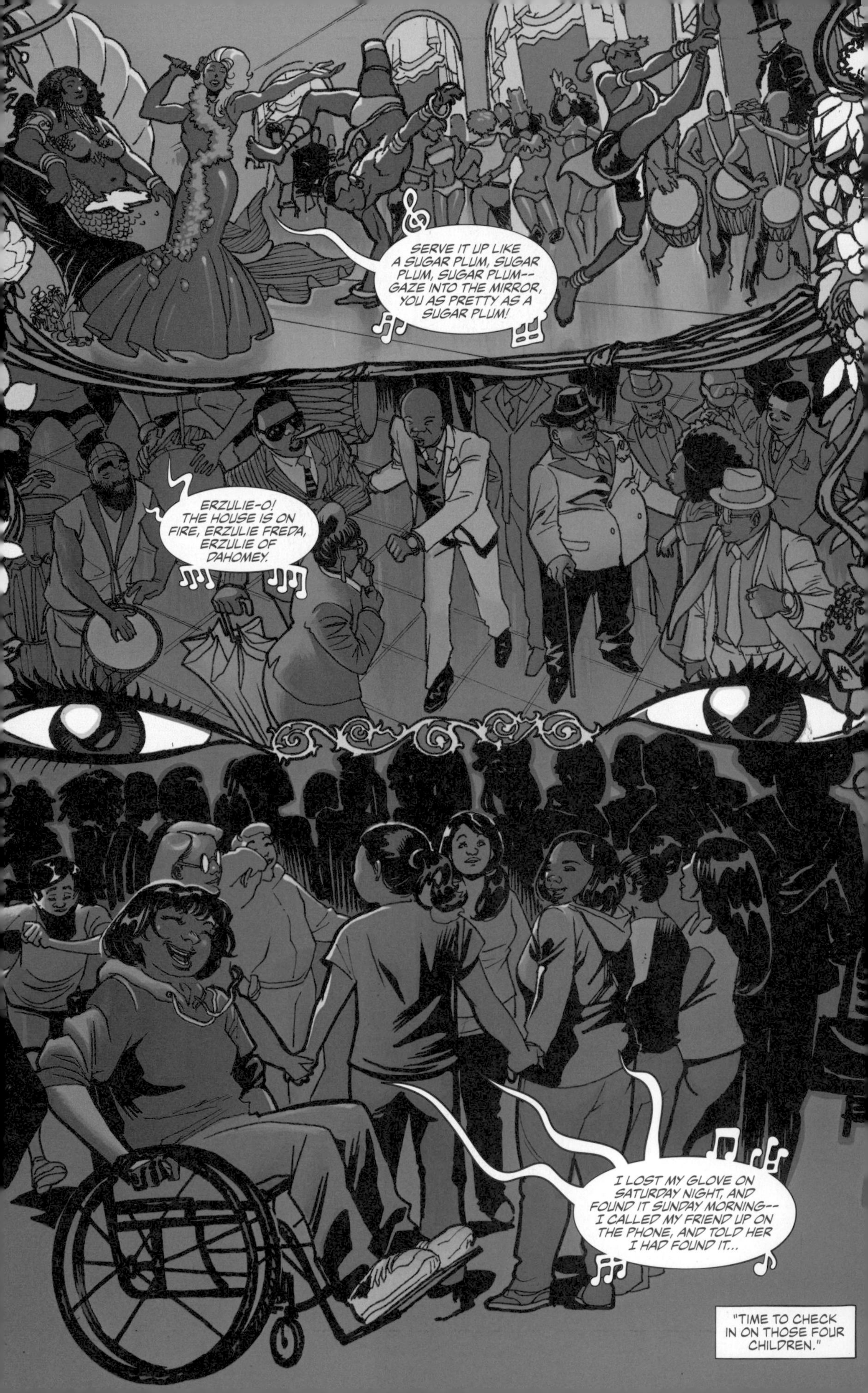
SERVE IT UP LIKE A SUGAR PLUM, SUGAR PLUM, SUGAR PLUM-- GAZE INTO THE MIRROR, YOU AS PRETTY AS A SUGAR PLUM!
ERZULIE-O! THE HOUSE IS ON FIRE, ERZULIE FREDA, ERZULIE OF DAHOMEY.
I LOST MY GLOVE ON SATURDAY NIGHT, AND FOUND IT SUNDAY MORNING-- I CALLED MY FRIEND UP ON THE PHONE, AND TOLD HER I HAD FOUND IT...
"TIME TO CHECK IN ON THOSE FOUR CHILDREN."

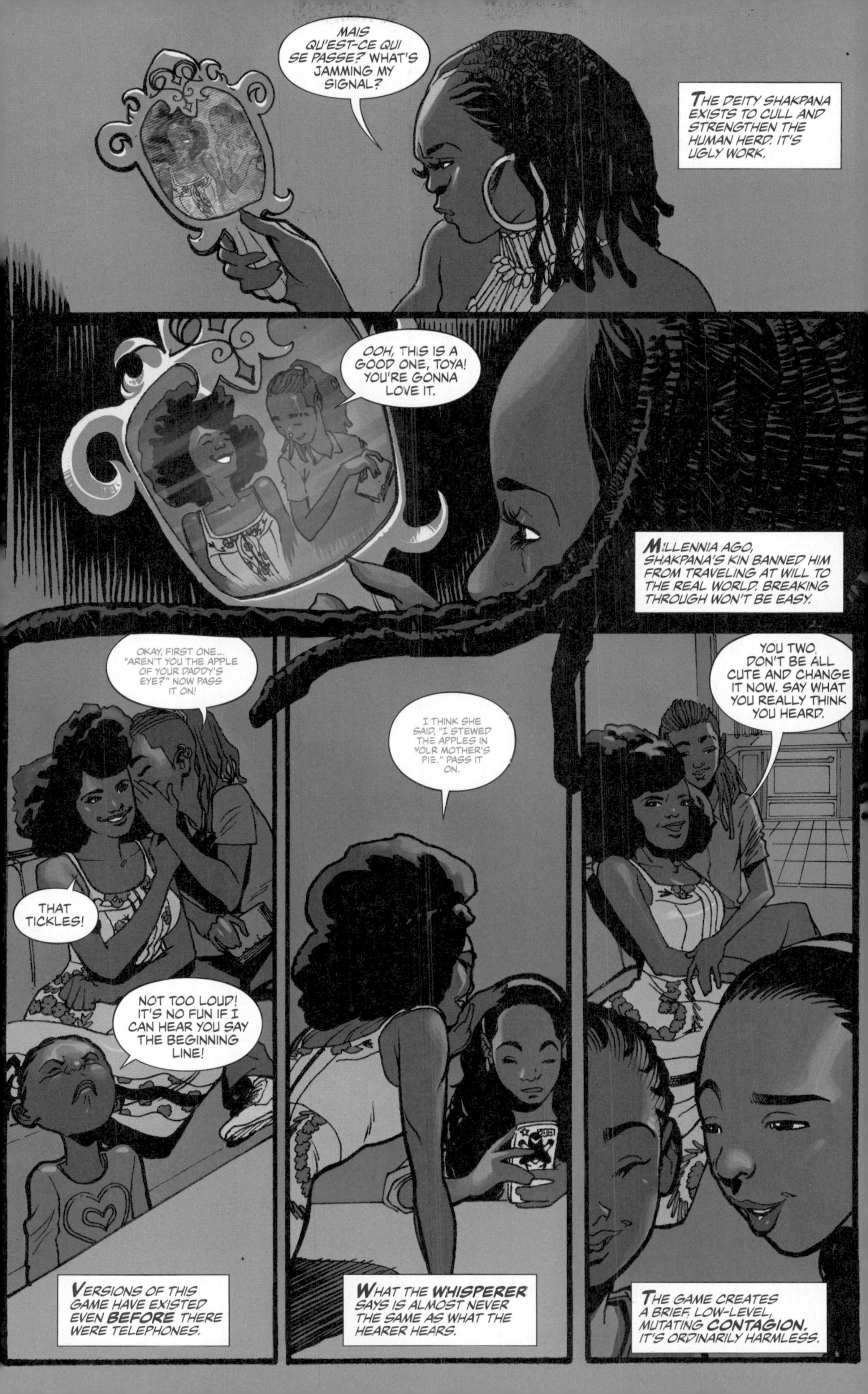
MAIS QU'EST-CE QUI SE PASSE? WHAT'S JAMMING MY SIGNAL?
THE DEITY SHAKPANA EXISTS TO CULL AND STRENGTHEN THE HUMAN HERD. IT'S UGLY WORK.
OOH, THIS IS A GOOD ONE, TOYA! YOU'RE GONNA LOVE IT.
MILLENNIA AGO, SHAKPANA'S KIN BANNED HIM FROM TRAVELING AT WILL TO THE REAL WORLD. BREAKING THROUGH WON'T BE EASY.
OKAY, FIRST ONE... "AREN'T YOU THE APPLE OF YOUR DADDY'S EYE?" NOW PASS IT ON!
THAT TICKLES!
NOT TOO LOUD! IT'S NO FUN IF I CAN HEAR YOU SAY THE BEGINNING LINE!
VERSIONS OF THIS GAME HAVE EXISTED EVEN BEFORE THERE WERE TELEPHONES.
I THINK SHE SAID, "I STEWED THE APPLES IN YOUR MOTHER'S PIE." PASS IT ON.
WHAT THE WHISPERER SAYS IS ALMOST NEVER THE SAME AS WHAT THE HEARER HEARS.
YOU TWO DON'T BE ALL CUTE AND CHANGE IT NOW. SAY WHAT YOU REALLY THINK YOU HEARD.
THE GAME CREATES A BRIEF, LOW-LEVEL, MUTATING CONTAGION. IT'S ORDINARILY HARMLESS.

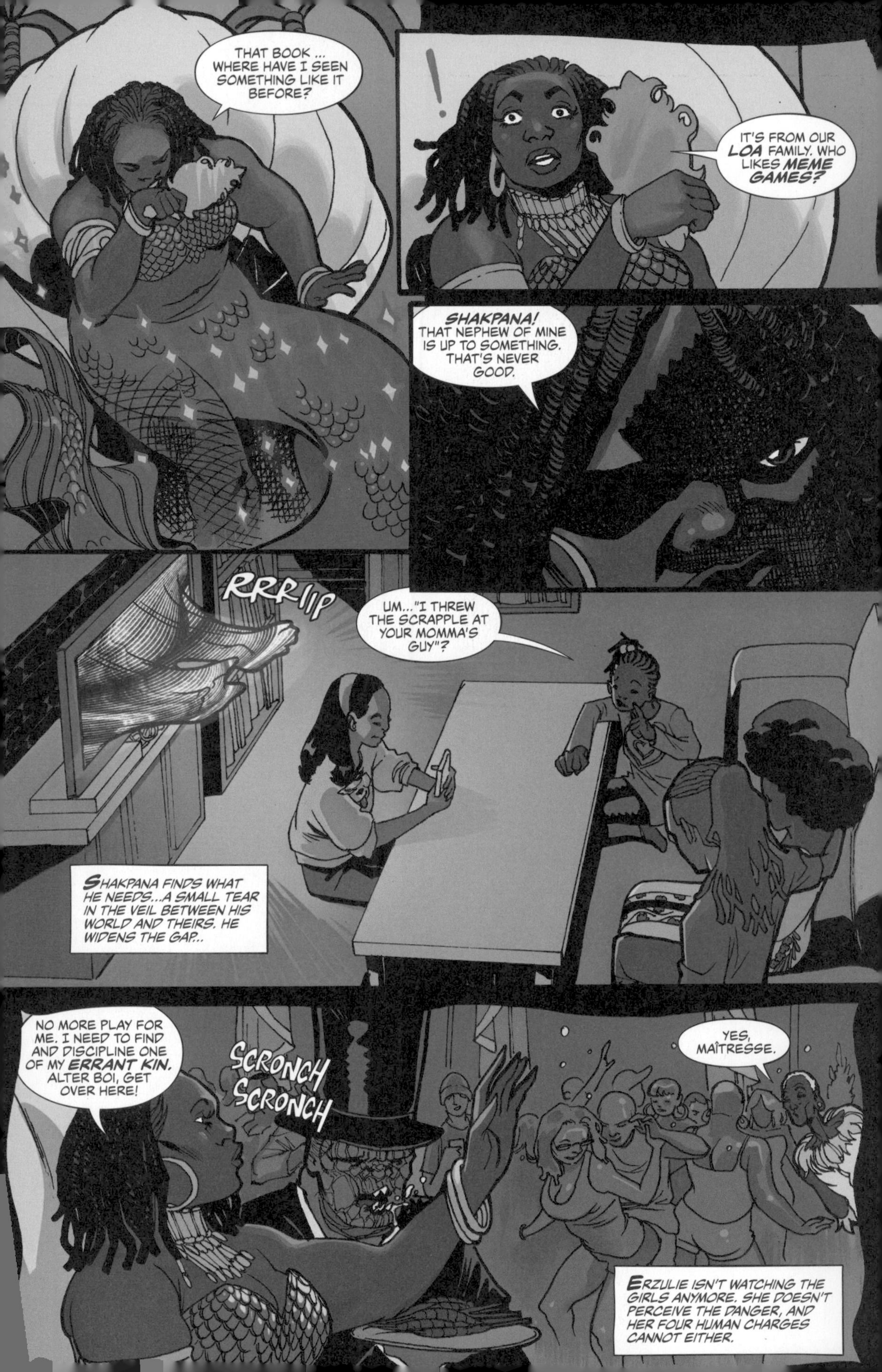
THAT BOOK ... WHERE HAVE I SEEN SOMETHING LIKE IT BEFORE?
!
IT'S FROM OUR LOA FAMILY. WHO LIKES MEME GAMES?
SHAKPANA! THAT NEPHEW OF MINE IS UP TO SOMETHING. THAT'S NEVER GOOD.
RRRIIP
UM..."I THREW THE SCRAPPLE AT YOUR MOMMA'S GUY"?
SHAKPANA FINDS WHAT HE NEEDS...A SMALL TEAR IN THE VEIL BETWEEN HIS WORLD AND THEIRS. HE WIDENS THE GAP...
NO MORE PLAY FOR ME. I NEED TO FIND AND DISCIPLINE ONE OF MY ERRANT KIN. ALTER BOI, GET OVER HERE!
SCRONCH SCRONCH
YES, MAÎTRESSE.
ERZULIE ISN'T WATCHING THE GIRLS ANYMORE. SHE DOESN'T PERCEIVE THE DANGER, AND HER FOUR HUMAN CHARGES CANNOT EITHER.

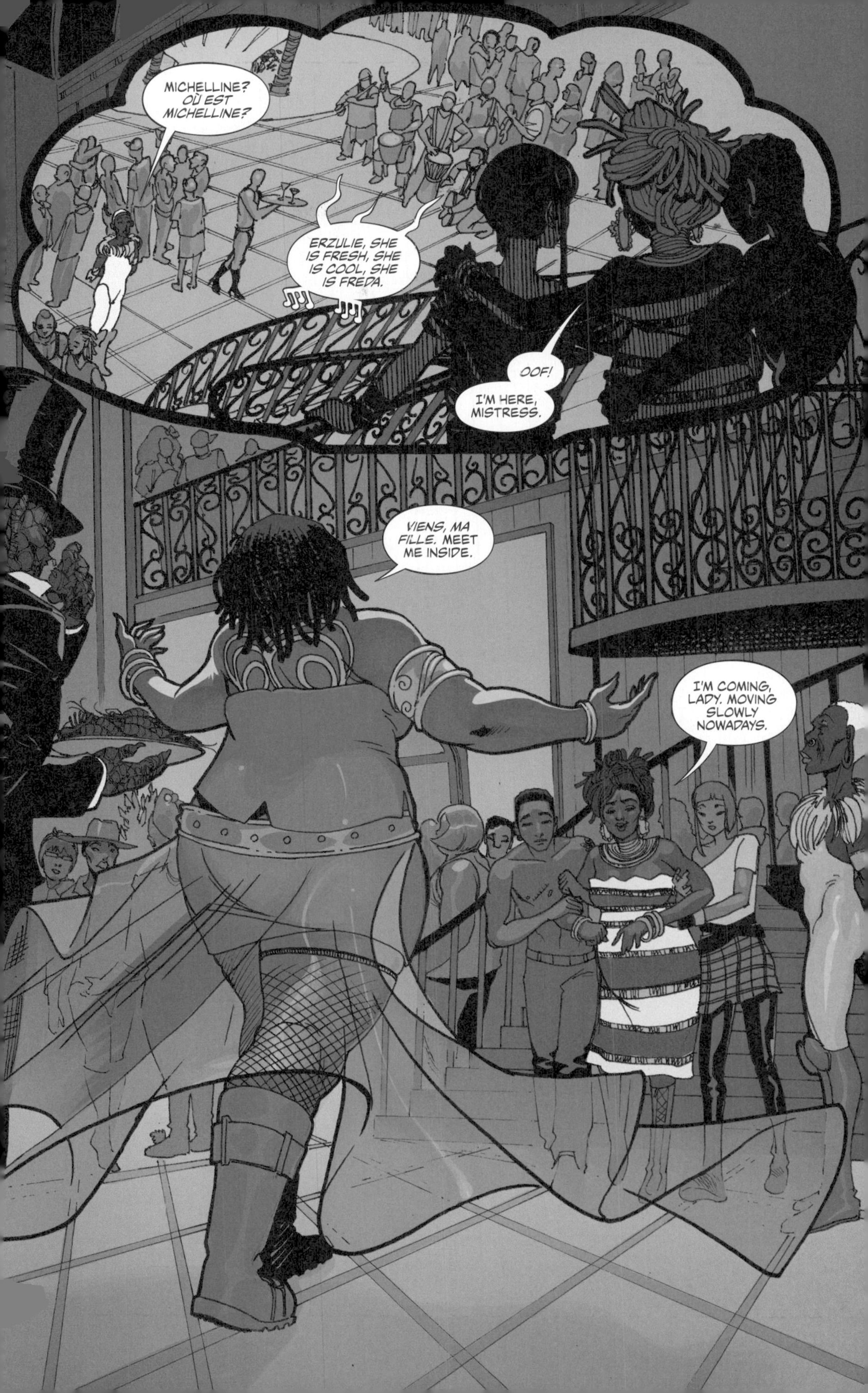
MICHELLINE? OÙ EST MICHELLINE?
ERZULIE, SHE IS FRESH, SHE IS COOL, SHE IS FREDA.
OOF!
I'M HERE, MISTRESS.
VIENS, MA FILLE. MEET ME INSIDE.
I'M COMING, LADY. MOVING SLOWLY NOWADAYS.

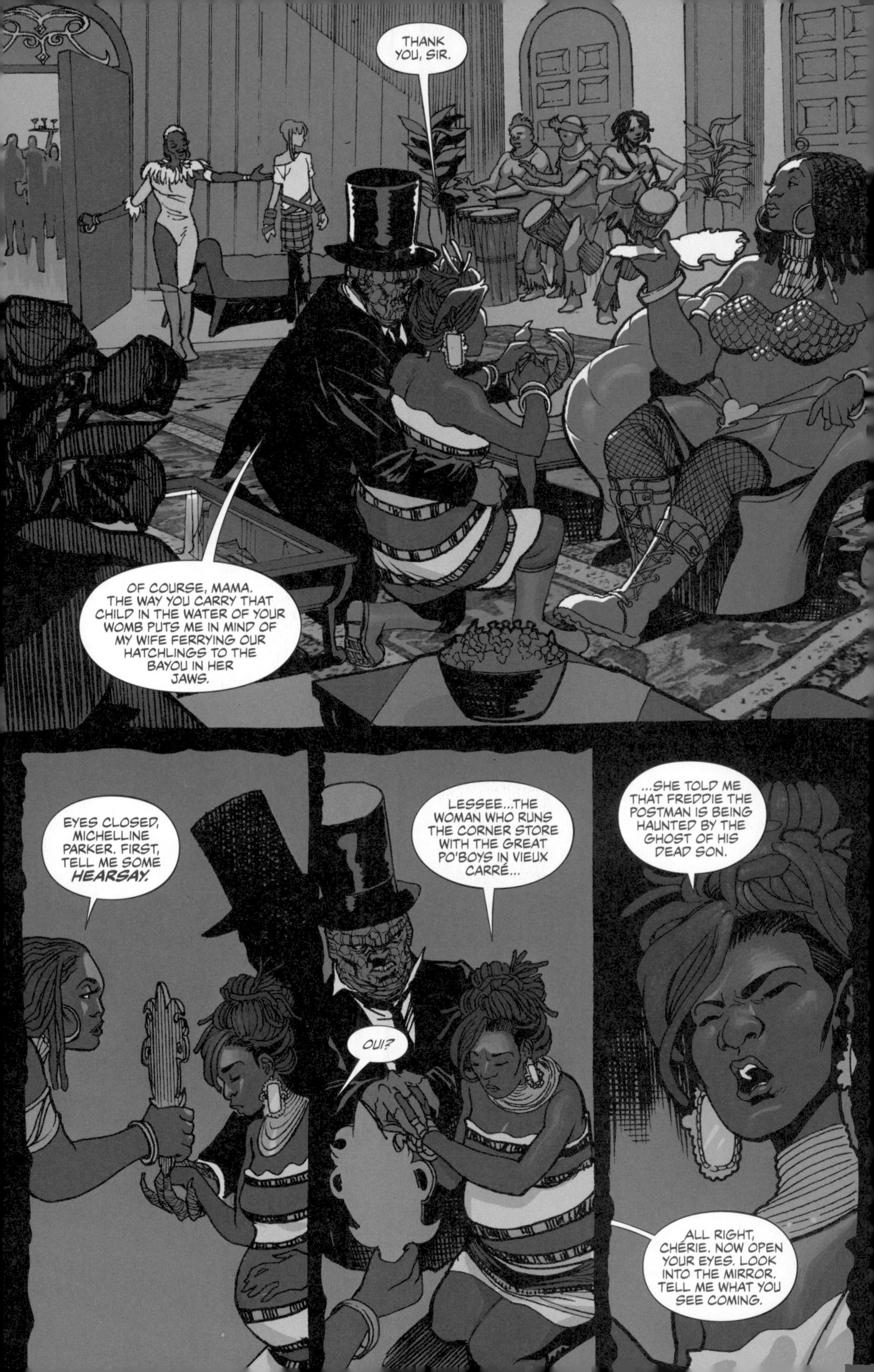
THANK YOU, SIR.
OF COURSE, MAMA. THE WAY YOU CARRY THAT CHILD IN THE WATER OF YOUR WOMB PUTS ME IN MIND OF MY WIFE FERRYING OUR HATCHLINGS TO THE BAYOU IN HER JAWS.
EYES CLOSED, MICHELLINE PARKER. FIRST, TELL ME SOME HEARSAY.
LESSEE...THE WOMAN WHO RUNS THE CORNER STORE WITH THE GREAT PO'BOYS IN VIEUX CARRÉ...
OUI?
...SHE TOLD ME THAT FREDDIE THE POSTMAN IS BEING HAUNTED BY THE GHOST OF HIS DEAD SON.
ALL RIGHT, CHÉRIE. NOW OPEN YOUR EYES. LOOK INTO THE MIRROR. TELL ME WHAT YOU SEE COMING.

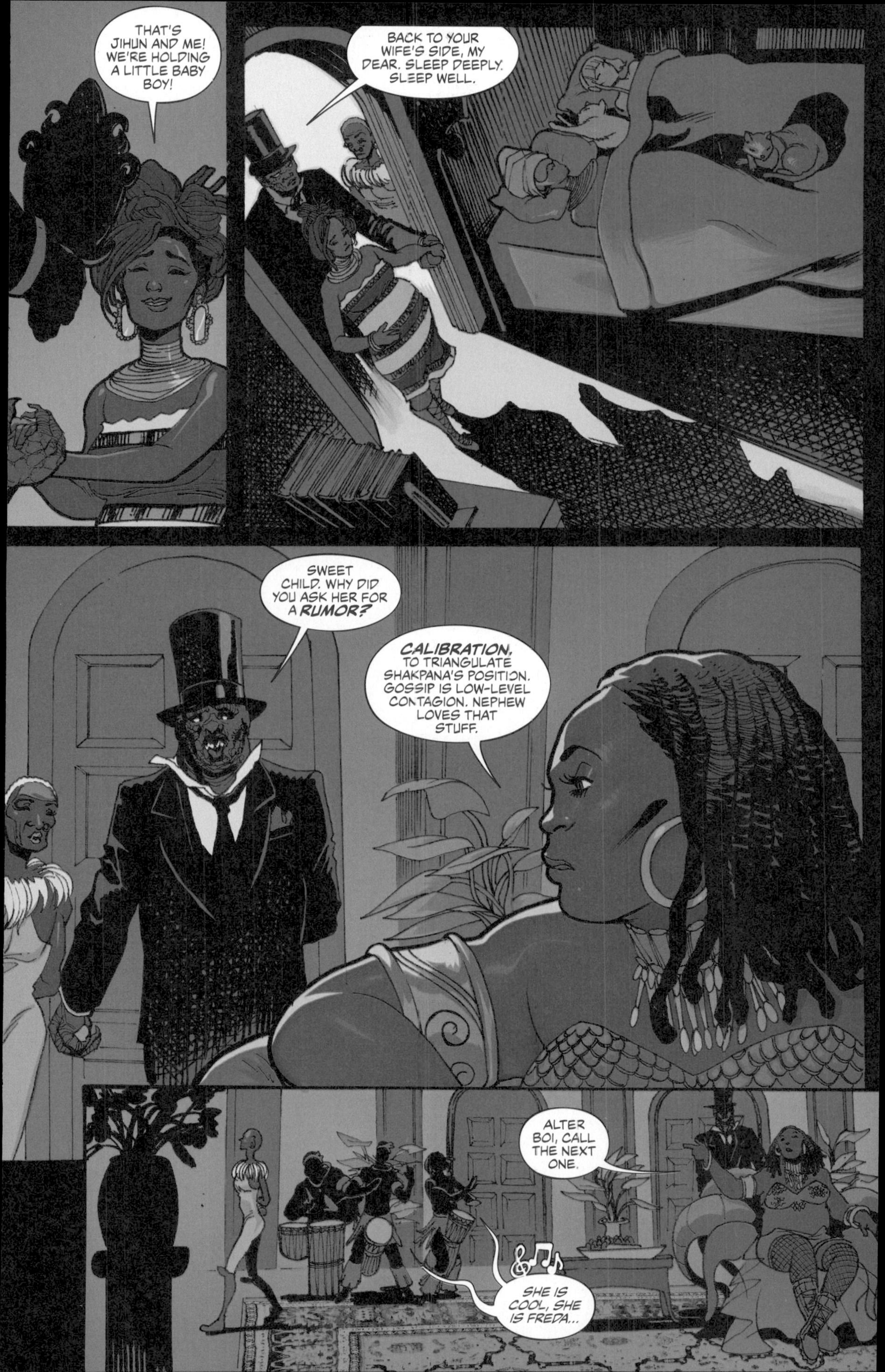
THAT'S JIHUN AND ME! WE'RE HOLDING A LITTLE BABY BOY!
BACK TO YOUR WIFE'S SIDE, MY DEAR. SLEEP DEEPLY. SLEEP WELL.
SWEET CHILD. WHY DID YOU ASK HER FOR A **RUMOR?**
CALIBRATION, TO TRIANGULATE SHAKPANA'S POSITION. GOSSIP IS LOW-LEVEL CONTAGION. NEPHEW LOVES THAT STUFF.
ALTER BOI, CALL THE NEXT ONE.
SHE IS COOL, SHE IS FREDA...

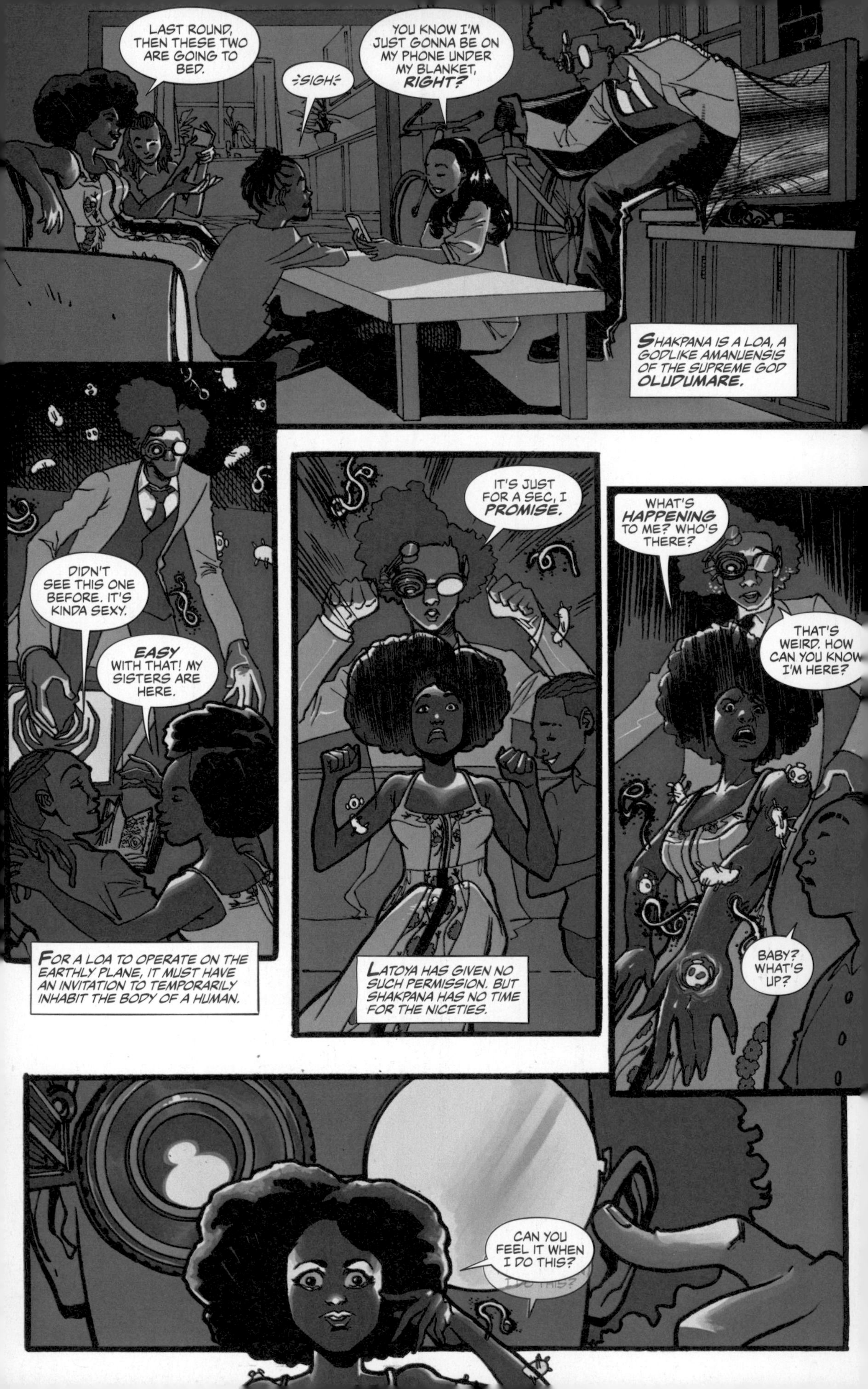
LAST ROUND, THEN THESE TWO ARE GOING TO BED.
-SIGH-
YOU KNOW I'M JUST GONNA BE ON MY PHONE UNDER MY BLANKET, RIGHT?
SHAKPANA IS A LOA, A GODLIKE AMANUENSIS OF THE SUPREME GOD OLUDUMARE.
DIDN'T SEE THIS ONE BEFORE. IT'S KINDA SEXY.
EASY WITH THAT! MY SISTERS ARE HERE.
FOR A LOA TO OPERATE ON THE EARTHLY PLANE, IT MUST HAVE AN INVITATION TO TEMPORARILY INHABIT THE BODY OF A HUMAN.
IT'S JUST FOR A SEC, I PROMISE.
LATOYA HAS GIVEN NO SUCH PERMISSION. BUT SHAKPANA HAS NO TIME FOR THE NICETIES.
WHAT'S HAPPENING TO ME? WHO'S THERE?
THAT'S WEIRD. HOW CAN YOU KNOW I'M HERE?
BABY? WHAT'S UP?
CAN YOU FEEL IT WHEN I DO THIS?
I DO THIS?

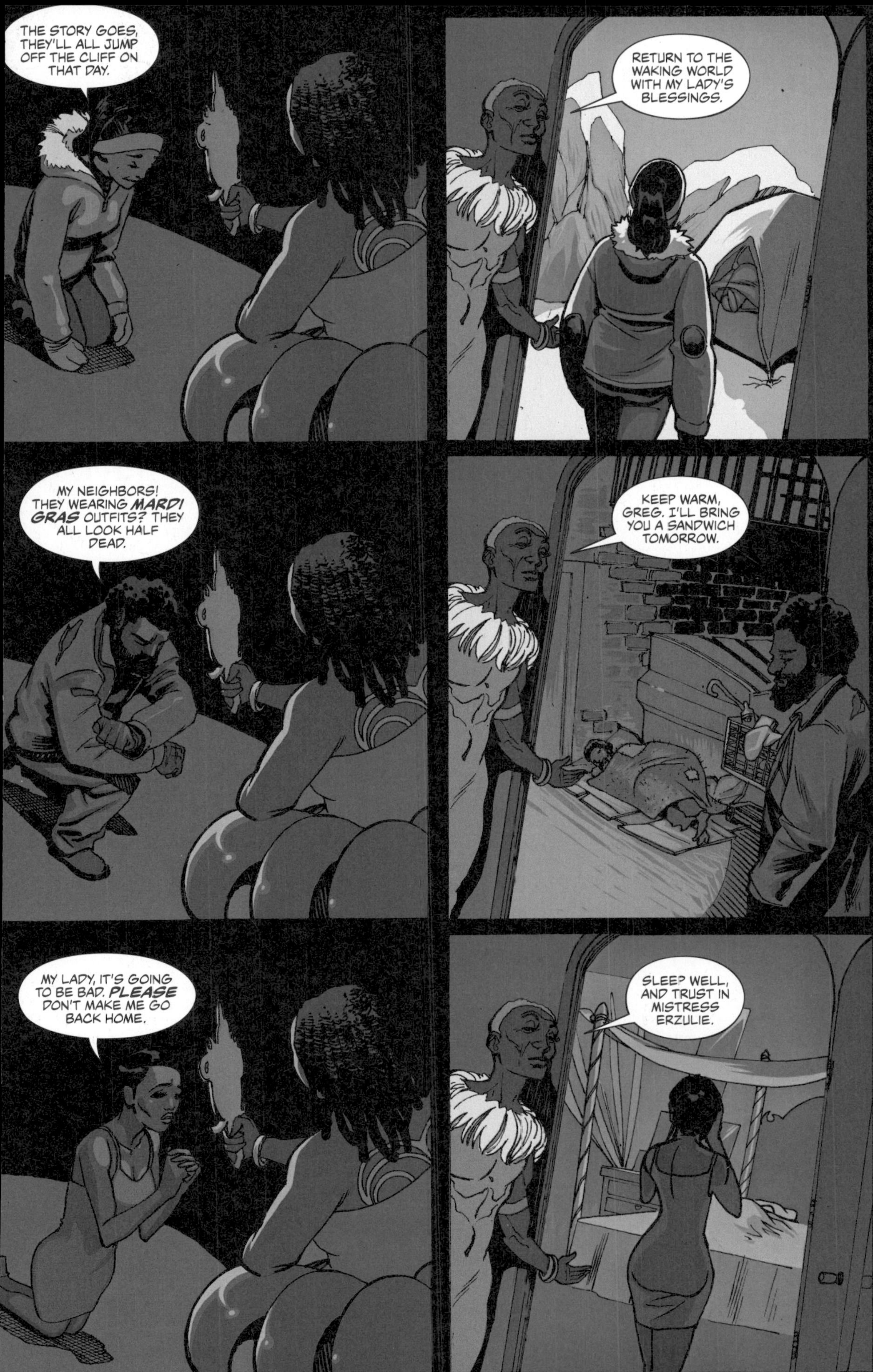
THE STORY GOES, THEY'LL ALL JUMP OFF THE CLIFF ON THAT DAY.
RETURN TO THE WAKING WORLD WITH MY LADY'S BLESSINGS.
MY NEIGHBORS! THEY WEARING MARDI GRAS OUTFITS? THEY ALL LOOK HALF DEAD.
KEEP WARM, GREG. I'LL BRING YOU A SANDWICH TOMORROW.
MY LADY, IT'S GOING TO BE BAD. PLEASE DON'T MAKE ME GO BACK HOME.
SLEEP WELL, AND TRUST IN MISTRESS ERZULIE.

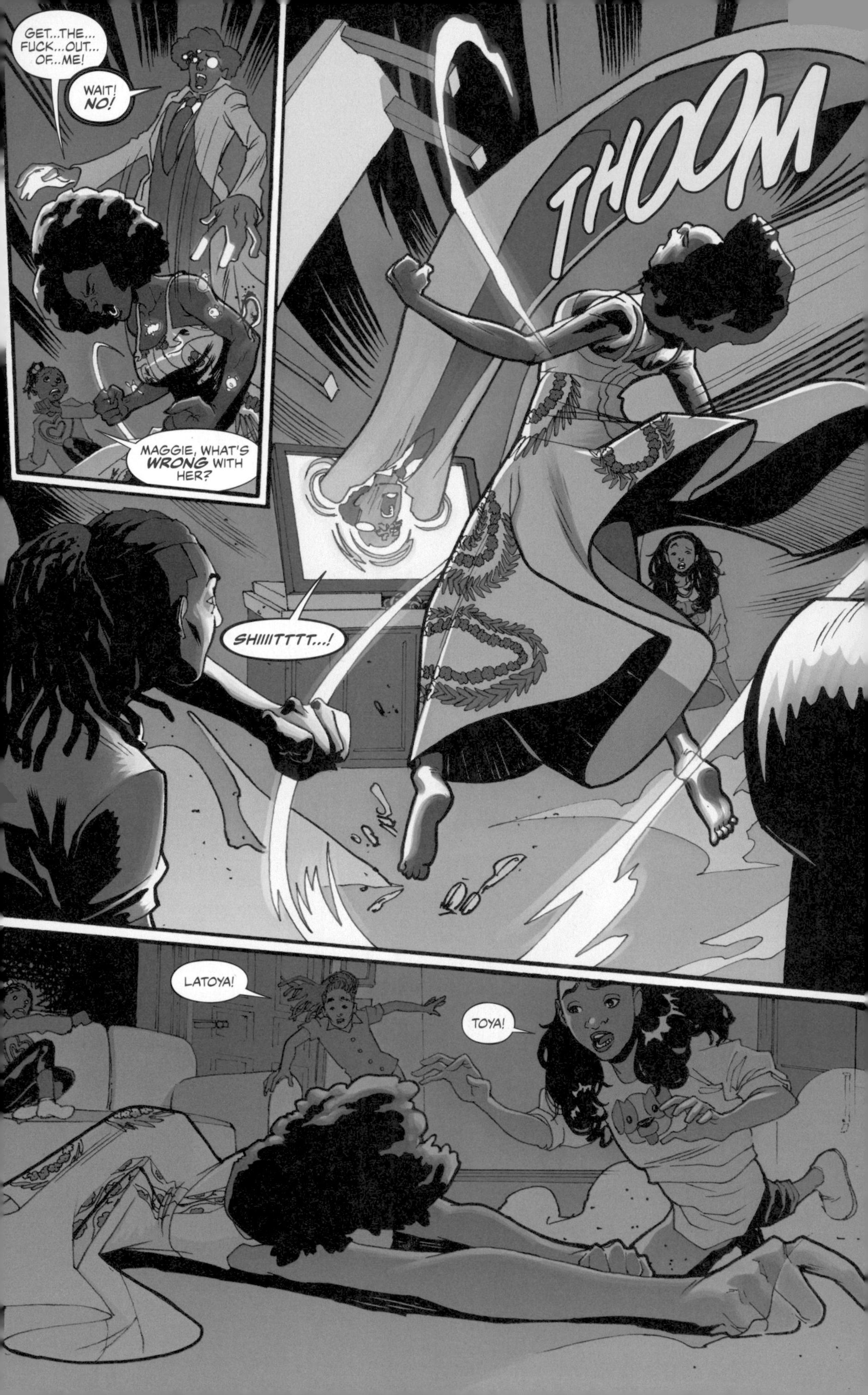
GET...THE... FUCK...OUT... OF...ME!
WAIT! NO!
MAGGIE, WHAT'S WRONG WITH HER?
THOOM
SHIIIITTTT...!
LATOYA!
TOYA!

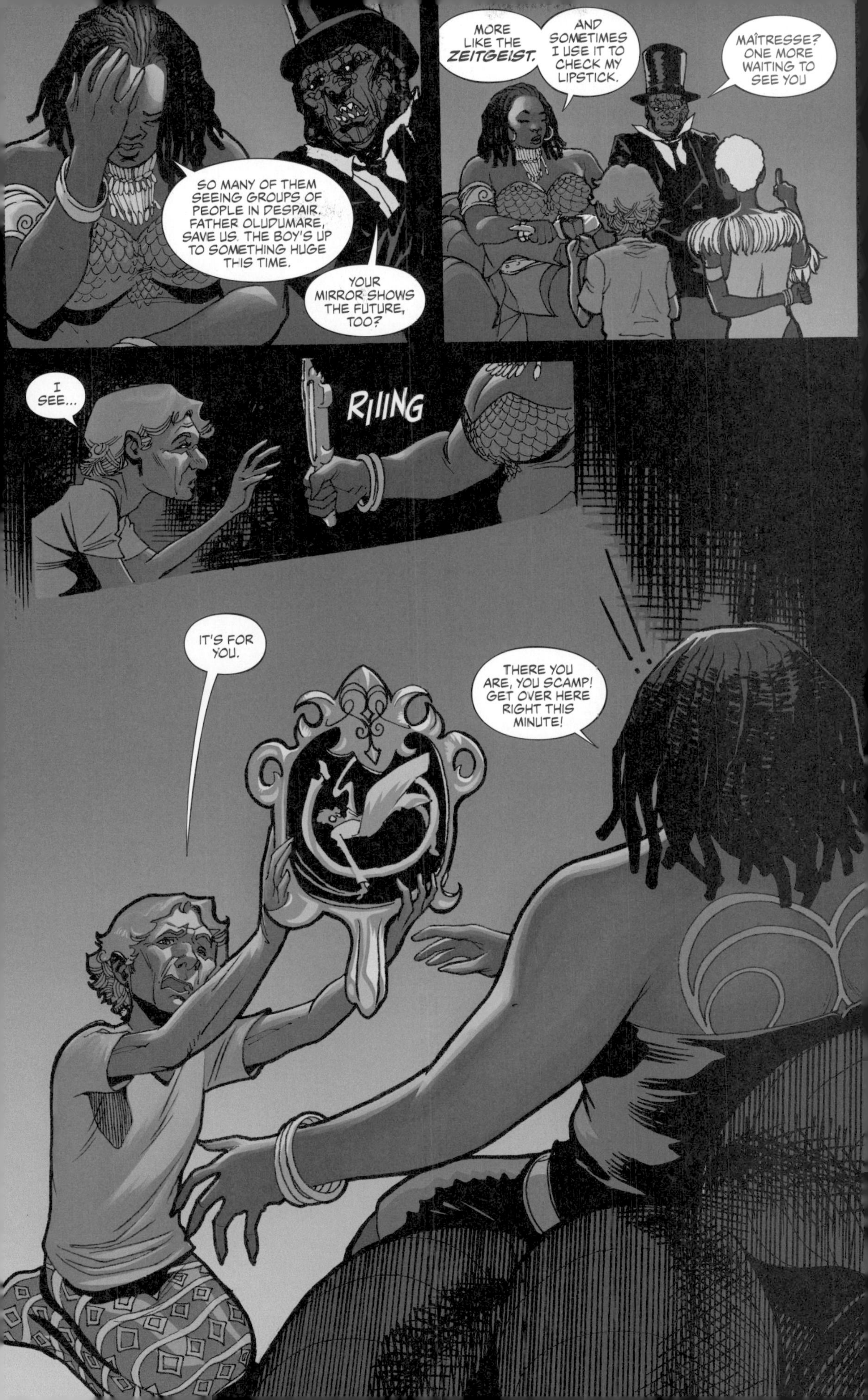
SO MANY OF THEM SEEING GROUPS OF PEOPLE IN DESPAIR. FATHER OLUDUMARE, SAVE US. THE BOY'S UP TO SOMETHING HUGE THIS TIME.
YOUR MIRROR SHOWS THE FUTURE, TOO?
MORE LIKE THE *ZEITGEIST.*
AND SOMETIMES I USE IT TO CHECK MY LIPSTICK.
MAÎTRESSE? ONE MORE WAITING TO SEE YOU
I SEE...
RIIING
IT'S FOR YOU.
THERE YOU ARE, YOU SCAMP! GET OVER HERE RIGHT THIS MINUTE!

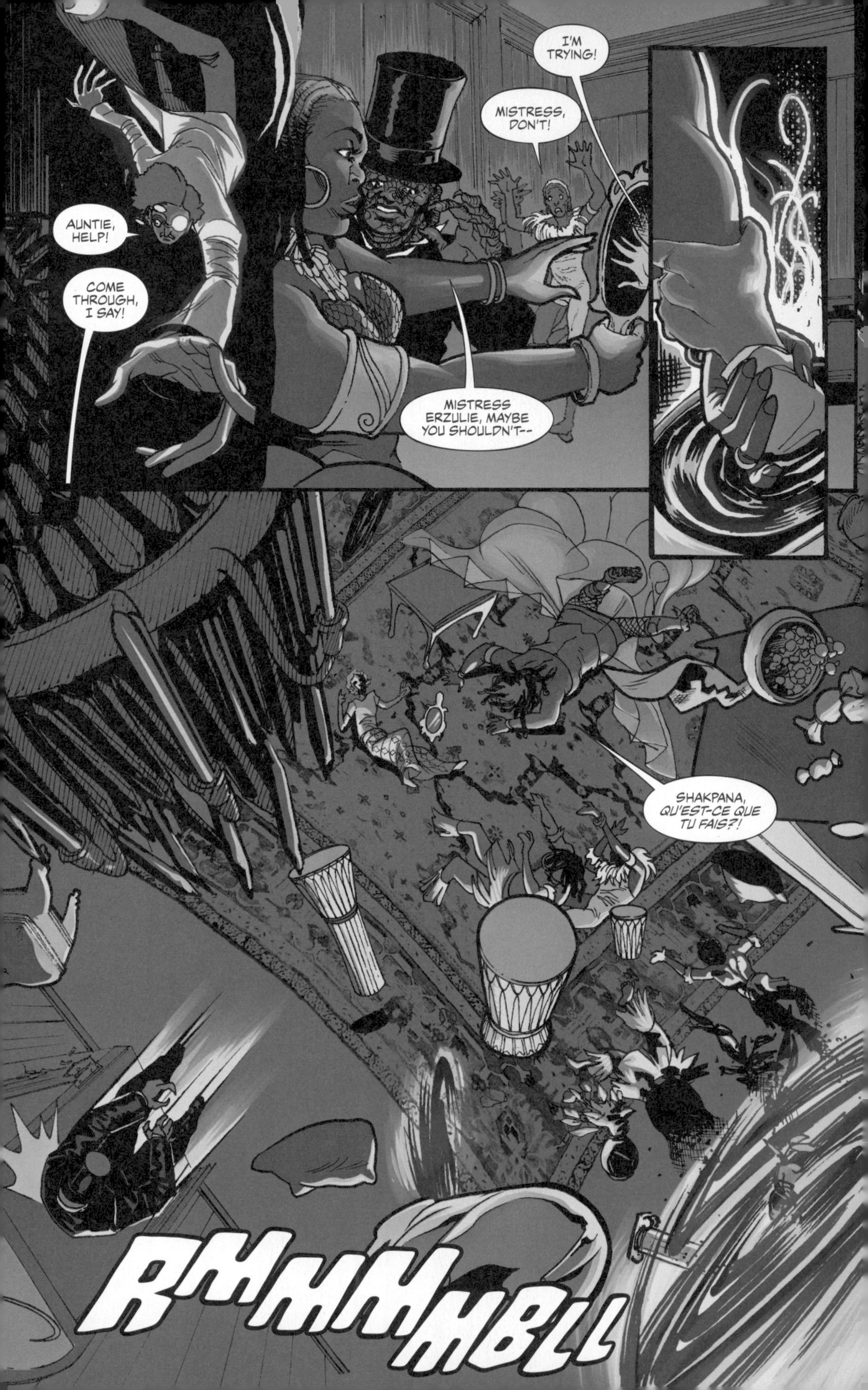
AUNTIE, HELP!
COME THROUGH, I SAY!
MISTRESS, DON'T!
I'M TRYING!
MISTRESS ERZULIE, MAYBE YOU SHOULDN'T--
SHAKPANA, QU'EST-CE QUE TU FAIS?!
RMMMMBLL

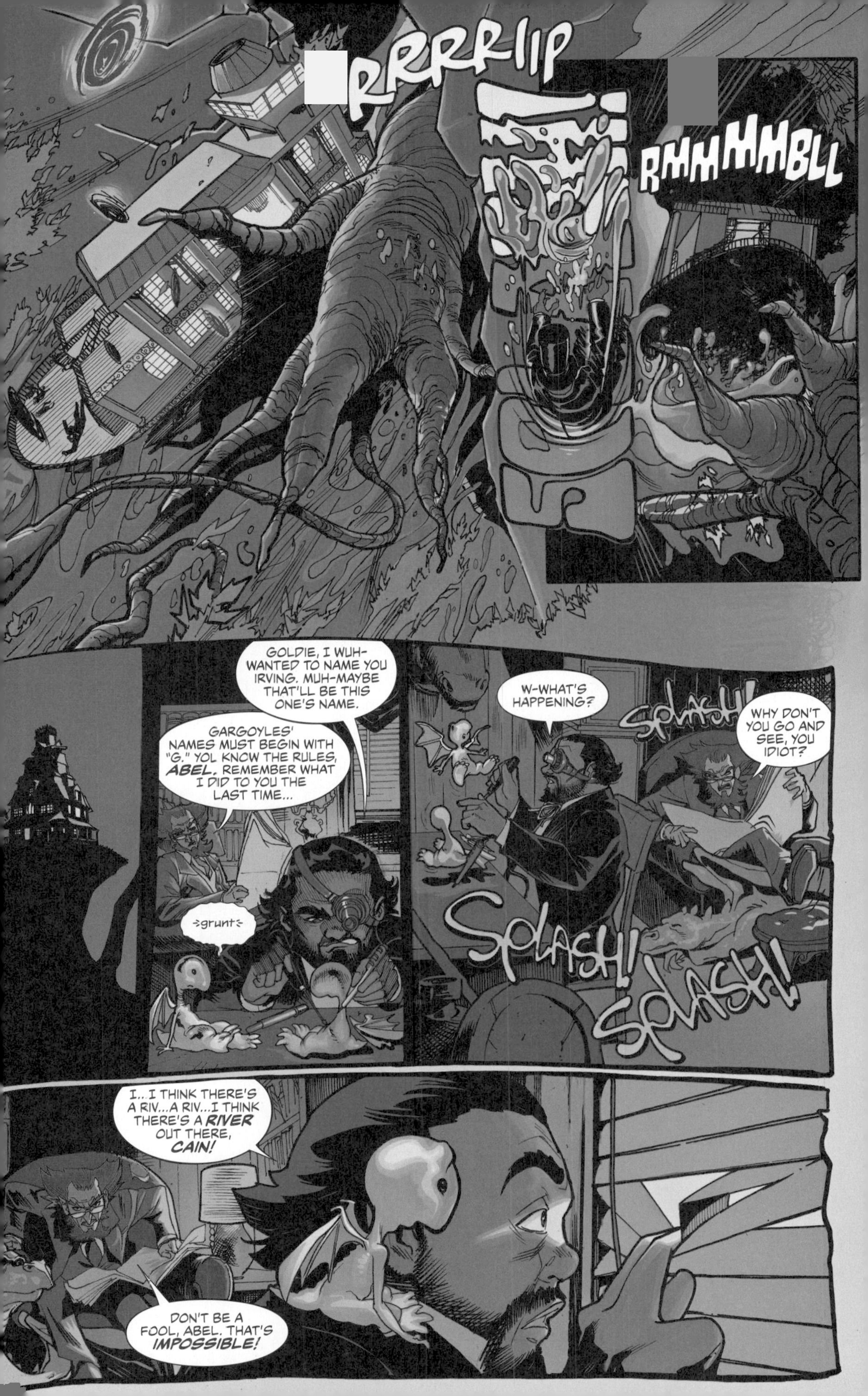
RRRRIIP
RMMMMMBLL
GOLDIE, I WUH-WANTED TO NAME YOU IRVING. MUH-MAYBE THAT'LL BE THIS ONE'S NAME.
GARGOYLES' NAMES MUST BEGIN WITH "G." YOU KNOW THE RULES, ABEL. REMEMBER WHAT I DID TO YOU THE LAST TIME...
grunt
W-WHAT'S HAPPENING?
SPLASH!
WHY DON'T YOU GO AND SEE, YOU IDIOT?
SPLASH!
SPLASH!
I...I THINK THERE'S A RIV...A RIV...I THINK THERE'S A RIVER OUT THERE, CAIN!
DON'T BE A FOOL, ABEL. THAT'S IMPOSSIBLE!

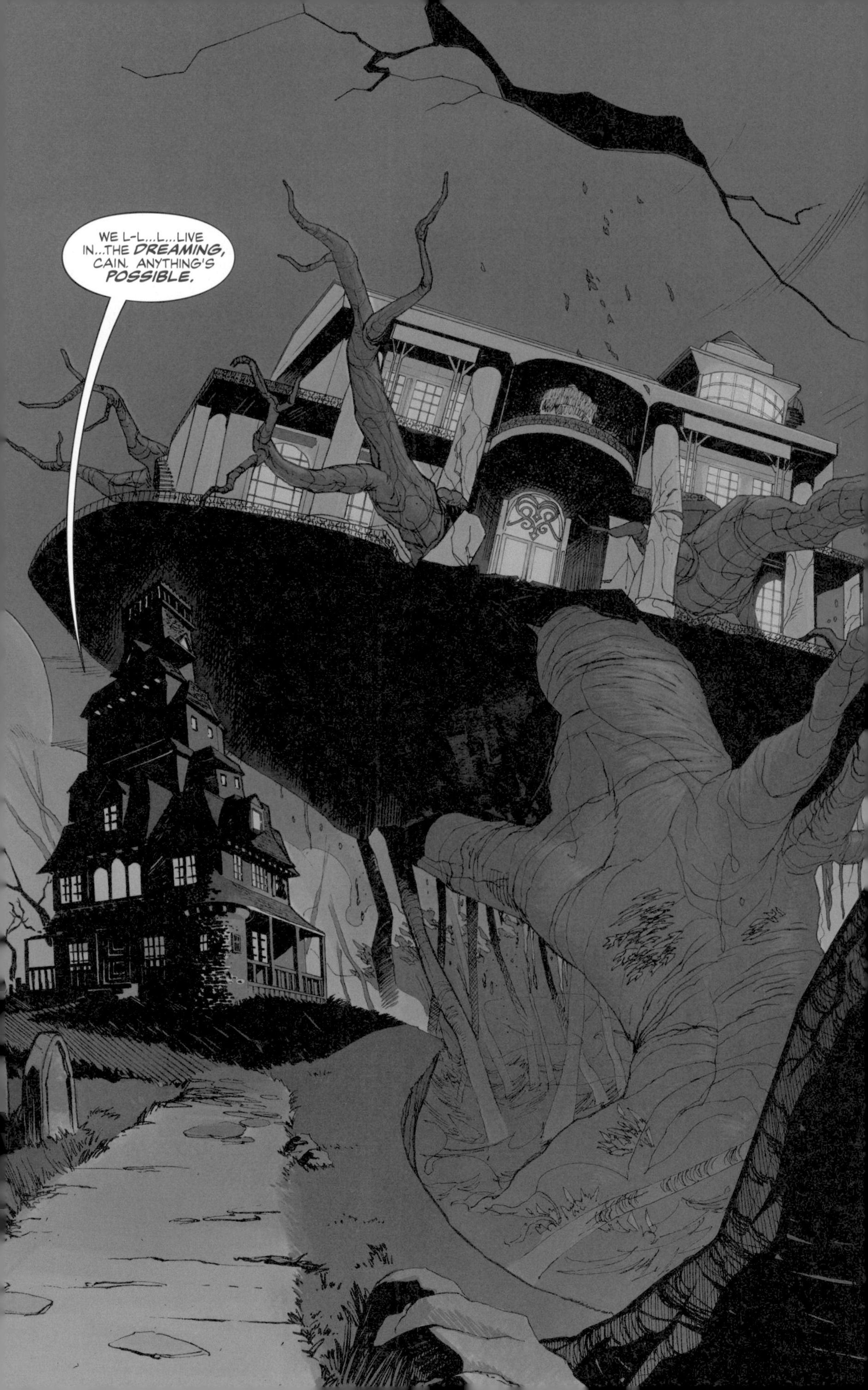
WE L-L...L...LIVE IN...THE *DREAMING*, CAIN. ANYTHING'S *POSSIBLE.*

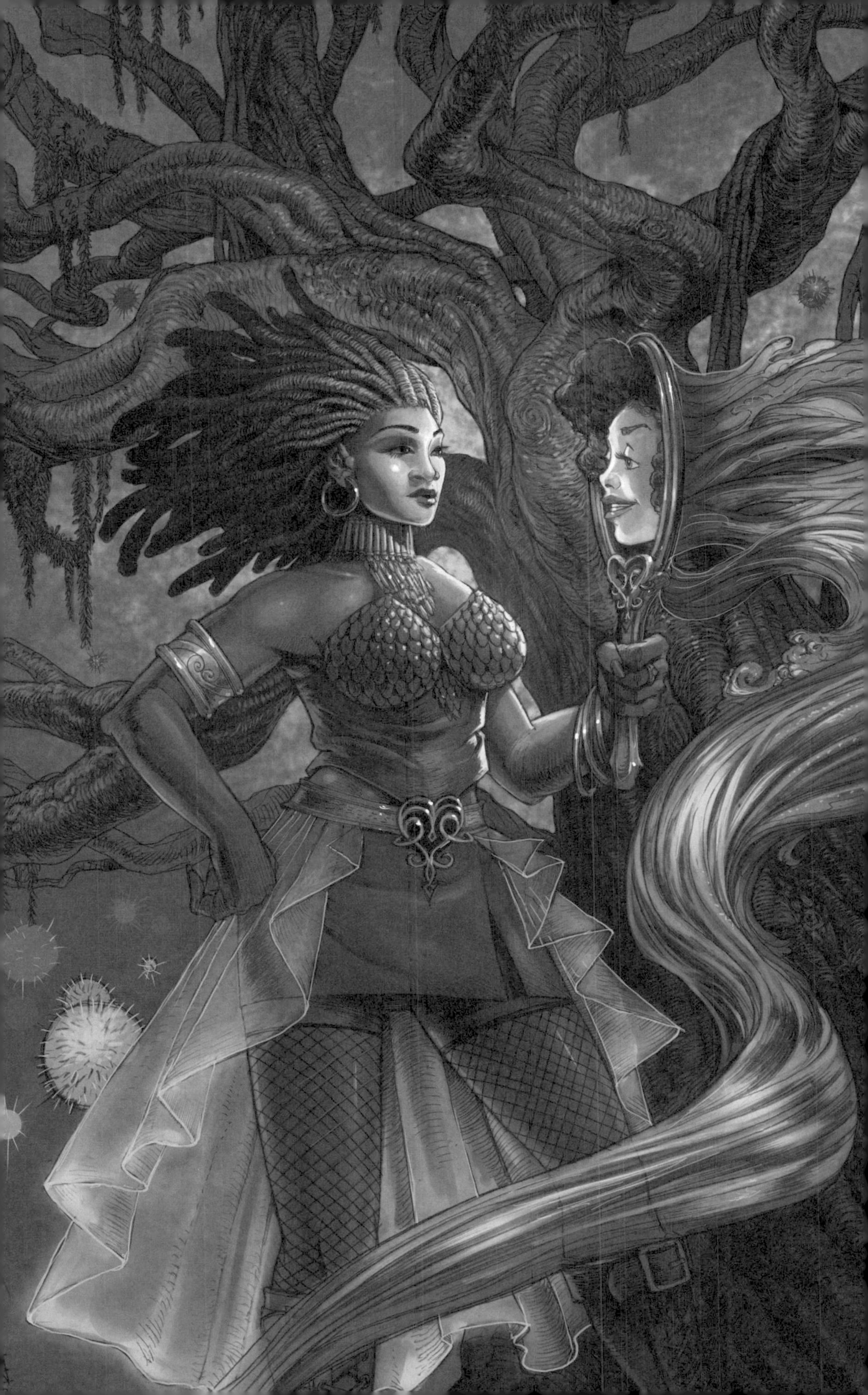

HOUSE OF WHISPERS

The Power Divided

WRITTEN BY
Nalo Hopkinson

ILLUSTRATED BY
Dominike "DOMO" Stanton

COLORS BY
John Rauch

LETTERS BY
AndWorld Design

COVER ART BY
Sean Andrew Murray

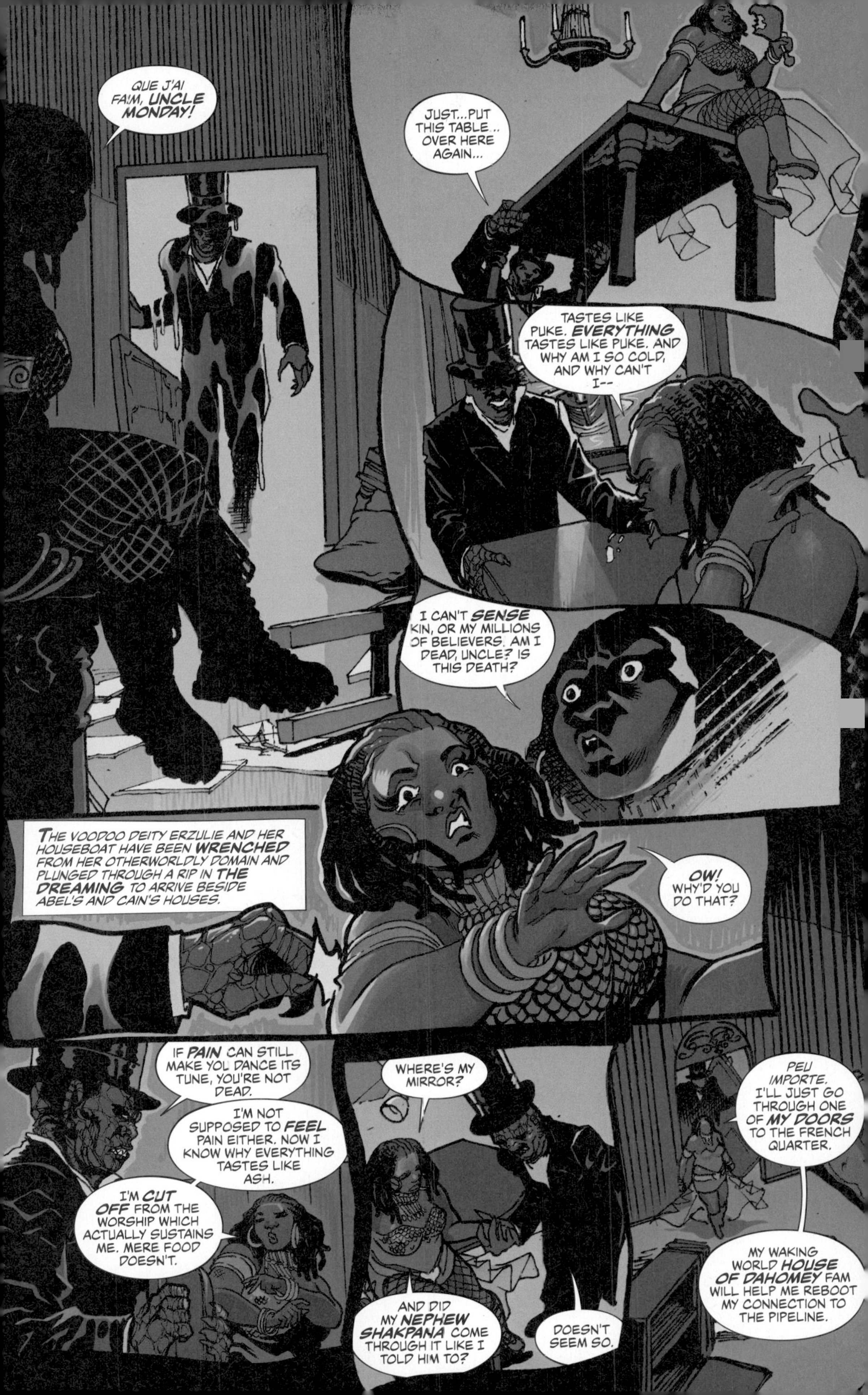
QUE J'AI FAIM, UNCLE MONDAY!
JUST...PUT THIS TABLE.. OVER HERE AGAIN...
TASTES LIKE PUKE. EVERYTHING TASTES LIKE PUKE. AND WHY AM I SO COLD, AND WHY CAN'T I--
I CAN'T SENSE KIN, OR MY MILLIONS OF BELIEVERS. AM I DEAD, UNCLE? IS THIS DEATH?
THE VOODOO DEITY ERZULIE AND HER HOUSEBOAT HAVE BEEN WRENCHED FROM HER OTHERWORLDLY DOMAIN AND PLUNGED THROUGH A RIP IN THE DREAMING TO ARRIVE BESIDE ABEL'S AND CAIN'S HOUSES.
OW! WHY'D YOU DO THAT?
IF PAIN CAN STILL MAKE YOU DANCE ITS TUNE, YOU'RE NOT DEAD.
I'M NOT SUPPOSED TO FEEL PAIN EITHER. NOW I KNOW WHY EVERYTHING TASTES LIKE ASH.
I'M CUT OFF FROM THE WORSHIP WHICH ACTUALLY SUSTAINS ME. MERE FOOD DOESN'T.
WHERE'S MY MIRROR?
AND DID MY NEPHEW SHAKPANA COME THROUGH IT LIKE I TOLD HIM TO?
DOESN'T SEEM SO.
PEU IMPORTE. I'LL JUST GO THROUGH ONE OF MY DOORS TO THE FRENCH QUARTER.
MY WAKING WORLD HOUSE OF DAHOMEY FAM WILL HELP ME REBOOT MY CONNECTION TO THE PIPELINE.

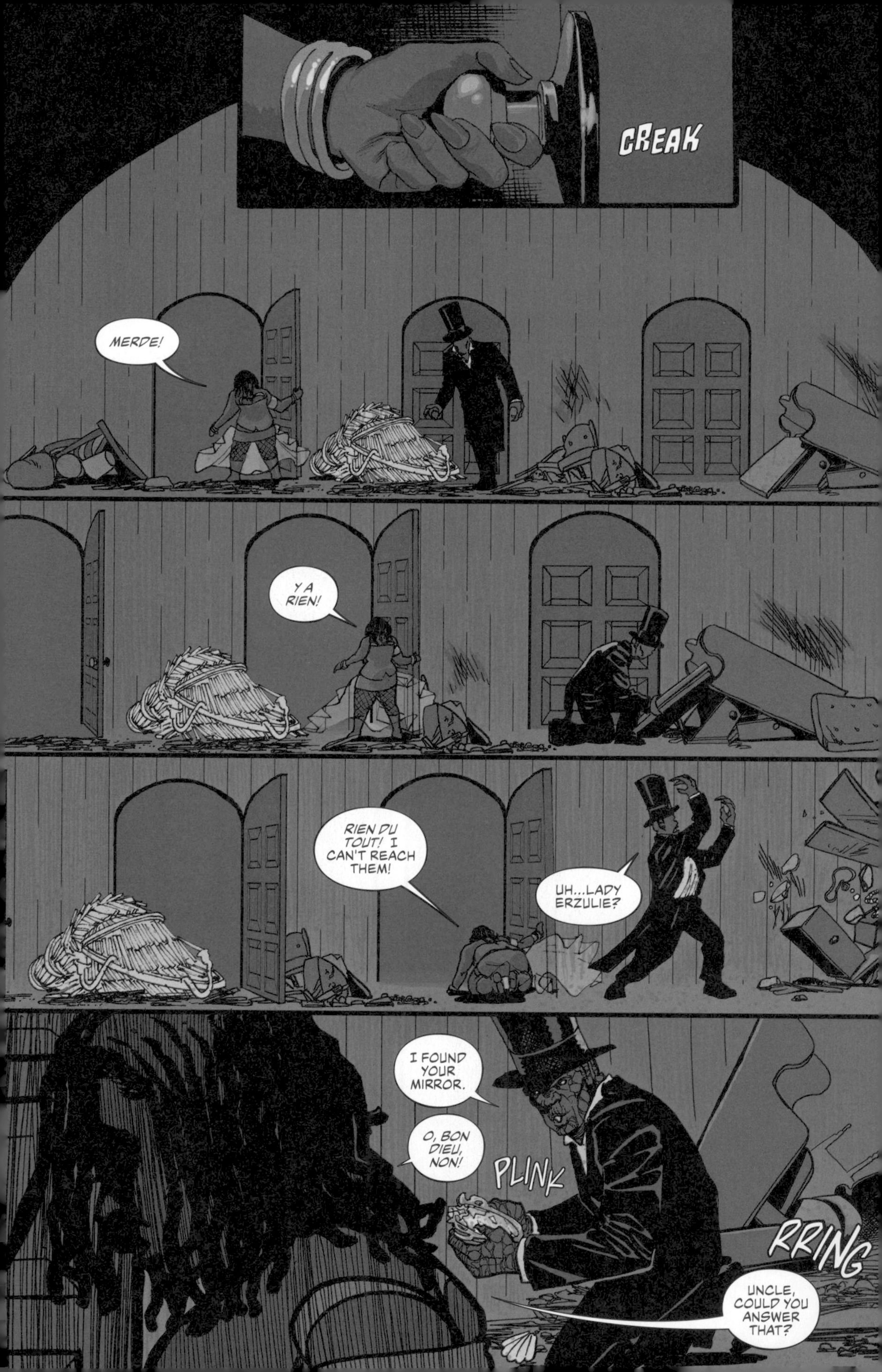
CREAK
MERDE!
Y A RIEN!
RIEN DU TOUT! I CAN'T REACH THEM!
UH...LADY ERZULIE?
I FOUND YOUR MIRROR.
O, BON DIEU, NON!
PLINK
RRING
UNCLE, COULD YOU ANSWER THAT?

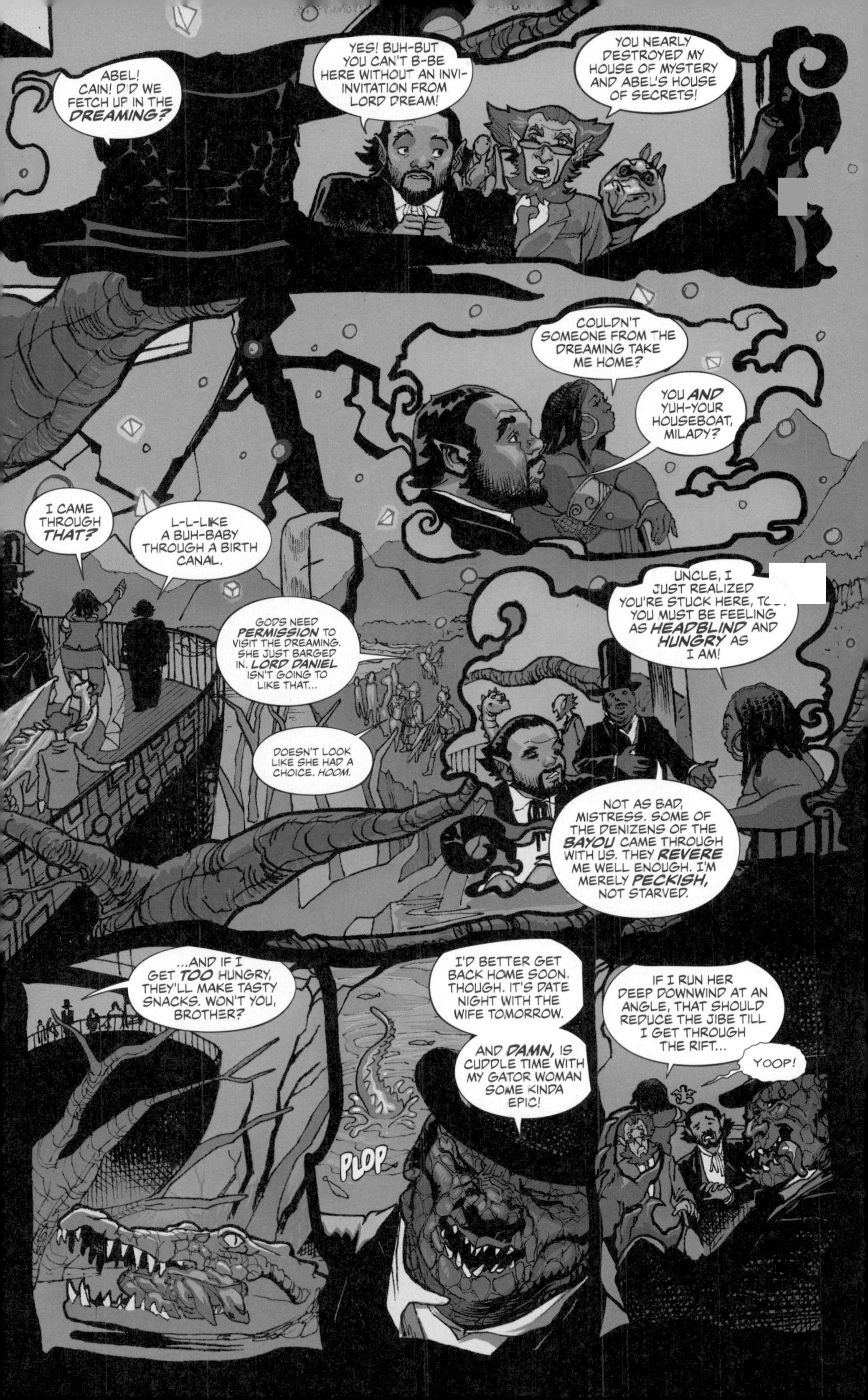
ABEL! CAIN! DID WE FETCH UP IN THE DREAMING?
YES! BUH-BUT YOU CAN'T B-BE HERE WITHOUT AN INVI-INVITATION FROM LORD DREAM!
YOU NEARLY DESTROYED MY HOUSE OF MYSTERY AND ABEL'S HOUSE OF SECRETS!
COULDN'T SOMEONE FROM THE DREAMING TAKE ME HOME?
YOU AND YUH-YOUR HOUSEBOAT, MILADY?
I CAME THROUGH THAT?
L-L-LIKE A BUH-BABY THROUGH A BIRTH CANAL.
GODS NEED PERMISSION TO VISIT THE DREAMING. SHE JUST BARGED IN. LORD DANIEL ISN'T GOING TO LIKE THAT...
DOESN'T LOOK LIKE SHE HAD A CHOICE. HOOM.
UNCLE, I JUST REALIZED YOU'RE STUCK HERE, TO YOU MUST BE FEELING AS HEADBLIND AND HUNGRY AS I AM!
NOT AS BAD, MISTRESS. SOME OF THE DENIZENS OF THE BAYOU CAME THROUGH WITH US. THEY REVERE ME WELL ENOUGH. I'M MERELY PECKISH, NOT STARVED.
...AND IF I GET TOO HUNGRY, THEY'LL MAKE TASTY SNACKS. WON'T YOU, BROTHER?
PLOP
I'D BETTER GET BACK HOME SOON, THOUGH. IT'S DATE NIGHT WITH THE WIFE TOMORROW.
AND DAMN, IS CUDDLE TIME WITH MY GATOR WOMAN SOME KINDA EPIC!
IF I RUN HER DEEP DOWNWIND AT AN ANGLE, THAT SHOULD REDUCE THE JIBE TILL I GET THROUGH THE RIFT...
YOOP!

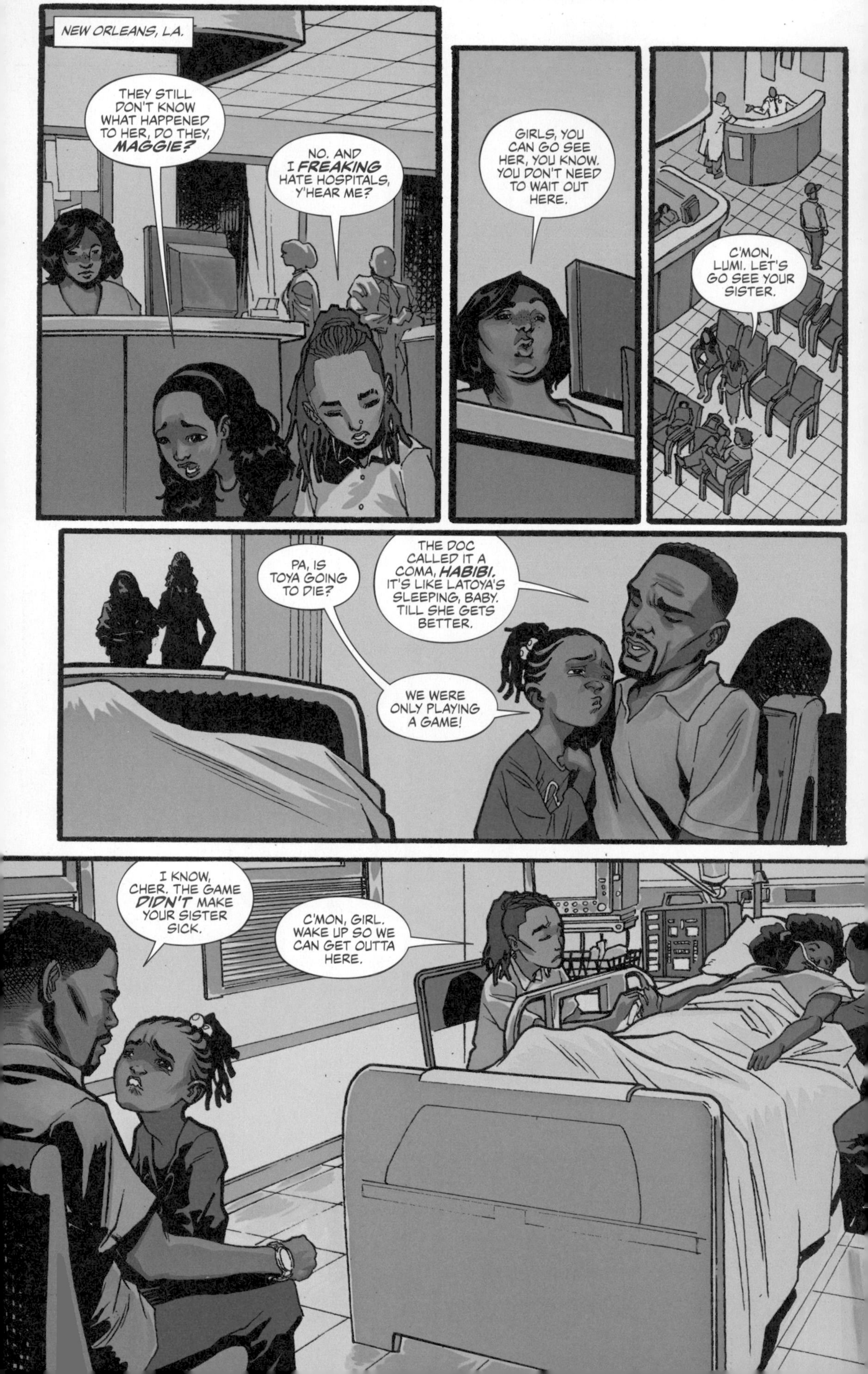
NEW ORLEANS, LA.
THEY STILL DON'T KNOW WHAT HAPPENED TO HER, DO THEY, MAGGIE?
NO. AND I FREAKING HATE HOSPITALS, Y'HEAR ME?
GIRLS, YOU CAN GO SEE HER, YOU KNOW. YOU DON'T NEED TO WAIT OUT HERE.
C'MON, LUMI. LET'S GO SEE YOUR SISTER.
PA, IS TOYA GOING TO DIE?
THE DOC CALLED IT A COMA, HABIBI. IT'S LIKE LATOYA'S SLEEPING, BABY. TILL SHE GETS BETTER.
WE WERE ONLY PLAYING A GAME!
I KNOW, CHER. THE GAME DIDN'T MAKE YOUR SISTER SICK.
C'MON, GIRL. WAKE UP SO WE CAN GET OUTTA HERE.

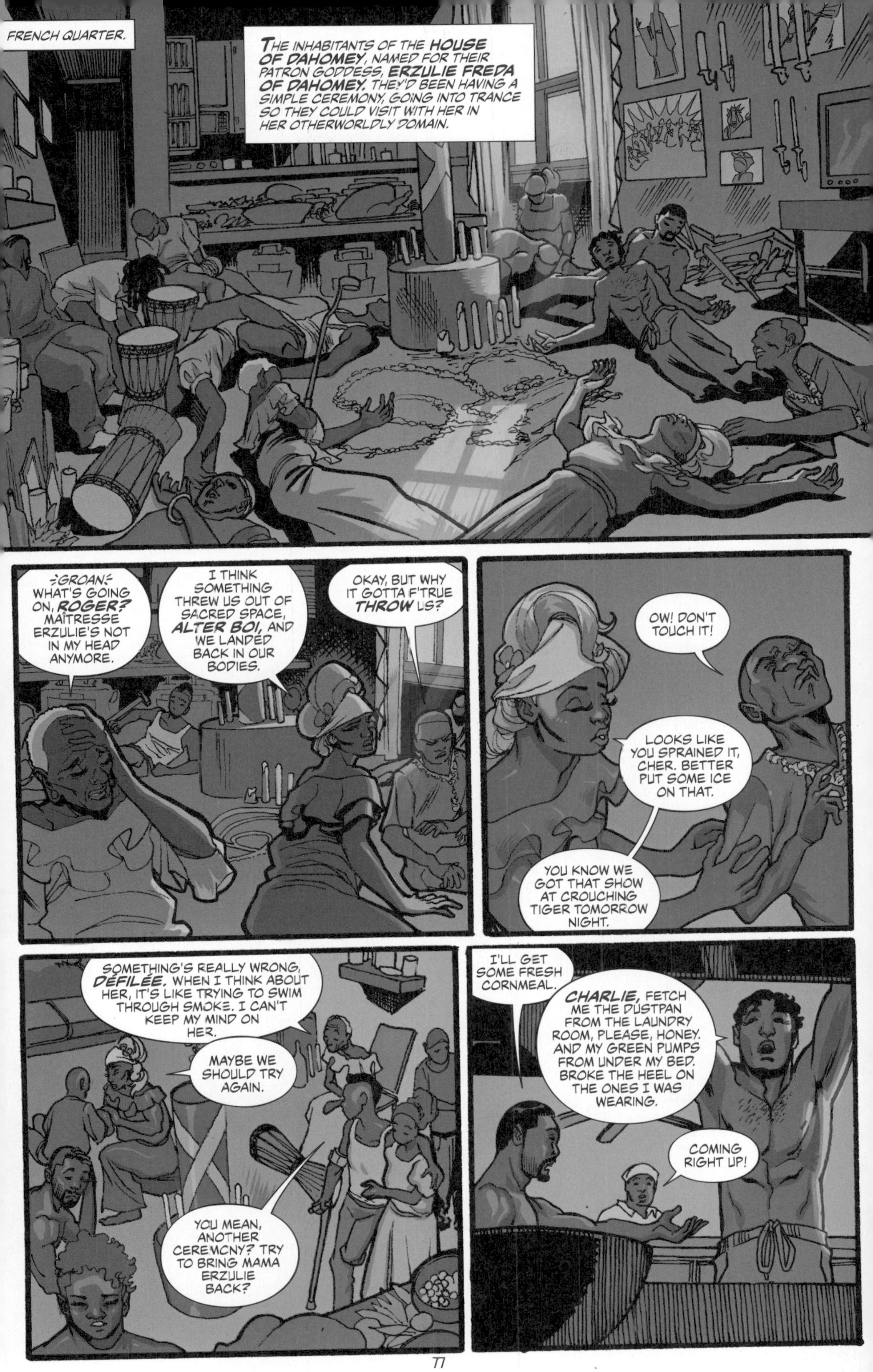
FRENCH QUARTER.
THE INHABITANTS OF THE HOUSE OF DAHOMEY, NAMED FOR THEIR PATRON GODDESS, ERZULIE FREDA OF DAHOMEY. THEY'D BEEN HAVING A SIMPLE CEREMONY, GOING INTO TRANCE SO THEY COULD VISIT WITH HER IN HER OTHERWORLDLY DOMAIN.
GROAN WHAT'S GOING ON, ROGER? MAÎTRESSE ERZULIE'S NOT IN MY HEAD ANYMORE.
I THINK SOMETHING THREW US OUT OF SACRED SPACE, ALTER BOI, AND WE LANDED BACK IN OUR BODIES.
OKAY, BUT WHY IT GOTTA F'TRUE THROW US?
OW! DON'T TOUCH IT!
LOOKS LIKE YOU SPRAINED IT, CHER. BETTER PUT SOME ICE ON THAT.
YOU KNOW WE GOT THAT SHOW AT CROUCHING TIGER TOMORROW NIGHT.
SOMETHING'S REALLY WRONG, DÉFILÉE. WHEN I THINK ABOUT HER, IT'S LIKE TRYING TO SWIM THROUGH SMOKE. I CAN'T KEEP MY MIND ON HER.
MAYBE WE SHOULD TRY AGAIN.
YOU MEAN, ANOTHER CEREMONY? TRY TO BRING MAMA ERZULIE BACK?
I'LL GET SOME FRESH CORNMEAL.
CHARLIE, FETCH ME THE DUSTPAN FROM THE LAUNDRY ROOM, PLEASE, HONEY. AND MY GREEN PUMPS FROM UNDER MY BED. BROKE THE HEEL ON THE ONES I WAS WEARING.
COMING RIGHT UP!

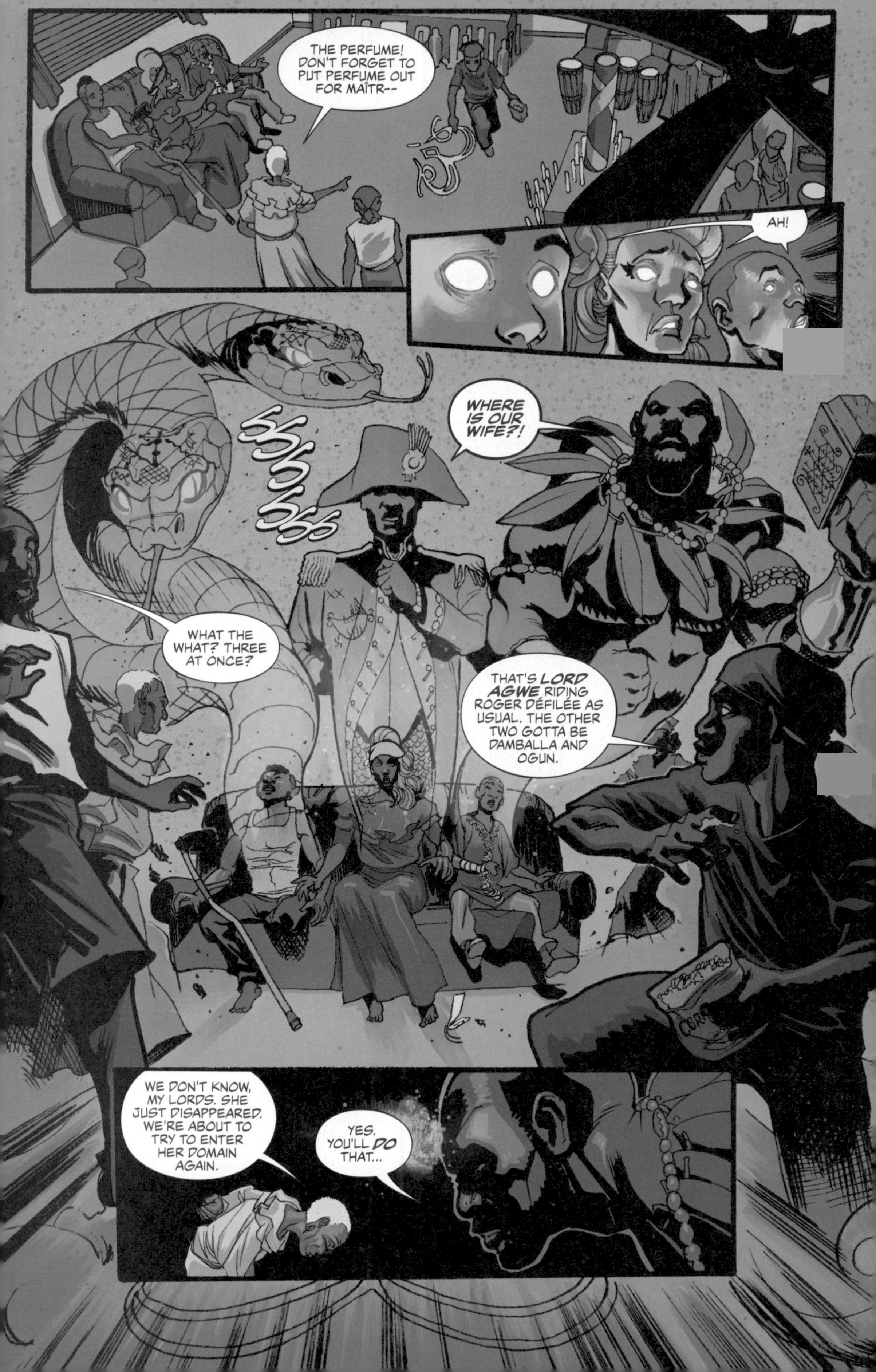
THE PERFUME! DON'T FORGET TO PUT PERFUME OUT FOR MAÎTR--
AH!
SSSSSSSSS
WHERE IS OUR WIFE?!
WHAT THE WHAT? THREE AT ONCE?
THAT'S LORD AGWE RIDING ROGER DÉFILÉE AS USUAL. THE OTHER TWO GOTTA BE DAMBALLA AND OGUN.
WE DON'T KNOW, MY LORDS. SHE JUST DISAPPEARED. WE'RE ABOUT TO TRY TO ENTER HER DOMAIN AGAIN.
YES. YOU'LL DO THAT...

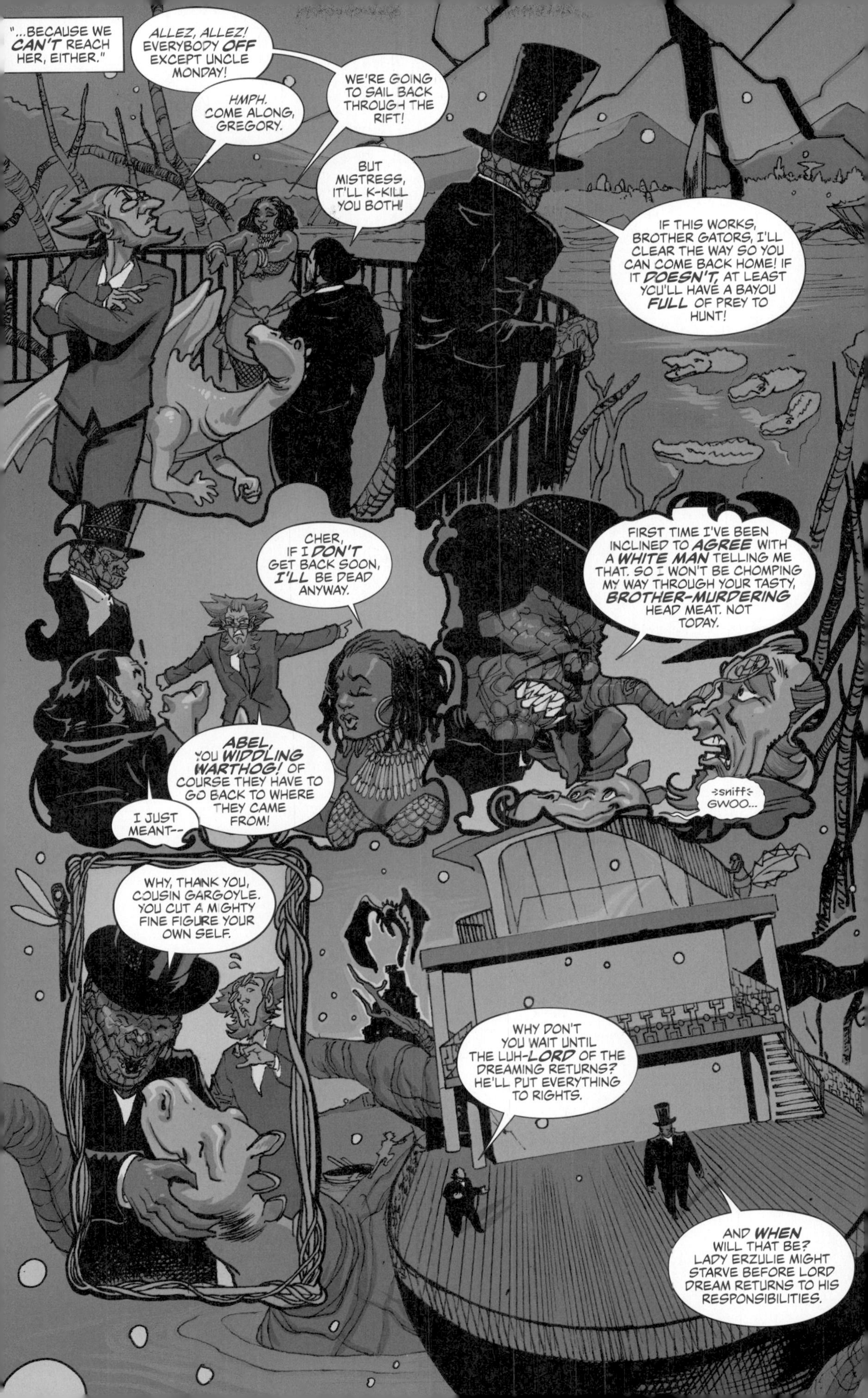
"...BECAUSE WE CAN'T REACH HER, EITHER."
ALLEZ, ALLEZ! EVERYBODY OFF EXCEPT UNCLE MONDAY!
HMPH. COME ALONG, GREGORY.
WE'RE GOING TO SAIL BACK THROUGH THE RIFT!
BUT MISTRESS, IT'LL K-KILL YOU BOTH!
IF THIS WORKS, BROTHER GATORS, I'LL CLEAR THE WAY SO YOU CAN COME BACK HOME! IF IT DOESN'T, AT LEAST YOU'LL HAVE A BAYOU FULL OF PREY TO HUNT!
CHER, IF I DON'T GET BACK SOON, I'LL BE DEAD ANYWAY.
FIRST TIME I'VE BEEN INCLINED TO AGREE WITH A WHITE MAN TELLING ME THAT. SO I WON'T BE CHOMPING MY WAY THROUGH YOUR TASTY, BROTHER-MURDERING HEAD MEAT. NOT TODAY.
ABEL, YOU WIDDLING WARTHOG! OF COURSE THEY HAVE TO GO BACK TO WHERE THEY CAME FROM!
I JUST MEANT--
=sniff= GWOO...
WHY, THANK YOU, COUSIN GARGOYLE. YOU CUT A MIGHTY FINE FIGURE YOUR OWN SELF.
WHY DON'T YOU WAIT UNTIL THE LUH-LORD OF THE DREAMING RETURNS? HE'LL PUT EVERYTHING TO RIGHTS.
AND WHEN WILL THAT BE? LADY ERZULIE MIGHT STARVE BEFORE LORD DREAM RETURNS TO HIS RESPONSIBILITIES.

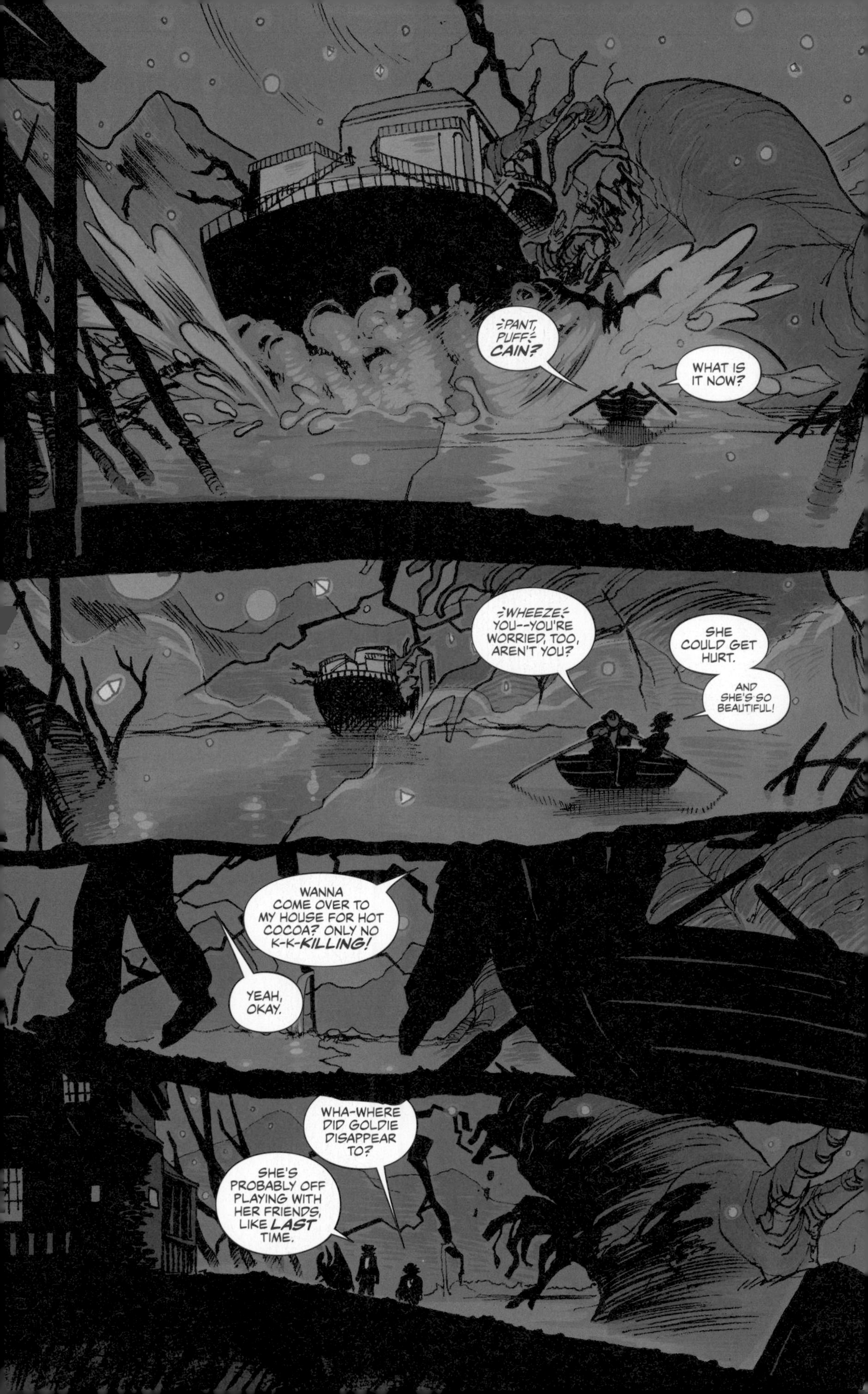

PANT, PUFF CAIN?
WHAT IS IT NOW?
WHEEZE YOU--YOU'RE WORRIED, TOO, AREN'T YOU?
SHE COULD GET HURT.
AND SHE'S SO BEAUTIFUL!
WANNA COME OVER TO MY HOUSE FOR HOT COCOA? ONLY NO K-K-KILLING!
YEAH, OKAY.
WHA-WHERE DID GOLDIE DISAPPEAR TO?
SHE'S PROBABLY OFF PLAYING WITH HER FRIENDS, LIKE LAST TIME.

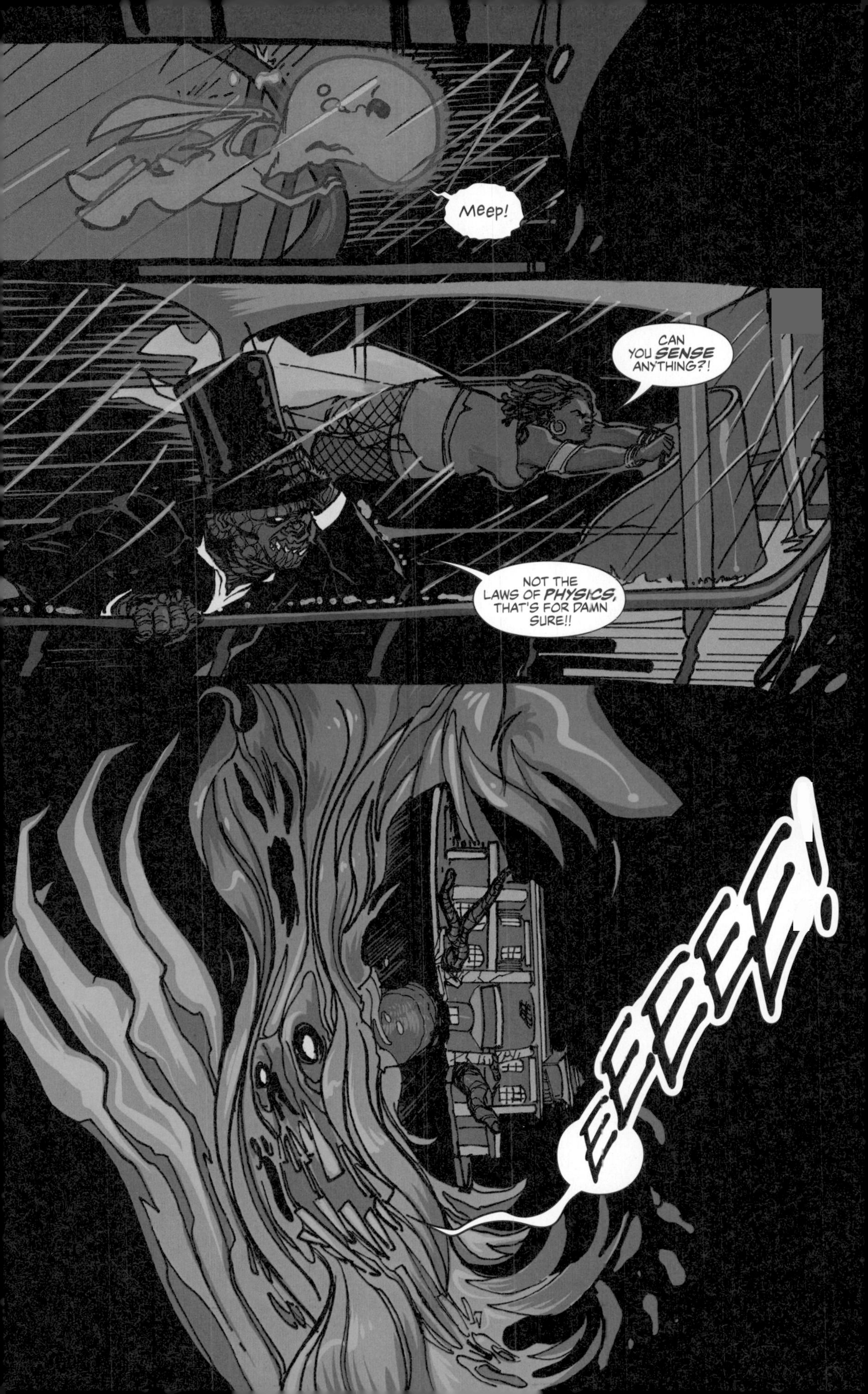
Meep!
CAN YOU SENSE ANYTHING?!
NOT THE LAWS OF PHYSICS, THAT'S FOR DAMN SURE!!

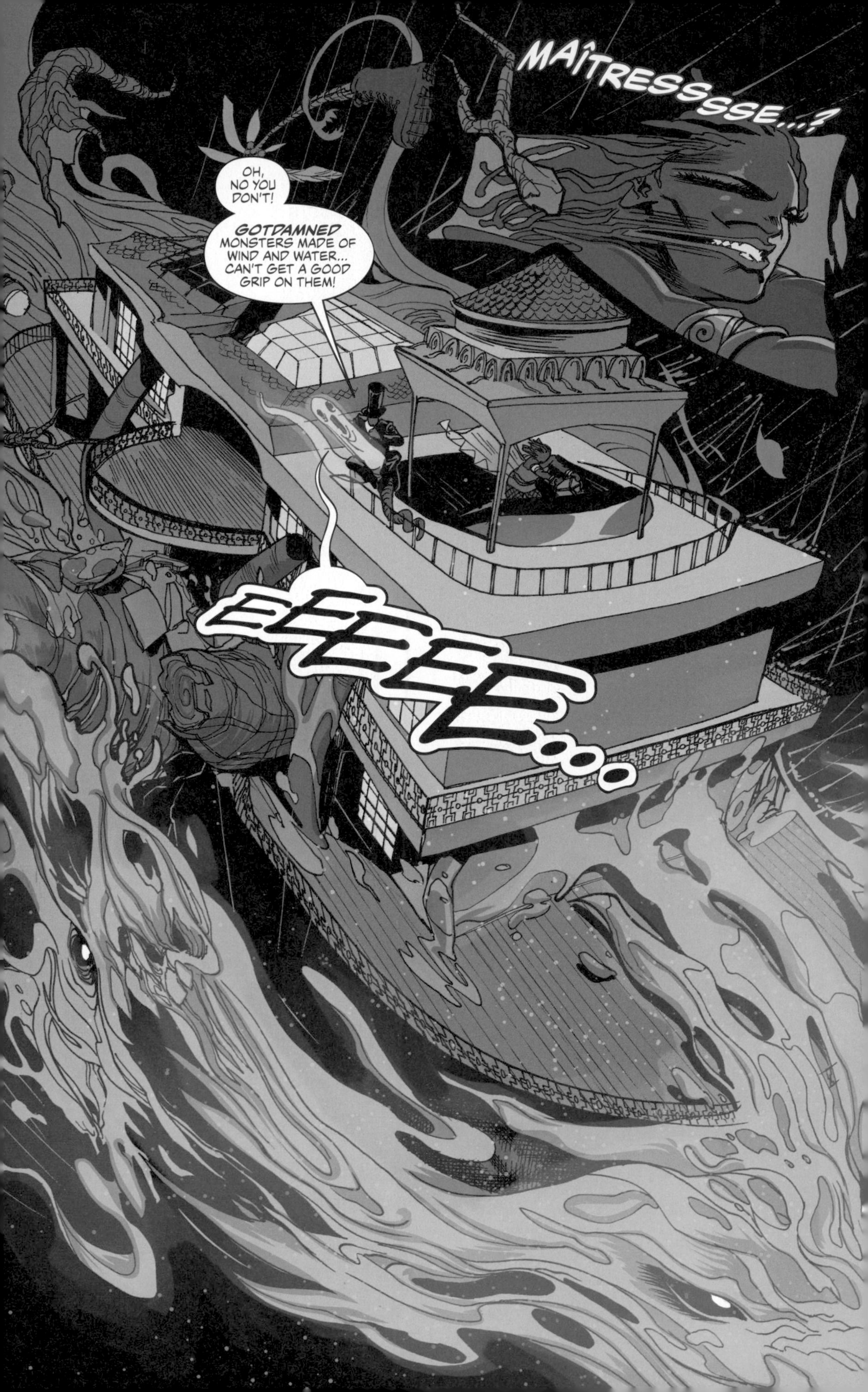
MAÎTRESSSSSE...?
OH, NO YOU DON'T!
GOTDAMNED MONSTERS MADE OF WIND AND WATER... CAN'T GET A GOOD GRIP ON THEM!
EEEEE...

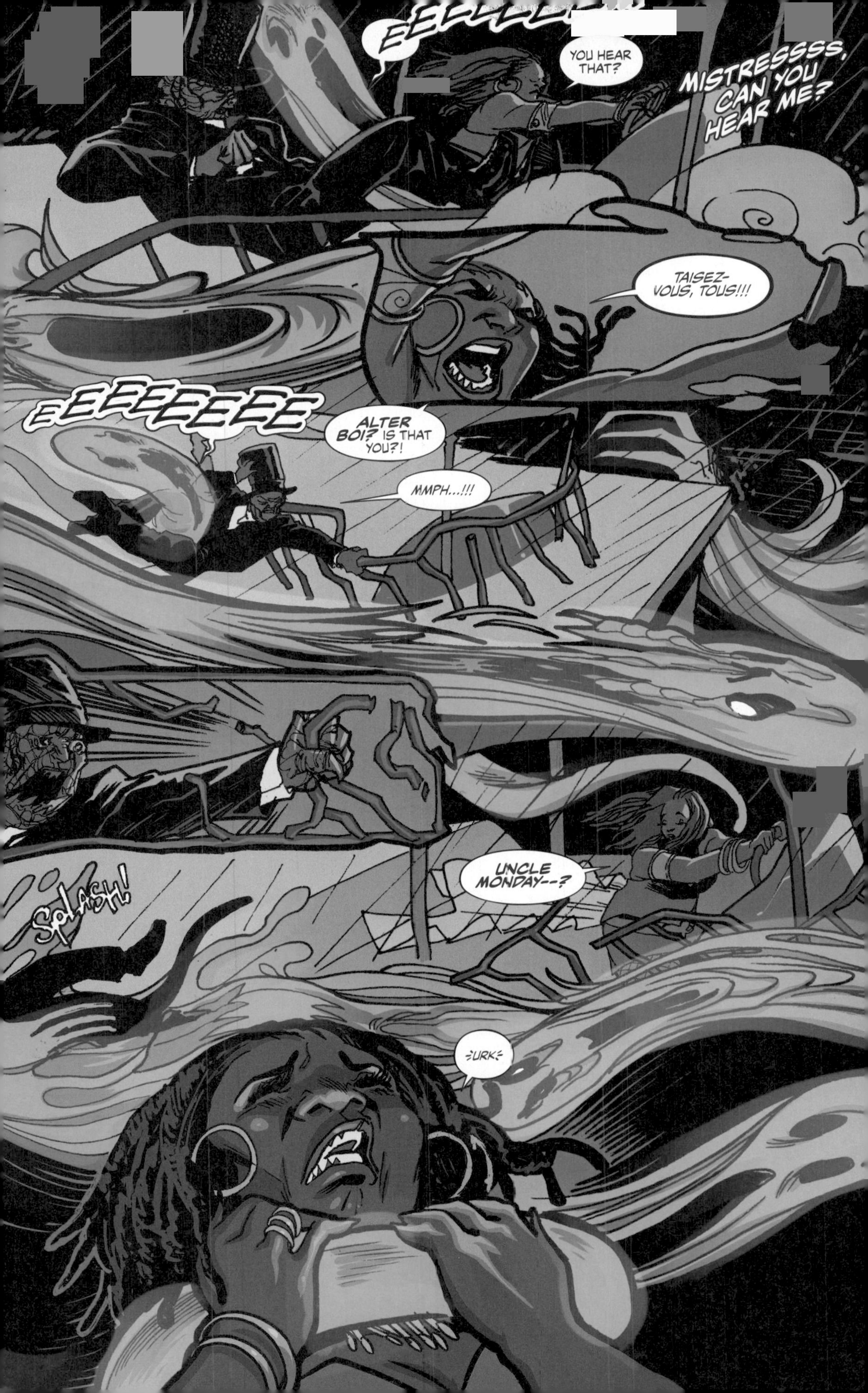
YOU HEAR THAT?
MISTRESSSS, CAN YOU HEAR ME?
TAISEZ-VOUS, TOUS!!!
EEEEEEEEEE
ALTER BOI? IS THAT YOU?!
MMPH...!!!
SPLASH!
UNCLE MONDAY--?
URK

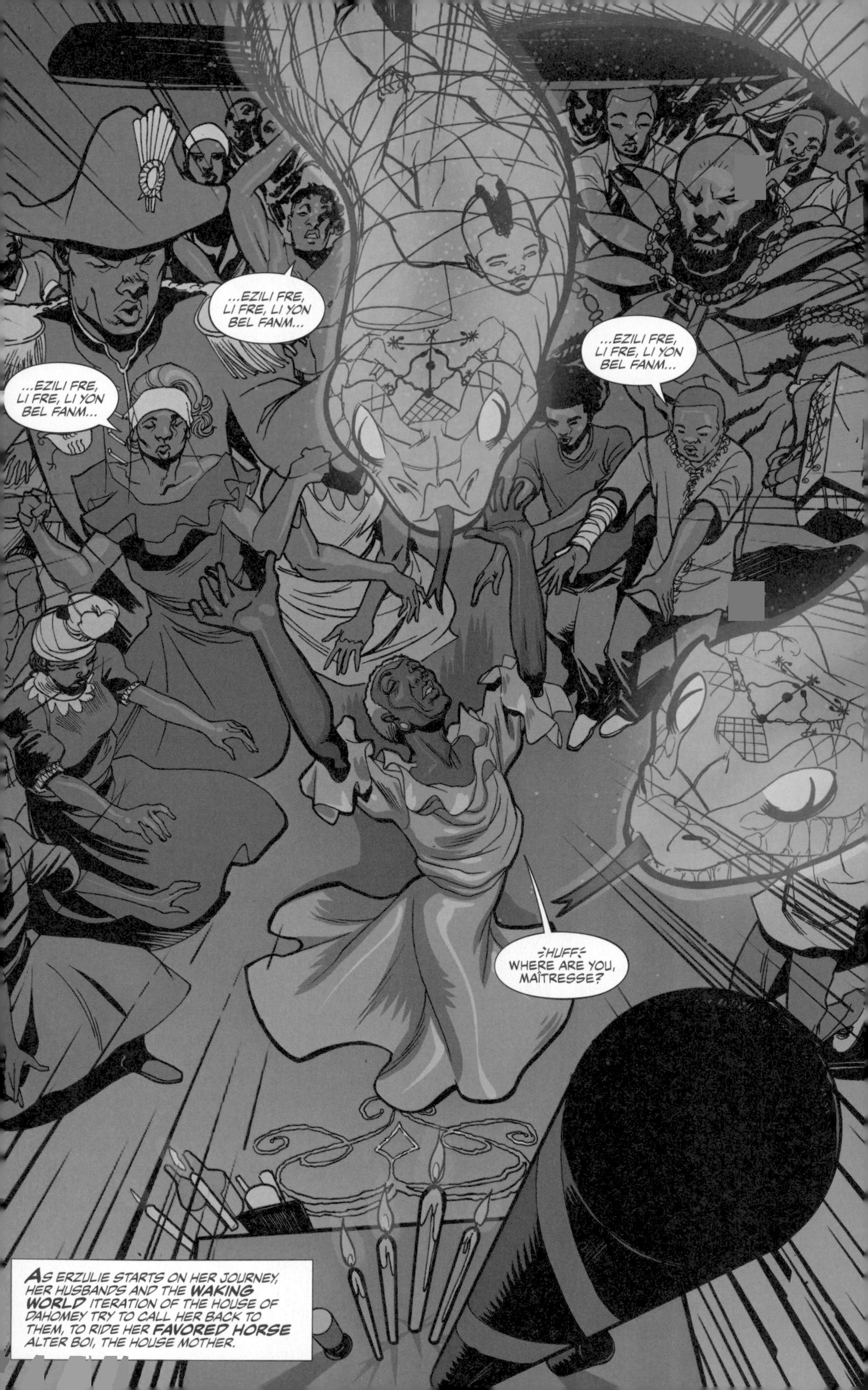
...EZILI FRE, LI FRE, LI YON BEL FANM...
...EZILI FRE, LI FRE, LI YON BEL FANM...
...EZILI FRE, LI FRE, LI YON BEL FANM...
-HUFF- WHERE ARE YOU, MAÎTRESSE?
AS ERZULIE STARTS ON HER JOURNEY, HER HUSBANDS AND THE WAKING WORLD ITERATION OF THE HOUSE OF DAHOMEY TRY TO CALL HER BACK TO THEM, TO RIDE HER FAVORED HORSE ALTER BOI, THE HOUSE MOTHER.

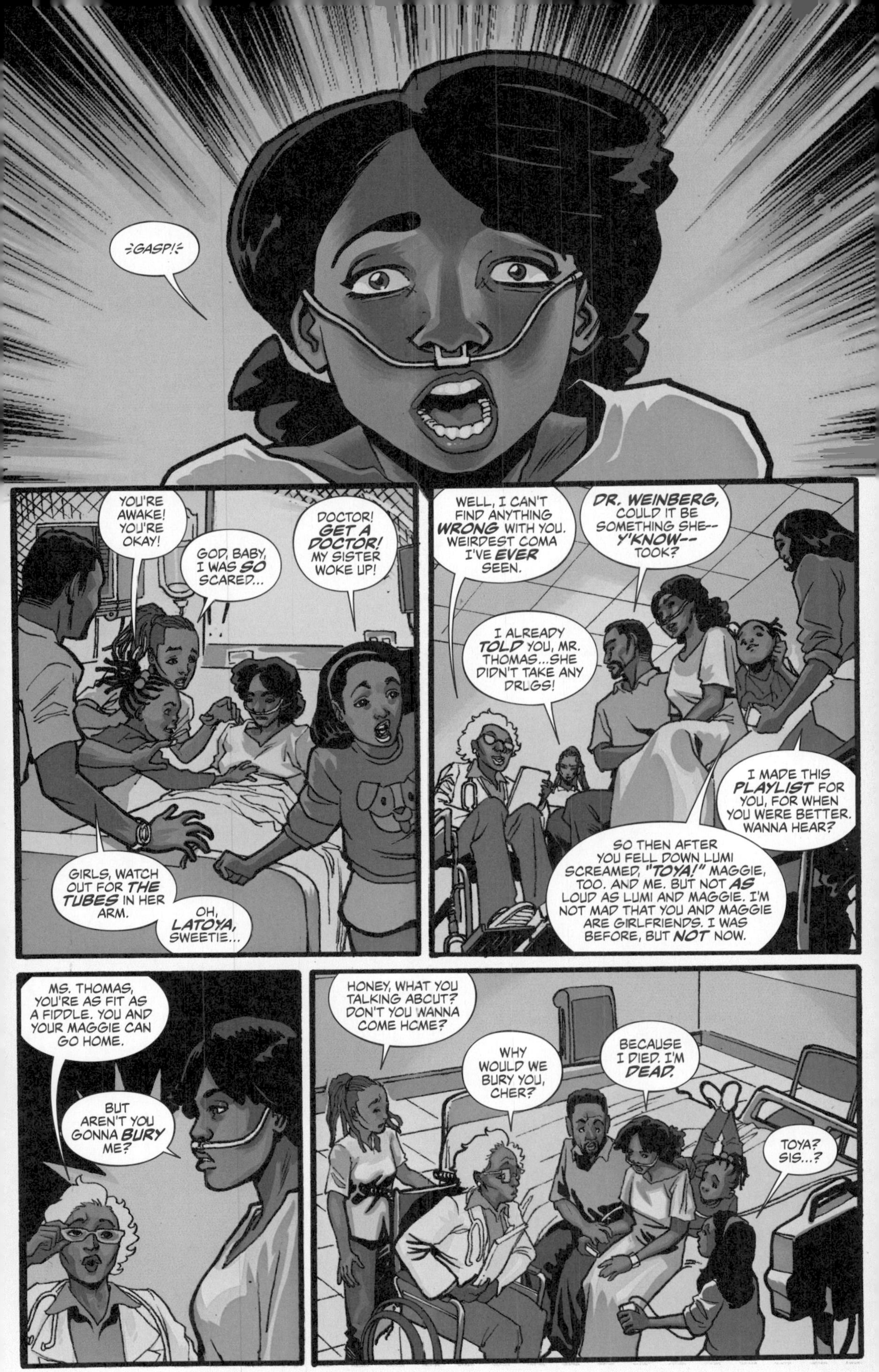

≈GASP!≈
YOU'RE AWAKE! YOU'RE OKAY!
GOD, BABY, I WAS SO SCARED...
DOCTOR! GET A DOCTOR! MY SISTER WOKE UP!
GIRLS, WATCH OUT FOR THE TUBES IN HER ARM.
OH, LATOYA, SWEETIE...
WELL, I CAN'T FIND ANYTHING WRONG WITH YOU. WEIRDEST COMA I'VE EVER SEEN.
DR. WEINBERG, COULD IT BE SOMETHING SHE-- Y'KNOW-- TOOK?
I ALREADY TOLD YOU, MR. THOMAS...SHE DIDN'T TAKE ANY DRUGS!
I MADE THIS PLAYLIST FOR YOU, FOR WHEN YOU WERE BETTER. WANNA HEAR?
SO THEN AFTER YOU FELL DOWN LUMI SCREAMED, "TOYA!" MAGGIE, TOO. AND ME. BUT NOT AS LOUD AS LUMI AND MAGGIE. I'M NOT MAD THAT YOU AND MAGGIE ARE GIRLFRIENDS. I WAS BEFORE, BUT NOT NOW.
MS. THOMAS, YOU'RE AS FIT AS A FIDDLE. YOU AND YOUR MAGGIE CAN GO HOME.
BUT AREN'T YOU GONNA BURY ME?
HONEY, WHAT YOU TALKING ABOUT? DON'T YOU WANNA COME HOME?
WHY WOULD WE BURY YOU, CHER?
BECAUSE I DIED. I'M DEAD.
TOYA? SIS...?

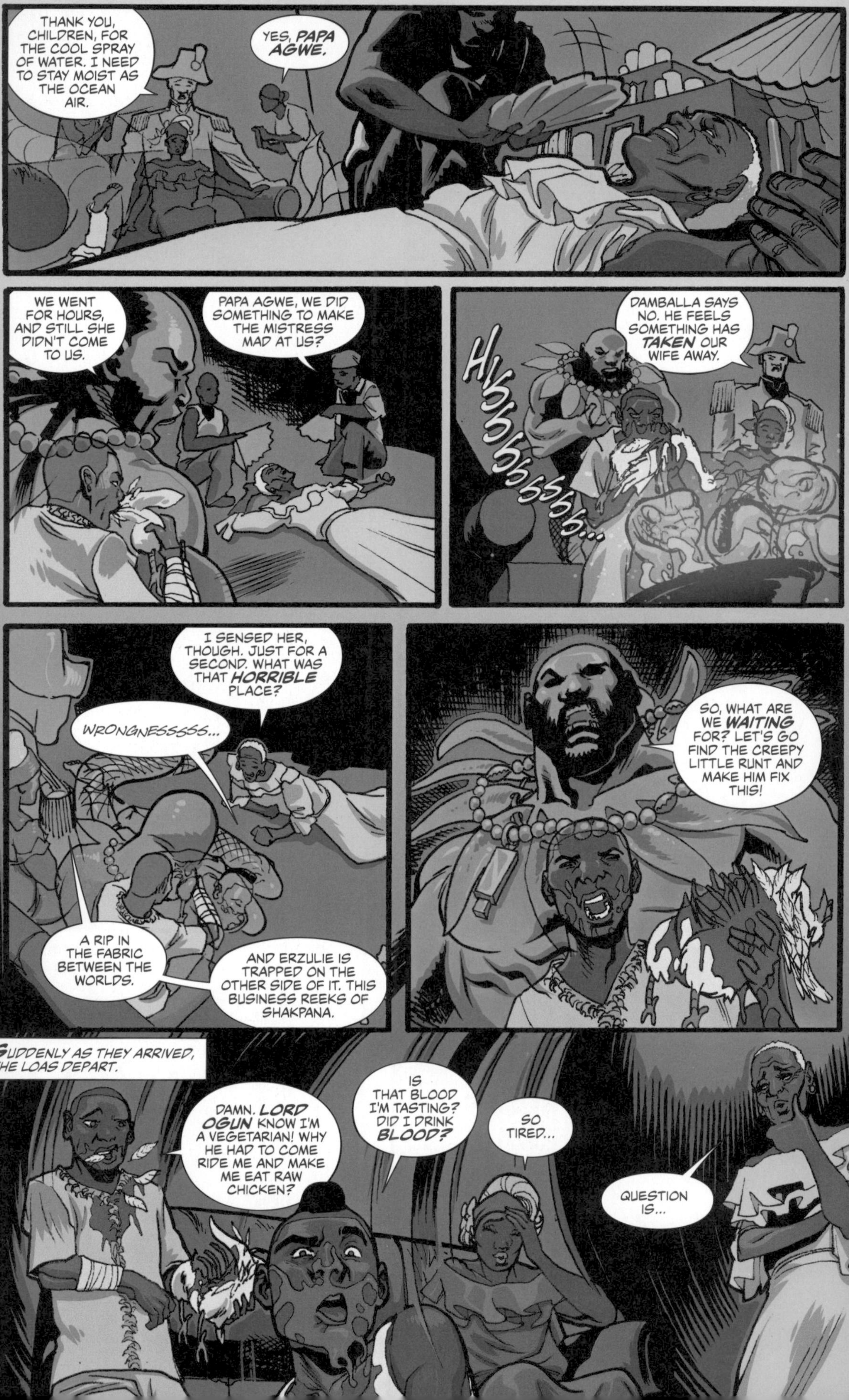
THANK YOU, CHILDREN, FOR THE COOL SPRAY OF WATER. I NEED TO STAY MOIST AS THE OCEAN AIR.
YES, PAPA AGWE.
WE WENT FOR HOURS, AND STILL SHE DIDN'T COME TO US.
PAPA AGWE, WE DID SOMETHING TO MAKE THE MISTRESS MAD AT US?
DAMBALLA SAYS NO. HE FEELS SOMETHING HAS TAKEN OUR WIFE AWAY.
HISSSSSSSSS...
I SENSED HER, THOUGH. JUST FOR A SECOND. WHAT WAS THAT HORRIBLE PLACE?
WRONGNESSSSS...
A RIP IN THE FABRIC BETWEEN THE WORLDS.
AND ERZULIE IS TRAPPED ON THE OTHER SIDE OF IT. THIS BUSINESS REEKS OF SHAKPANA.
SO, WHAT ARE WE WAITING FOR? LET'S GO FIND THE CREEPY LITTLE RUNT AND MAKE HIM FIX THIS!
SUDDENLY AS THEY ARRIVED, THE LOAS DEPART.
DAMN. LORD OGUN KNOW I'M A VEGETARIAN! WHY HE HAD TO COME RIDE ME AND MAKE ME EAT RAW CHICKEN?
IS THAT BLOOD I'M TASTING? DID I DRINK BLOOD?
SO TIRED...
QUESTION IS...

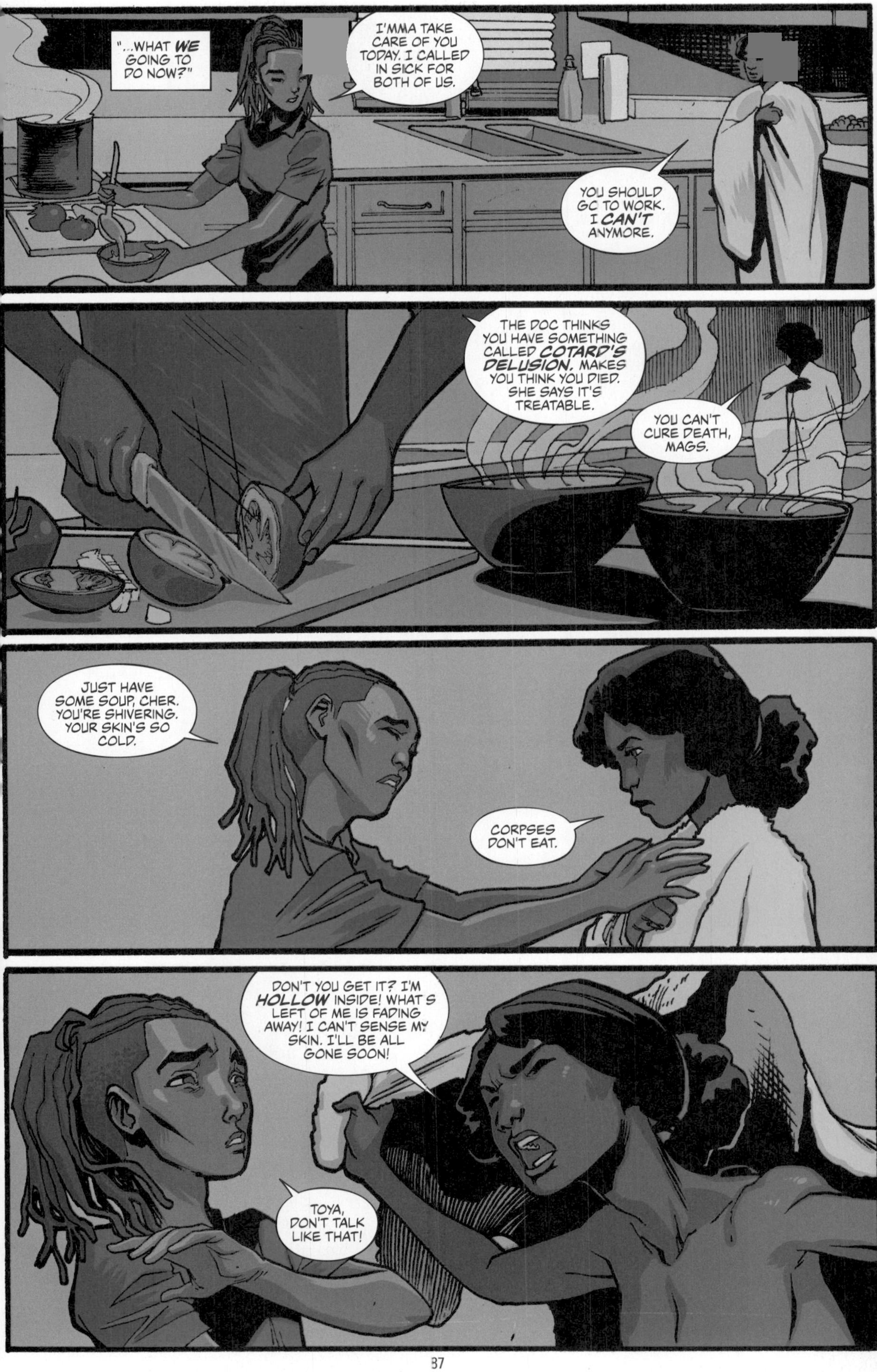
"...WHAT WE GOING TO DO NOW?"
I'MMA TAKE CARE OF YOU TODAY. I CALLED IN SICK FOR BOTH OF US.
YOU SHOULD GO TO WORK. I CAN'T ANYMORE.
THE DOC THINKS YOU HAVE SOMETHING CALLED COTARD'S DELUSION. MAKES YOU THINK YOU DIED. SHE SAYS IT'S TREATABLE.
YOU CAN'T CURE DEATH, MAGS.
JUST HAVE SOME SOUP, CHER. YOU'RE SHIVERING. YOUR SKIN'S SO COLD.
CORPSES DON'T EAT.
DON'T YOU GET IT? I'M HOLLOW INSIDE! WHAT'S LEFT OF ME IS FADING AWAY! I CAN'T SENSE MY SKIN. I'LL BE ALL GONE SOON!
TOYA, DON'T TALK LIKE THAT!

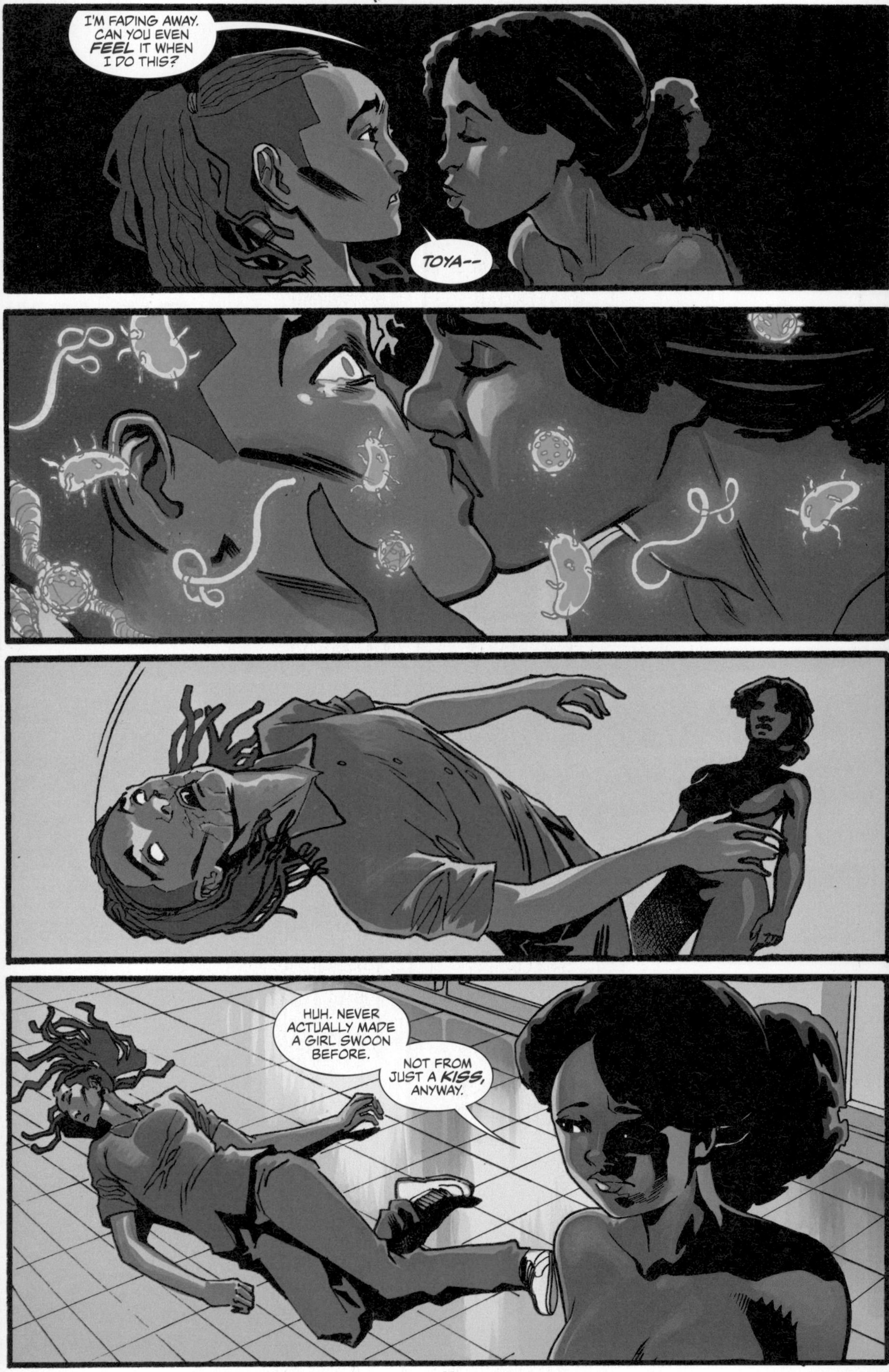

I'M FADING AWAY. CAN YOU EVEN FEEL IT WHEN I DO THIS?
TOYA--
HUH. NEVER ACTUALLY MADE A GIRL SWOON BEFORE.
NOT FROM JUST A KISS, ANYWAY.

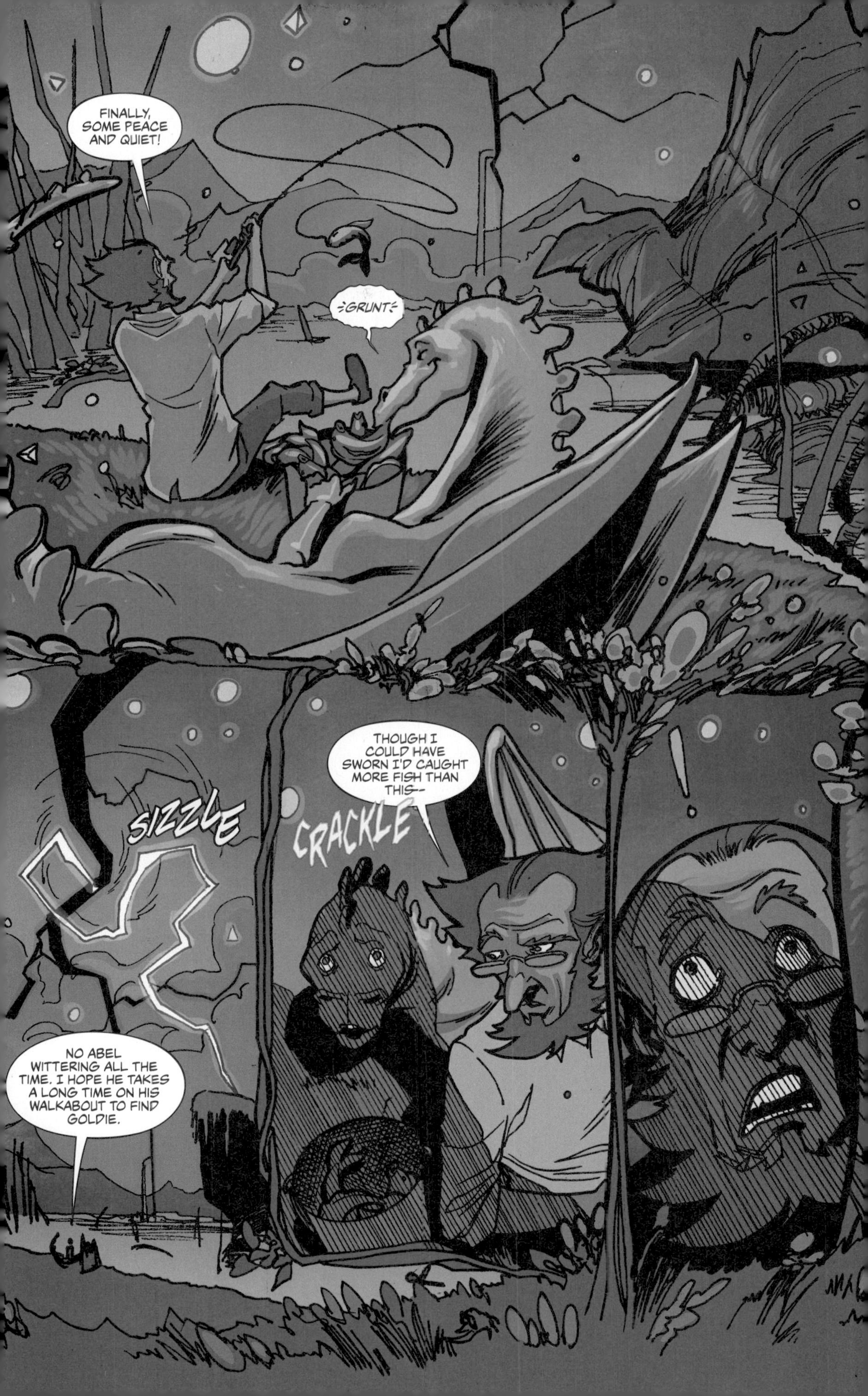
FINALLY, SOME PEACE AND QUIET!
GRUNT
NO ABEL WITTERING ALL THE TIME. I HOPE HE TAKES A LONG TIME ON HIS WALKABOUT TO FIND GOLDIE.
SIZZLE
CRACKLE
THOUGH I COULD HAVE SWORN I'D CAUGHT MORE FISH THAN THIS--
!

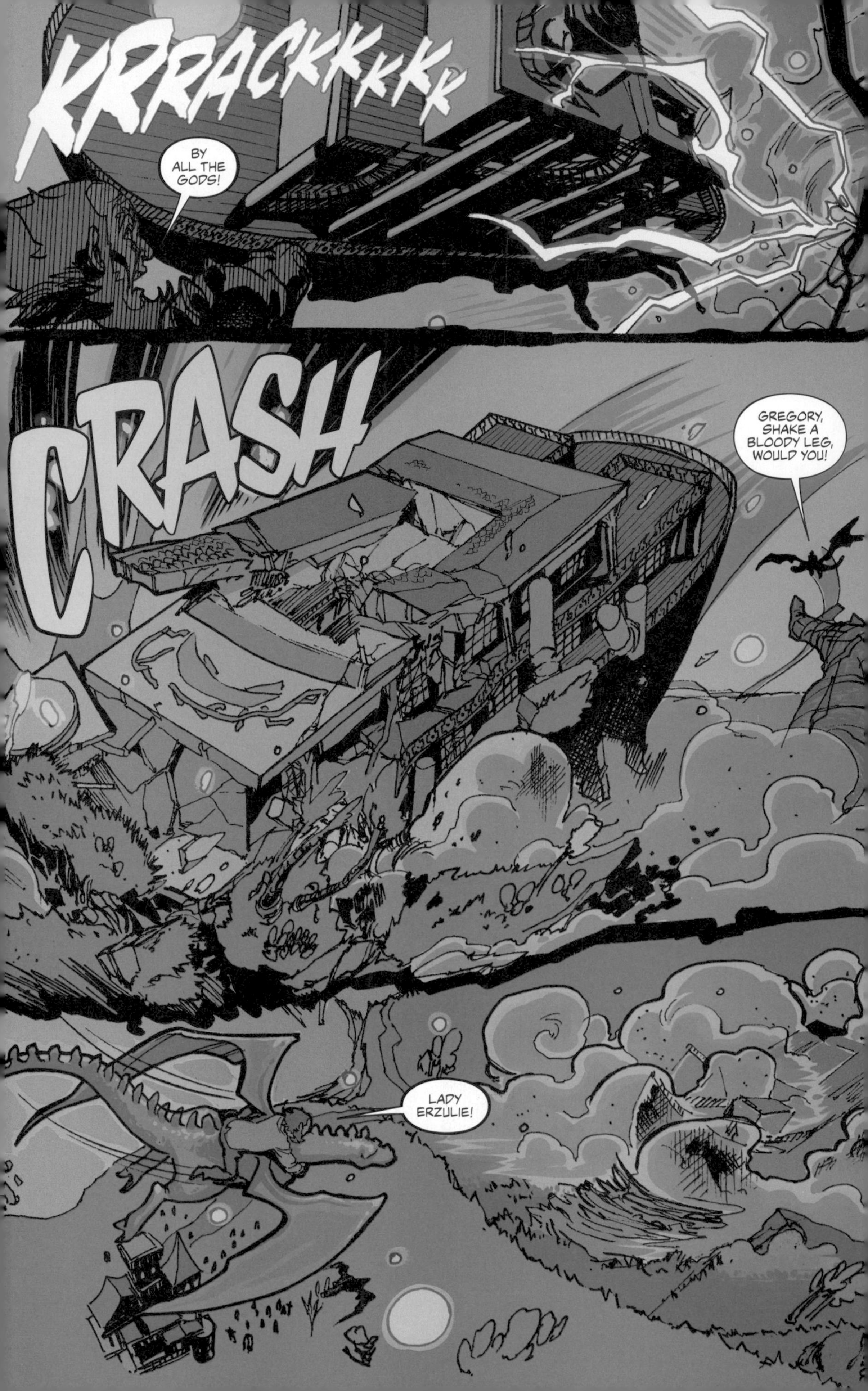
KRRACKKKKK
BY ALL THE GODS!
CRASH
GREGORY, SHAKE A BLOODY LEG, WOULD YOU!
LADY ERZULIE!

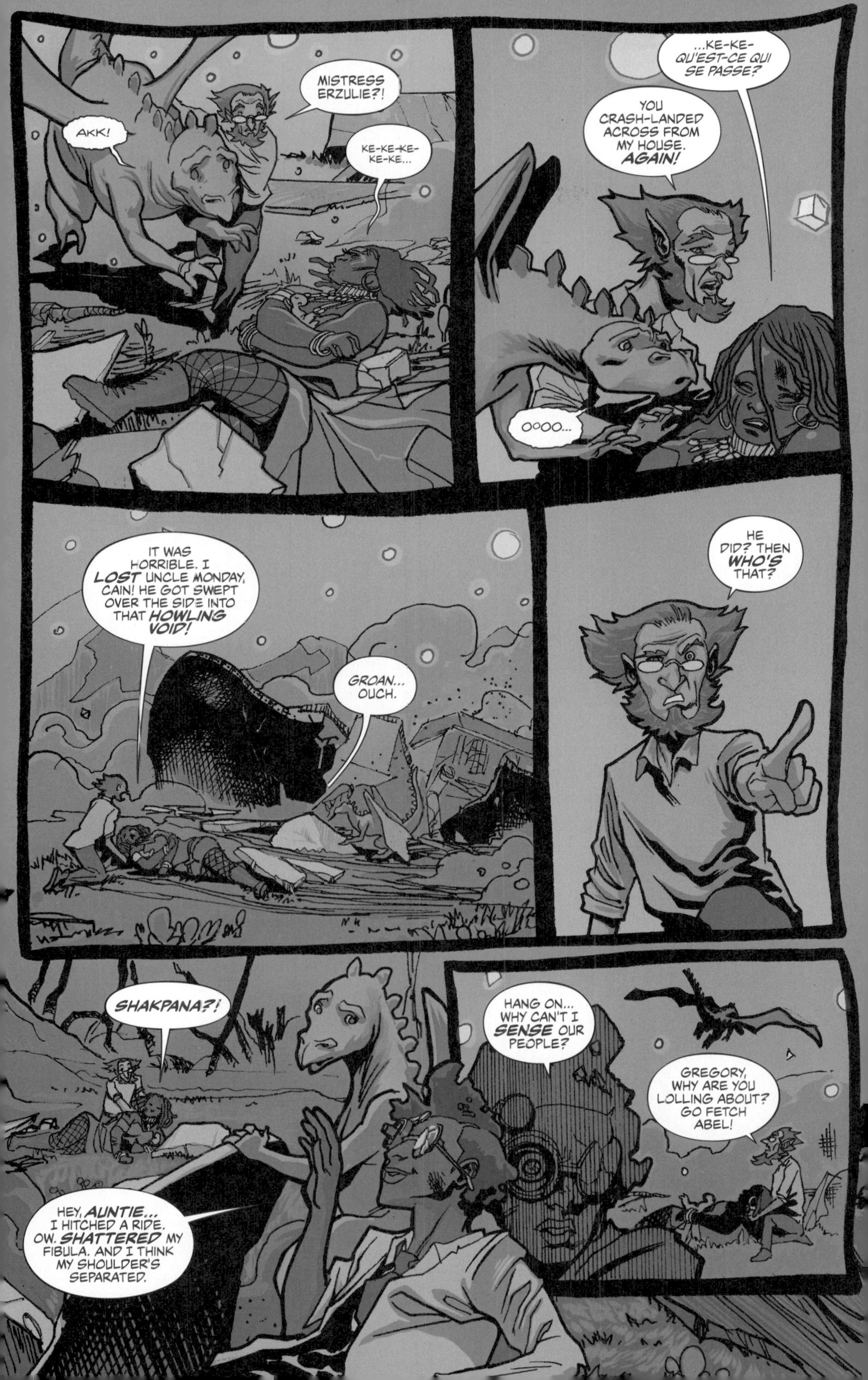
MISTRESS ERZULIE?!
AKK!
KE-KE-KE-KE-KE...
...KE-KE- QU'EST-CE QUI SE PASSE?
YOU CRASH-LANDED ACROSS FROM MY HOUSE. AGAIN!
OOOO...
IT WAS HORRIBLE. I LOST UNCLE MONDAY, CAIN! HE GOT SWEPT OVER THE SIDE INTO THAT HOWLING VOID!
GROAN... OUCH.
HE DID? THEN WHO'S THAT?
SHAKPANA?!
HEY, AUNTIE... I HITCHED A RIDE. OW. SHATTERED MY FIBULA. AND I THINK MY SHOULDER'S SEPARATED.
HANG ON... WHY CAN'T I SENSE OUR PEOPLE?
GREGORY, WHY ARE YOU LOLLING ABOUT? GO FETCH ABEL!

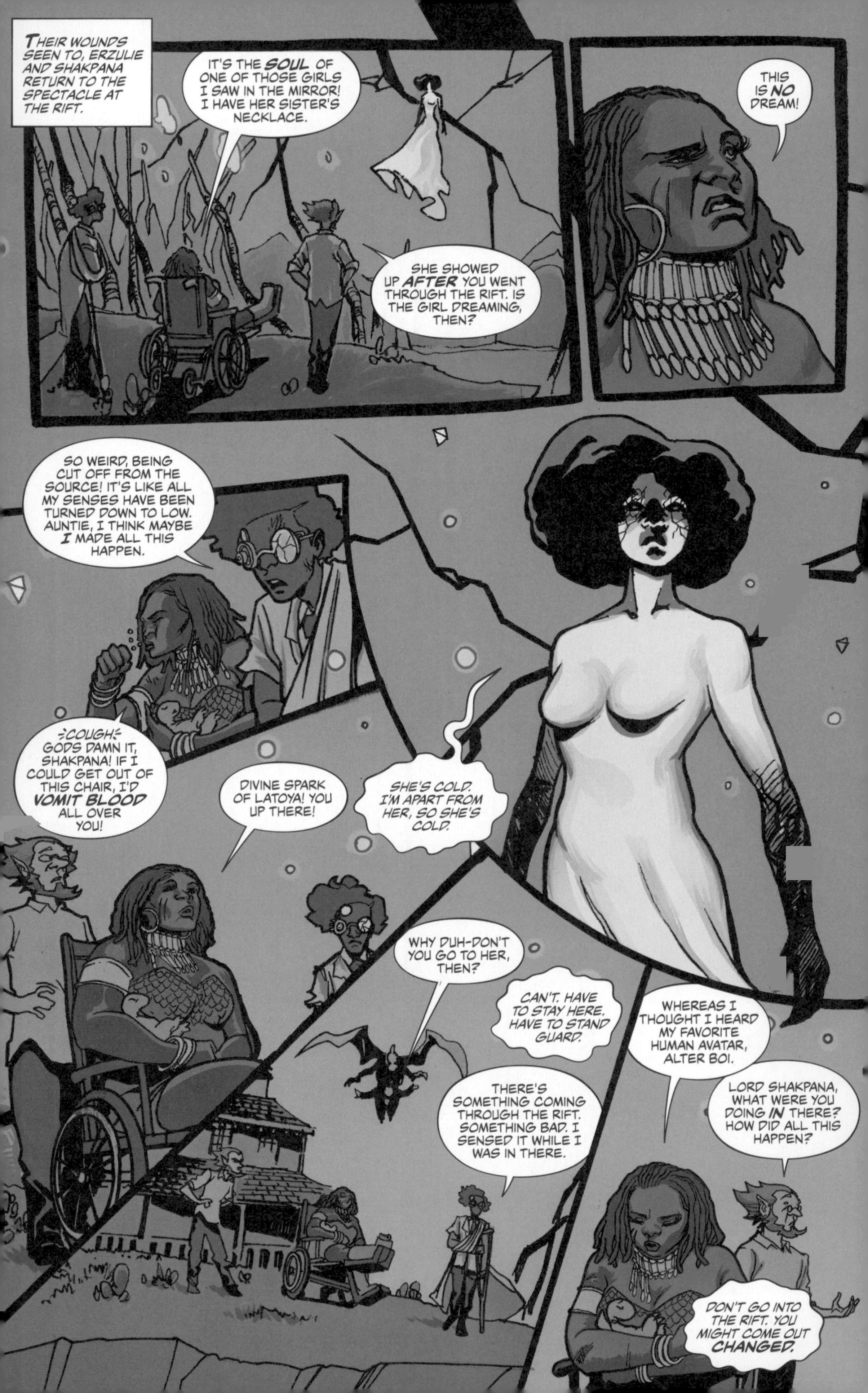
THEIR WOUNDS SEEN TO, ERZULIE AND SHAKPANA RETURN TO THE SPECTACLE AT THE RIFT.
IT'S THE SOUL OF ONE OF THOSE GIRLS I SAW IN THE MIRROR! I HAVE HER SISTER'S NECKLACE.
SHE SHOWED UP AFTER YOU WENT THROUGH THE RIFT. IS THE GIRL DREAMING, THEN?
THIS IS NO DREAM!
SO WEIRD, BEING CUT OFF FROM THE SOURCE! IT'S LIKE ALL MY SENSES HAVE BEEN TURNED DOWN TO LOW. AUNTIE, I THINK MAYBE I MADE ALL THIS HAPPEN.
COUGH GODS DAMN IT, SHAKPANA! IF I COULD GET OUT OF THIS CHAIR, I'D VOMIT BLOOD ALL OVER YOU!
DIVINE SPARK OF LATOYA! YOU UP THERE!
SHE'S COLD. I'M APART FROM HER, SO SHE'S COLD.
WHY DUH-DON'T YOU GO TO HER, THEN?
CAN'T. HAVE TO STAY HERE. HAVE TO STAND GUARD.
THERE'S SOMETHING COMING THROUGH THE RIFT. SOMETHING BAD. I SENSED IT WHILE I WAS IN THERE.
WHEREAS I THOUGHT I HEARD MY FAVORITE HUMAN AVATAR, ALTER BOI.
LORD SHAKPANA, WHAT WERE YOU DOING IN THERE? HOW DID ALL THIS HAPPEN?
DON'T GO INTO THE RIFT. YOU MIGHT COME OUT CHANGED.

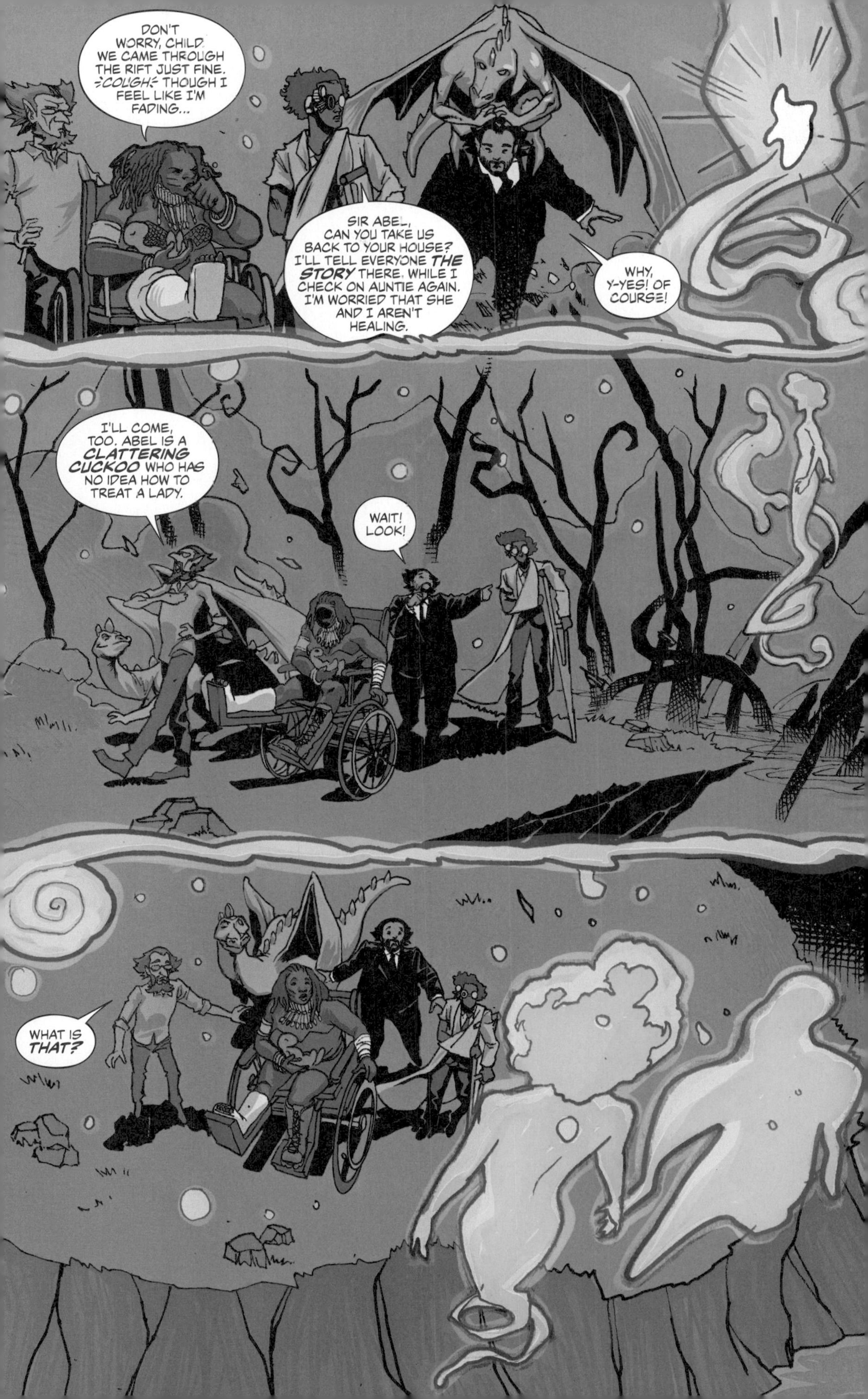
DON'T WORRY, CHILD. WE CAME THROUGH THE RIFT JUST FINE. *COUGH* THOUGH I FEEL LIKE I'M FADING...
SIR ABEL, CAN YOU TAKE US BACK TO YOUR HOUSE? I'LL TELL EVERYONE THE STORY THERE, WHILE I CHECK ON AUNTIE AGAIN. I'M WORRIED THAT SHE AND I AREN'T HEALING.
WHY, Y-YES! OF COURSE!
I'LL COME, TOO. ABEL IS A CLATTERING CUCKOO WHO HAS NO IDEA HOW TO TREAT A LADY.
WAIT! LOOK!
WHAT IS THAT?

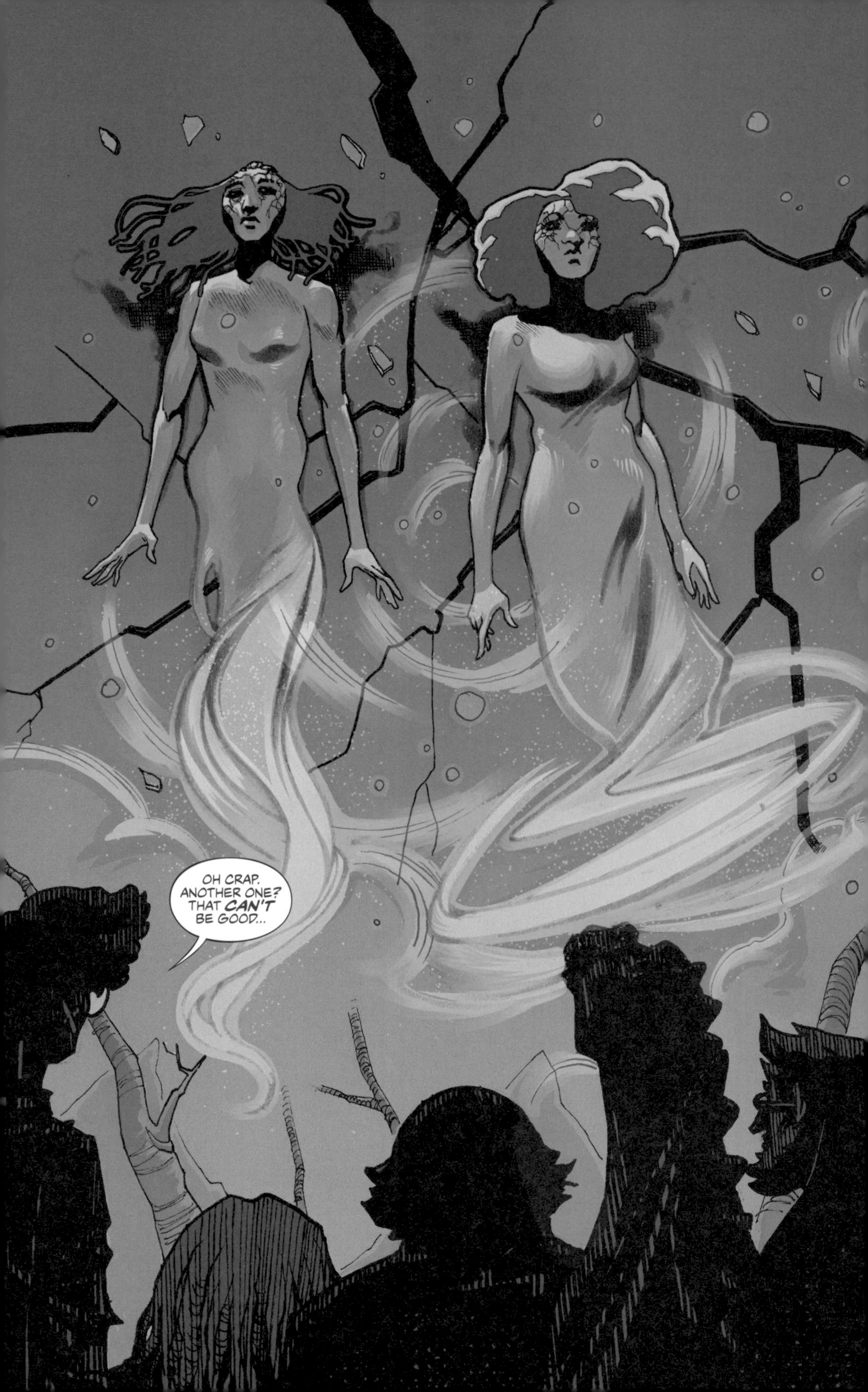
OH CRAP. ANOTHER ONE? THAT CAN'T BE GOOD...

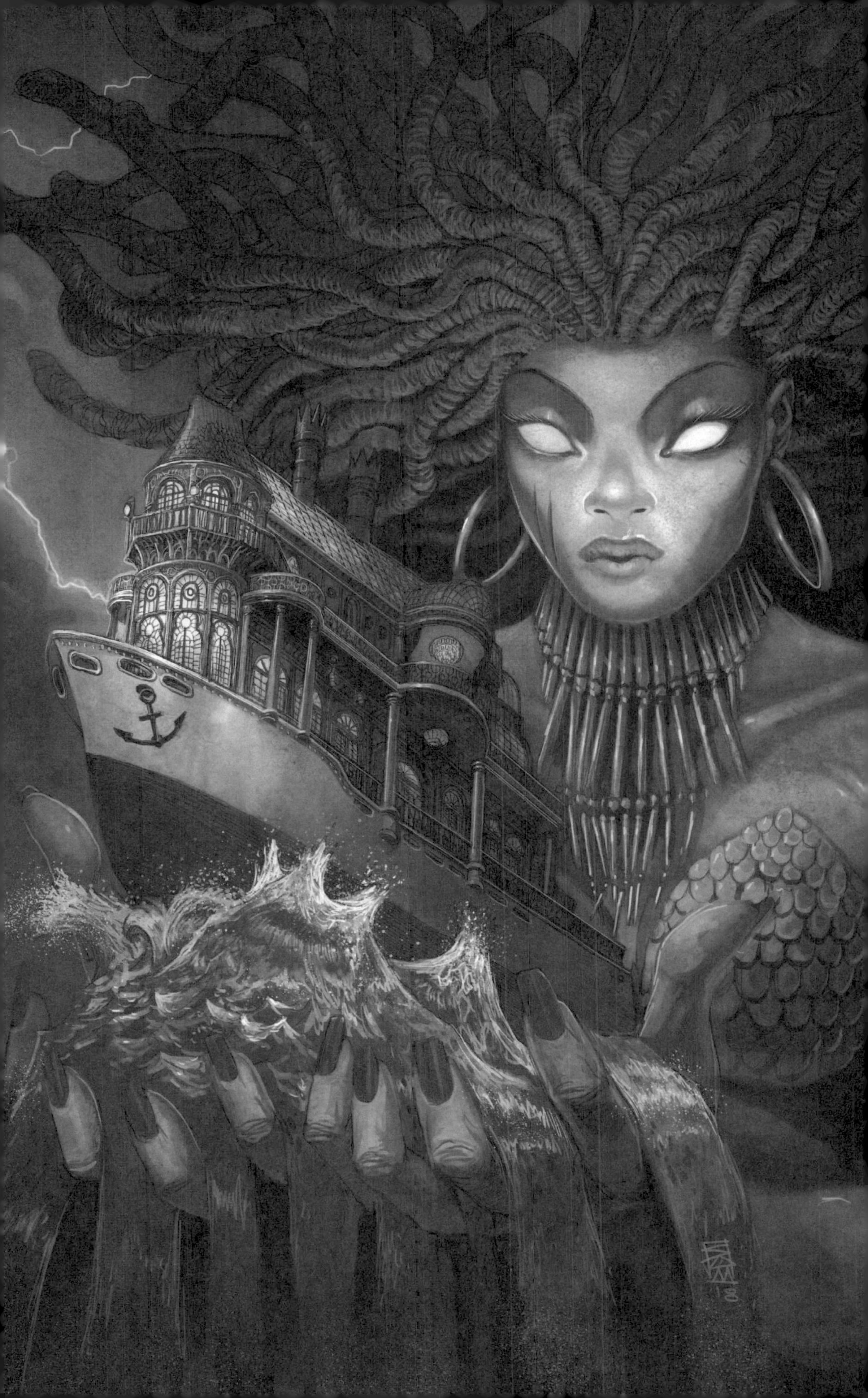

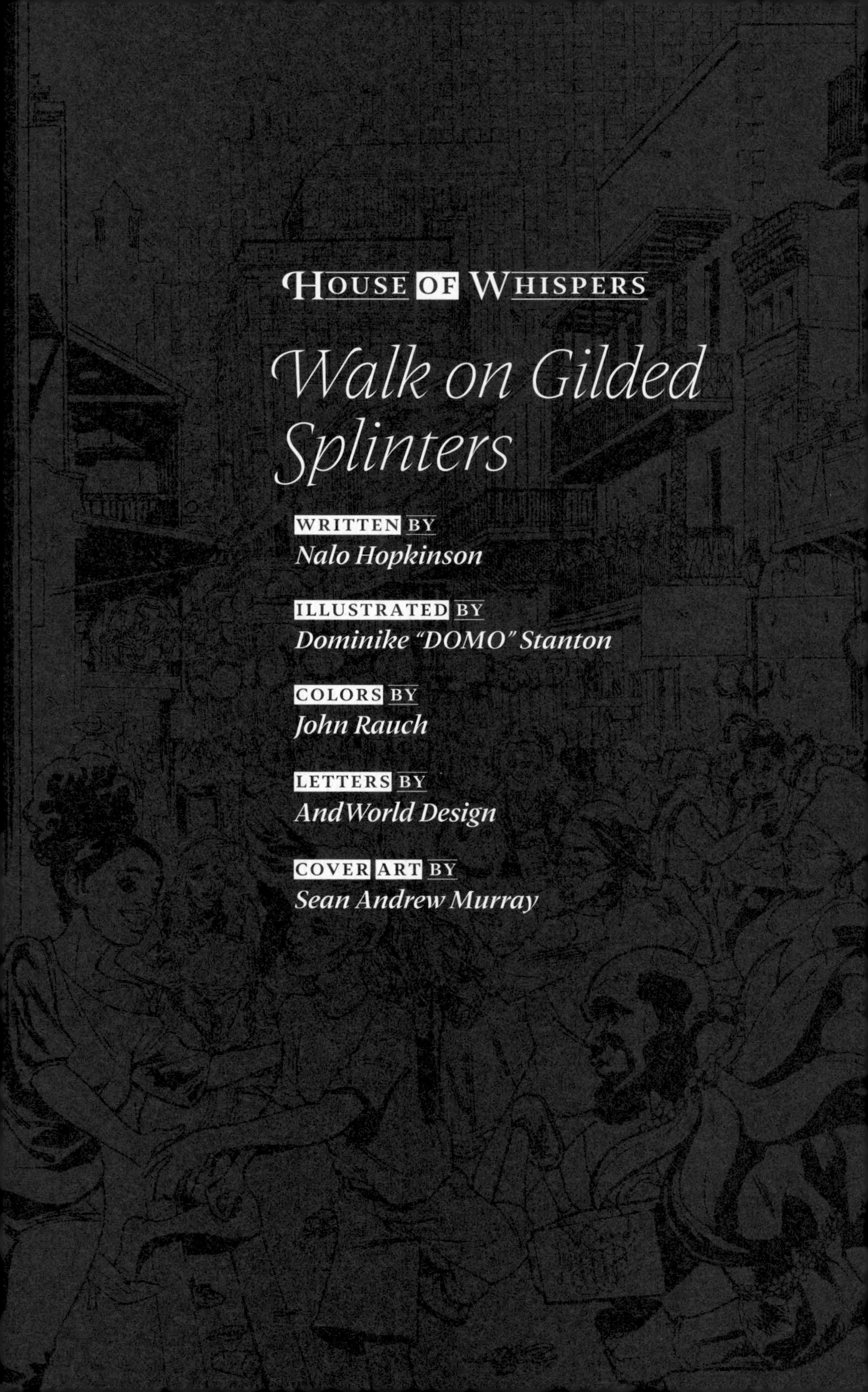

HOUSE OF WHISPERS

Walk on Gilded Splinters

WRITTEN BY
Nalo Hopkinson

ILLUSTRATED BY
Dominike "DOMO" Stanton

COLORS BY
John Rauch

LETTERS BY
AndWorld Design

COVER ART BY
Sean Andrew Murray

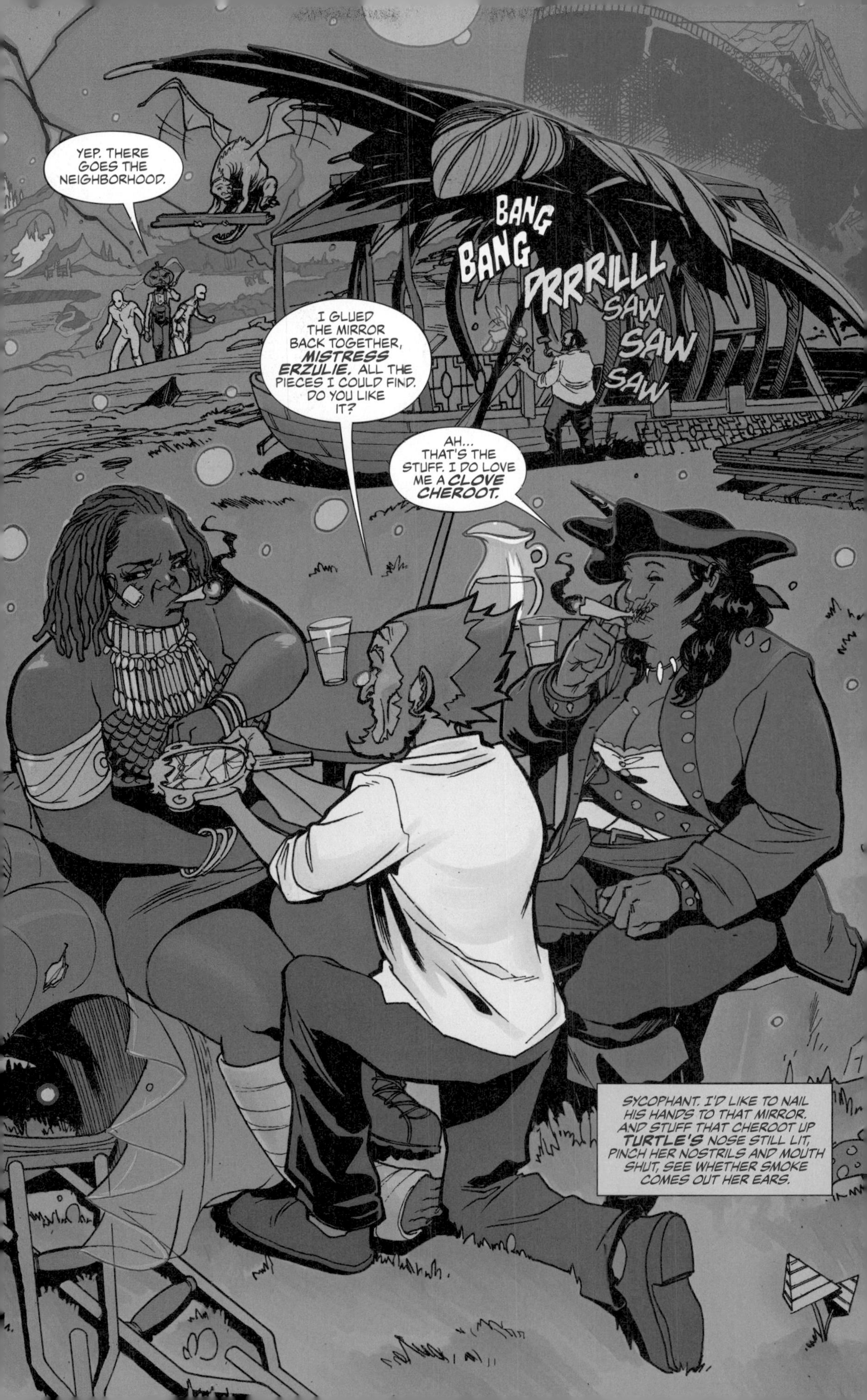
YEP. THERE GOES THE NEIGHBORHOOD.
BANG BANG DRRRILLL SAW SAW SAW
I GLUED THE MIRROR BACK TOGETHER, MISTRESS ERZULIE. ALL THE PIECES I COULD FIND. DO YOU LIKE IT?
AH... THAT'S THE STUFF. I DO LOVE ME A CLOVE CHEROOT.
SYCOPHANT. I'D LIKE TO NAIL HIS HANDS TO THAT MIRROR. AND STUFF THAT CHEROOT UP TURTLE'S NOSE STILL LIT, PINCH HER NOSTRILS AND MOUTH SHUT, SEE WHETHER SMOKE COMES OUT HER EARS.

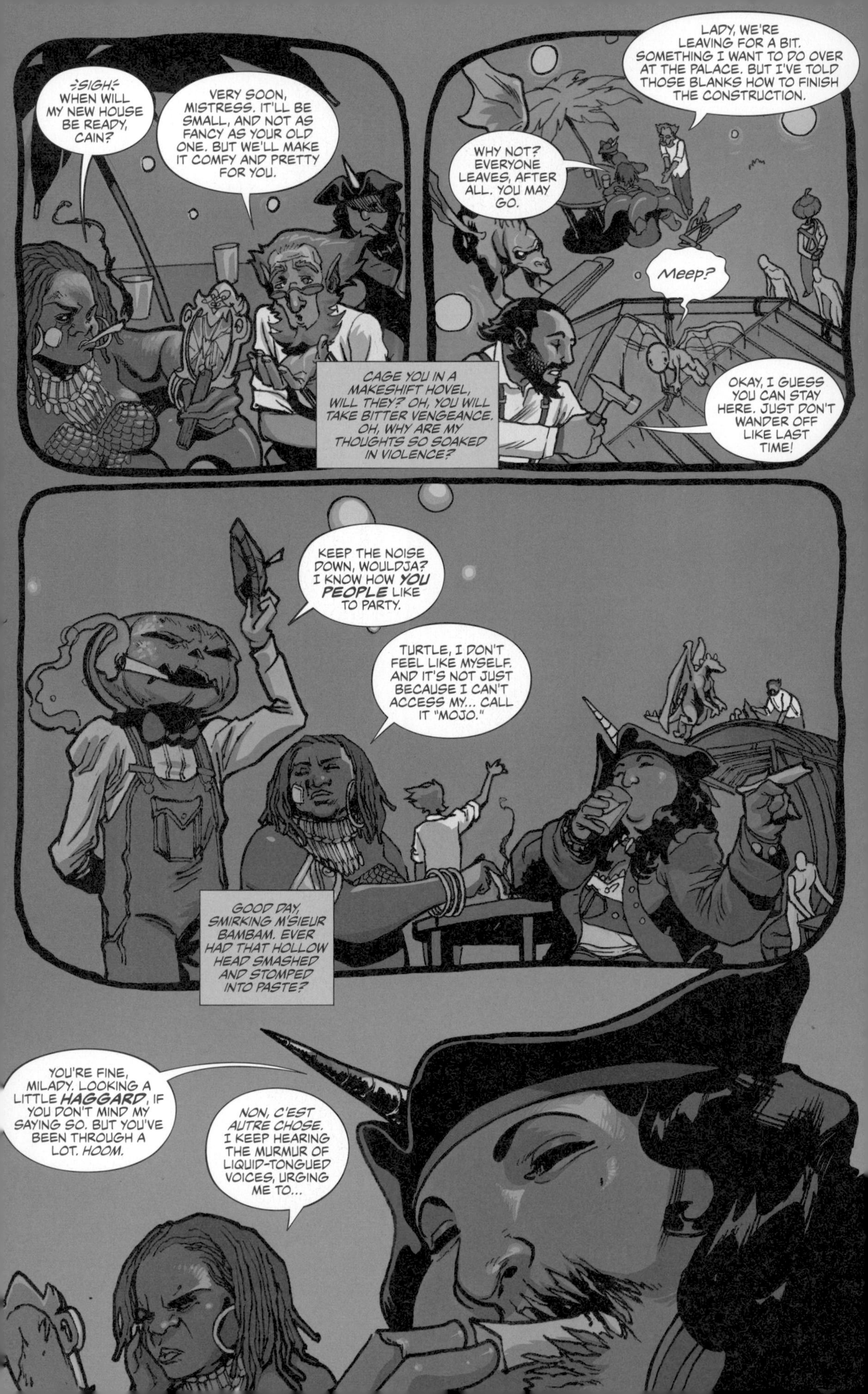
~SIGH~ WHEN WILL MY NEW HOUSE BE READY, CAIN?
VERY SOON, MISTRESS. IT'LL BE SMALL, AND NOT AS FANCY AS YOUR OLD ONE. BUT WE'LL MAKE IT COMFY AND PRETTY FOR YOU.
CAGE YOU IN A MAKESHIFT HOVEL, WILL THEY? OH, YOU WILL TAKE BITTER VENGEANCE. OH, WHY ARE MY THOUGHTS SO SOAKED IN VIOLENCE?
LADY, WE'RE LEAVING FOR A BIT. SOMETHING I WANT TO DO OVER AT THE PALACE. BUT I'VE TOLD THOSE BLANKS HOW TO FINISH THE CONSTRUCTION.
WHY NOT? EVERYONE LEAVES, AFTER ALL. YOU MAY GO.
Meep?
OKAY, I GUESS YOU CAN STAY HERE. JUST DON'T WANDER OFF LIKE LAST TIME!
KEEP THE NOISE DOWN, WOULDJA? I KNOW HOW ***YOU PEOPLE*** LIKE TO PARTY.
TURTLE, I DON'T FEEL LIKE MYSELF. AND IT'S NOT JUST BECAUSE I CAN'T ACCESS MY... CALL IT "MOJO."
GOOD DAY, SMIRKING M'SIEUR BAMBAM. EVER HAD THAT HOLLOW HEAD SMASHED AND STOMPED INTO PASTE?
YOU'RE FINE, MILADY. LOOKING A LITTLE ***HAGGARD***, IF YOU DON'T MIND MY SAYING SO. BUT YOU'VE BEEN THROUGH A LOT. *HOOM.*
NON, C'EST AUTRE CHOSE. I KEEP HEARING THE MURMUR OF LIQUID-TONGUED VOICES, URGING ME TO...

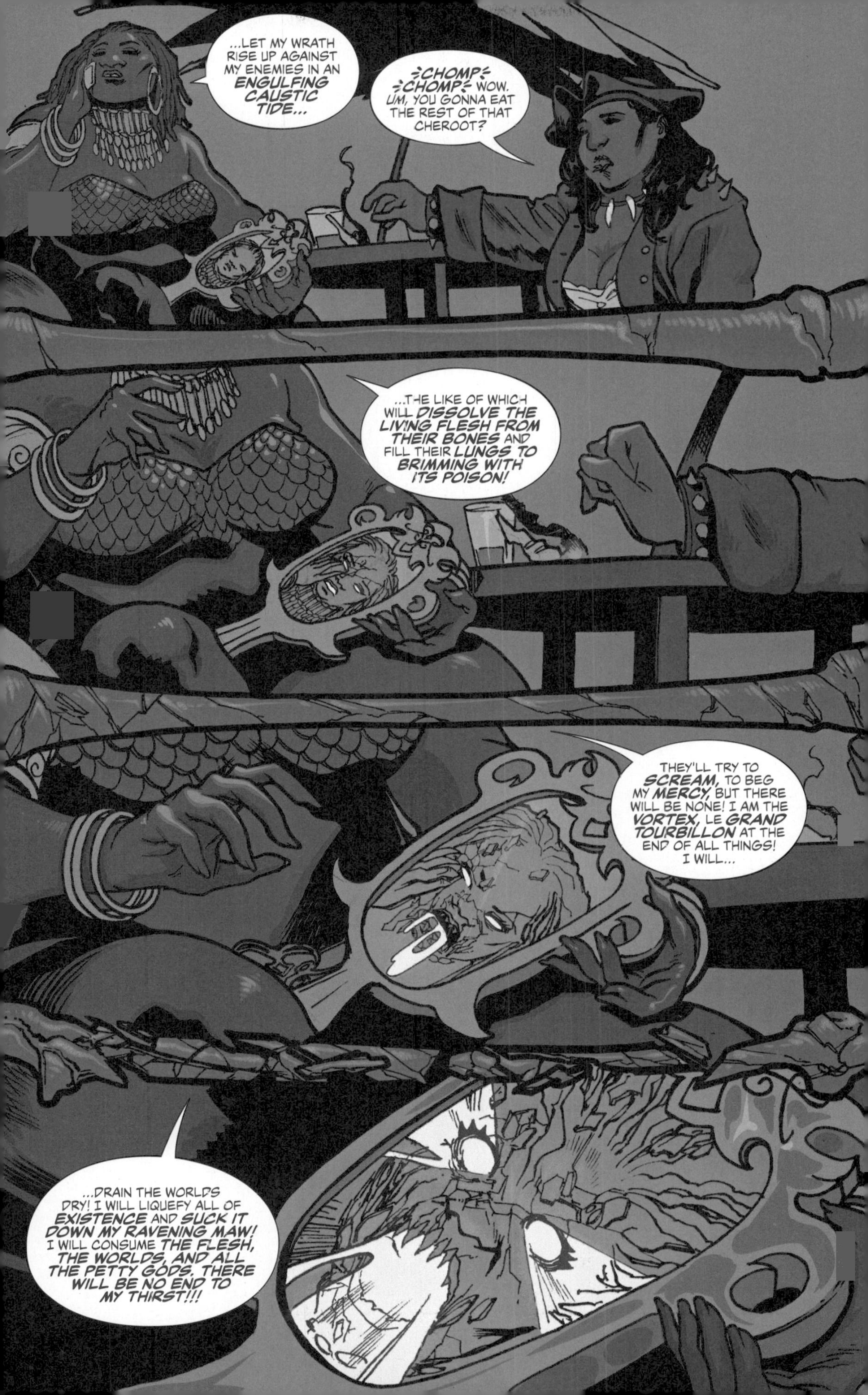
...LET MY WRATH RISE UP AGAINST MY ENEMIES IN AN ENGULFING CAUSTIC TIDE...
CHOMP CHOMP WOW. UM, YOU GONNA EAT THE REST OF THAT CHEROOT?
...THE LIKE OF WHICH WILL DISSOLVE THE LIVING FLESH FROM THEIR BONES AND FILL THEIR LUNGS TO BRIMMING WITH ITS POISON!
THEY'LL TRY TO SCREAM, TO BEG MY MERCY, BUT THERE WILL BE NONE! I AM THE VORTEX, LE GRAND TOURBILLON AT THE END OF ALL THINGS! I WILL...
...DRAIN THE WORLDS DRY! I WILL LIQUEFY ALL OF EXISTENCE AND SUCK IT DOWN MY RAVENING MAW! I WILL CONSUME THE FLESH, THE WORLDS, AND ALL THE PETTY GODS. THERE WILL BE NO END TO MY THIRST!!!

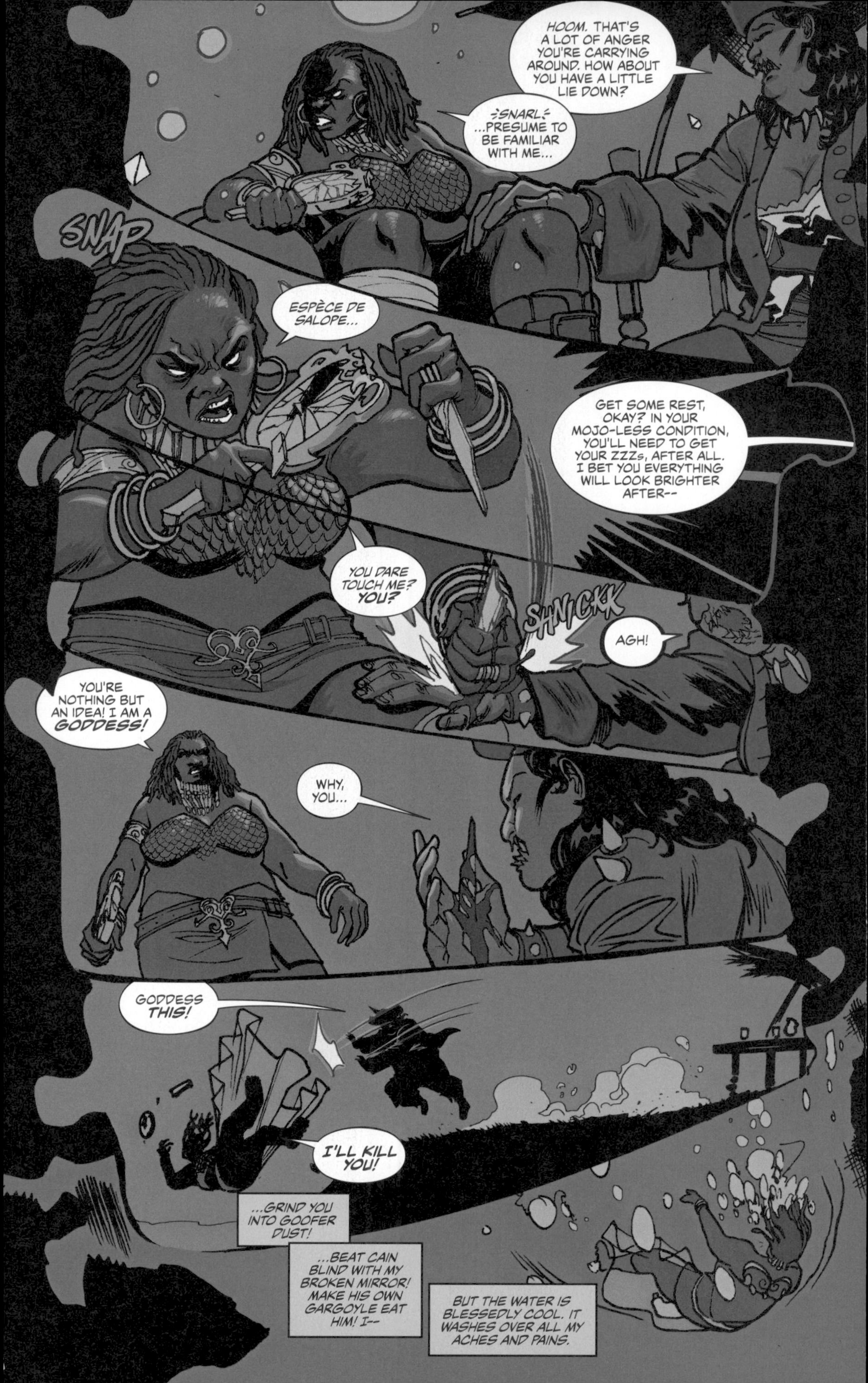
HOOM. THAT'S A LOT OF ANGER YOU'RE CARRYING AROUND. HOW ABOUT YOU HAVE A LITTLE LIE DOWN?
SNARL ...PRESUME TO BE FAMILIAR WITH ME...
SNAP
ESPÈCE DE SALOPE...
GET SOME REST, OKAY? IN YOUR MOJO-LESS CONDITION, YOU'LL NEED TO GET YOUR ZZZs, AFTER ALL. I BET YOU EVERYTHING WILL LOOK BRIGHTER AFTER--
YOU DARE TOUCH ME? YOU?
SHNICKK
AGH!
YOU'RE NOTHING BUT AN IDEA! I AM A GODDESS!
WHY, YOU...
GODDESS THIS!
I'LL KILL YOU!
...GRIND YOU INTO GOOFER DUST!
...BEAT CAIN BLIND WITH MY BROKEN MIRROR! MAKE HIS OWN GARGOYLE EAT HIM! I--
BUT THE WATER IS BLESSEDLY COOL. IT WASHES OVER ALL MY ACHES AND PAINS.

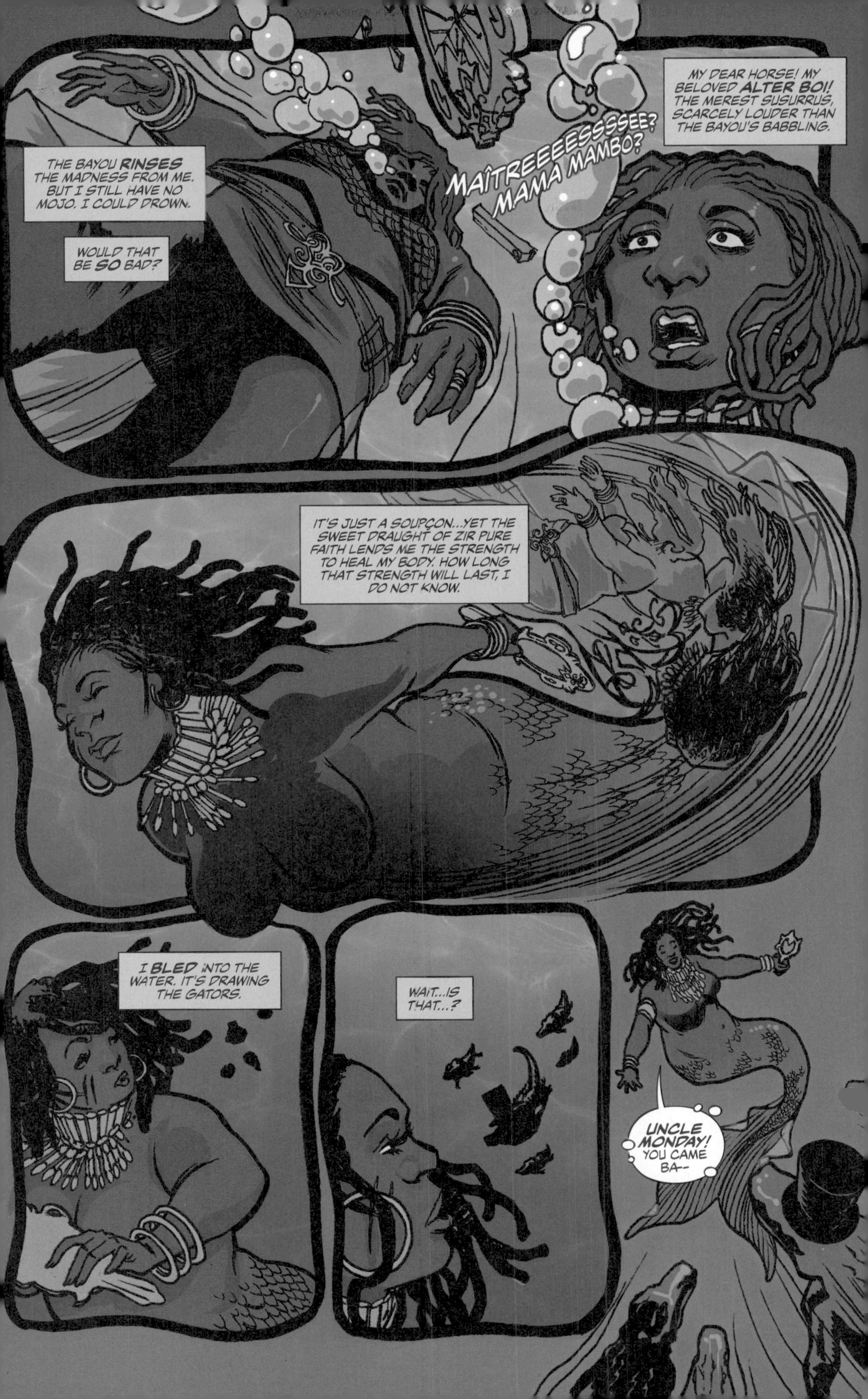
THE BAYOU RINSES THE MADNESS FROM ME. BUT I STILL HAVE NO MOJO. I COULD DROWN.
WOULD THAT BE SO BAD?
MAÎTREEEEESSSSEE? MAMA MAMBO?
MY DEAR HORSE! MY BELOVED ALTER BOI! THE MEREST SUSURRUS, SCARCELY LOUDER THAN THE BAYOU'S BABBLING.
IT'S JUST A SOUPÇON...YET THE SWEET DRAUGHT OF ZIR PURE FAITH LENDS ME THE STRENGTH TO HEAL MY BODY. HOW LONG THAT STRENGTH WILL LAST, I DO NOT KNOW.
I BLED INTO THE WATER. IT'S DRAWING THE GATORS.
WAIT...IS THAT...?
UNCLE MONDAY! YOU CAME BA--

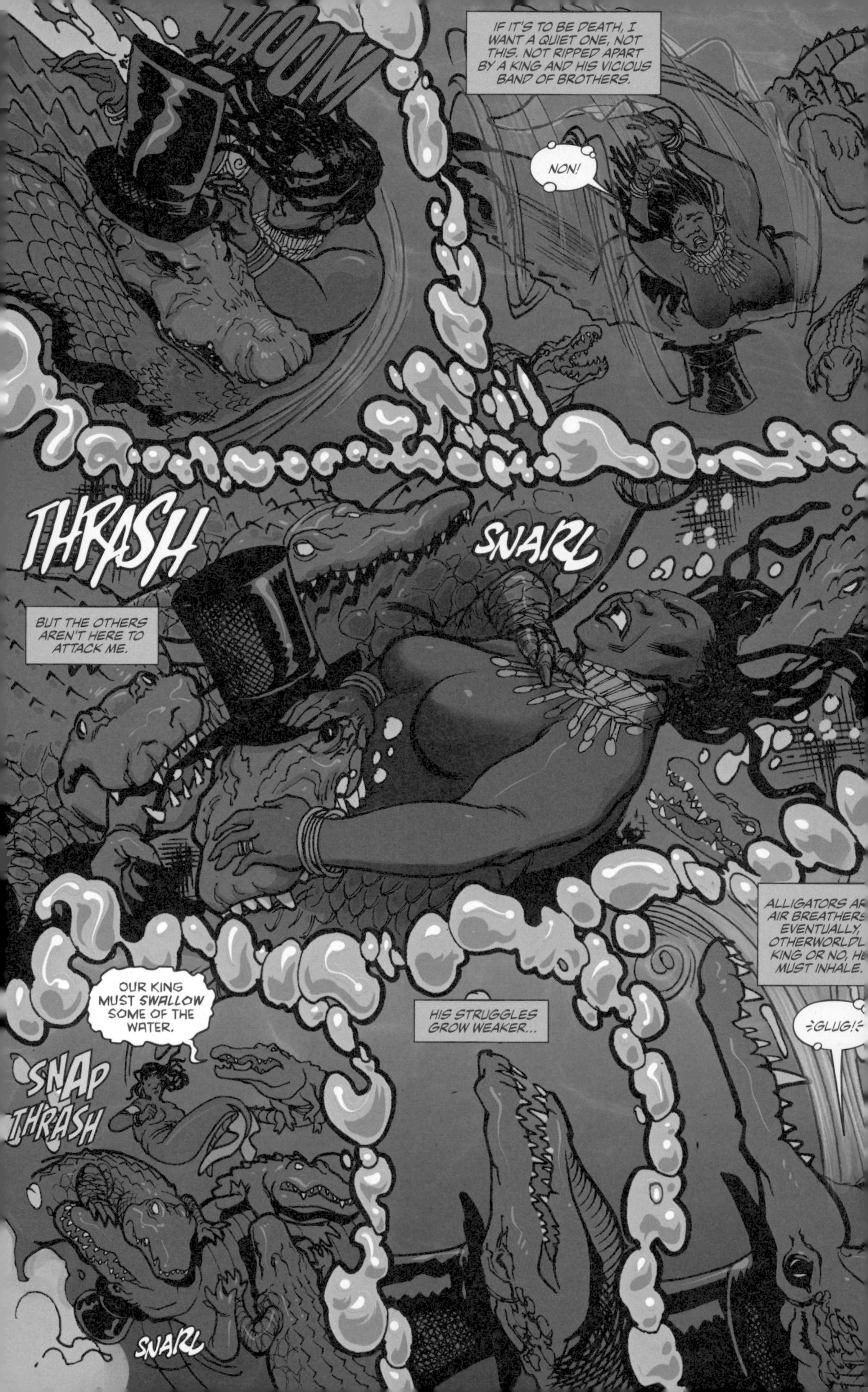
WHOOM
IF IT'S TO BE DEATH, I WANT A QUIET ONE, NOT THIS. NOT RIPPED APART BY A KING AND HIS VICIOUS BAND OF BROTHERS.
NON!
THRASH
SNARL
BUT THE OTHERS AREN'T HERE TO ATTACK ME.
OUR KING MUST SWALLOW SOME OF THE WATER.
SNAP
THRASH
SNARL
HIS STRUGGLES GROW WEAKER...
ALLIGATORS AR
AIR BREATHERS
EVENTUALLY,
OTHERWORLDL
KING OR NO, H
MUST INHALE.
GLUG!

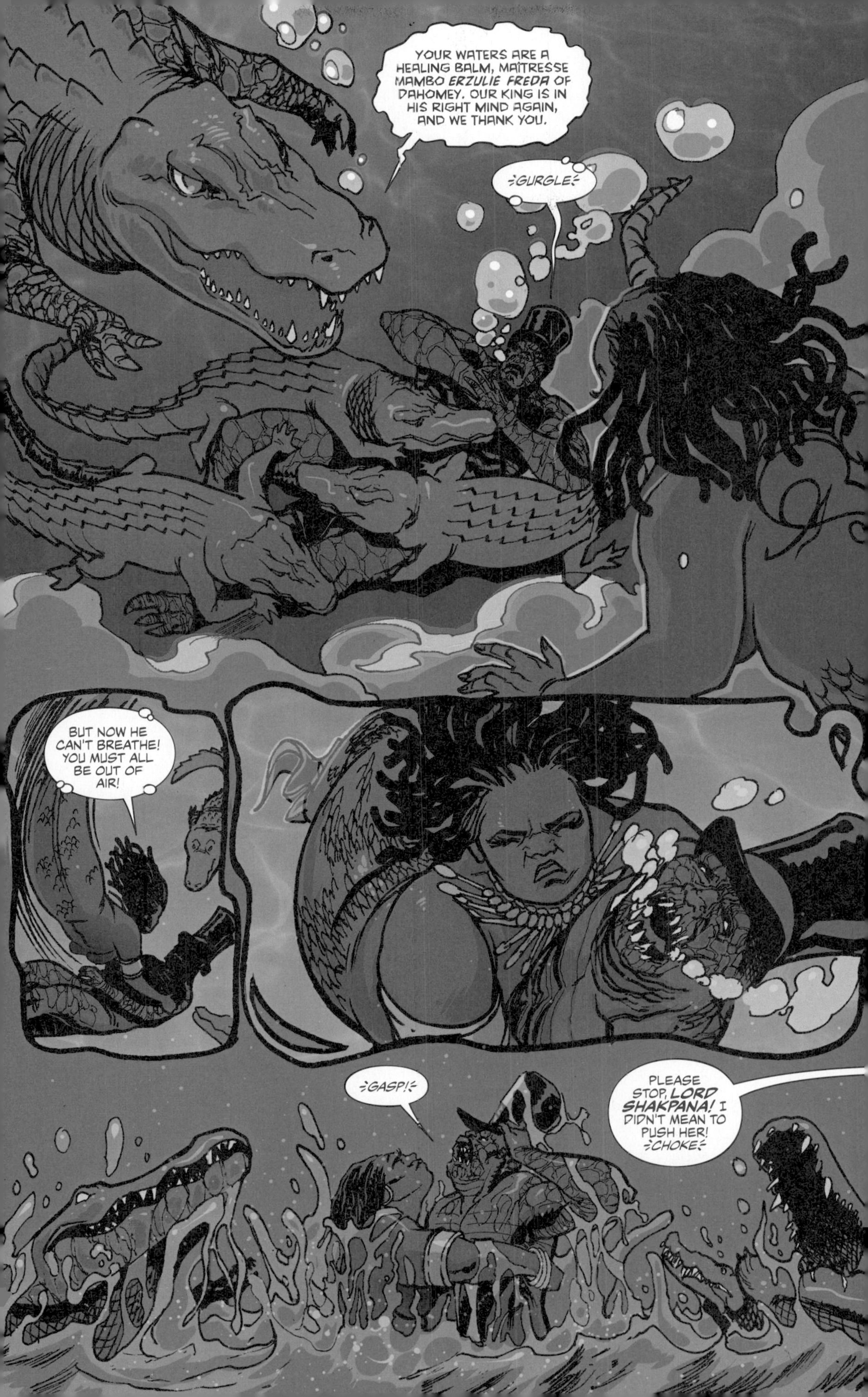
YOUR WATERS ARE A HEALING BALM, MAÎTRESSE MAMBO *ERZULIE FREDA* OF DAHOMEY. OUR KING IS IN HIS RIGHT MIND AGAIN, AND WE THANK YOU.
GURGLE
BUT NOW HE CAN'T BREATHE! YOU MUST ALL BE OUT OF AIR!
GASP!
PLEASE STOP, **LORD SHAKPANA!** I DIDN'T MEAN TO PUSH HER! CHOKE

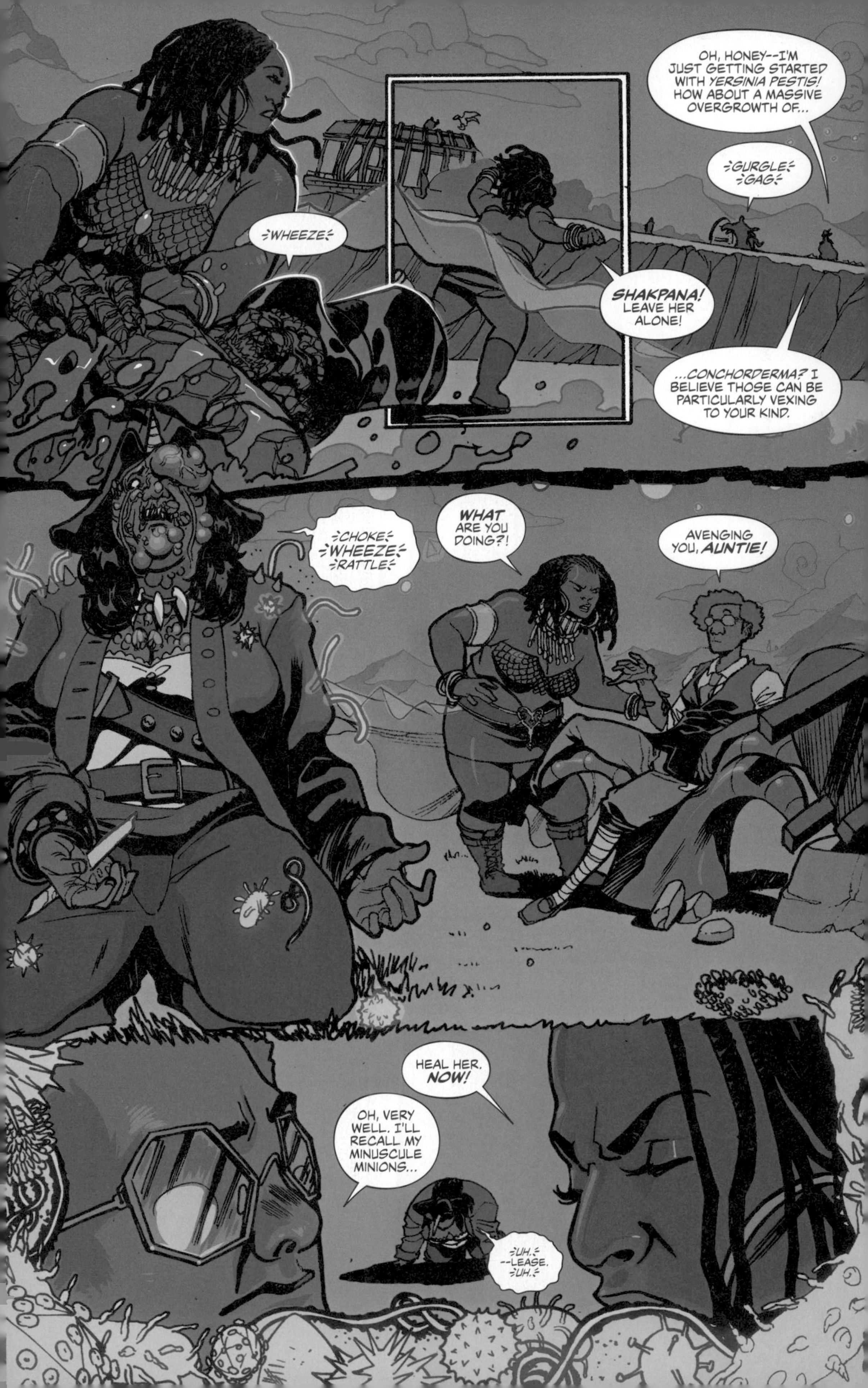

OH, HONEY--I'M JUST GETTING STARTED WITH *YERSINIA PESTIS!* HOW ABOUT A MASSIVE OVERGROWTH OF...
GURGLE GAG
WHEEZE
SHAKPANA! LEAVE HER ALONE!
...*CONCHORDERMA?* I BELIEVE THOSE CAN BE PARTICULARLY VEXING TO YOUR KIND.
CHOKE WHEEZE RATTLE
WHAT ARE YOU DOING?!
AVENGING YOU, **AUNTIE!**
HEAL HER. **NOW!**
OH, VERY WELL. I'LL RECALL MY MINUSCULE MINIONS...
UH. --LEASE. UH.

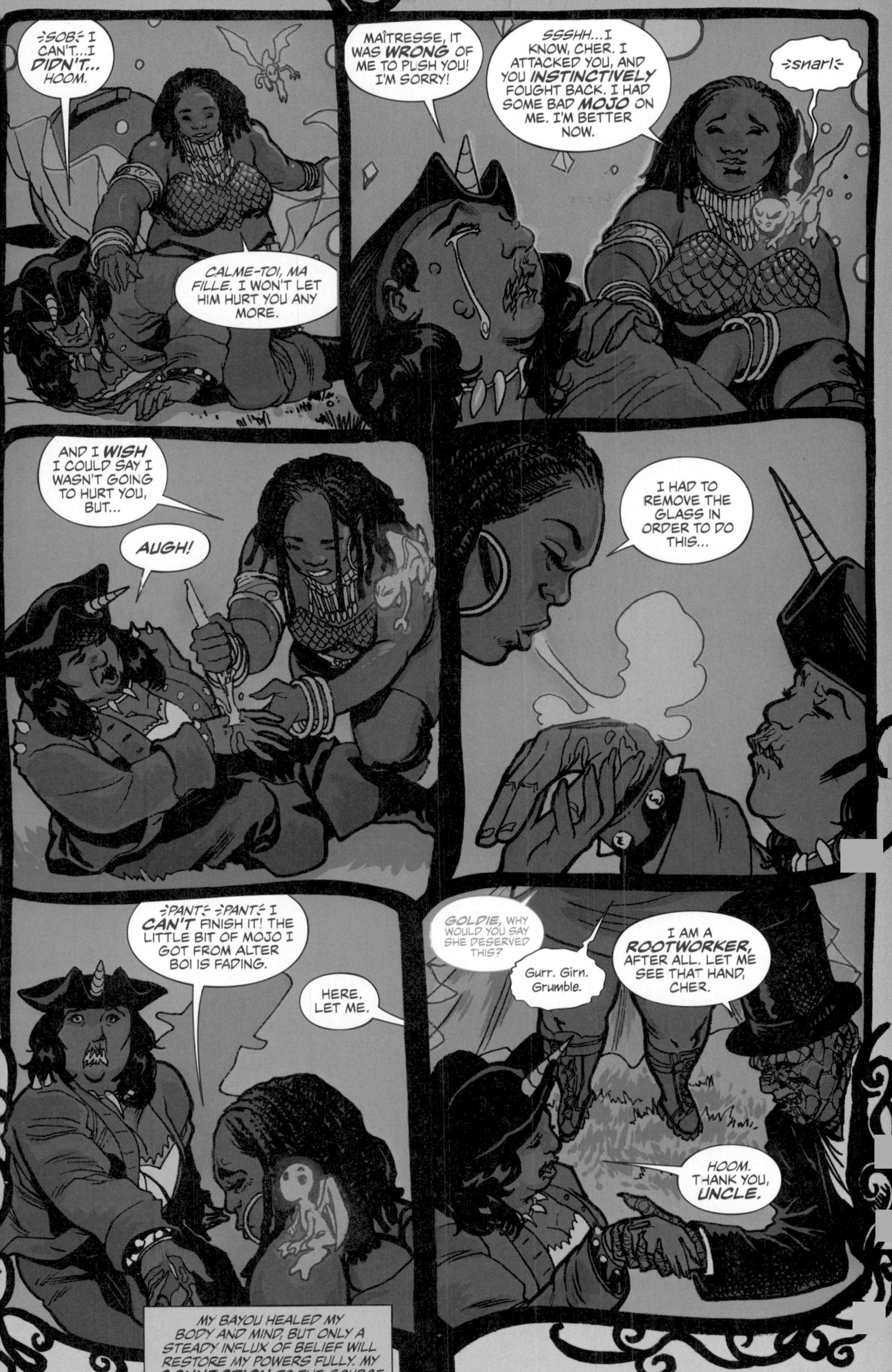

≈SOB≈ I CAN'T...I DIDN'T... HOOM.
CALME-TOI, MA FILLE. I WON'T LET HIM HURT YOU ANY MORE.
MAÎTRESSE, IT WAS WRONG OF ME TO PUSH YOU! I'M SORRY!
SSSHH...I KNOW, CHER. I ATTACKED YOU, AND YOU INSTINCTIVELY FOUGHT BACK. I HAD SOME BAD MOJO ON ME. I'M BETTER NOW.
≈snarl≈
AND I WISH I COULD SAY I WASN'T GOING TO HURT YOU, BUT...
AUGH!
I HAD TO REMOVE THE GLASS IN ORDER TO DO THIS...
≈PANT≈ ≈PANT≈ I CAN'T FINISH IT! THE LITTLE BIT OF MOJO I GOT FROM ALTER BOI IS FADING.
HERE. LET ME.
MY BAYOU HEALED MY BODY AND MIND, BUT ONLY A STEADY INFLUX OF BELIEF WILL RESTORE MY POWERS FULLY. MY CONNECTION TO THE SOURCE IS STILL COMPROMISED.
GOLDIE, WHY WOULD YOU SAY SHE DESERVED THIS?
Gurr. Girn. Grumble.
I AM A ROOTWORKER, AFTER ALL. LET ME SEE THAT HAND, CHER.
HOOM. THANK YOU, UNCLE.

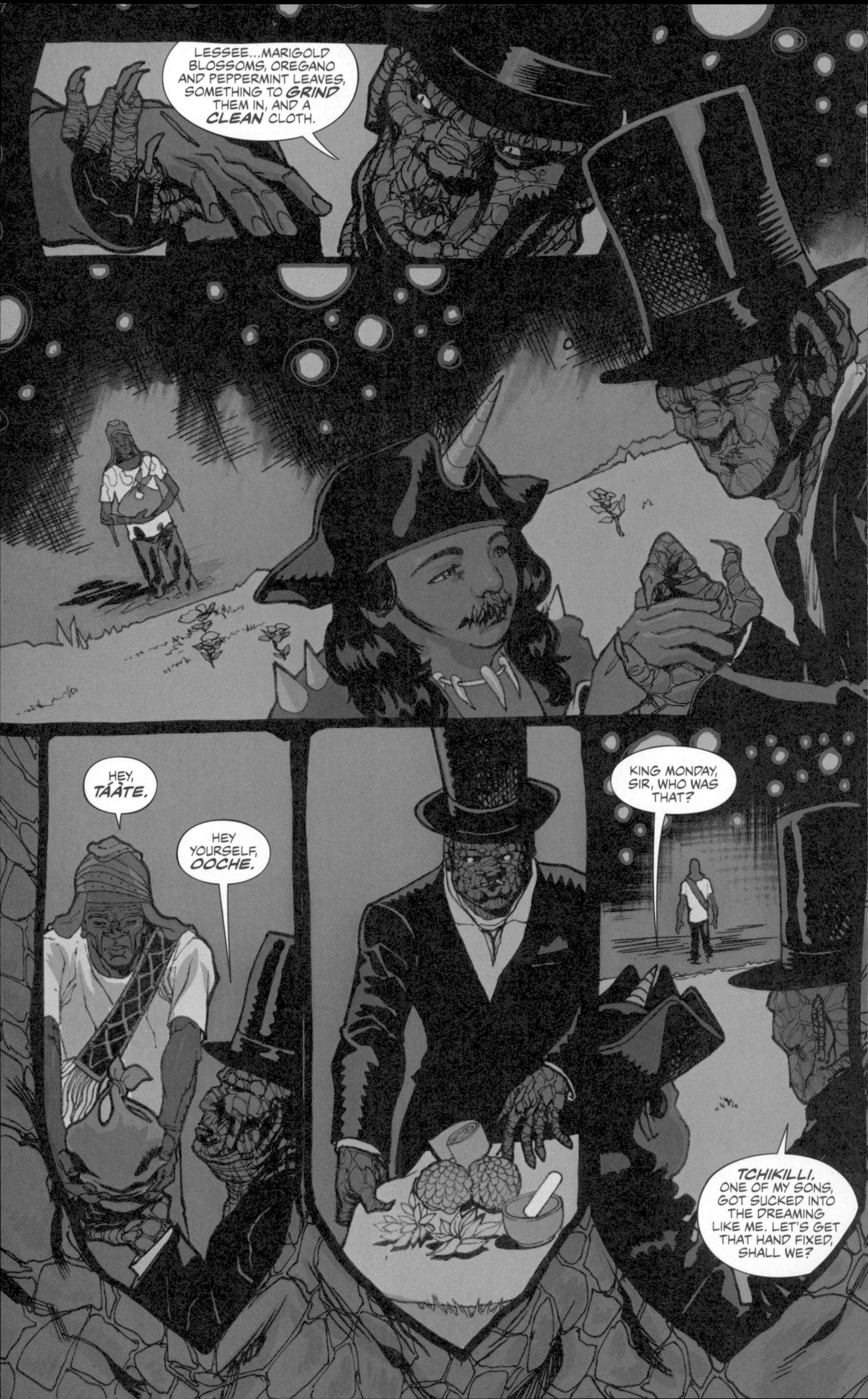
LESSEE...MARIGOLD BLOSSOMS, OREGANO AND PEPPERMINT LEAVES, SOMETHING TO GRIND THEM IN, AND A CLEAN CLOTH.
HEY, TÁÂTE.
HEY YOURSELF, OOCHE.
KING MONDAY, SIR, WHO WAS THAT?
TCHIKILLI. ONE OF MY SONS, GOT SUCKED INTO THE DREAMING LIKE ME. LET'S GET THAT HAND FIXED, SHALL WE?

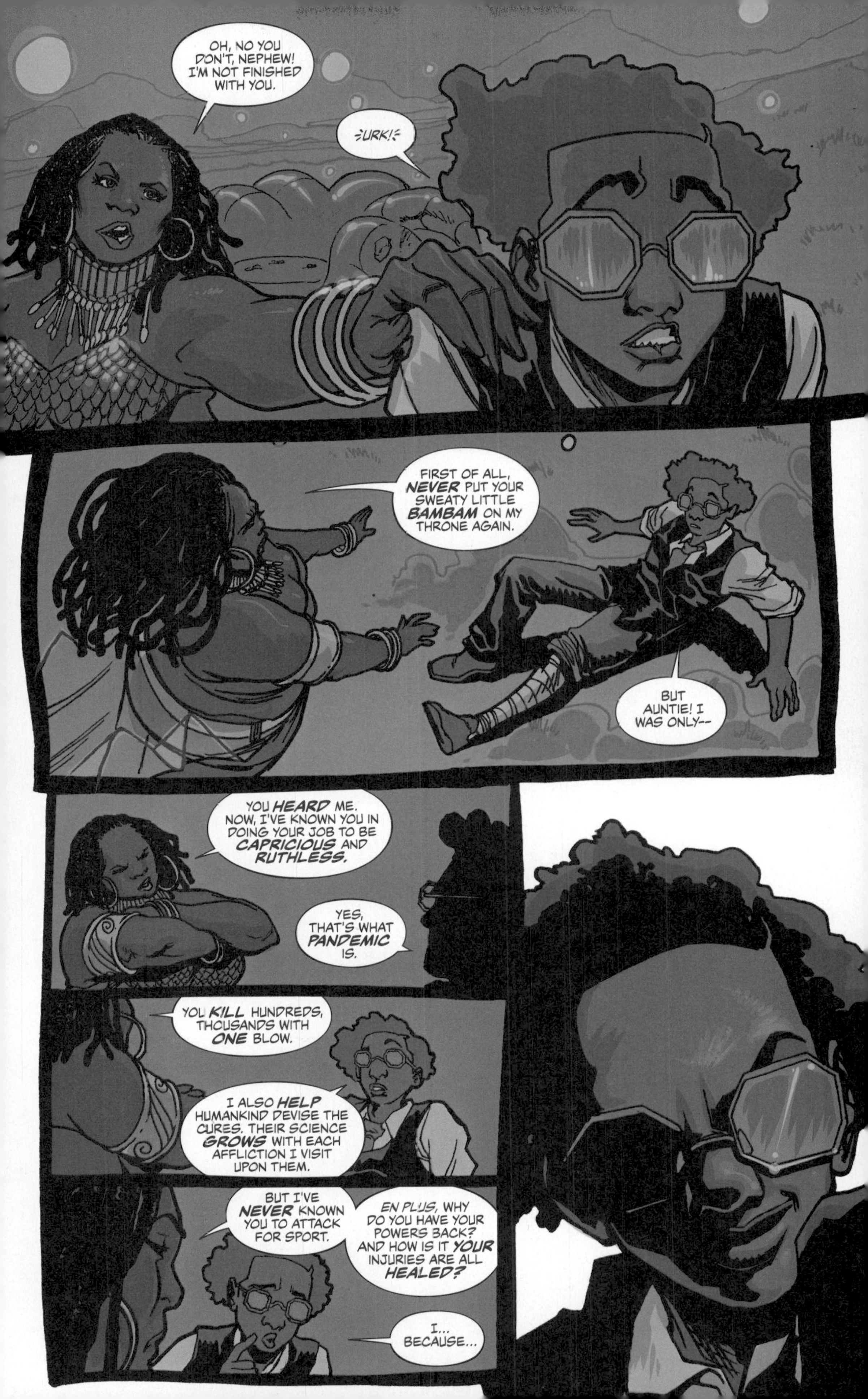

OH, NO YOU DON'T, NEPHEW! I'M NOT FINISHED WITH YOU.
URK!
FIRST OF ALL, NEVER PUT YOUR SWEATY LITTLE BAMBAM ON MY THRONE AGAIN.
BUT AUNTIE! I WAS ONLY--
YOU HEARD ME. NOW, I'VE KNOWN YOU IN DOING YOUR JOB TO BE CAPRICIOUS AND RUTHLESS.
YES, THAT'S WHAT PANDEMIC IS.
YOU KILL HUNDREDS, THOUSANDS WITH ONE BLOW.
I ALSO HELP HUMANKIND DEVISE THE CURES. THEIR SCIENCE GROWS WITH EACH AFFLICTION I VISIT UPON THEM.
BUT I'VE NEVER KNOWN YOU TO ATTACK FOR SPORT.
EN PLUS, WHY DO YOU HAVE YOUR POWERS BACK? AND HOW IS IT YOUR INJURIES ARE ALL HEALED?
I... BECAUSE...

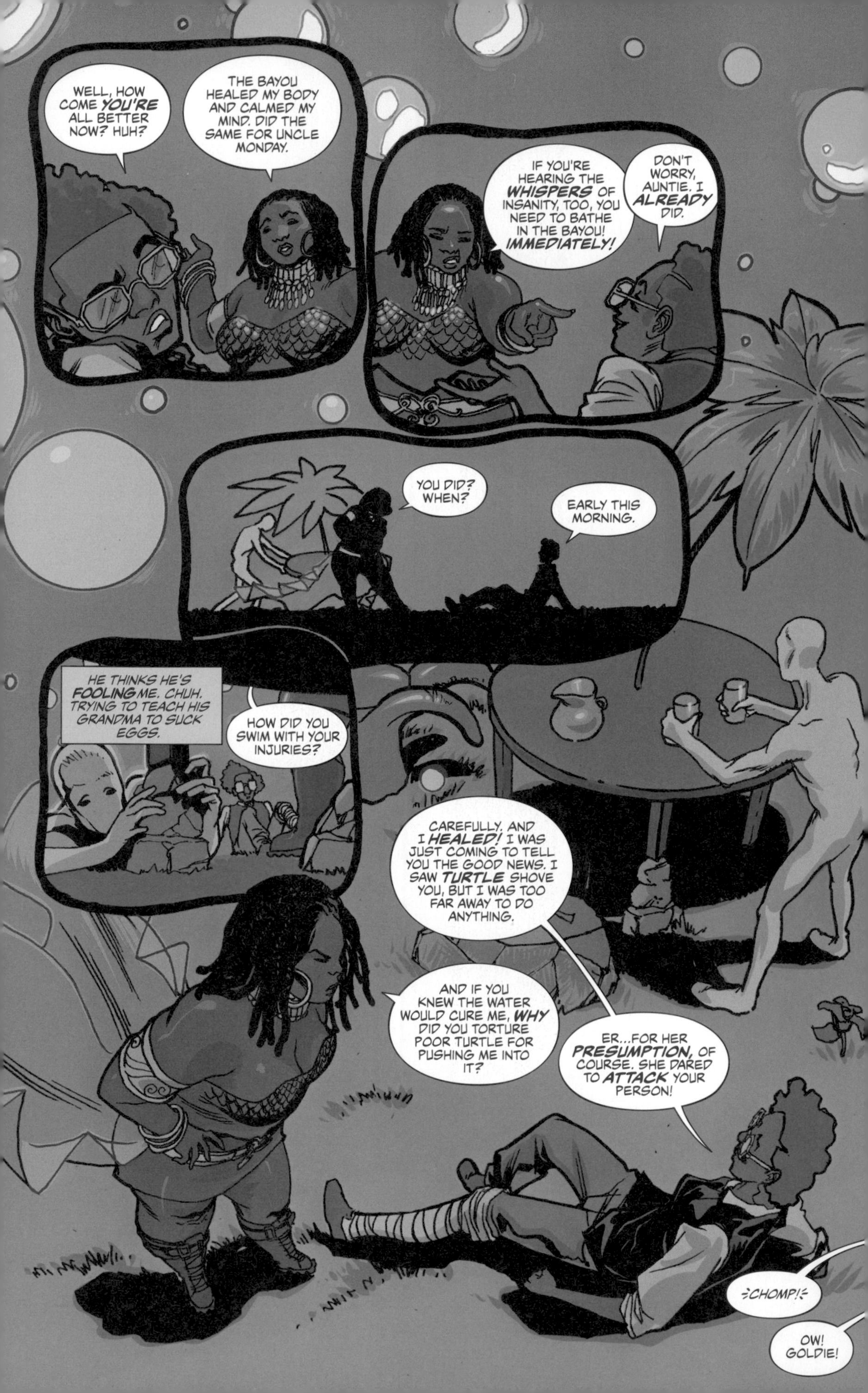
WELL, HOW COME YOU'RE ALL BETTER NOW? HUH?
THE BAYOU HEALED MY BODY AND CALMED MY MIND. DID THE SAME FOR UNCLE MONDAY.
IF YOU'RE HEARING THE WHISPERS OF INSANITY, TOO, YOU NEED TO BATHE IN THE BAYOU! IMMEDIATELY!
DON'T WORRY, AUNTIE. I ALREADY DID.
YOU DID? WHEN?
EARLY THIS MORNING.
HE THINKS HE'S FOOLING ME. CHUH. TRYING TO TEACH HIS GRANDMA TO SUCK EGGS.
HOW DID YOU SWIM WITH YOUR INJURIES?
CAREFULLY. AND I HEALED! I WAS JUST COMING TO TELL YOU THE GOOD NEWS. I SAW TURTLE SHOVE YOU, BUT I WAS TOO FAR AWAY TO DO ANYTHING.
AND IF YOU KNEW THE WATER WOULD CURE ME, WHY DID YOU TORTURE POOR TURTLE FOR PUSHING ME INTO IT?
ER...FOR HER PRESUMPTION, OF COURSE. SHE DARED TO ATTACK YOUR PERSON!
CHOMP!
OW! GOLDIE!

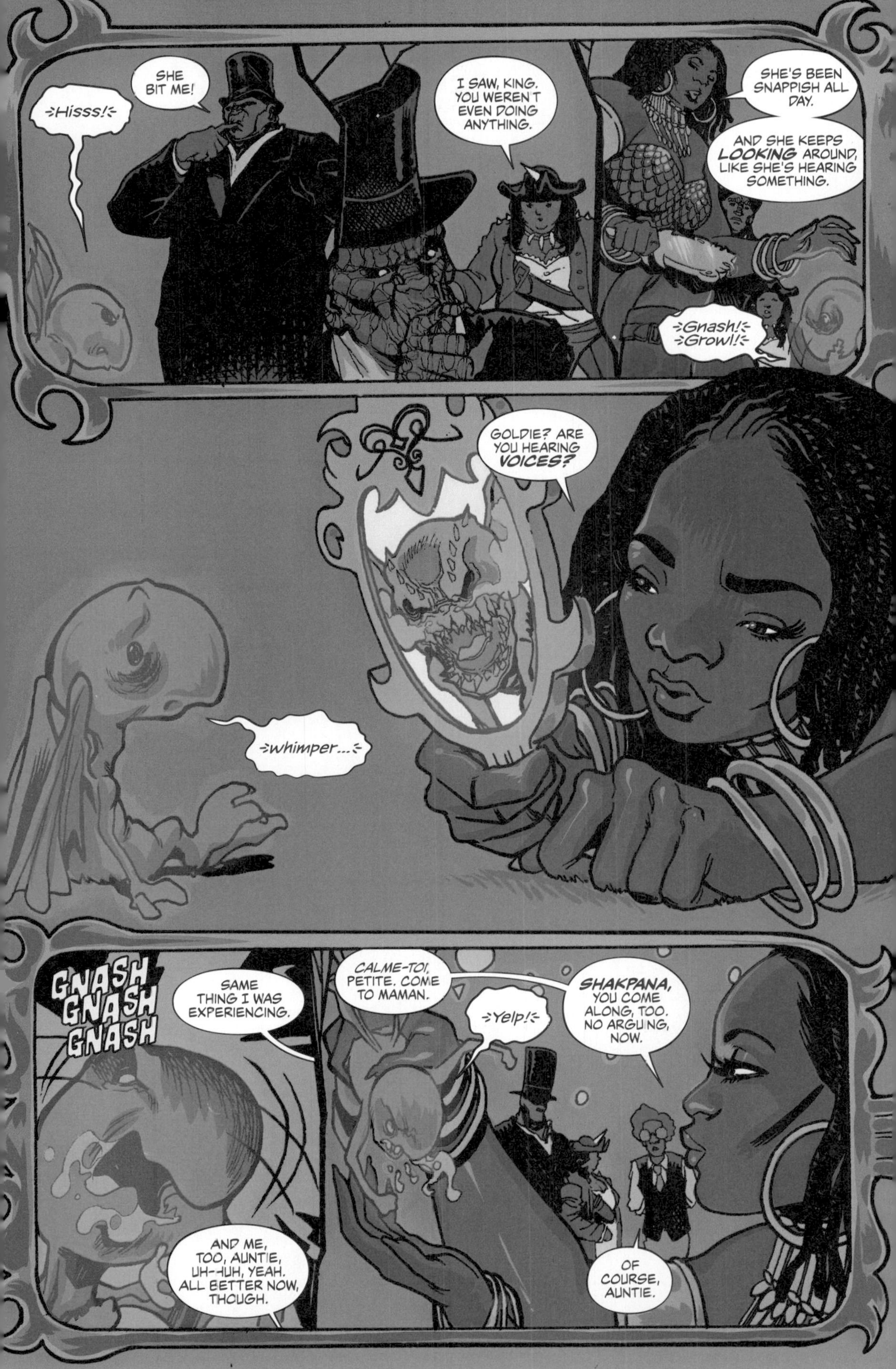

-Hisss!-
SHE BIT ME!
I SAW, KING. YOU WEREN'T EVEN DOING ANYTHING.
SHE'S BEEN SNAPPISH ALL DAY.
AND SHE KEEPS LOOKING AROUND, LIKE SHE'S HEARING SOMETHING.
-Gnash! -Growl!-
GOLDIE? ARE YOU HEARING VOICES?
-whimper...-
GNASH GNASH GNASH
SAME THING I WAS EXPERIENCING.
AND ME, TOO, AUNTIE, UH-HUH, YEAH. ALL BETTER NOW, THOUGH.
CALME-TOI, PETITE. COME TO MAMAN.
-Yelp!-
SHAKPANA, YOU COME ALONG, TOO. NO ARGUING, NOW.
OF COURSE, AUNTIE.

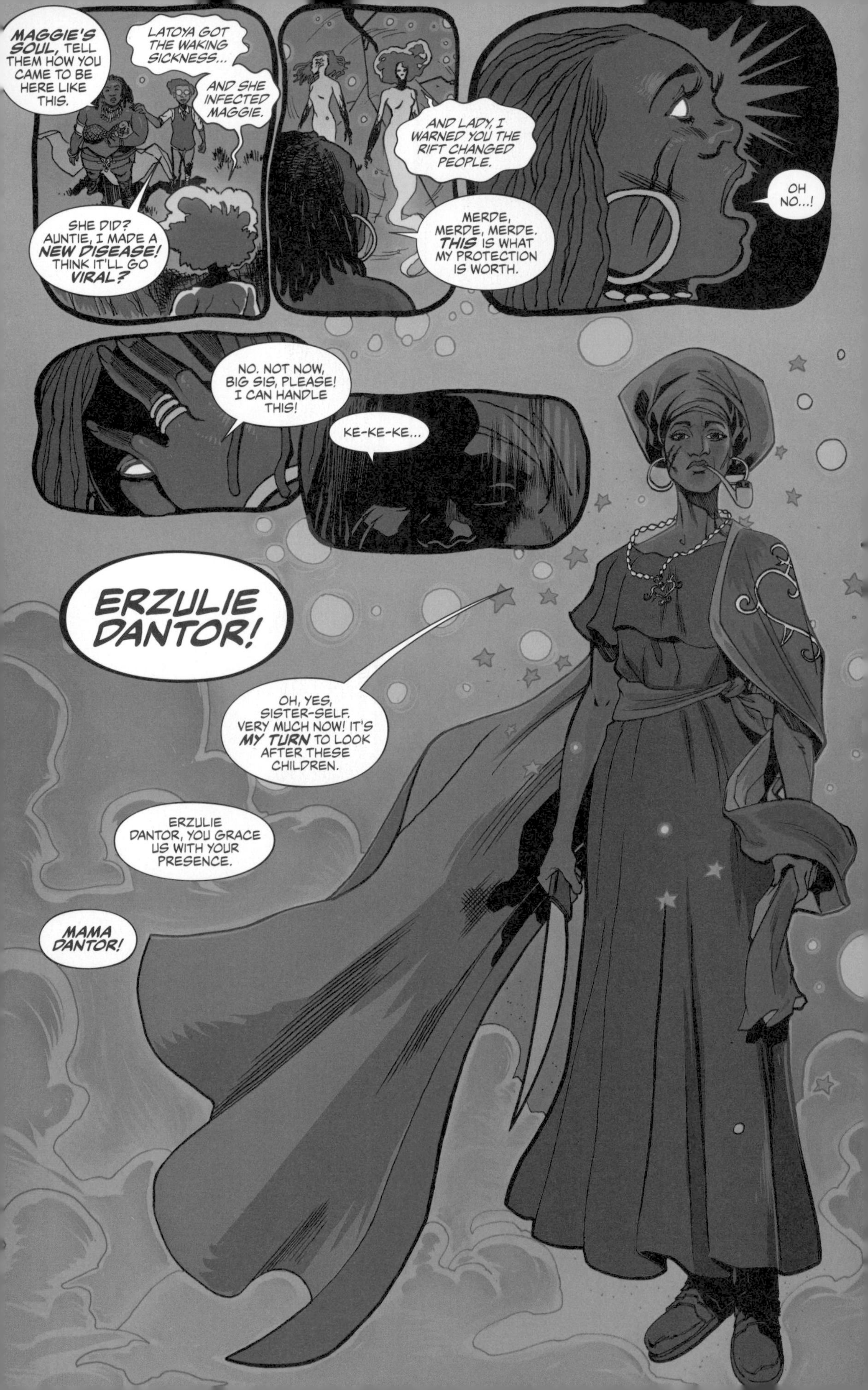
MAGGIE'S SOUL, TELL THEM HOW YOU CAME TO BE HERE LIKE THIS.
LATOYA GOT THE WAKING SICKNESS...
AND SHE INFECTED MAGGIE.
SHE DID? AUNTIE, I MADE A NEW DISEASE! THINK IT'LL GO VIRAL?
AND LADY, I WARNED YOU THE RIFT CHANGED PEOPLE.
MERDE, MERDE, MERDE. THIS IS WHAT MY PROTECTION IS WORTH.
OH NO...!
NO. NOT NOW, BIG SIS, PLEASE! I CAN HANDLE THIS!
KE-KE-KE...
ERZULIE DANTOR!
OH, YES, SISTER-SELF. VERY MUCH NOW! IT'S MY TURN TO LOOK AFTER THESE CHILDREN.
ERZULIE DANTOR, YOU GRACE US WITH YOUR PRESENCE.
MAMA DANTOR!

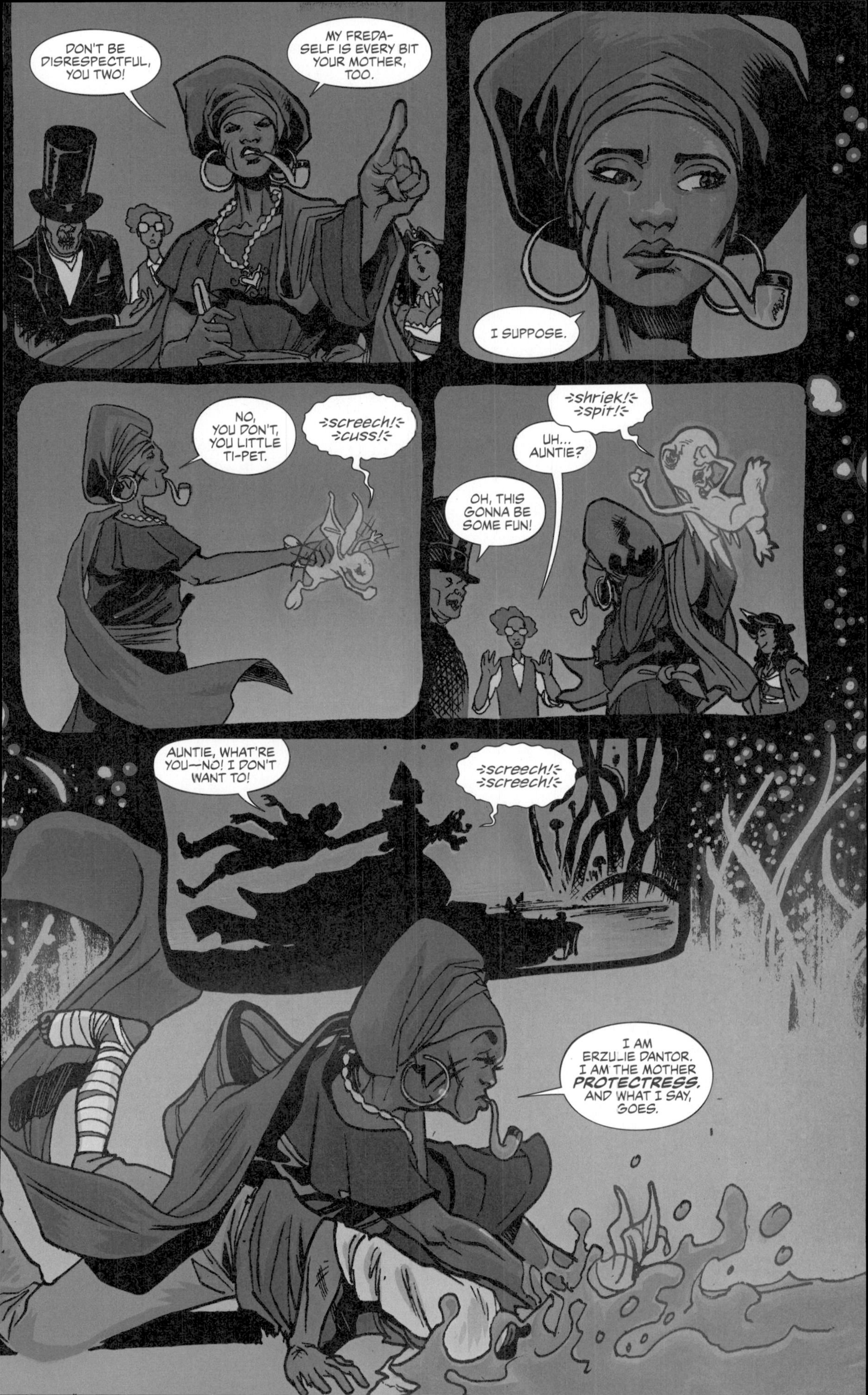
DON'T BE DISRESPECTFUL, YOU TWO!
MY FREDA-SELF IS EVERY BIT YOUR MOTHER, TOO.
I SUPPOSE.
NO, YOU DON'T, YOU LITTLE TI-PET.
>screech!< >cuss!<
>shriek!< >spit!<
UH... AUNTIE?
OH, THIS GONNA BE SOME FUN!
AUNTIE, WHAT'RE YOU—NO! I DON'T WANT TO!
>screech!< >screech!<
I AM ERZULIE DANTOR. I AM THE MOTHER PROTECTRESS. AND WHAT I SAY, GOES.

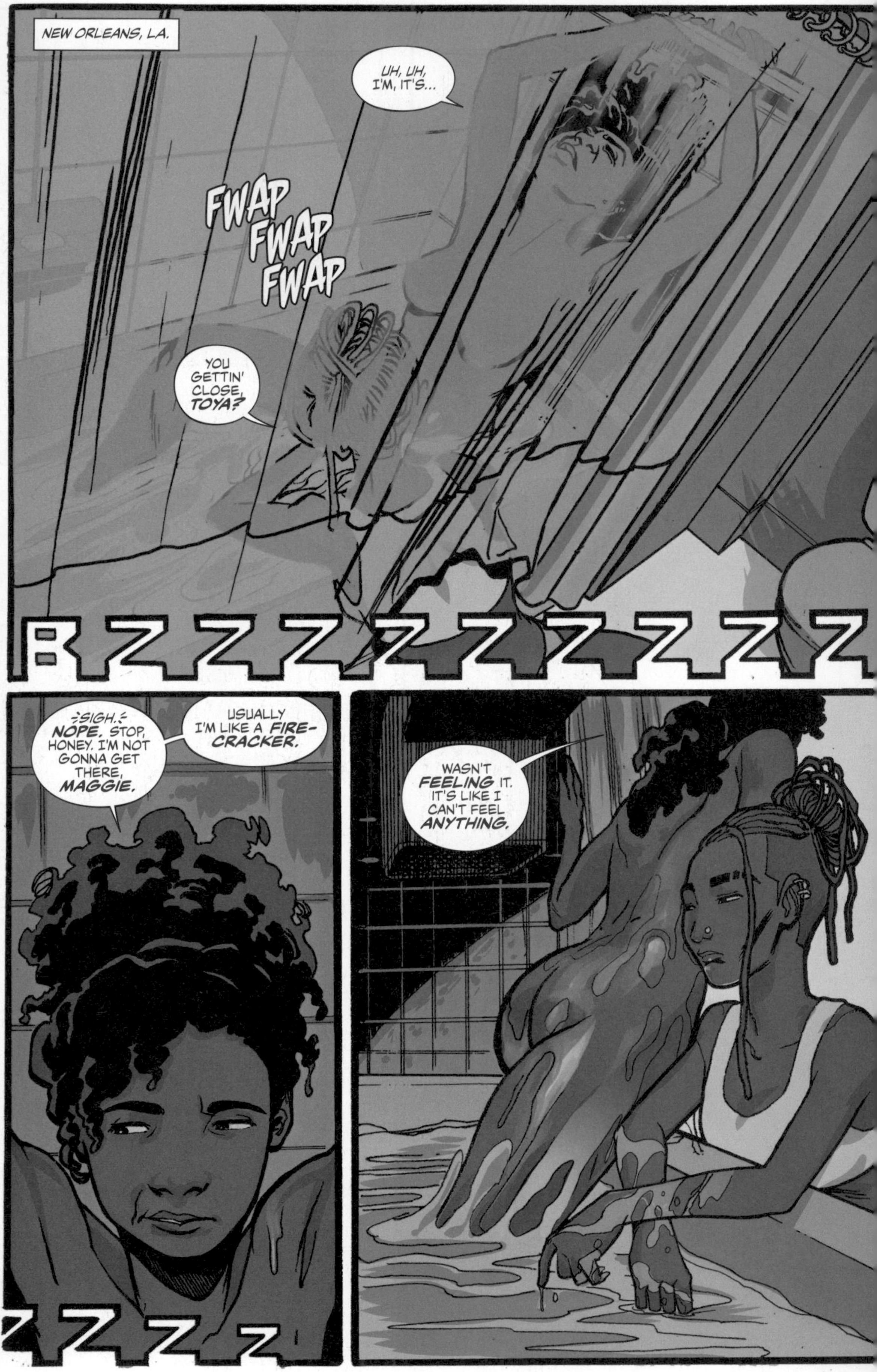
NEW ORLEANS, LA.
UH, UH, I'M, IT'S...
FWAP FWAP FWAP
YOU GETTIN' CLOSE, TOYA?
BZZZZZZZZZ
ZZZZ
⁼SIGH.⁼ NOPE. STOP, HONEY. I'M NOT GONNA GET THERE, MAGGIE.
USUALLY I'M LIKE A FIRE-CRACKER.
WASN'T FEELING IT. IT'S LIKE I CAN'T FEEL ANYTHING.

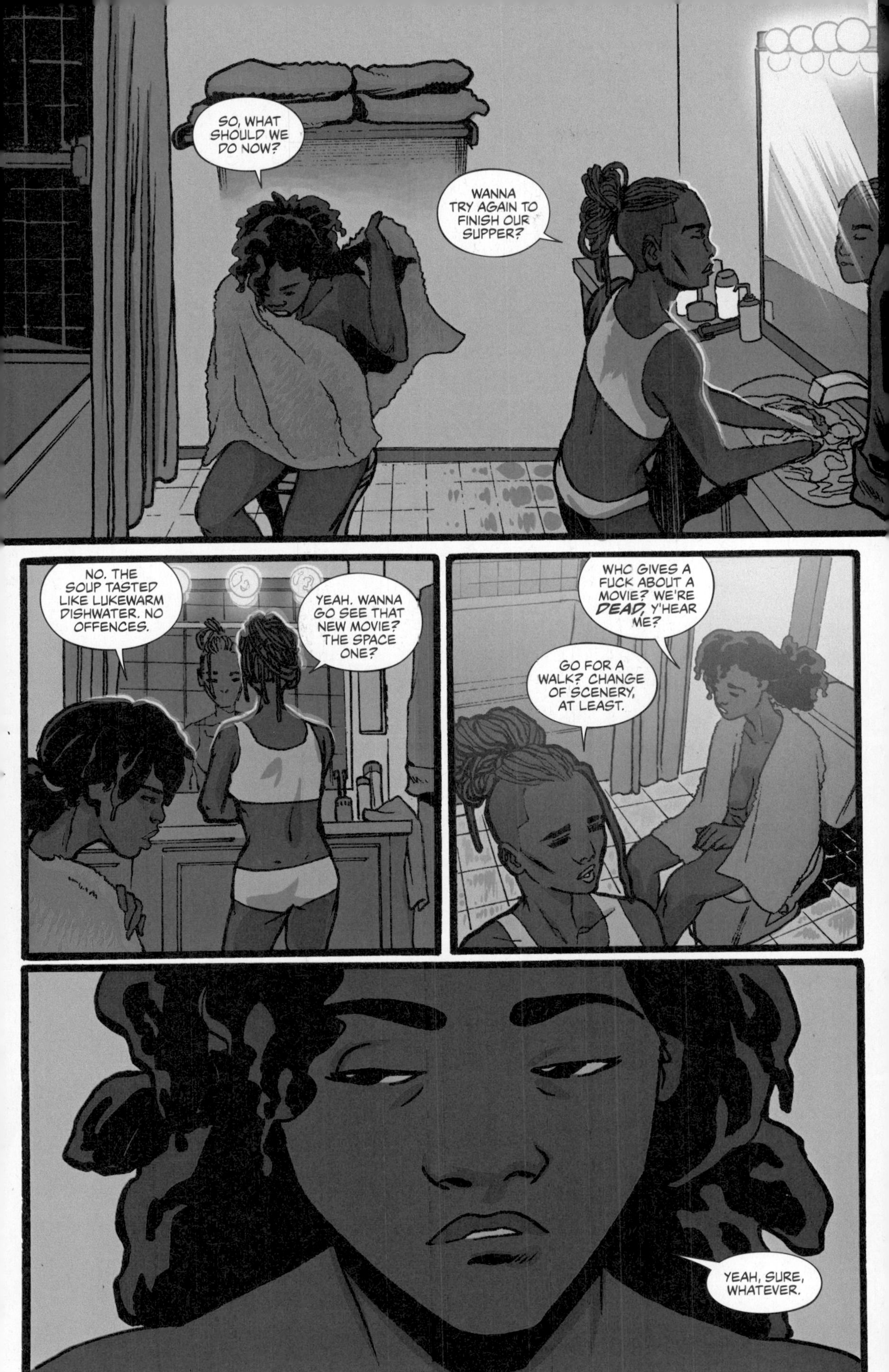
SO, WHAT SHOULD WE DO NOW?
WANNA TRY AGAIN TO FINISH OUR SUPPER?
NO. THE SOUP TASTED LIKE LUKEWARM DISHWATER. NO OFFENCES.
YEAH. WANNA GO SEE THAT NEW MOVIE? THE SPACE ONE?
WHC GIVES A FUCK ABOUT A MOVIE? WE'RE *DEAD*, Y'HEAR ME?
GO FOR A WALK? CHANGE OF SCENERY, AT LEAST.
YEAH, SURE, WHATEVER.

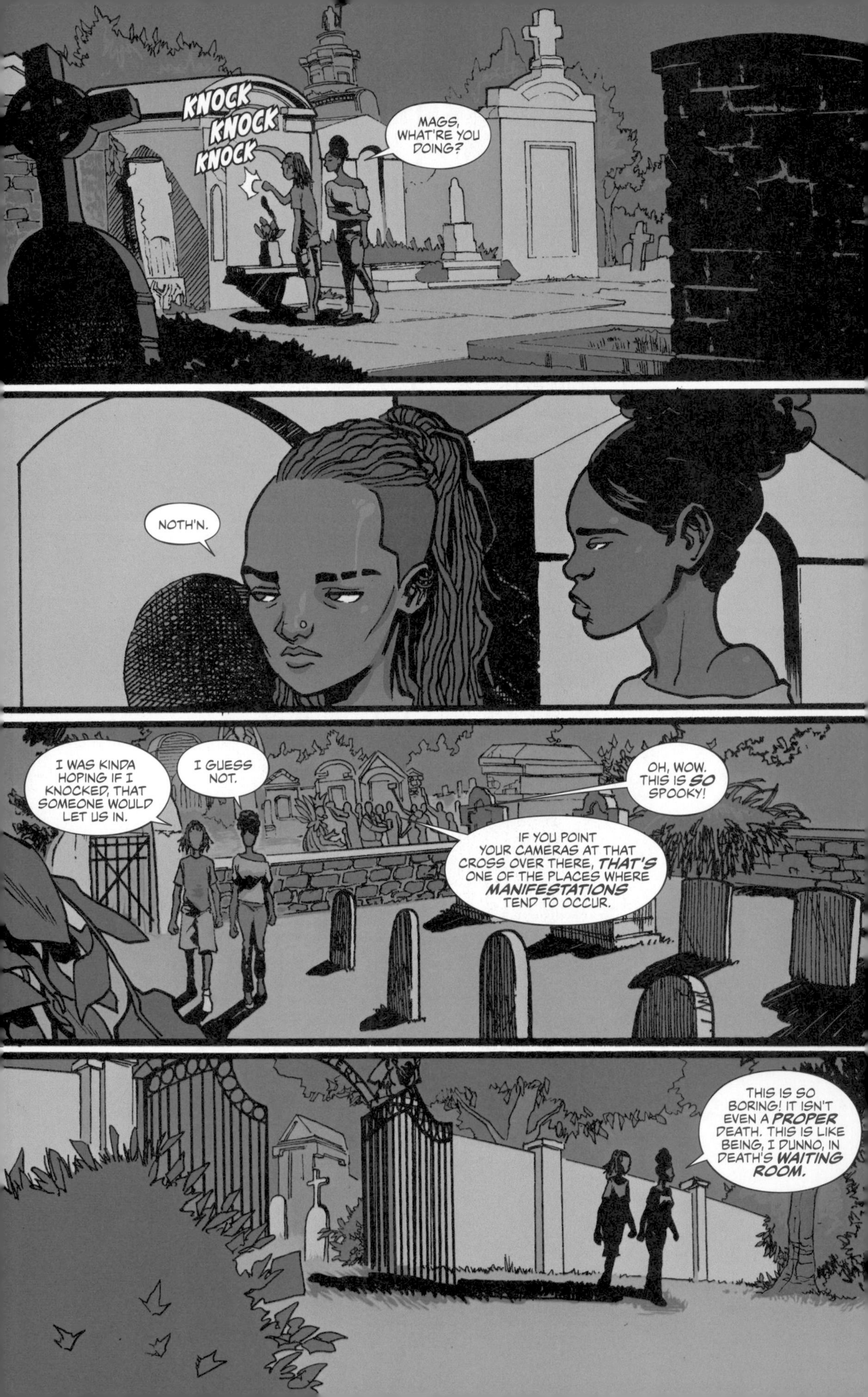
KNOCK KNOCK KNOCK
MAGS, WHAT'RE YOU DOING?
NOTH'N.
I WAS KINDA HOPING IF I KNOCKED, THAT SOMEONE WOULD LET US IN.
I GUESS NOT.
OH, WOW. THIS IS SO SPOOKY!
IF YOU POINT YOUR CAMERAS AT THAT CROSS OVER THERE, THAT'S ONE OF THE PLACES WHERE MANIFESTATIONS TEND TO OCCUR.
THIS IS SO BORING! IT ISN'T EVEN A PROPER DEATH. THIS IS LIKE BEING, I DUNNO, IN DEATH'S WAITING ROOM.

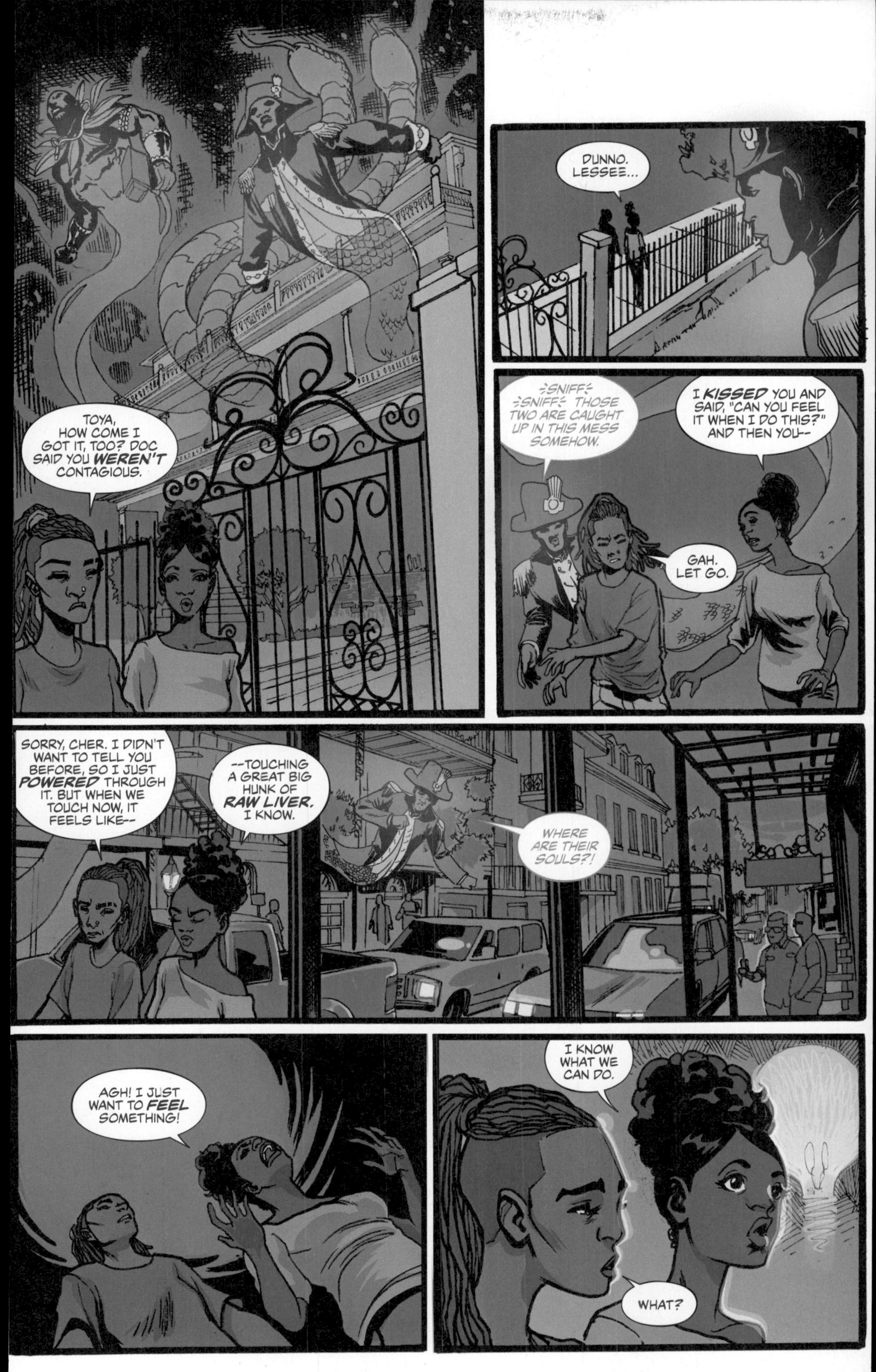
TOYA, HOW COME I GOT IT, TOO? DOC SAID YOU WEREN'T CONTAGIOUS.
DUNNO. LESSEE...
SNIFF SNIFF THOSE TWO ARE CAUGHT UP IN THIS MESS SOMEHOW.
I KISSED YOU AND SAID, "CAN YOU FEEL IT WHEN I DO THIS?" AND THEN YOU--
GAH. LET GO.
SORRY, CHER. I DIDN'T WANT TO TELL YOU BEFORE, SO I JUST POWERED THROUGH IT. BUT WHEN WE TOUCH NOW, IT FEELS LIKE--
--TOUCHING A GREAT BIG HUNK OF RAW LIVER. I KNOW.
WHERE ARE THEIR SOULS?!
AGH! I JUST WANT TO FEEL SOMETHING!
I KNOW WHAT WE CAN DO.
WHAT?

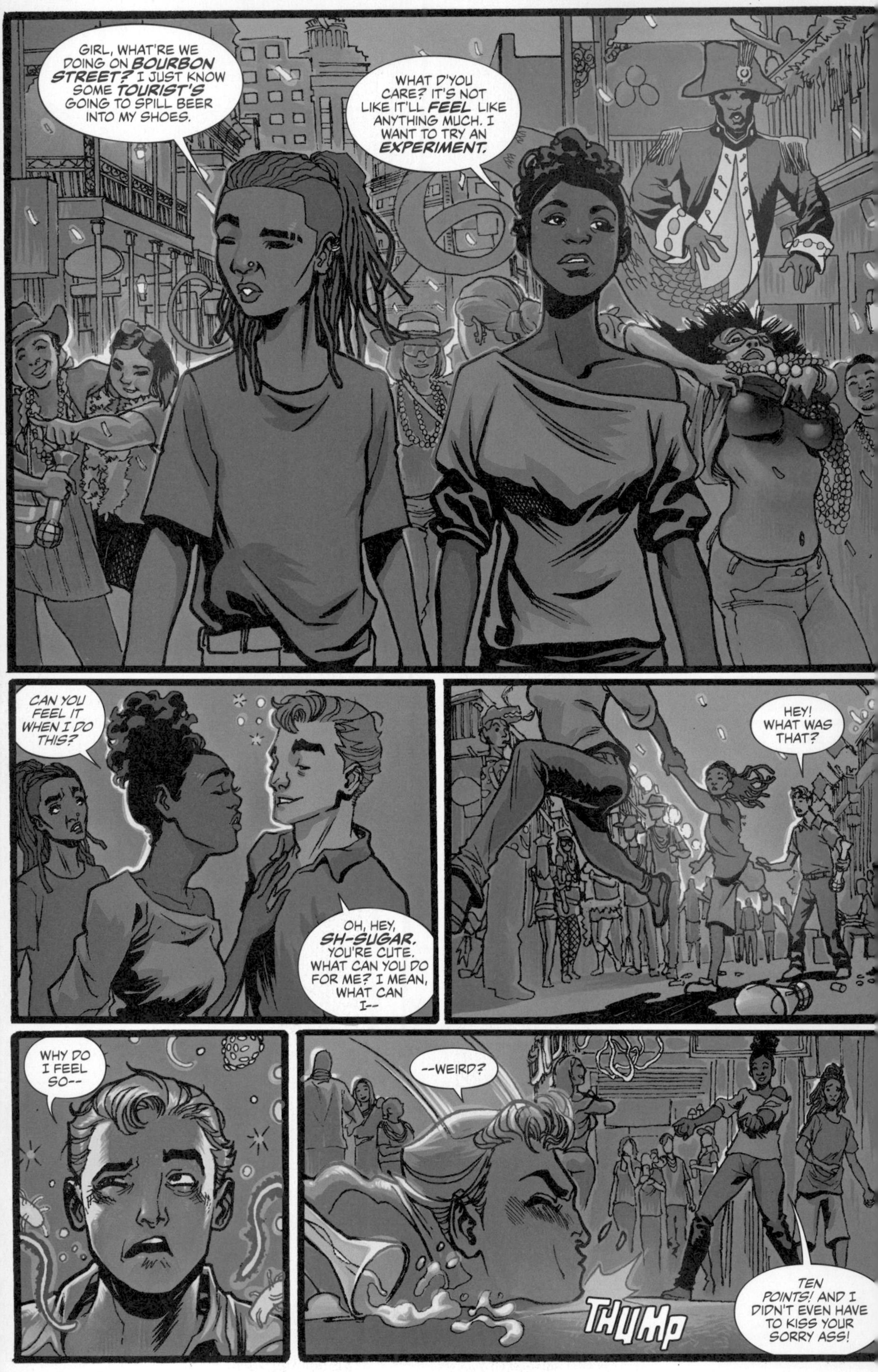
GIRL, WHAT'RE WE DOING ON BOURBON STREET? I JUST KNOW SOME TOURIST'S GOING TO SPILL BEER INTO MY SHOES.
WHAT D'YOU CARE? IT'S NOT LIKE IT'LL FEEL LIKE ANYTHING MUCH. I WANT TO TRY AN EXPERIMENT.
CAN YOU FEEL IT WHEN I DO THIS?
OH, HEY, SH-SUGAR. YOU'RE CUTE. WHAT CAN YOU DO FOR ME? I MEAN, WHAT CAN I--
HEY! WHAT WAS THAT?
WHY DO I FEEL SO--
--WEIRD?
THUMP
TEN POINTS! AND I DIDN'T EVEN HAVE TO KISS YOUR SORRY ASS!

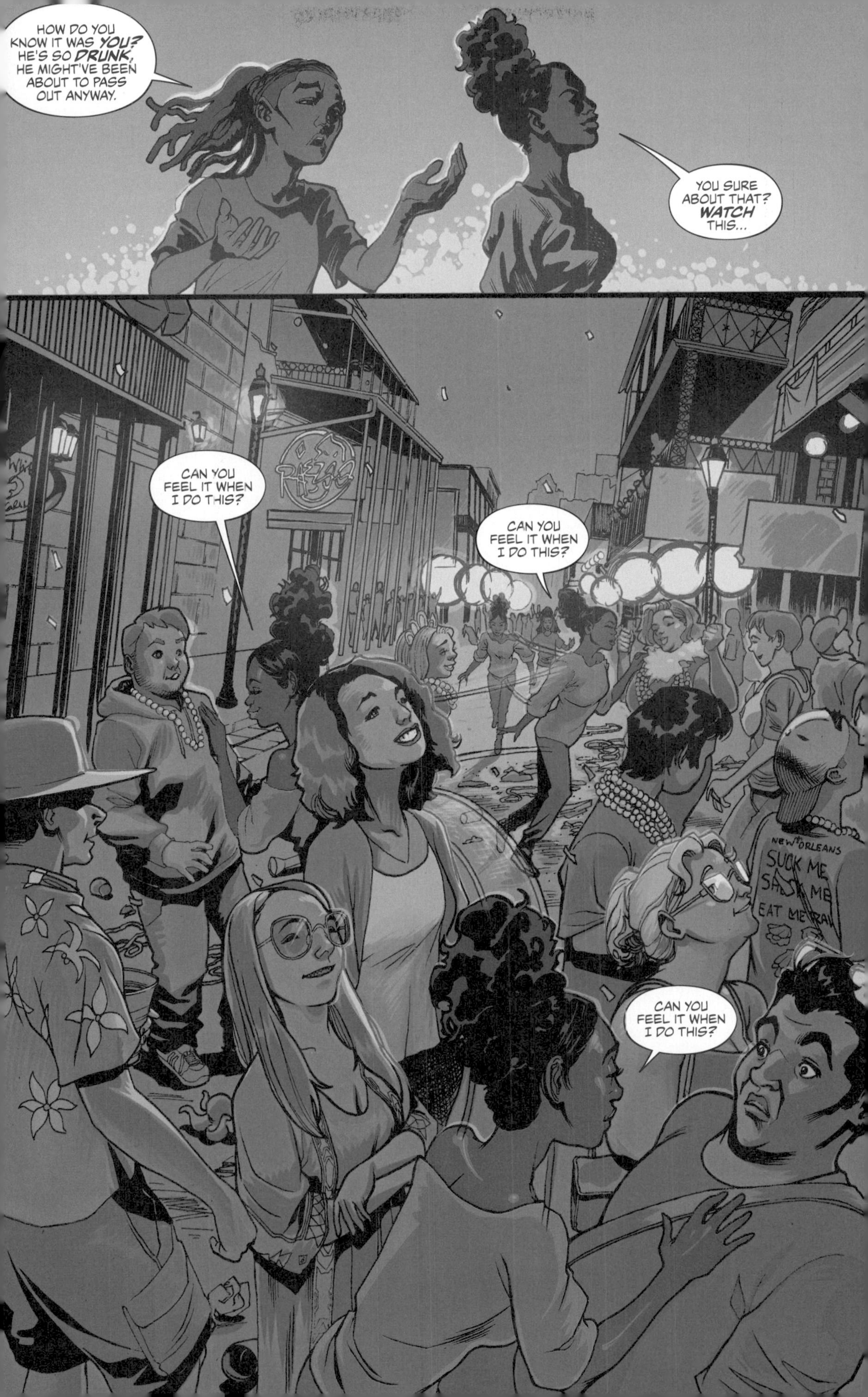
HOW DO YOU KNOW IT WAS *YOU?* HE'S SO *DRUNK,* HE MIGHT'VE BEEN ABOUT TO PASS OUT ANYWAY.
YOU SURE ABOUT THAT? *WATCH* THIS...
CAN YOU FEEL IT WHEN I DO THIS?
CAN YOU FEEL IT WHEN I DO THIS?
NEW ORLEANS
SUCK ME
EAT ME RAW
CAN YOU FEEL IT WHEN I DO THIS?

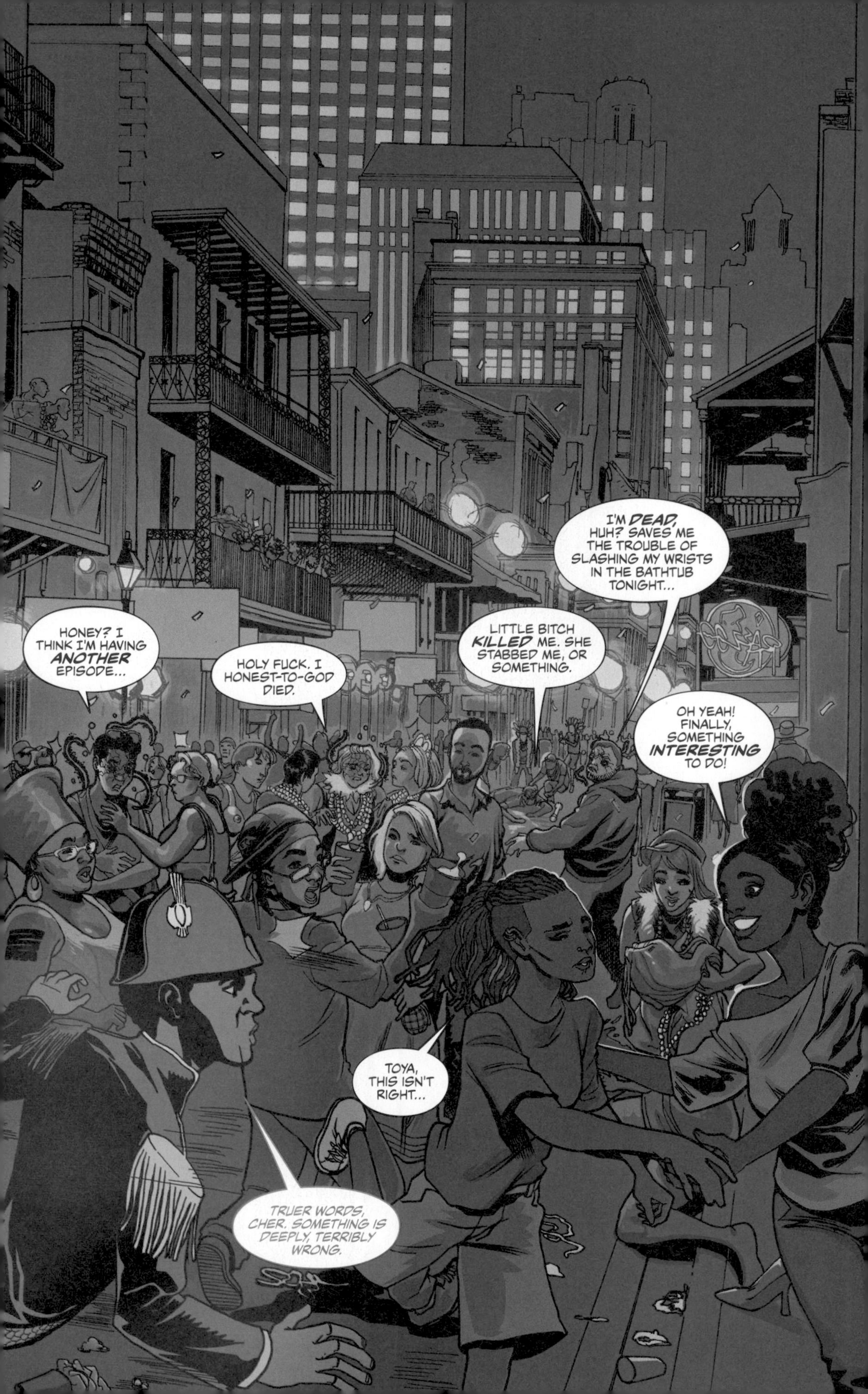
HONEY? I THINK I'M HAVING ANOTHER EPISODE...
HOLY FUCK. I HONEST-TO-GOD DIED.
LITTLE BITCH KILLED ME. SHE STABBED ME, OR SOMETHING.
I'M DEAD, HUH? SAVES ME THE TROUBLE OF SLASHING MY WRISTS IN THE BATHTUB TONIGHT...
OH YEAH! FINALLY, SOMETHING INTERESTING TO DO!
TOYA, THIS ISN'T RIGHT...
TRUER WORDS, CHER. SOMETHING IS DEEPLY, TERRIBLY WRONG.

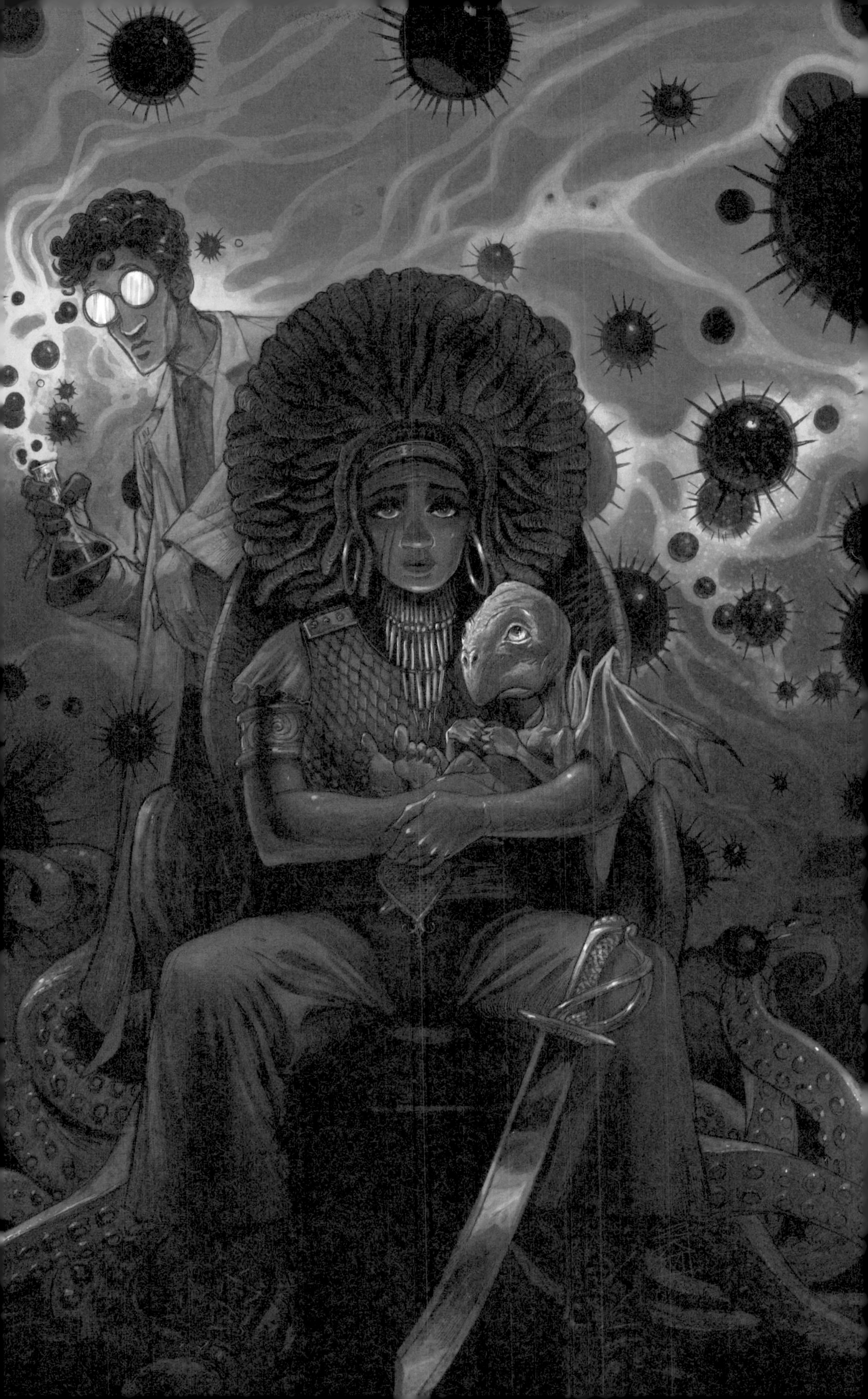

HOUSE OF WHISPERS

Dip Me in the Healing Stream

WRITTEN BY
Nalo Hopkinson

ILLUSTRATED BY
Dominike "DOMO" Stanton
and *Aneke*

COLORS BY
John Rauch

LETTERS BY
AndWorld Design

COVER ART BY
Sean Andrew Murray

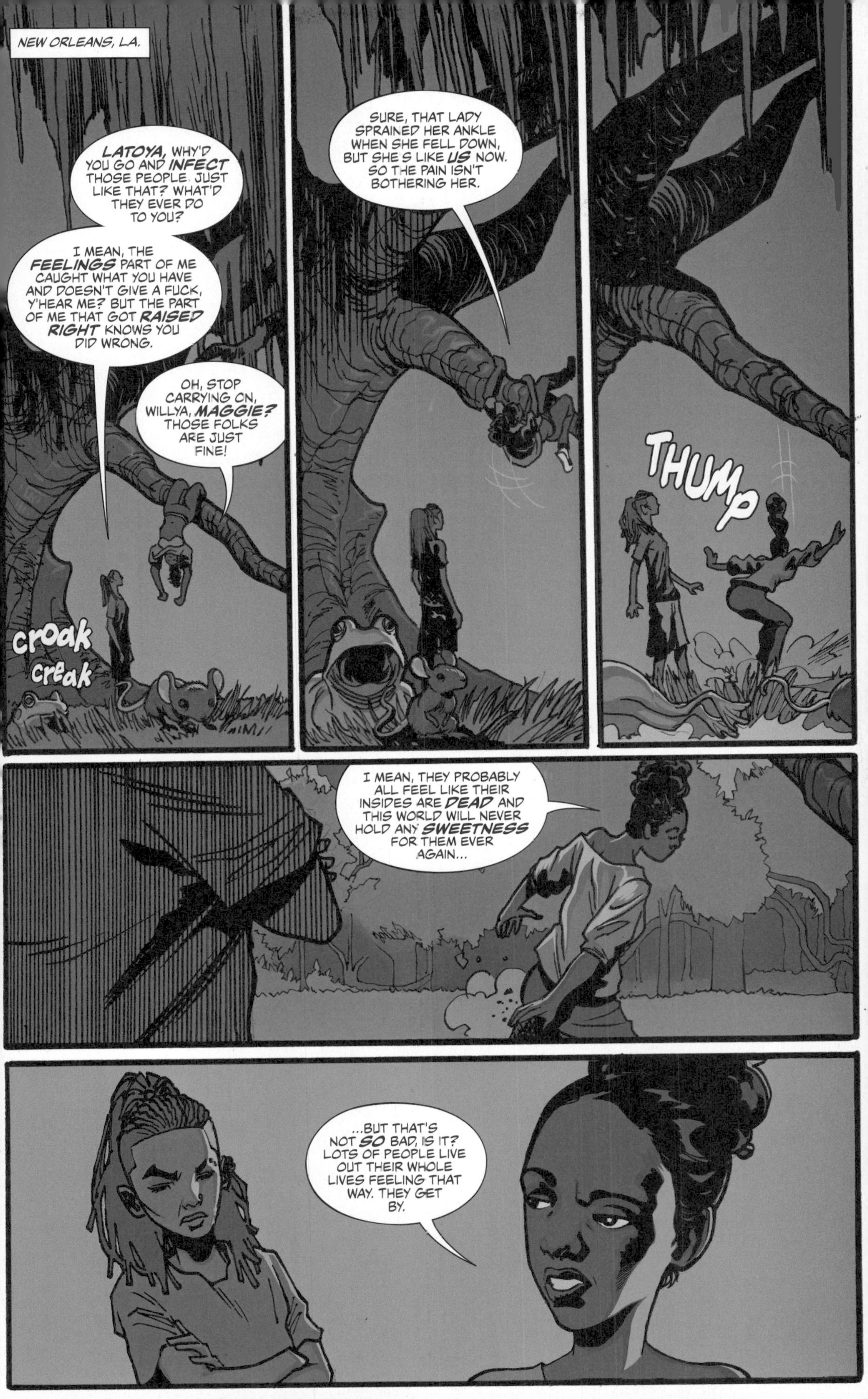
NEW ORLEANS, LA.
LATOYA, WHY'D YOU GO AND INFECT THOSE PEOPLE JUST LIKE THAT? WHAT'D THEY EVER DO TO YOU?
I MEAN, THE FEELINGS PART OF ME CAUGHT WHAT YOU HAVE AND DOESN'T GIVE A FUCK, Y'HEAR ME? BUT THE PART OF ME THAT GOT RAISED RIGHT KNOWS YOU DID WRONG.
OH, STOP CARRYING ON, WILLYA, MAGGIE? THOSE FOLKS ARE JUST FINE!
croak
creak
SURE, THAT LADY SPRAINED HER ANKLE WHEN SHE FELL DOWN, BUT SHE'S LIKE US NOW. SO THE PAIN ISN'T BOTHERING HER.
THUMP
I MEAN, THEY PROBABLY ALL FEEL LIKE THEIR INSIDES ARE DEAD AND THIS WORLD WILL NEVER HOLD ANY SWEETNESS FOR THEM EVER AGAIN...
...BUT THAT'S NOT SO BAD, IS IT? LOTS OF PEOPLE LIVE OUT THEIR WHOLE LIVES FEELING THAT WAY. THEY GET BY.

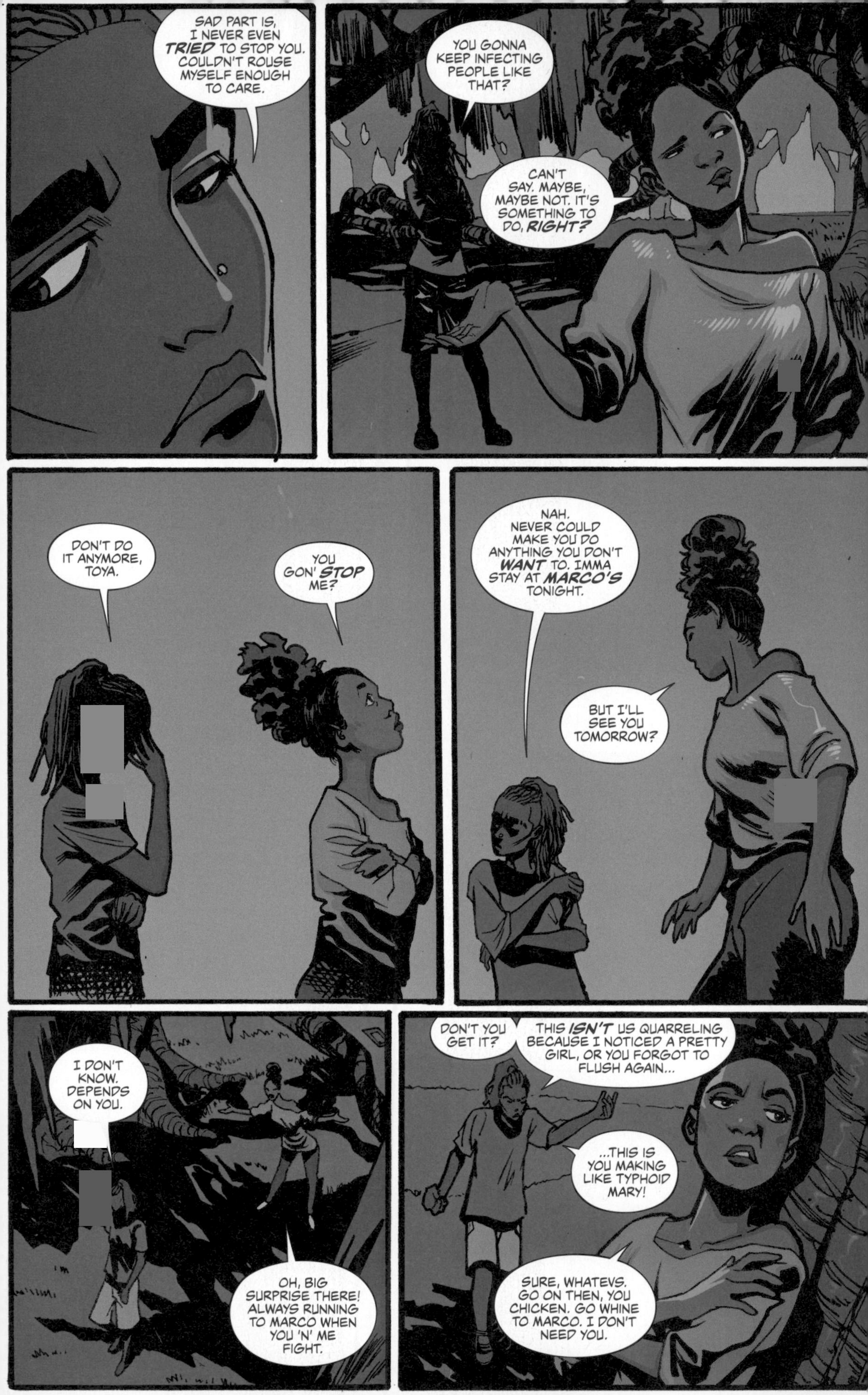
SAD PART IS, I NEVER EVEN TRIED TO STOP YOU. COULDN'T ROUSE MYSELF ENOUGH TO CARE.
YOU GONNA KEEP INFECTING PEOPLE LIKE THAT?
CAN'T SAY. MAYBE, MAYBE NOT. IT'S SOMETHING TO DO, RIGHT?
DON'T DO IT ANYMORE, TOYA.
YOU GON' STOP ME?
NAH. NEVER COULD MAKE YOU DO ANYTHING YOU DON'T WANT TO. IMMA STAY AT MARCO'S TONIGHT.
BUT I'LL SEE YOU TOMORROW?
I DON'T KNOW. DEPENDS ON YOU.
OH, BIG SURPRISE THERE! ALWAYS RUNNING TO MARCO WHEN YOU 'N' ME FIGHT.
DON'T YOU GET IT?
THIS ISN'T US QUARRELING BECAUSE I NOTICED A PRETTY GIRL, OR YOU FORGOT TO FLUSH AGAIN...
...THIS IS YOU MAKING LIKE TYPHOID MARY!
SURE, WHATEVS. GO ON THEN, YOU CHICKEN. GO WHINE TO MARCO. I DON'T NEED YOU.

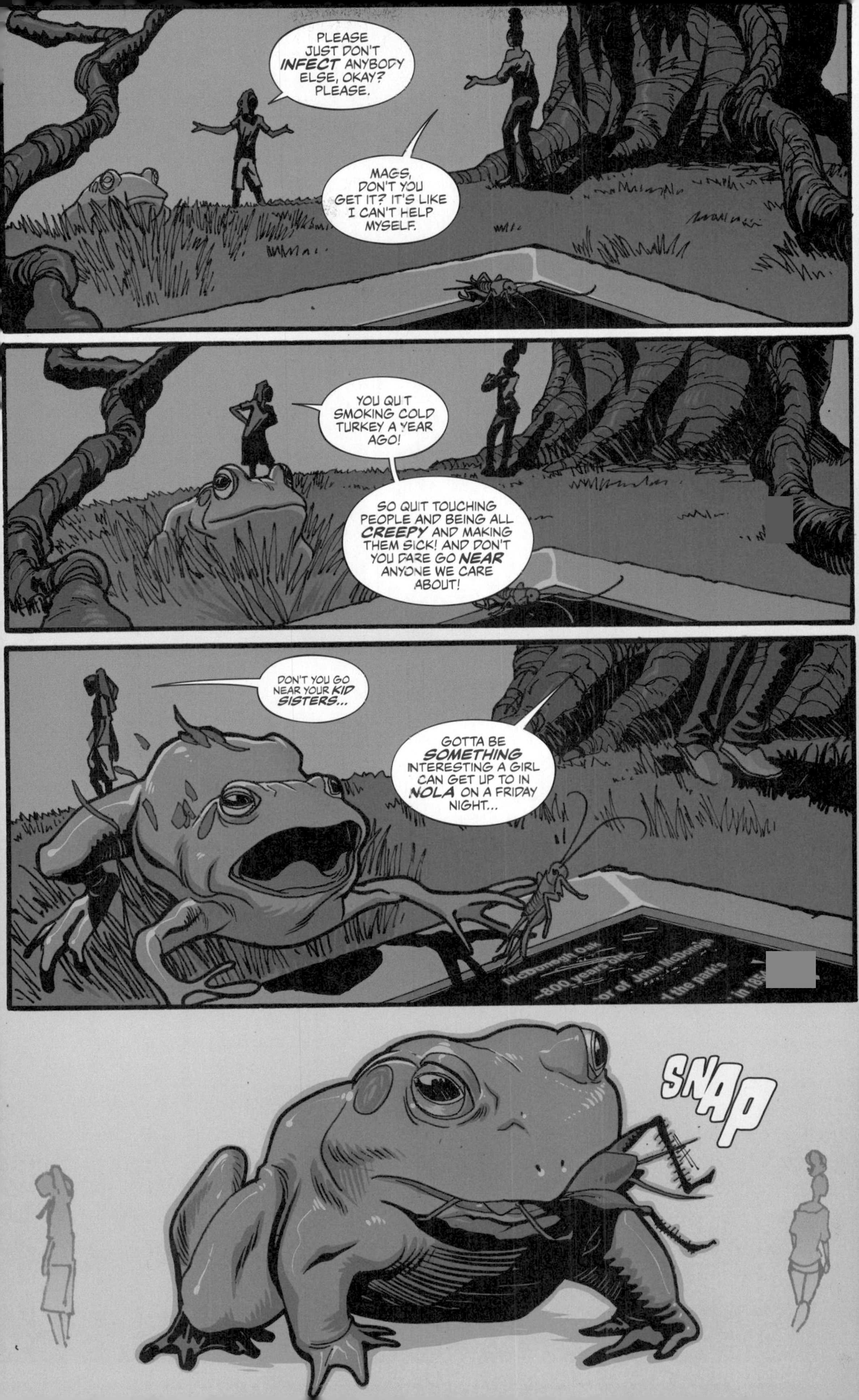
PLEASE JUST DON'T INFECT ANYBODY ELSE, OKAY? PLEASE.
MAGS, DON'T YOU GET IT? IT'S LIKE I CAN'T HELP MYSELF.
YOU QUIT SMOKING COLD TURKEY A YEAR AGO!
SO QUIT TOUCHING PEOPLE AND BEING ALL CREEPY AND MAKING THEM SICK! AND DON'T YOU DARE GO NEAR ANYONE WE CARE ABOUT!
DON'T YOU GO NEAR YOUR KID SISTERS...
GOTTA BE SOMETHING INTERESTING A GIRL CAN GET UP TO IN NOLA ON A FRIDAY NIGHT...
McDonogh Oak
800 years old
SNAP

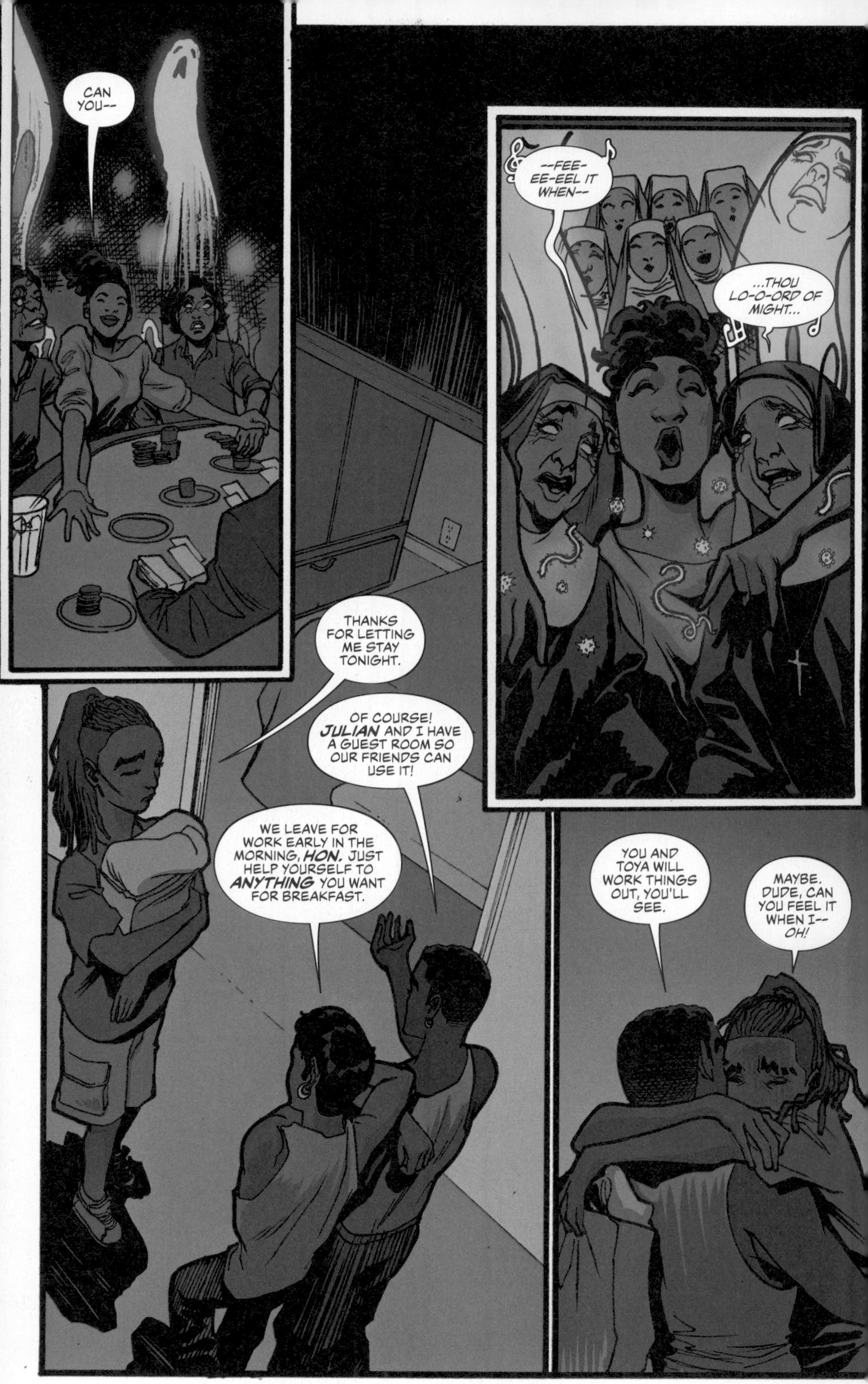
CAN YOU--
--FEE-EE-EEL IT WHEN--
...THOU LO-O-ORD OF MIGHT...
THANKS FOR LETTING ME STAY TONIGHT.
OF COURSE! JULIAN AND I HAVE A GUEST ROOM SO OUR FRIENDS CAN USE IT!
WE LEAVE FOR WORK EARLY IN THE MORNING, HON. JUST HELP YOURSELF TO ANYTHING YOU WANT FOR BREAKFAST.
YOU AND TOYA WILL WORK THINGS OUT, YOU'LL SEE.
MAYBE. DUDE, CAN YOU FEEL IT WHEN I-- OH!

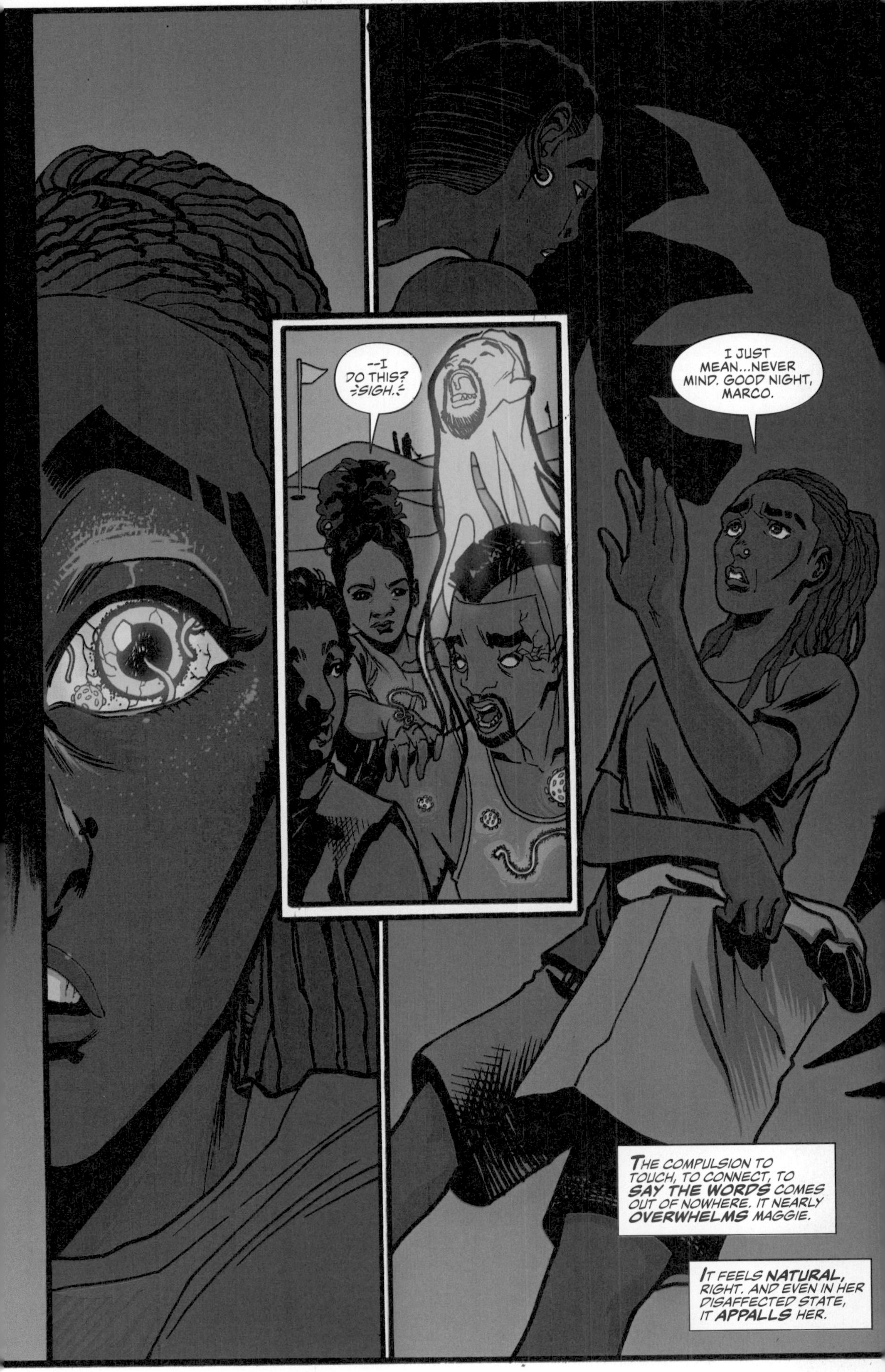
--I DO THIS? *SIGH.*
I JUST MEAN...NEVER MIND. GOOD NIGHT, MARCO.
THE COMPULSION TO TOUCH, TO CONNECT, TO SAY THE WORDS COMES OUT OF NOWHERE. IT NEARLY OVERWHELMS MAGGIE.
IT FEELS NATURAL, RIGHT. AND EVEN IN HER DISAFFECTED STATE, IT APPALLS HER.

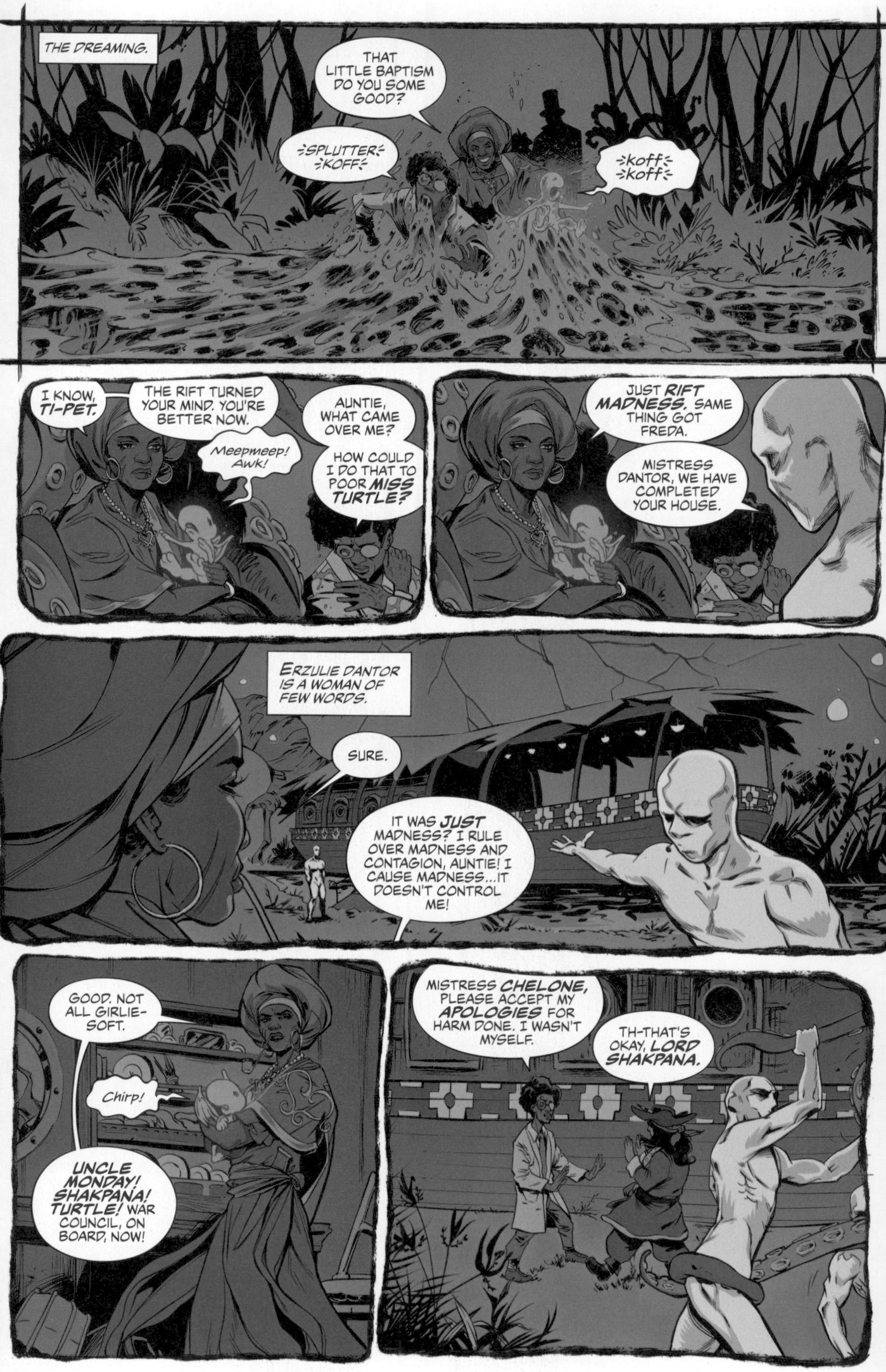

THE DREAMING.
THAT LITTLE BAPTISM DO YOU SOME GOOD?
-SPLUTTER- -KOFF-
-koff- -koff-
I KNOW, TI-PET.
THE RIFT TURNED YOUR MIND. YOU'RE BETTER NOW.
Meepmeep! Awk!
AUNTIE, WHAT CAME OVER ME?
HOW COULD I DO THAT TO POOR MISS TURTLE?
JUST RIFT MADNESS. SAME THING GOT FREDA.
MISTRESS DANTOR, WE HAVE COMPLETED YOUR HOUSE.
ERZULIE DANTOR IS A WOMAN OF FEW WORDS.
SURE.
IT WAS JUST MADNESS? I RULE OVER MADNESS AND CONTAGION, AUNTIE! I CAUSE MADNESS...IT DOESN'T CONTROL ME!
GOOD. NOT ALL GIRLIE-SOFT.
Chirp!
UNCLE MONDAY! SHAKPANA! TURTLE! WAR COUNCIL, ON BOARD, NOW!
MISTRESS CHELONE, PLEASE ACCEPT MY APOLOGIES FOR HARM DONE. I WASN'T MYSELF.
TH-THAT'S OKAY, LORD SHAKPANA.

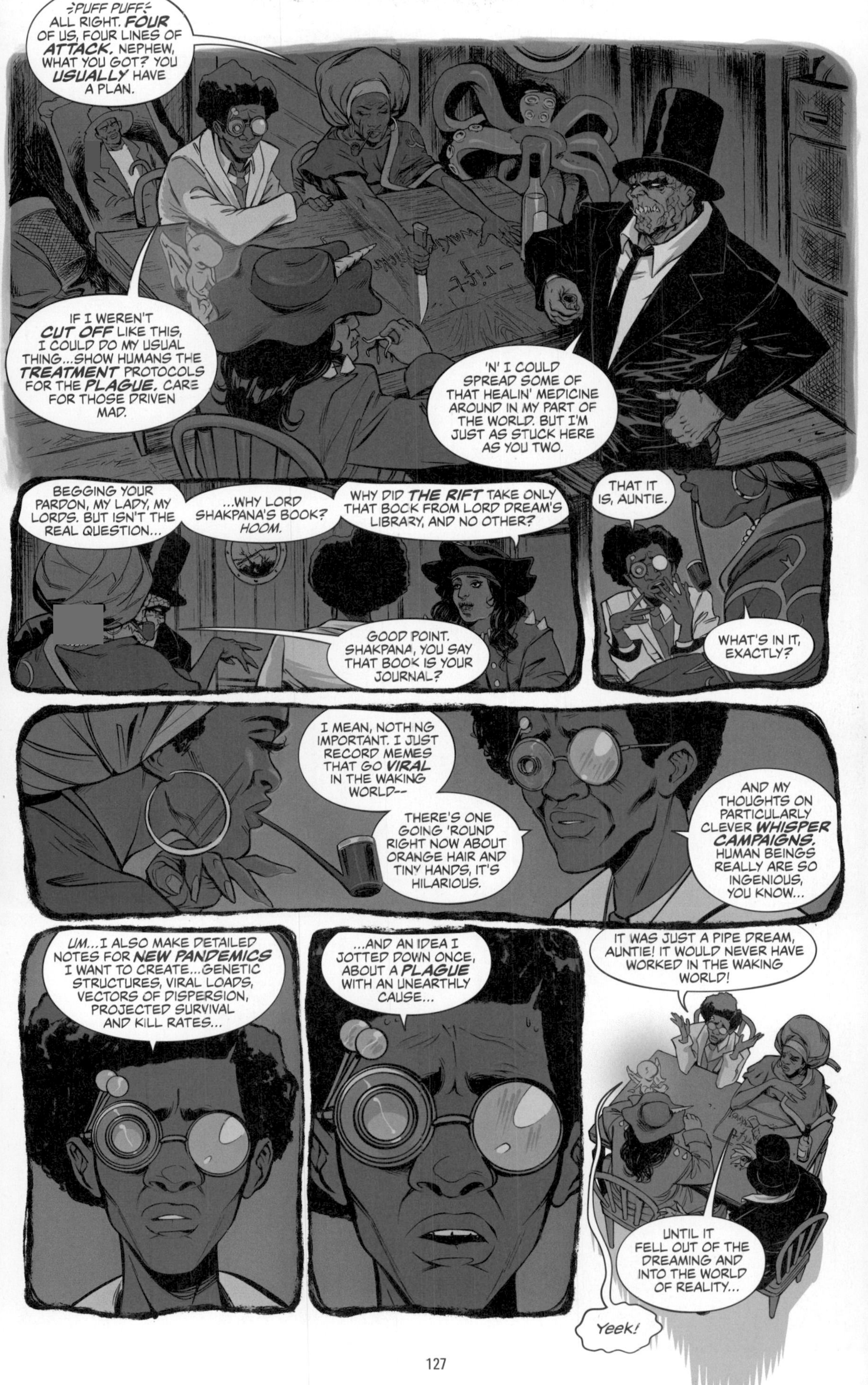

PUFF PUFF
ALL RIGHT. **FOUR** OF US, FOUR LINES OF **ATTACK.** NEPHEW, WHAT YOU GOT? YOU **USUALLY** HAVE A PLAN.
IF I WEREN'T **CUT OFF** LIKE THIS, I COULD DO MY USUAL THING...SHOW HUMANS THE **TREATMENT** PROTOCOLS FOR THE **PLAGUE.** CARE FOR THOSE DRIVEN MAD.
'N' I COULD SPREAD SOME OF THAT HEALIN' MEDICINE AROUND IN MY PART OF THE WORLD. BUT I'M JUST AS STUCK HERE AS YOU TWO.
BEGGING YOUR PARDON, MY LADY, MY LORDS. BUT ISN'T THE REAL QUESTION...
...WHY LORD SHAKPANA'S BOOK? *HOOM.*
WHY DID **THE RIFT** TAKE ONLY THAT BOCK FROM LORD DREAM'S LIBRARY, AND NO OTHER?
GOOD POINT. SHAKPANA, YOU SAY THAT BOOK IS YOUR JOURNAL?
THAT IT IS, AUNTIE.
WHAT'S IN IT, EXACTLY?
I MEAN, NOTH NG IMPORTANT. I JUST RECORD MEMES THAT GO **VIRAL** IN THE WAKING WORLD--
THERE'S ONE GOING 'ROUND RIGHT NOW ABOUT ORANGE HAIR AND TINY HANDS, IT'S HILARIOUS.
AND MY THOUGHTS ON PARTICULARLY CLEVER **WHISPER CAMPAIGNS.** HUMAN BEINGS REALLY ARE SO INGENIOUS, YOU KNOW...
UM...I ALSO MAKE DETAILED NOTES FOR **NEW PANDEMICS** I WANT TO CREATE...GENETIC STRUCTURES, VIRAL LOADS, VECTORS OF DISPERSION, PROJECTED SURVIVAL AND KILL RATES...
...AND AN IDEA I JOTTED DOWN ONCE, ABOUT A **PLAGUE** WITH AN UNEARTHLY CAUSE...
IT WAS JUST A PIPE DREAM, AUNTIE! IT WOULD NEVER HAVE WORKED IN THE WAKING WORLD!
UNTIL IT FELL OUT OF THE DREAMING AND INTO THE WORLD OF REALITY...
Yeek!

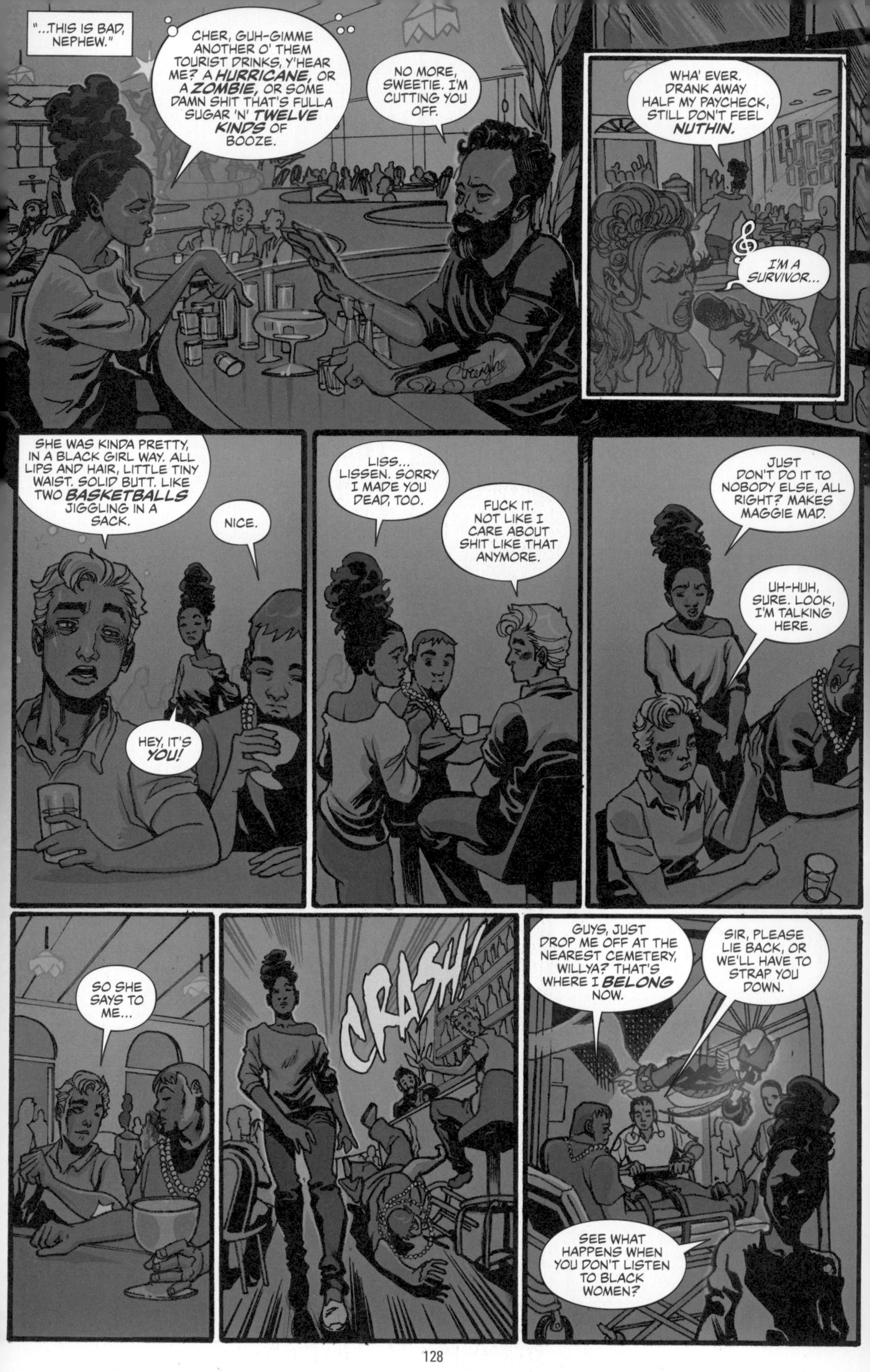
"...THIS IS BAD, NEPHEW."
CHER, GUH-GIMME ANOTHER O' THEM TOURIST DRINKS, Y'HEAR ME? A HURRICANE, OR A ZOMBIE, OR SOME DAMN SHIT THAT'S FULLA SUGAR 'N' TWELVE KINDS OF BOOZE.
NO MORE, SWEETIE. I'M CUTTING YOU OFF.
WHA' EVER. DRANK AWAY HALF MY PAYCHECK, STILL DON'T FEEL NUTHIN.
I'M A SURVIVOR...
SHE WAS KINDA PRETTY, IN A BLACK GIRL WAY. ALL LIPS AND HAIR, LITTLE TINY WAIST. SOLID BUTT. LIKE TWO BASKETBALLS JIGGLING IN A SACK.
NICE.
HEY, IT'S YOU!
LISS... LISSEN. SORRY I MADE YOU DEAD, TOO.
FUCK IT. NOT LIKE I CARE ABOUT SHIT LIKE THAT ANYMORE.
JUST DON'T DO IT TO NOBODY ELSE, ALL RIGHT? MAKES MAGGIE MAD.
UH-HUH, SURE. LOOK, I'M TALKING HERE.
SO SHE SAYS TO ME...
CRASH!
GUYS, JUST DROP ME OFF AT THE NEAREST CEMETERY, WILLYA? THAT'S WHERE I BELONG NOW.
SIR, PLEASE LIE BACK, OR WE'LL HAVE TO STRAP YOU DOWN.
SEE WHAT HAPPENS WHEN YOU DON'T LISTEN TO BLACK WOMEN?

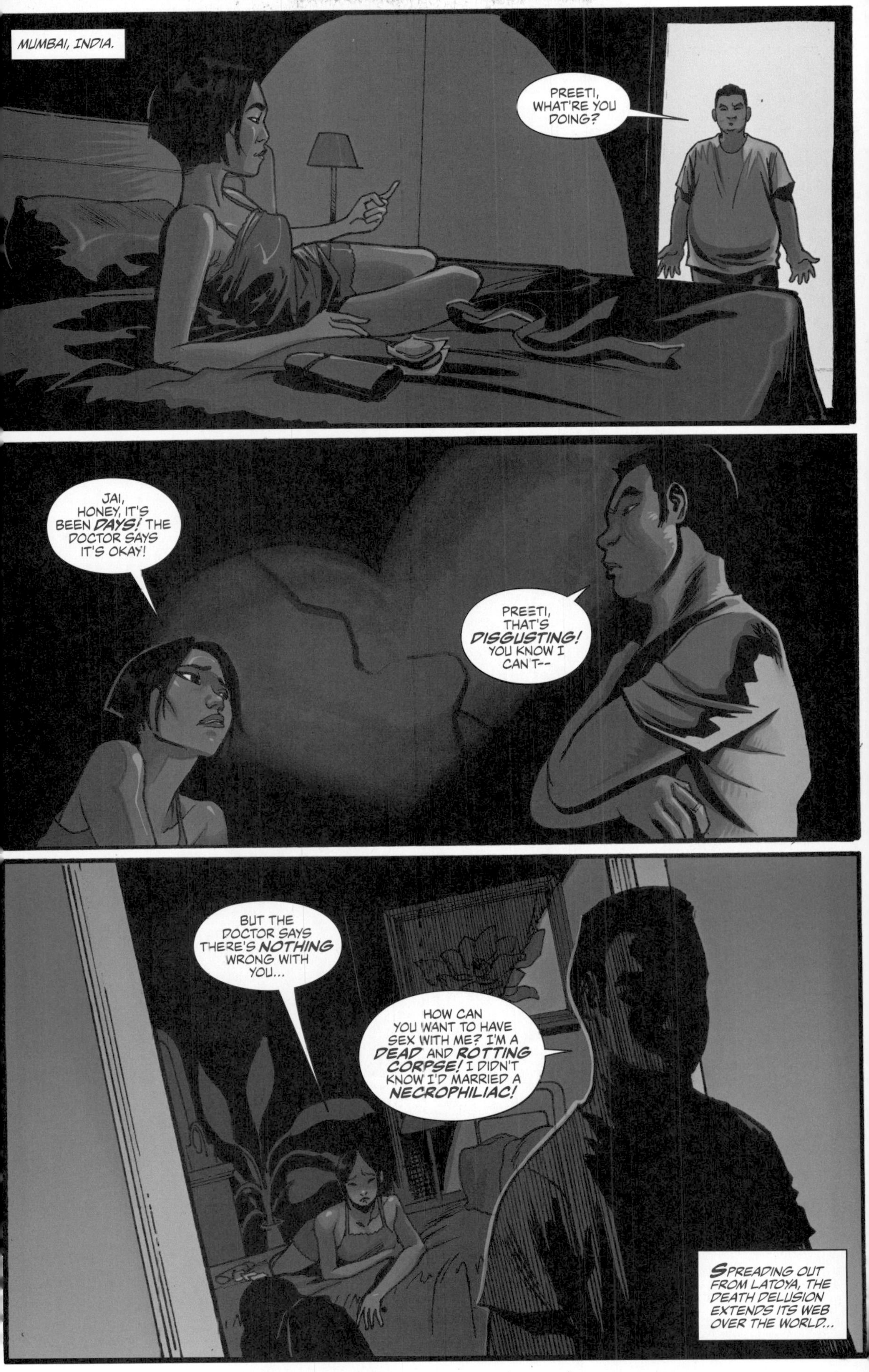
MUMBAI, INDIA.
PREETI, WHAT'RE YOU DOING?
JAI, HONEY, IT'S BEEN DAYS! THE DOCTOR SAYS IT'S OKAY!
PREETI, THAT'S DISGUSTING! YOU KNOW I CAN'T--
BUT THE DOCTOR SAYS THERE'S NOTHING WRONG WITH YOU...
HOW CAN YOU WANT TO HAVE SEX WITH ME? I'M A DEAD AND ROTTING CORPSE! I DIDN'T KNOW I'D MARRIED A NECROPHILIAC!
SPREADING OUT FROM LATOYA, THE DEATH DELUSION EXTENDS ITS WEB OVER THE WORLD...

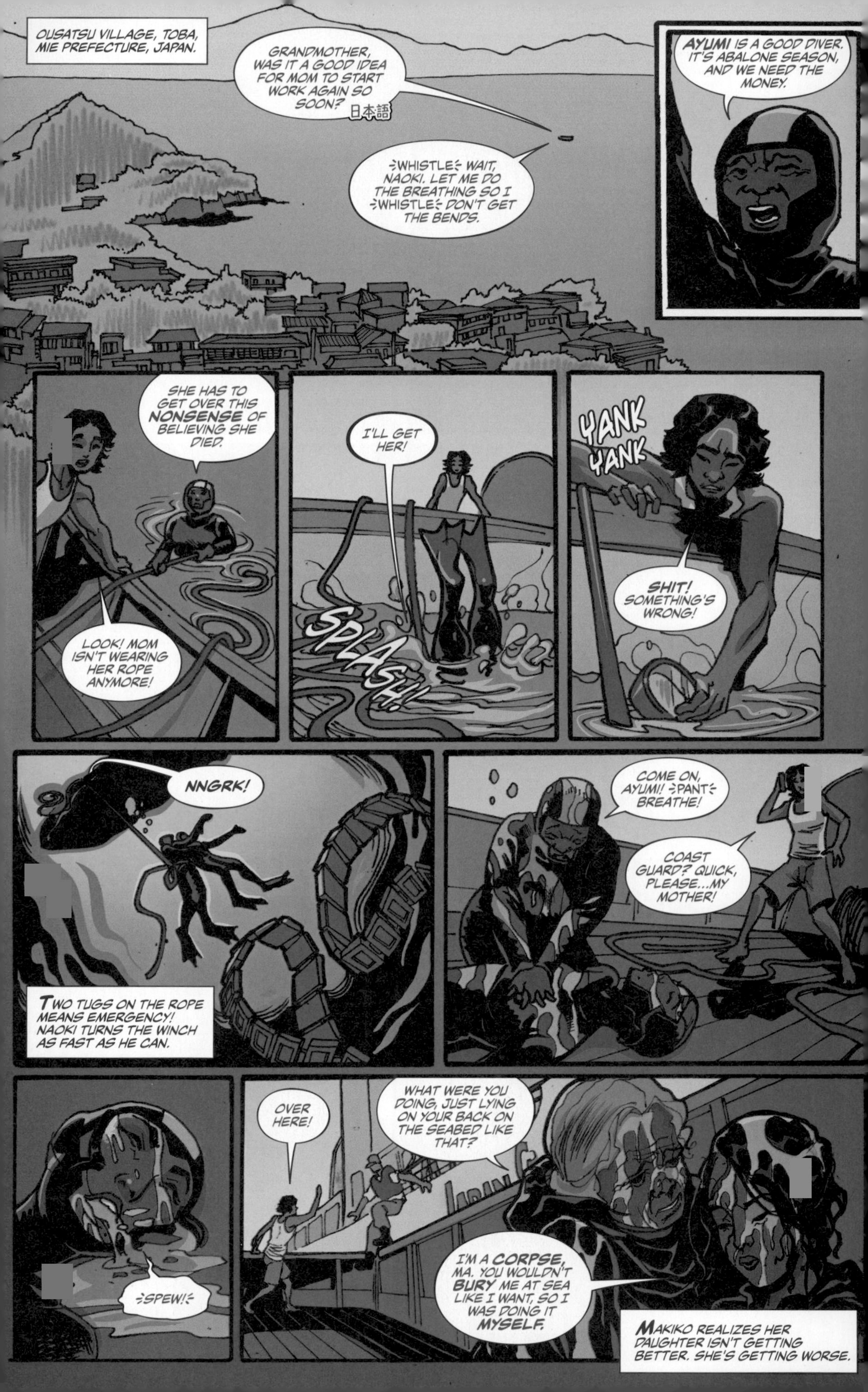
OUSATSU VILLAGE, TOBA, MIE PREFECTURE, JAPAN.
GRANDMOTHER, WAS IT A GOOD IDEA FOR MOM TO START WORK AGAIN SO SOON? 日本語
⇉WHISTLE⇇ WAIT, NAOKI. LET ME DO THE BREATHING SO I ⇉WHISTLE⇇ DON'T GET THE BENDS.
AYUMI IS A GOOD DIVER. IT'S ABALONE SEASON, AND WE NEED THE MONEY.
SHE HAS TO GET OVER THIS NONSENSE OF BELIEVING SHE DIED.
LOOK! MOM ISN'T WEARING HER ROPE ANYMORE!
I'LL GET HER!
SPLASH!
YANK YANK
SHIT! SOMETHING'S WRONG!
NNGRK!
TWO TUGS ON THE ROPE MEANS EMERGENCY! NAOKI TURNS THE WINCH AS FAST AS HE CAN.
COME ON, AYUMI! ⇉PANT⇇ BREATHE!
COAST GUARD? QUICK, PLEASE...MY MOTHER!
⇉SPEW!⇇
OVER HERE!
WHAT WERE YOU DOING, JUST LYING ON YOUR BACK ON THE SEABED LIKE THAT?
I'M A CORPSE, MA. YOU WOULDN'T BURY ME AT SEA LIKE I WANT, SO I WAS DOING IT MYSELF.
MAKIKO REALIZES HER DAUGHTER ISN'T GETTING BETTER. SHE'S GETTING WORSE.

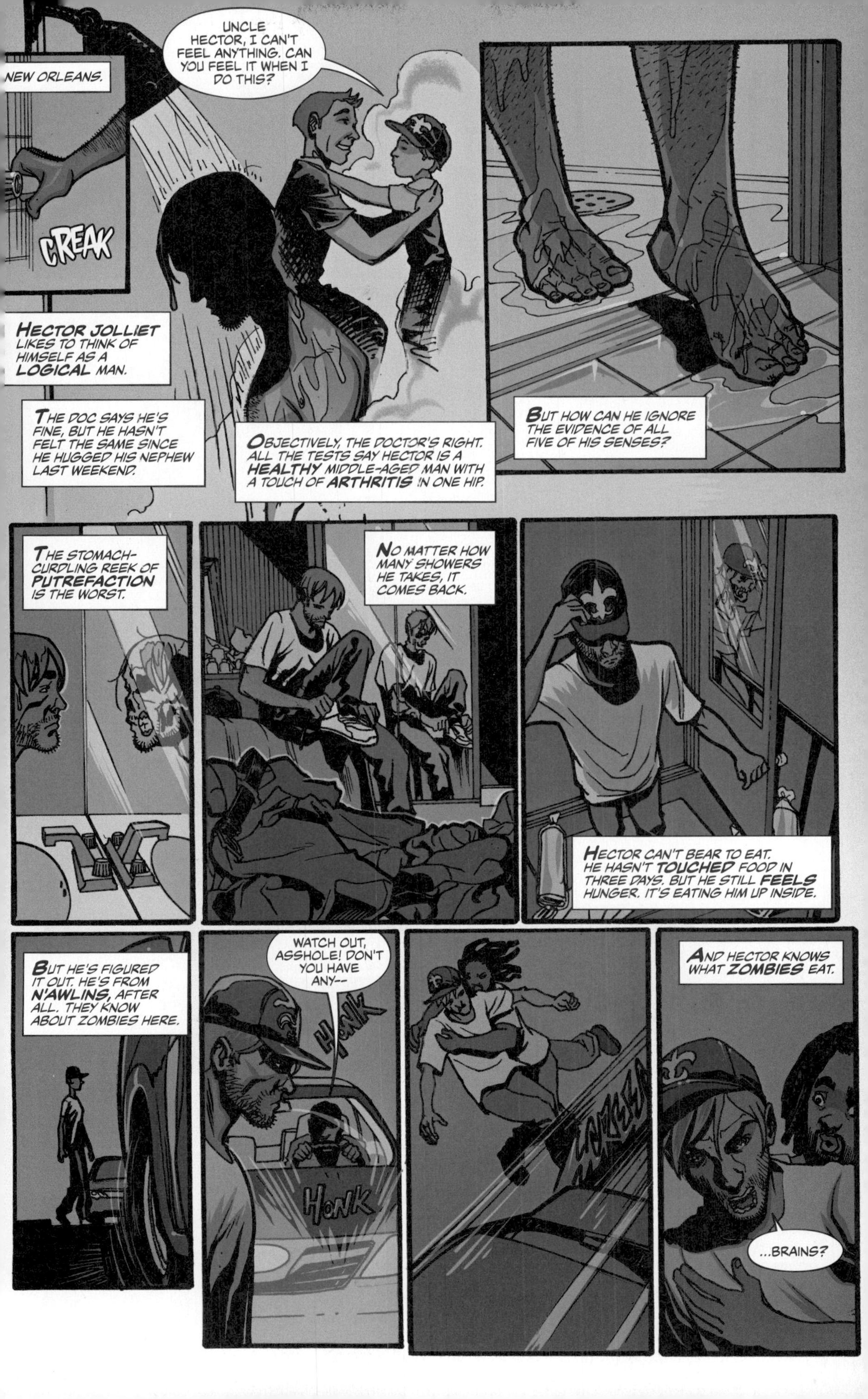

NEW ORLEANS.
UNCLE HECTOR, I CAN'T FEEL ANYTHING. CAN YOU FEEL IT WHEN I DO THIS?
CREAK
HECTOR JOLLIET LIKES TO THINK OF HIMSELF AS A LOGICAL MAN.
THE DOC SAYS HE'S FINE, BUT HE HASN'T FELT THE SAME SINCE HE HUGGED HIS NEPHEW LAST WEEKEND.
OBJECTIVELY, THE DOCTOR'S RIGHT. ALL THE TESTS SAY HECTOR IS A HEALTHY MIDDLE-AGED MAN WITH A TOUCH OF ARTHRITIS IN ONE HIP.
BUT HOW CAN HE IGNORE THE EVIDENCE OF ALL FIVE OF HIS SENSES?
THE STOMACH-CURDLING REEK OF PUTREFACTION IS THE WORST.
NO MATTER HOW MANY SHOWERS HE TAKES, IT COMES BACK.
HECTOR CAN'T BEAR TO EAT. HE HASN'T TOUCHED FOOD IN THREE DAYS. BUT HE STILL FEELS HUNGER. IT'S EATING HIM UP INSIDE.
BUT HE'S FIGURED IT OUT. HE'S FROM N'AWLINS, AFTER ALL. THEY KNOW ABOUT ZOMBIES HERE.
WATCH OUT, ASSHOLE! DON'T YOU HAVE ANY--
HONK
HONK
AND HECTOR KNOWS WHAT ZOMBIES EAT.
...BRAINS?

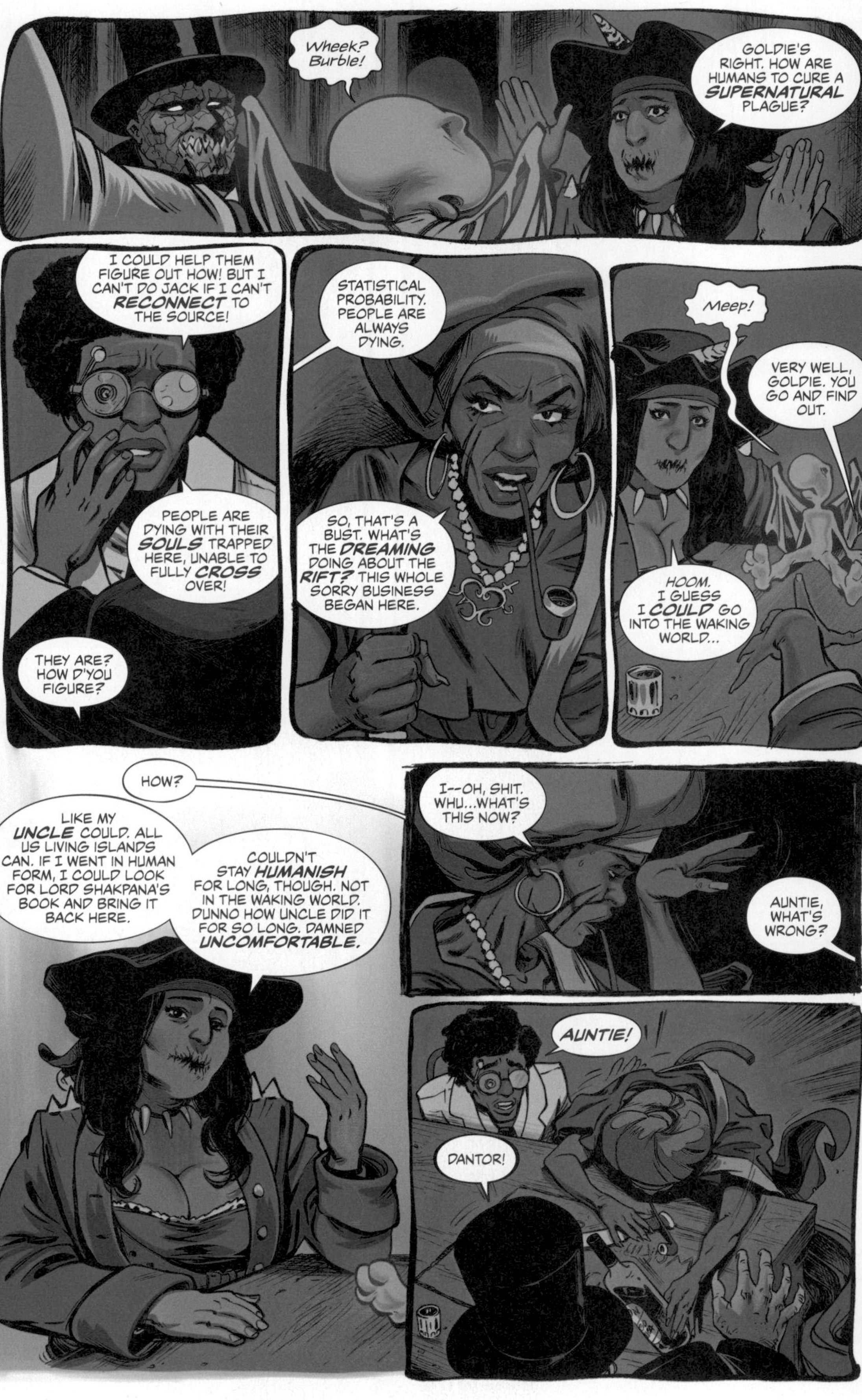
Wheek? Burble!
GOLDIE'S RIGHT. HOW ARE HUMANS TO CURE A SUPERNATURAL PLAGUE?
I COULD HELP THEM FIGURE OUT HOW! BUT I CAN'T DO JACK IF I CAN'T RECONNECT TO THE SOURCE!
PEOPLE ARE DYING WITH THEIR SOULS TRAPPED HERE, UNABLE TO FULLY CROSS OVER!
THEY ARE? HOW D'YOU FIGURE?
STATISTICAL PROBABILITY. PEOPLE ARE ALWAYS DYING.
SO, THAT'S A BUST. WHAT'S THE DREAMING DOING ABOUT THE RIFT? THIS WHOLE SORRY BUSINESS BEGAN HERE.
Meep!
VERY WELL, GOLDIE. YOU GO AND FIND OUT.
HOOM. I GUESS I COULD GO INTO THE WAKING WORLD...
HOW?
LIKE MY UNCLE COULD. ALL US LIVING ISLANDS CAN. IF I WENT IN HUMAN FORM, I COULD LOOK FOR LORD SHAKPANA'S BOOK AND BRING IT BACK HERE.
COULDN'T STAY HUMANISH FOR LONG, THOUGH. NOT IN THE WAKING WORLD. DUNNO HOW UNCLE DID IT FOR SO LONG. DAMNED UNCOMFORTABLE.
I--OH, SHIT. WHU...WHAT'S THIS NOW?
AUNTIE, WHAT'S WRONG?
AUNTIE!
DANTOR!

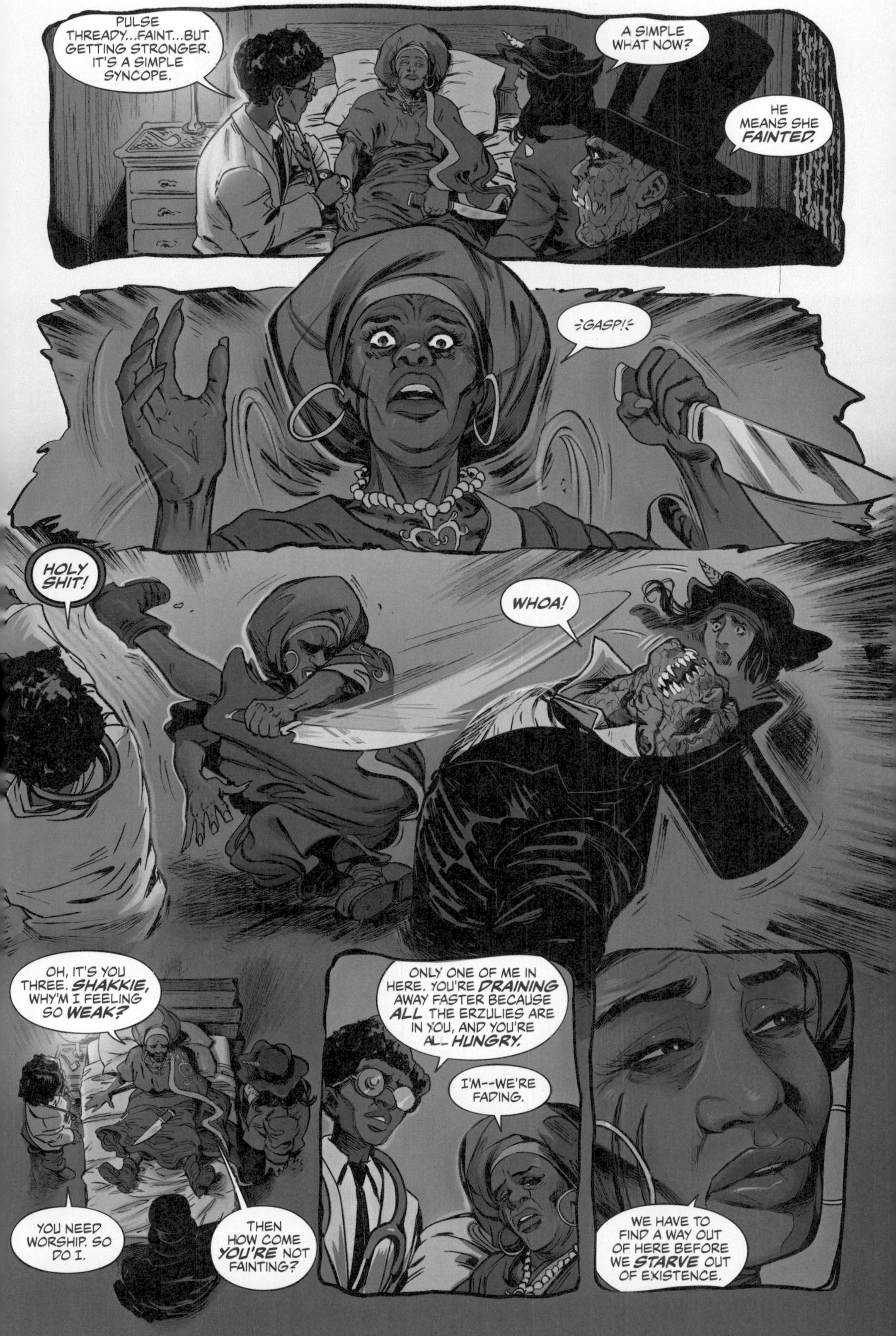
PULSE THREADY...FAINT...BUT GETTING STRONGER. IT'S A SIMPLE SYNCOPE.
A SIMPLE WHAT NOW?
HE MEANS SHE FAINTED.
GASP!
HOLY SHIT!
WHOA!
OH, IT'S YOU THREE. SHAKKIE, WHY'M I FEELING SO WEAK?
YOU NEED WORSHIP. SO DO I.
THEN HOW COME YOU'RE NOT FAINTING?
ONLY ONE OF ME IN HERE. YOU'RE DRAINING AWAY FASTER BECAUSE ALL THE ERZULIES ARE IN YOU, AND YOU'RE ALL HUNGRY.
I'M--WE'RE FADING.
WE HAVE TO FIND A WAY OUT OF HERE BEFORE WE STARVE OUT OF EXISTENCE.

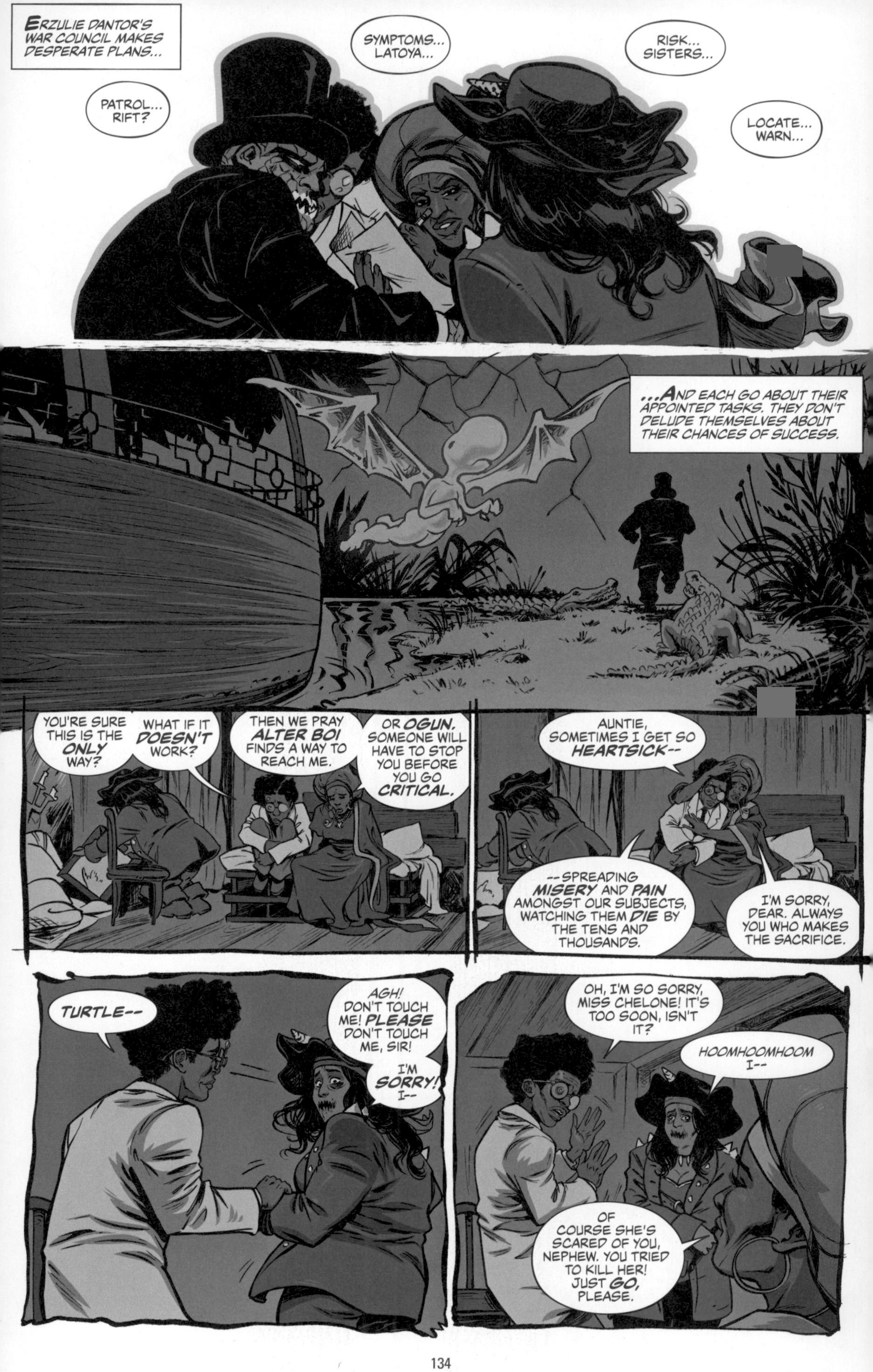
ERZULIE DANTOR'S WAR COUNCIL MAKES DESPERATE PLANS...
PATROL... RIFT?
SYMPTOMS... LATOYA...
RISK... SISTERS...
LOCATE... WARN...
...AND EACH GO ABOUT THEIR APPOINTED TASKS. THEY DON'T DELUDE THEMSELVES ABOUT THEIR CHANCES OF SUCCESS.
YOU'RE SURE THIS IS THE ONLY WAY?
WHAT IF IT DOESN'T WORK?
THEN WE PRAY ALTER BOI FINDS A WAY TO REACH ME.
OR OGUN. SOMEONE WILL HAVE TO STOP YOU BEFORE YOU GO CRITICAL.
AUNTIE, SOMETIMES I GET SO HEARTSICK--
--SPREADING MISERY AND PAIN AMONGST OUR SUBJECTS, WATCHING THEM DIE BY THE TENS AND THOUSANDS.
I'M SORRY, DEAR. ALWAYS YOU WHO MAKES THE SACRIFICE.
TURTLE--
AGH! DON'T TOUCH ME! PLEASE DON'T TOUCH ME, SIR!
I'M SORRY! I--
OH, I'M SO SORRY, MISS CHELONE! IT'S TOO SOON, ISN'T IT?
HOOMHOOMHOOM I--
OF COURSE SHE'S SCARED OF YOU, NEPHEW. YOU TRIED TO KILL HER! JUST GO, PLEASE.

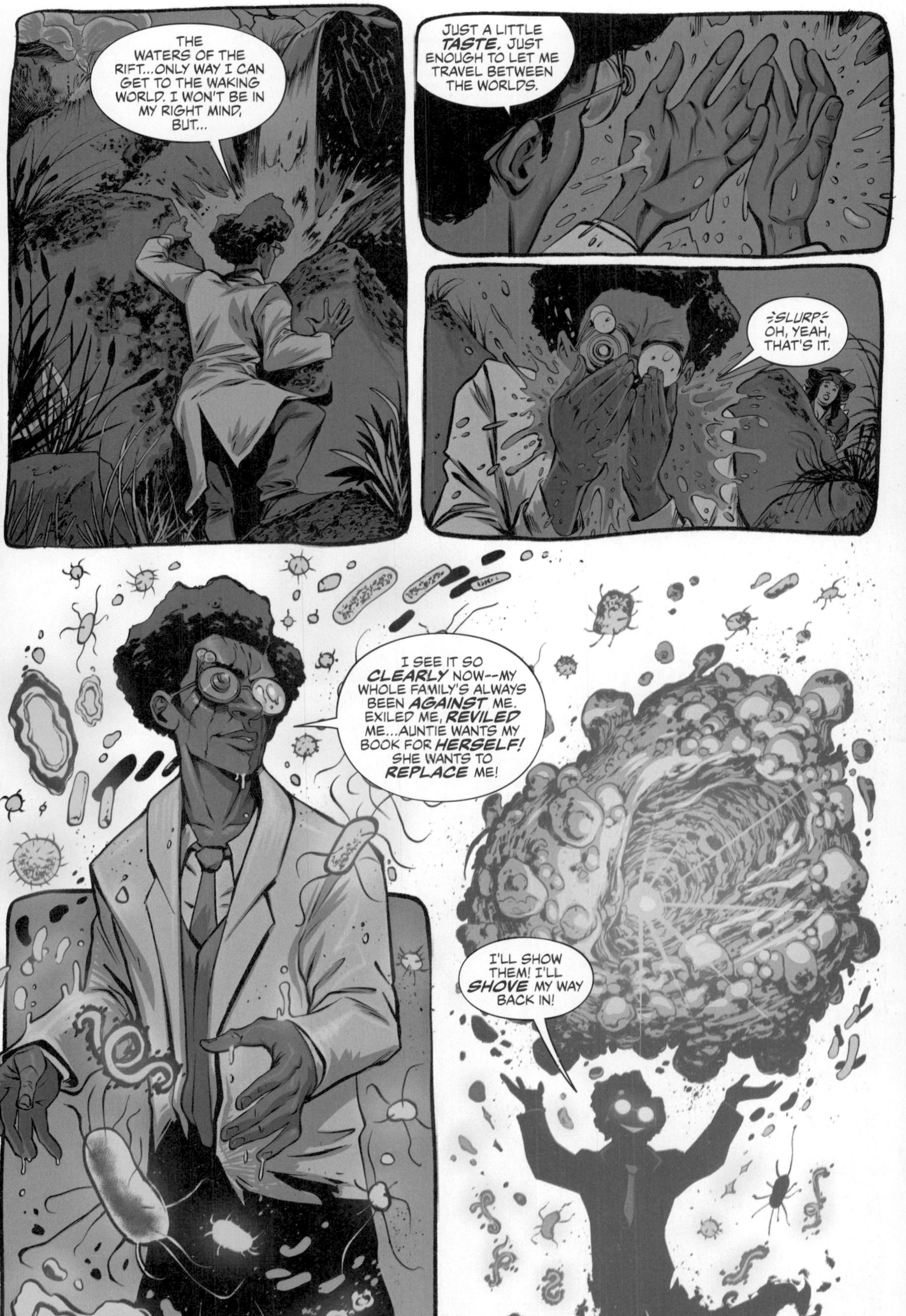
THE WATERS OF THE RIFT...ONLY WAY I CAN GET TO THE WAKING WORLD. I WON'T BE IN MY RIGHT MIND, BUT...
JUST A LITTLE TASTE. JUST ENOUGH TO LET ME TRAVEL BETWEEN THE WORLDS.
SLURP
OH, YEAH, THAT'S IT.
I SEE IT SO CLEARLY NOW--MY WHOLE FAMILY'S ALWAYS BEEN AGAINST ME. EXILED ME, REVILED ME...AUNTIE WANTS MY BOOK FOR HERSELF! SHE WANTS TO REPLACE ME!
I'LL SHOW THEM! I'LL SHOVE MY WAY BACK IN!

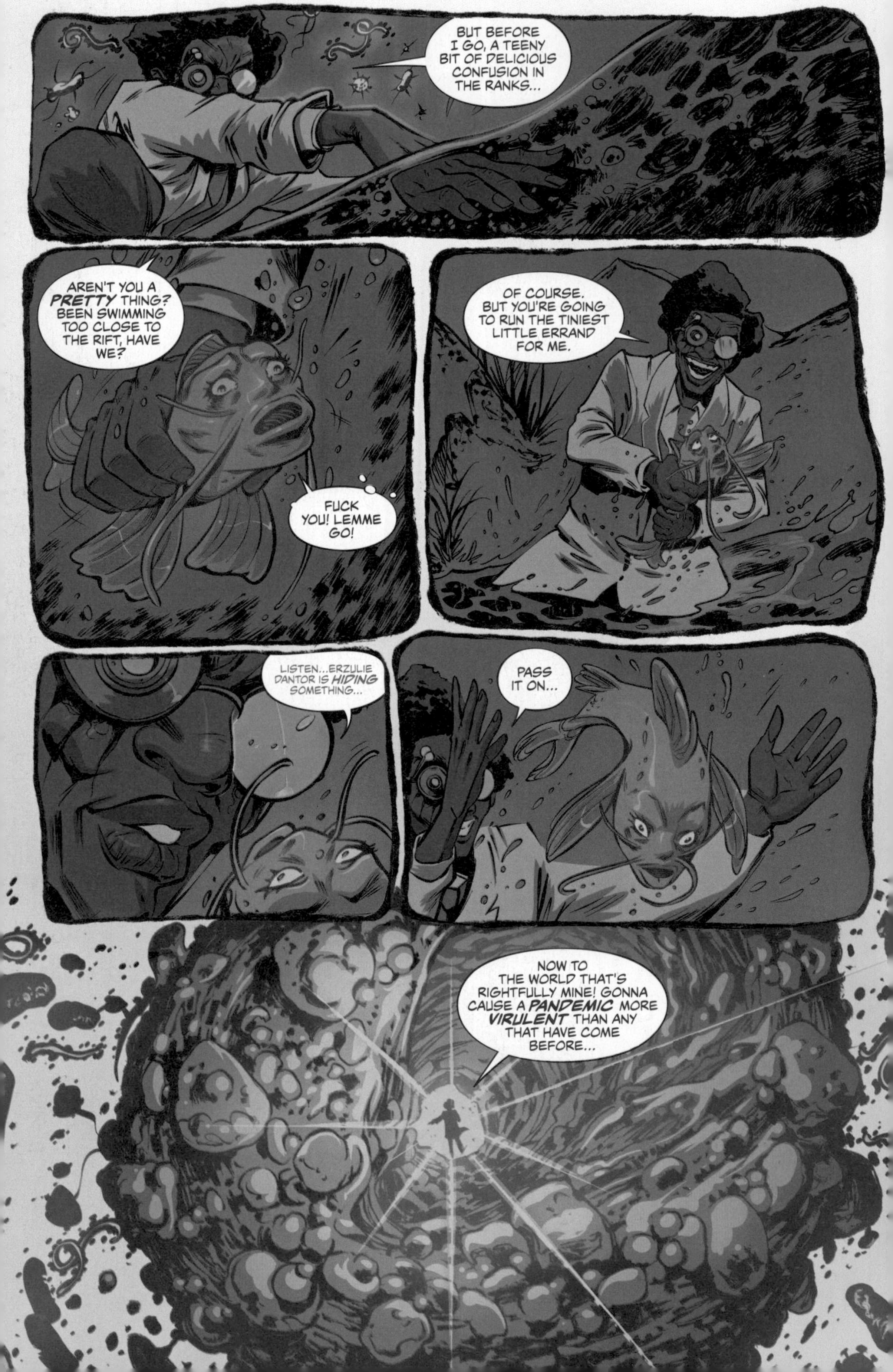
BUT BEFORE I GO, A TEENY BIT OF DELICIOUS CONFUSION IN THE RANKS...
AREN'T YOU A PRETTY THING? BEEN SWIMMING TOO CLOSE TO THE RIFT, HAVE WE?
FUCK YOU! LEMME GO!
OF COURSE. BUT YOU'RE GOING TO RUN THE TINIEST LITTLE ERRAND FOR ME.
LISTEN...ERZULIE DANTOR IS HIDING SOMETHING...
PASS IT ON...
NOW TO THE WORLD THAT'S RIGHTFULLY MINE! GONNA CAUSE A PANDEMIC MORE VIRULENT THAN ANY THAT HAVE COME BEFORE...

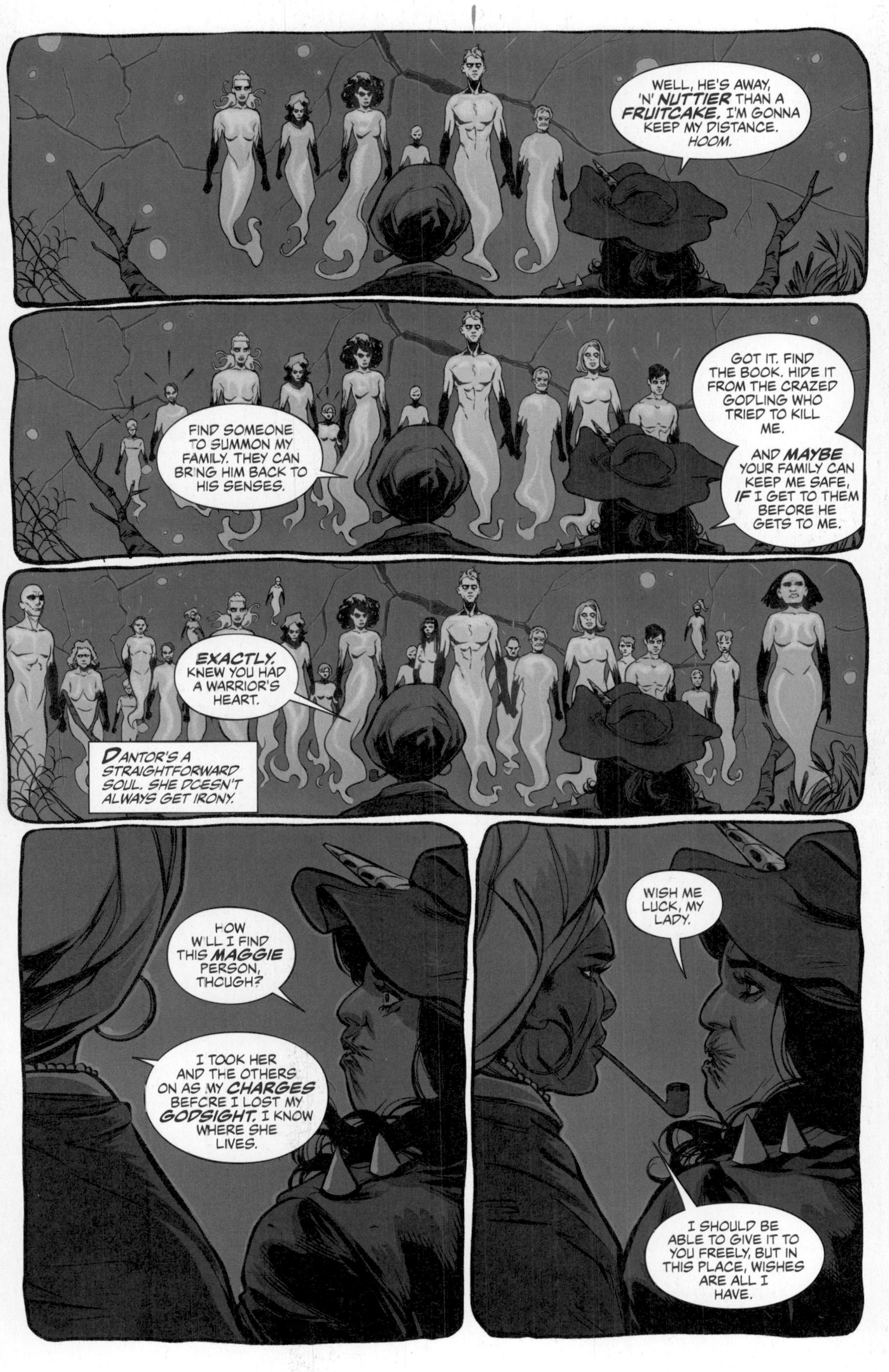
WELL, HE'S AWAY, 'N' NUTTIER THAN A FRUITCAKE. I'M GONNA KEEP MY DISTANCE. HOOM.
FIND SOMEONE TO SUMMON MY FAMILY. THEY CAN BRING HIM BACK TO HIS SENSES.
GOT IT. FIND THE BOOK. HIDE IT FROM THE CRAZED GODLING WHO TRIED TO KILL ME.
AND MAYBE YOUR FAMILY CAN KEEP ME SAFE, IF I GET TO THEM BEFORE HE GETS TO ME.
EXACTLY. KNEW YOU HAD A WARRIOR'S HEART.
DANTOR'S A STRAIGHTFORWARD SOUL. SHE DOESN'T ALWAYS GET IRONY.
HOW WILL I FIND THIS MAGGIE PERSON, THOUGH?
I TOOK HER AND THE OTHERS ON AS MY CHARGES BEFORE I LOST MY GODSIGHT. I KNOW WHERE SHE LIVES.
WISH ME LUCK, MY LADY.
I SHOULD BE ABLE TO GIVE IT TO YOU FREELY, BUT IN THIS PLACE, WISHES ARE ALL I HAVE.

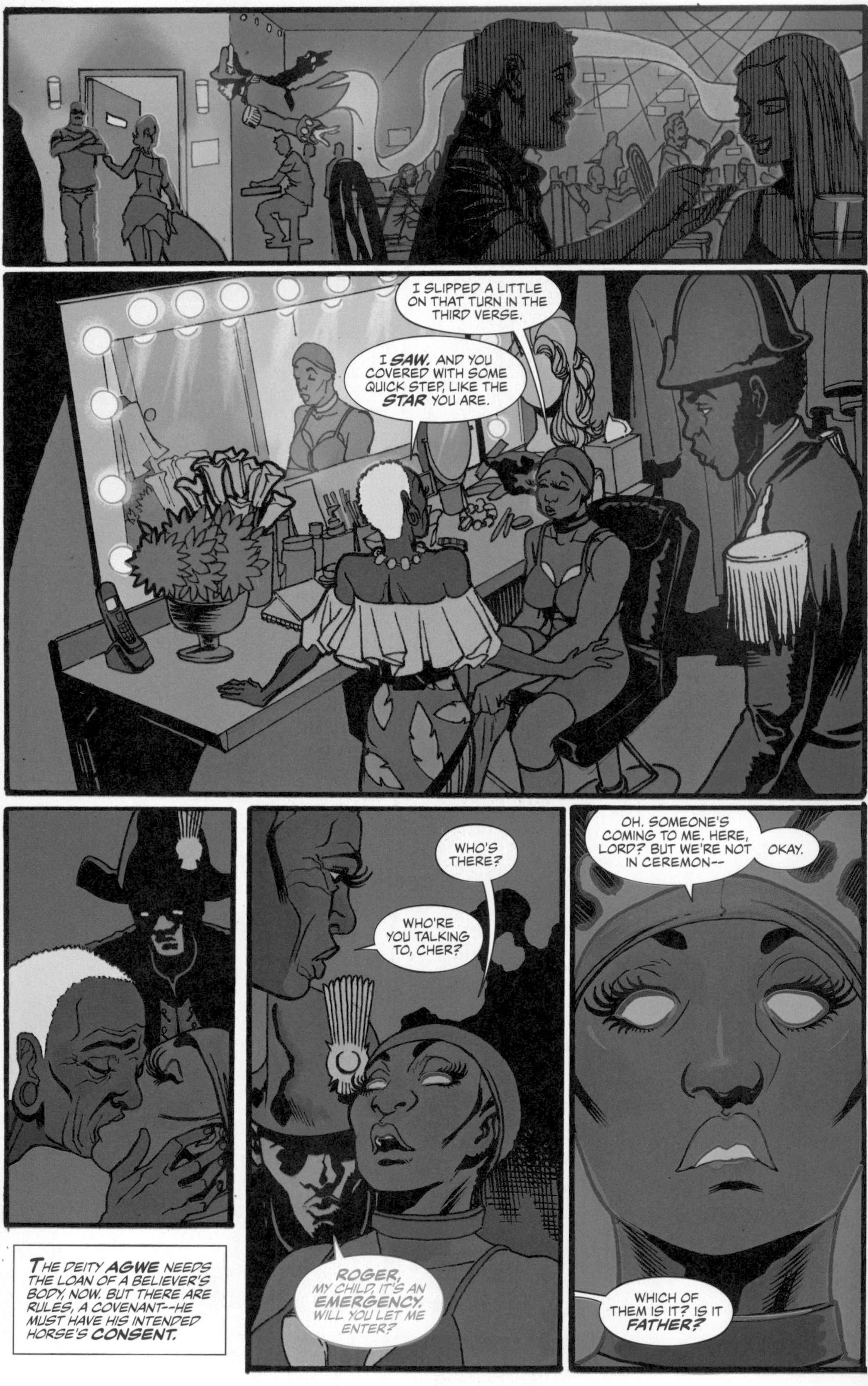
I SLIPPED A LITTLE ON THAT TURN IN THE THIRD VERSE.
I SAW. AND YOU COVERED WITH SOME QUICK STEP, LIKE THE STAR YOU ARE.
THE DEITY AGWE NEEDS THE LOAN OF A BELIEVER'S BODY, NOW. BUT THERE ARE RULES, A COVENANT--HE MUST HAVE HIS INTENDED HORSE'S CONSENT.
WHO'S THERE?
WHO'RE YOU TALKING TO, CHER?
ROGER, MY CHILD, IT'S AN EMERGENCY. WILL YOU LET ME ENTER?
OH. SOMEONE'S COMING TO ME. HERE, LORD? BUT WE'RE NOT IN CEREMON--
OKAY.
WHICH OF THEM IS IT? IS IT FATHER?

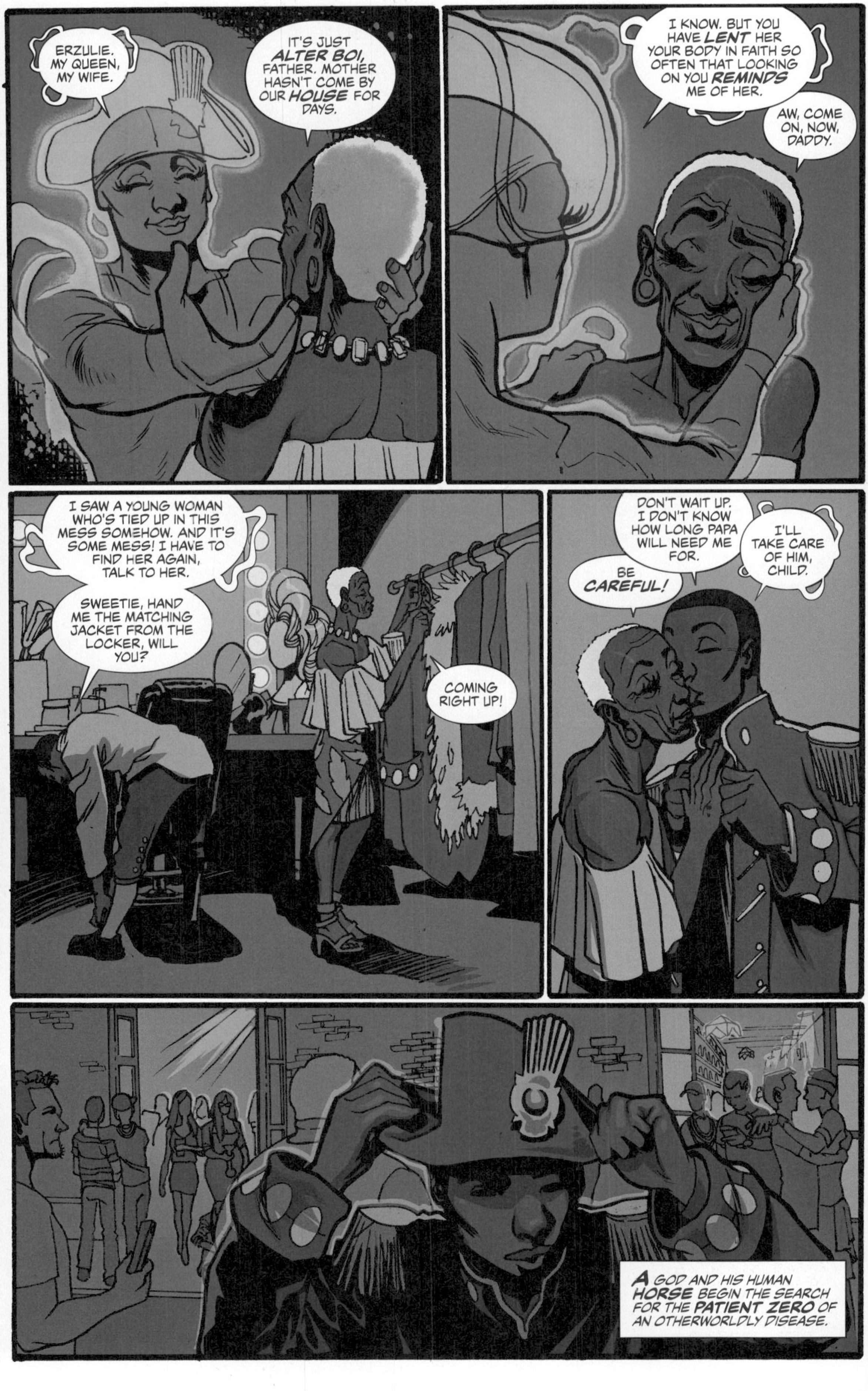
ERZULIE. MY QUEEN, MY WIFE.
IT'S JUST ALTER BOI, FATHER. MOTHER HASN'T COME BY OUR HOUSE FOR DAYS.
I KNOW. BUT YOU HAVE LENT HER YOUR BODY IN FAITH SO OFTEN THAT LOOKING ON YOU REMINDS ME OF HER.
AW, COME ON, NOW, DADDY.
I SAW A YOUNG WOMAN WHO'S TIED UP IN THIS MESS SOMEHOW. AND IT'S SOME MESS! I HAVE TO FIND HER AGAIN, TALK TO HER.
SWEETIE, HAND ME THE MATCHING JACKET FROM THE LOCKER, WILL YOU?
COMING RIGHT UP!
DON'T WAIT UP. I DON'T KNOW HOW LONG PAPA WILL NEED ME FOR.
BE CAREFUL!
I'LL TAKE CARE OF HIM, CHILD.
A GOD AND HIS HUMAN HORSE BEGIN THE SEARCH FOR THE PATIENT ZERO OF AN OTHERWORLDLY DISEASE.

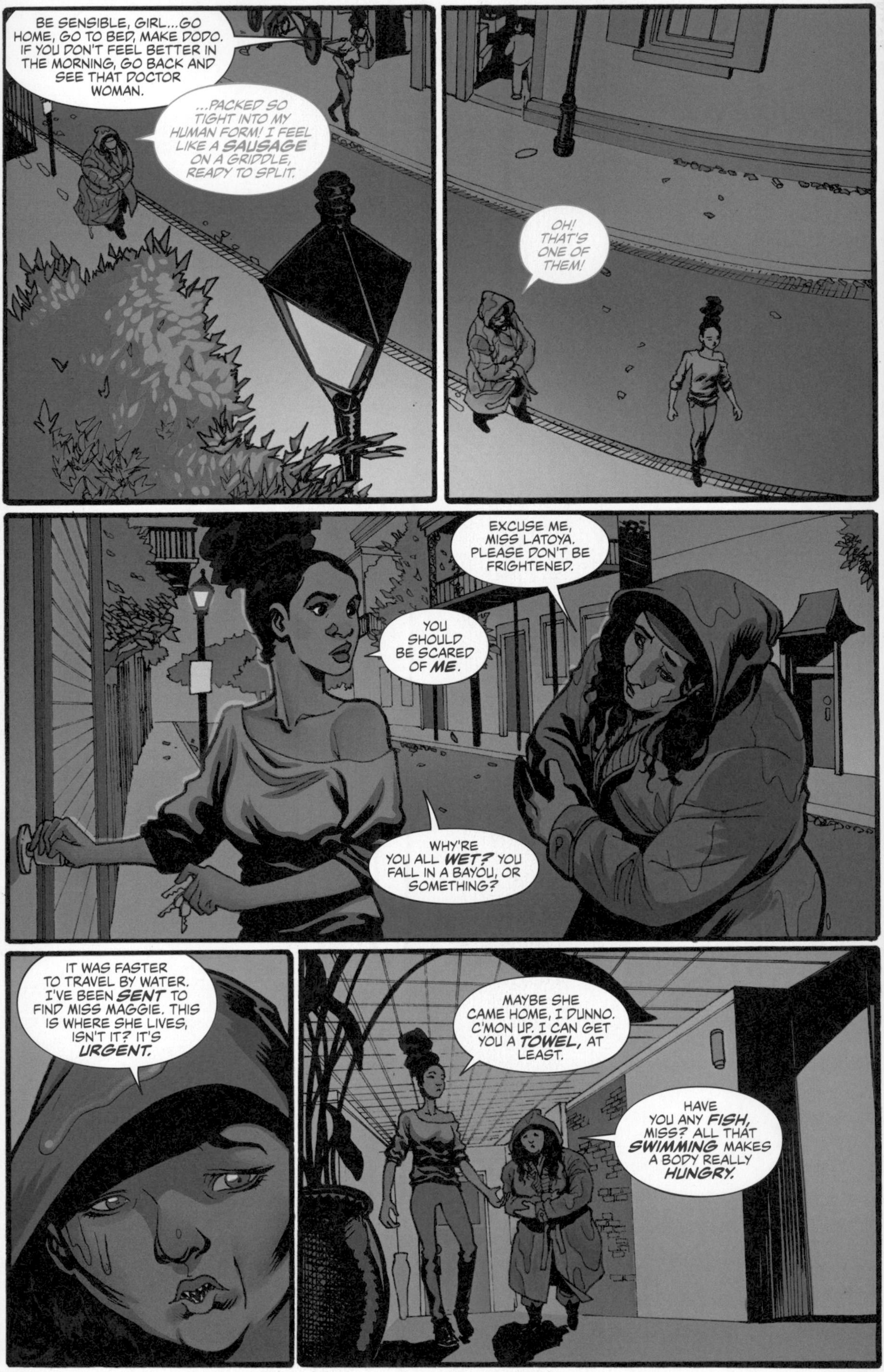
BE SENSIBLE, GIRL...GO HOME, GO TO BED, MAKE DODO. IF YOU DON'T FEEL BETTER IN THE MORNING, GO BACK AND SEE THAT DOCTOR WOMAN.
...PACKED SO TIGHT INTO MY HUMAN FORM! I FEEL LIKE A SAUSAGE ON A GRIDDLE, READY TO SPLIT.
OH! THAT'S ONE OF THEM!
EXCUSE ME, MISS LATOYA. PLEASE DON'T BE FRIGHTENED.
YOU SHOULD BE SCARED OF ME.
WHY'RE YOU ALL WET? YOU FALL IN A BAYOU, OR SOMETHING?
IT WAS FASTER TO TRAVEL BY WATER. I'VE BEEN SENT TO FIND MISS MAGGIE. THIS IS WHERE SHE LIVES, ISN'T IT? IT'S URGENT.
MAYBE SHE CAME HOME, I DUNNO. C'MON UP. I CAN GET YOU A TOWEL, AT LEAST.
HAVE YOU ANY FISH, MISS? ALL THAT SWIMMING MAKES A BODY REALLY HUNGRY.

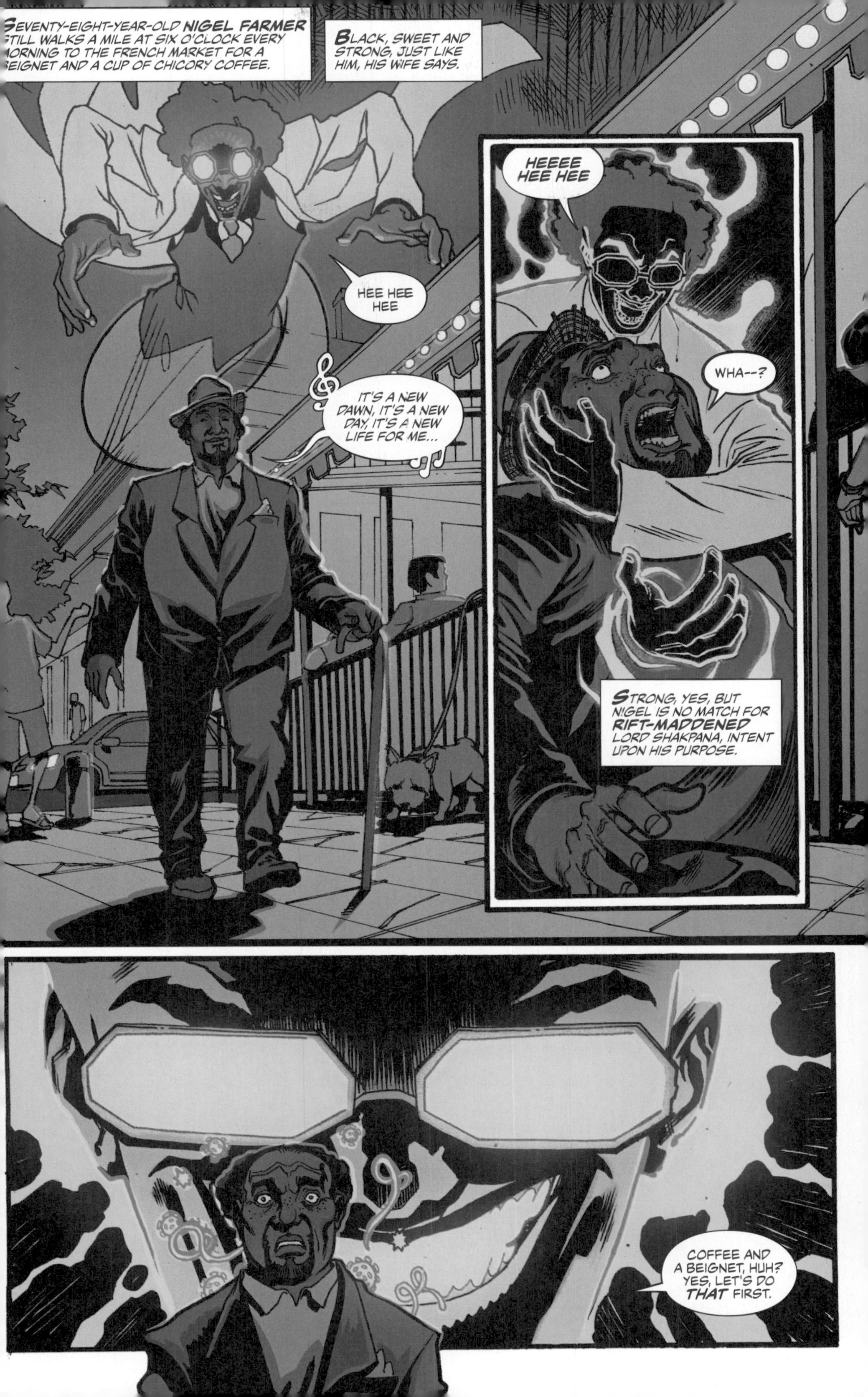
SEVENTY-EIGHT-YEAR-OLD NIGEL FARMER STILL WALKS A MILE AT SIX O'CLOCK EVERY MORNING TO THE FRENCH MARKET FOR A BEIGNET AND A CUP OF CHICORY COFFEE.
BLACK, SWEET AND STRONG, JUST LIKE HIM, HIS WIFE SAYS.
HEE HEE HEE
IT'S A NEW DAWN, IT'S A NEW DAY, IT'S A NEW LIFE FOR ME...
HEEEE HEE HEE
WHA--?
STRONG, YES, BUT NIGEL IS NO MATCH FOR RIFT-MADDENED LORD SHAKPANA, INTENT UPON HIS PURPOSE.
COFFEE AND A BEIGNET, HUH? YES, LET'S DO THAT FIRST.

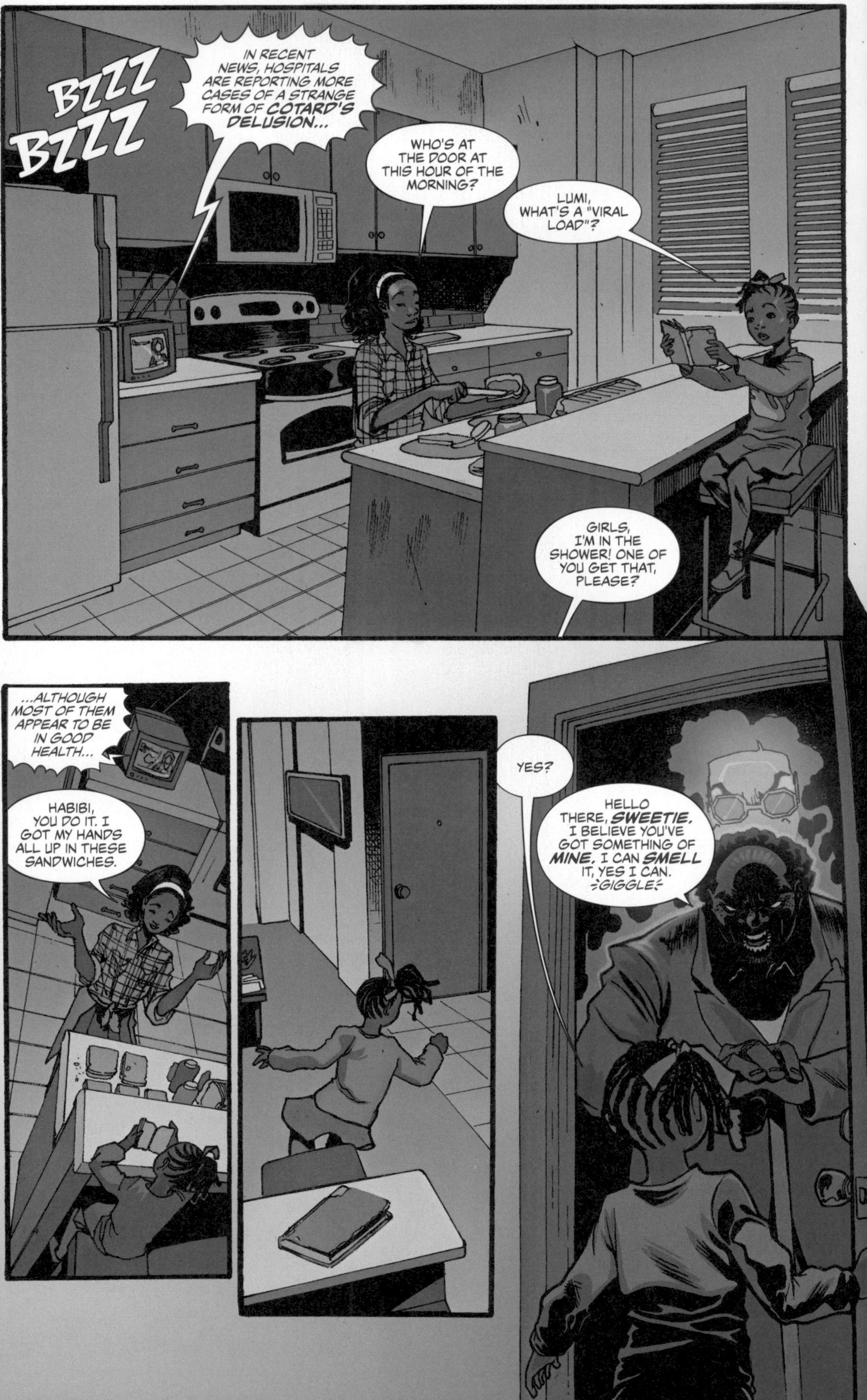
BZZZ BZZZ
IN RECENT NEWS, HOSPITALS ARE REPORTING MORE CASES OF A STRANGE FORM OF COTARD'S DELUSION...
WHO'S AT THE DOOR AT THIS HOUR OF THE MORNING?
LUMI, WHAT'S A "VIRAL LOAD"?
GIRLS, I'M IN THE SHOWER! ONE OF YOU GET THAT, PLEASE?
...ALTHOUGH MOST OF THEM APPEAR TO BE IN GOOD HEALTH...
HABIBI, YOU DO IT. I GOT MY HANDS ALL UP IN THESE SANDWICHES.
YES?
HELLO THERE, SWEETIE. I BELIEVE YOU'VE GOT SOMETHING OF MINE. I CAN SMELL IT, YES I CAN. ≈GIGGLE≈

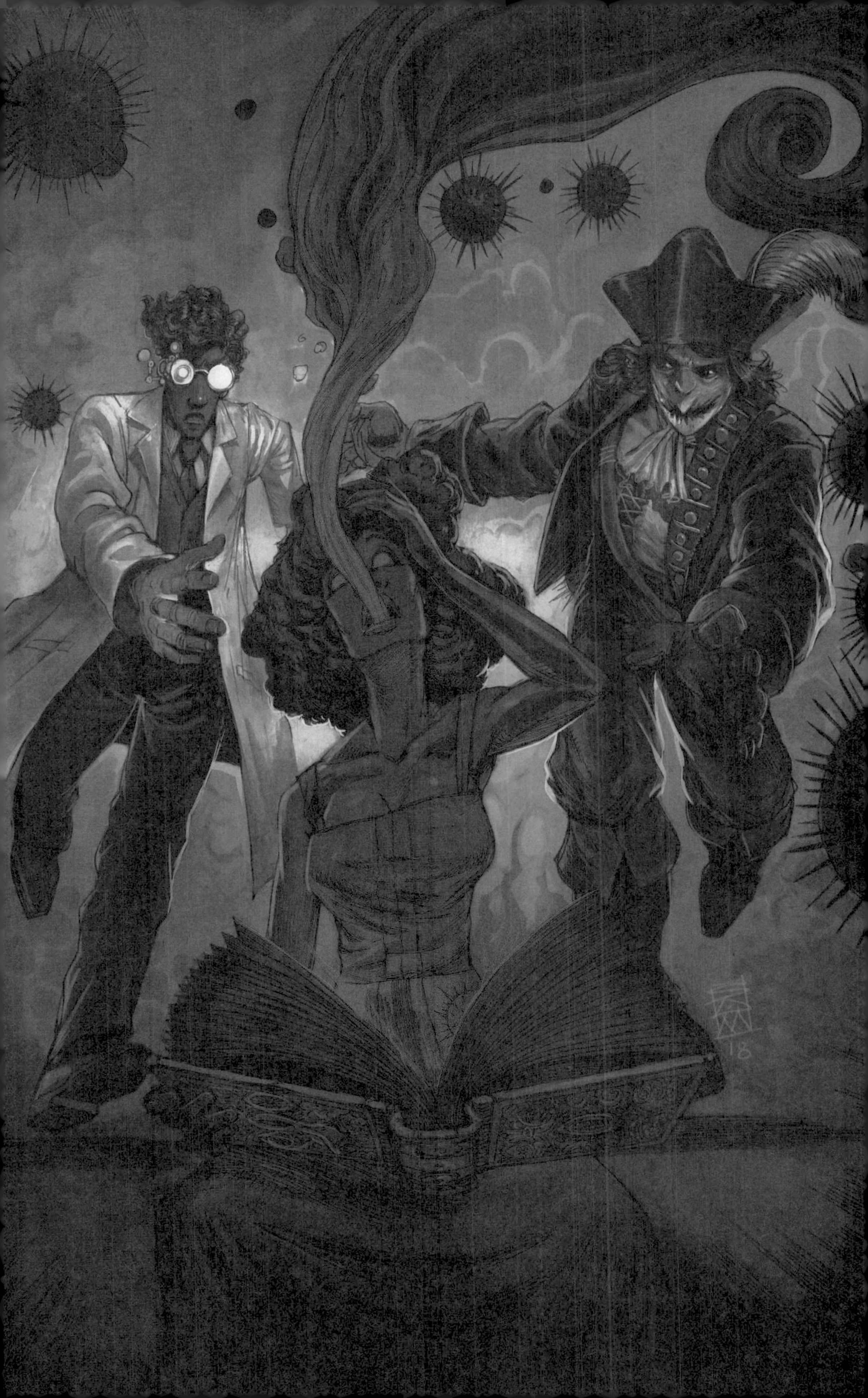

HOUSE OF WHISPERS

Rumors of Glory

WRITTEN BY
Nalo Hopkinson
and *Dan Watters*

ILLUSTRATED BY
Dominike "DOMO" Stanton

COLORS BY
John Rauch

LETTERS BY
AndWorld Design

COVER ART BY
Sean Andrew Murray

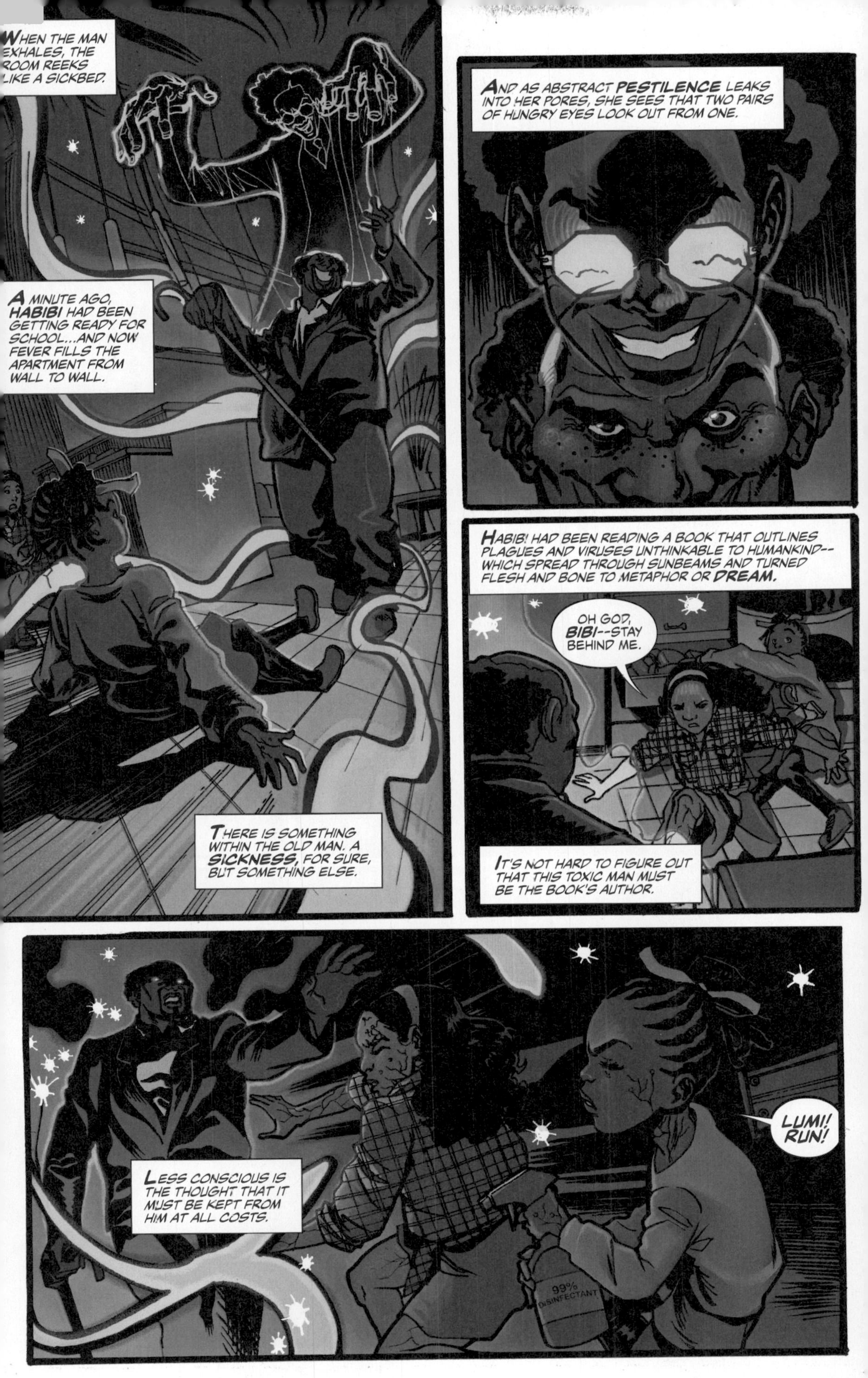
WHEN THE MAN EXHALES, THE ROOM REEKS LIKE A SICKBED.
A MINUTE AGO, HABIBI HAD BEEN GETTING READY FOR SCHOOL...AND NOW FEVER FILLS THE APARTMENT FROM WALL TO WALL.
THERE IS SOMETHING WITHIN THE OLD MAN. A SICKNESS, FOR SURE, BUT SOMETHING ELSE.
AND AS ABSTRACT PESTILENCE LEAKS INTO HER PORES, SHE SEES THAT TWO PAIRS OF HUNGRY EYES LOOK OUT FROM ONE.
HABIBI HAD BEEN READING A BOOK THAT OUTLINES PLAGUES AND VIRUSES UNTHINKABLE TO HUMANKIND--WHICH SPREAD THROUGH SUNBEAMS AND TURNED FLESH AND BONE TO METAPHOR OR DREAM.
OH GOD, BIBI--STAY BEHIND ME.
IT'S NOT HARD TO FIGURE OUT THAT THIS TOXIC MAN MUST BE THE BOOK'S AUTHOR.
LESS CONSCIOUS IS THE THOUGHT THAT IT MUST BE KEPT FROM HIM AT ALL COSTS.
LUMI! RUN!
99% DISINFECTANT

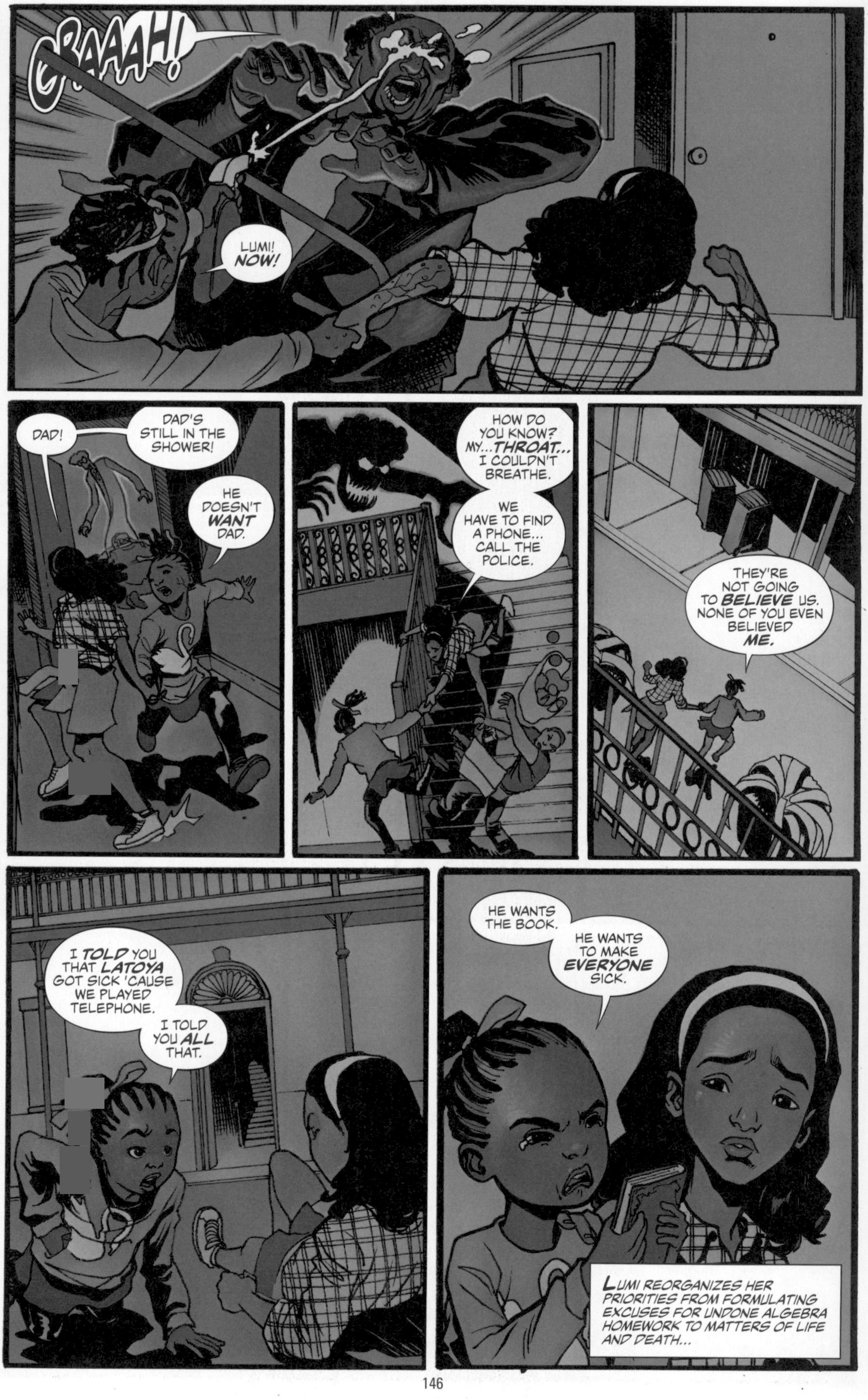
GRAAAH!
LUMI! NOW!
DAD!
DAD'S STILL IN THE SHOWER!
HE DOESN'T WANT DAD.
HOW DO YOU KNOW? MY...THROAT... I COULDN'T BREATHE.
WE HAVE TO FIND A PHONE... CALL THE POLICE.
THEY'RE NOT GOING TO BELIEVE US. NONE OF YOU EVEN BELIEVED ME.
I TOLD YOU THAT LATOYA GOT SICK 'CAUSE WE PLAYED TELEPHONE.
I TOLD YOU ALL THAT.
HE WANTS THE BOOK.
HE WANTS TO MAKE EVERYONE SICK.
LUMI REORGANIZES HER PRIORITIES FROM FORMULATING EXCUSES FOR UNDONE ALGEBRA HOMEWORK TO MATTERS OF LIFE AND DEATH...

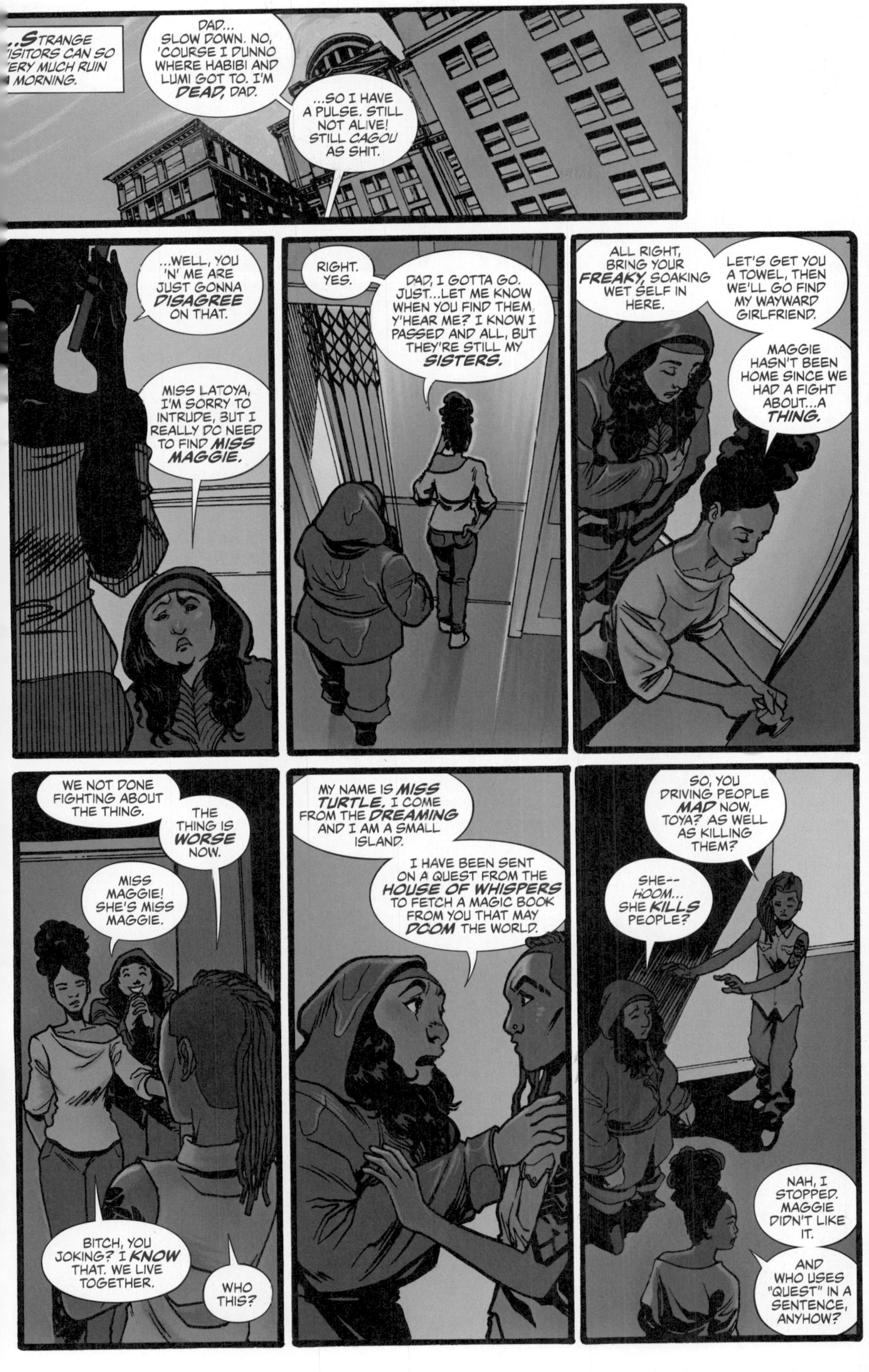

...STRANGE VISITORS CAN SO VERY MUCH RUIN A MORNING.
DAD... SLOW DOWN. NO, 'COURSE I DUNNO WHERE HABIBI AND LUMI GOT TO. I'M DEAD, DAD.
...SO I HAVE A PULSE. STILL NOT ALIVE! STILL CAGOU AS SHIT.
...WELL, YOU 'N' ME ARE JUST GONNA DISAGREE ON THAT.
MISS LATOYA, I'M SORRY TO INTRUDE, BUT I REALLY DO NEED TO FIND MISS MAGGIE.
RIGHT. YES.
DAD, I GOTTA GO. JUST...LET ME KNOW WHEN YOU FIND THEM, Y'HEAR ME? I KNOW I PASSED AND ALL, BUT THEY'RE STILL MY SISTERS.
ALL RIGHT, BRING YOUR FREAKY, SOAKING WET SELF IN HERE.
LET'S GET YOU A TOWEL, THEN WE'LL GO FIND MY WAYWARD GIRLFRIEND.
MAGGIE HASN'T BEEN HOME SINCE WE HAD A FIGHT ABOUT...A THING.
WE NOT DONE FIGHTING ABOUT THE THING.
THE THING IS WORSE NOW.
MISS MAGGIE! SHE'S MISS MAGGIE.
BITCH, YOU JOKING? I KNOW THAT. WE LIVE TOGETHER.
WHO THIS?
MY NAME IS MISS TURTLE. I COME FROM THE DREAMING AND I AM A SMALL ISLAND.
I HAVE BEEN SENT ON A QUEST FROM THE HOUSE OF WHISPERS TO FETCH A MAGIC BOOK FROM YOU THAT MAY DOOM THE WORLD.
SO, YOU DRIVING PEOPLE MAD NOW, TOYA? AS WELL AS KILLING THEM?
SHE-- HOOM... SHE KILLS PEOPLE?
NAH, I STOPPED. MAGGIE DIDN'T LIKE IT.
AND WHO USES "QUEST" IN A SENTENCE, ANYHOW?

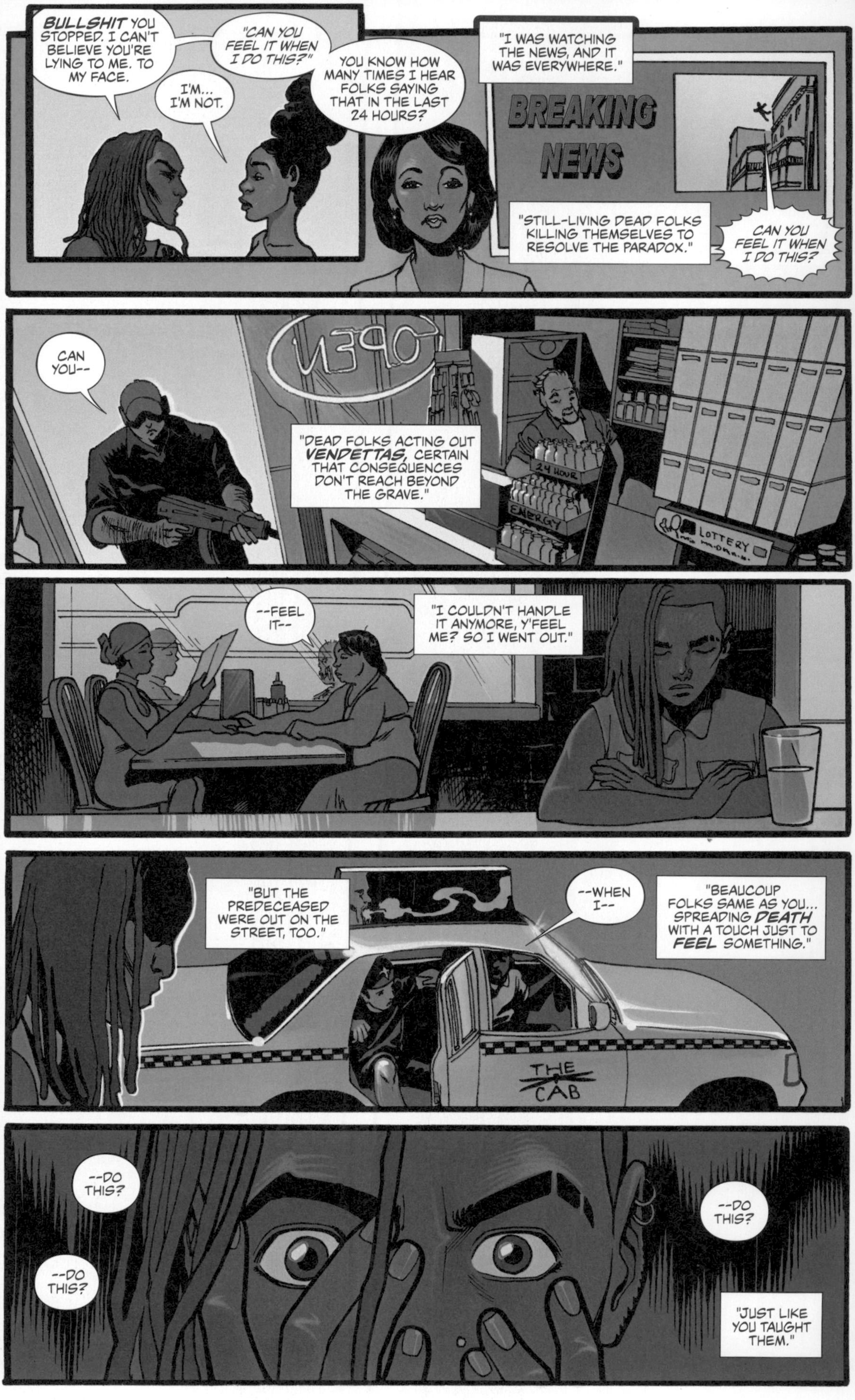
BULLSHIT YOU STOPPED. I CAN'T BELIEVE YOU'RE LYING TO ME. TO MY FACE.
"CAN YOU FEEL IT WHEN I DO THIS?"
I'M... I'M NOT.
YOU KNOW HOW MANY TIMES I HEAR FOLKS SAYING THAT IN THE LAST 24 HOURS?
"I WAS WATCHING THE NEWS, AND IT WAS EVERYWHERE."
BREAKING NEWS
"STILL-LIVING DEAD FOLKS KILLING THEMSELVES TO RESOLVE THE PARADOX."
CAN YOU FEEL IT WHEN I DO THIS?
CAN YOU--
OPEN
"DEAD FOLKS ACTING OUT VENDETTAS, CERTAIN THAT CONSEQUENCES DON'T REACH BEYOND THE GRAVE."
24 HOUR
ENERGY
LOTTERY
--FEEL IT--
"I COULDN'T HANDLE IT ANYMORE, Y'FEEL ME? SO I WENT OUT."
"BUT THE PREDECEASED WERE OUT ON THE STREET, TOO."
--WHEN I--
"BEAUCOUP FOLKS SAME AS YOU... SPREADING DEATH WITH A TOUCH JUST TO FEEL SOMETHING."
THE CAB
--DO THIS?
--DO THIS?
--DO THIS?
"JUST LIKE YOU TAUGHT THEM."

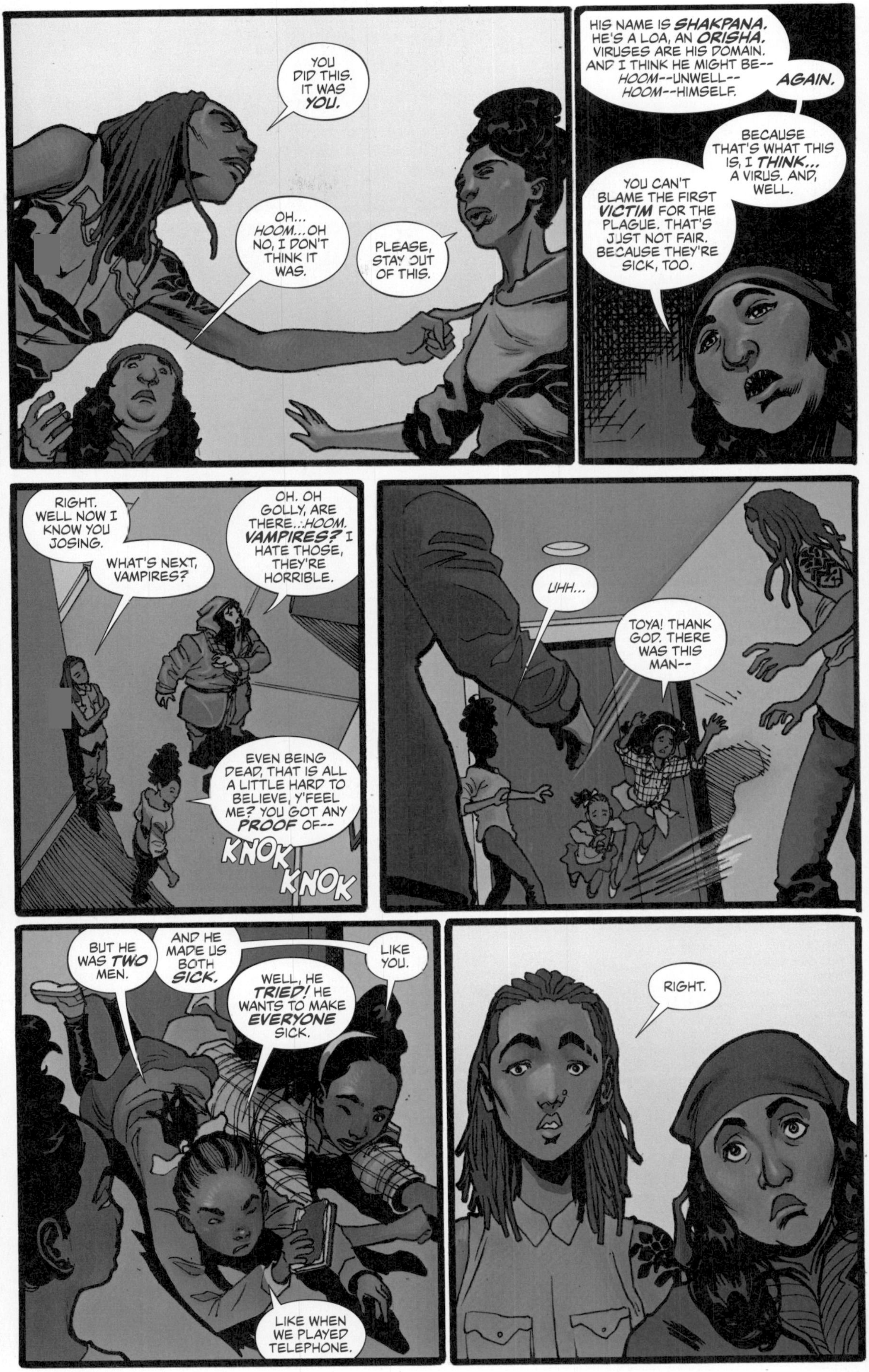
YOU DID THIS. IT WAS YOU.
OH... HOOM...OH NO, I DON'T THINK IT WAS.
PLEASE, STAY OUT OF THIS.
HIS NAME IS SHAKPANA. HE'S A LOA, AN ORISHA. VIRUSES ARE HIS DOMAIN. AND I THINK HE MIGHT BE-- HOOM--UNWELL-- HOOM--HIMSELF.
AGAIN.
BECAUSE THAT'S WHAT THIS IS, I THINK... A VIRUS. AND, WELL.
YOU CAN'T BLAME THE FIRST VICTIM FOR THE PLAGUE. THAT'S JUST NOT FAIR. BECAUSE THEY'RE SICK, TOO.
RIGHT. WELL NOW I KNOW YOU JOSING.
WHAT'S NEXT, VAMPIRES?
OH. OH GOLLY, ARE THERE...HOOM. VAMPIRES? I HATE THOSE, THEY'RE HORRIBLE.
EVEN BEING DEAD, THAT IS ALL A LITTLE HARD TO BELIEVE, Y'FEEL ME? YOU GOT ANY PROOF OF--
KNOK KNOK
UHH...
TOYA! THANK GOD. THERE WAS THIS MAN--
BUT HE WAS TWO MEN.
AND HE MADE US BOTH SICK.
LIKE YOU.
WELL, HE TRIED! HE WANTS TO MAKE EVERYONE SICK.
LIKE WHEN WE PLAYED TELEPHONE.
RIGHT.

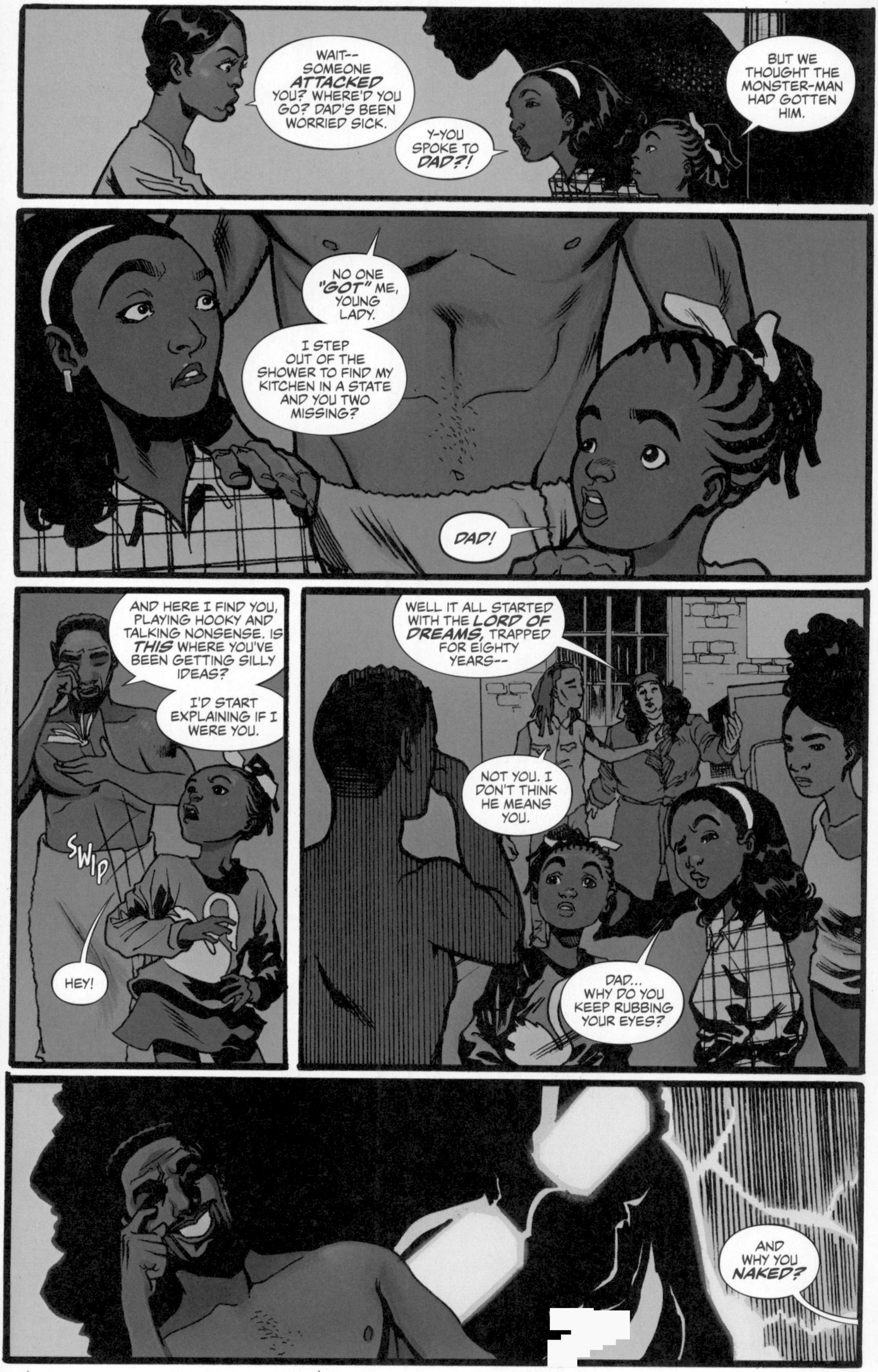
WAIT-- SOMEONE ATTACKED YOU? WHERE'D YOU GO? DAD'S BEEN WORRIED SICK.
Y-YOU SPOKE TO DAD?!
BUT WE THOUGHT THE MONSTER-MAN HAD GOTTEN HIM.
NO ONE "GOT" ME, YOUNG LADY.
I STEP OUT OF THE SHOWER TO FIND MY KITCHEN IN A STATE AND YOU TWO MISSING?
DAD!
AND HERE I FIND YOU, PLAYING HOOKY AND TALKING NONSENSE. IS THIS WHERE YOU'VE BEEN GETTING SILLY IDEAS?
I'D START EXPLAINING IF I WERE YOU.
SWIP
HEY!
WELL IT ALL STARTED WITH THE LORD OF DREAMS, TRAPPED FOR EIGHTY YEARS--
NOT YOU. I DON'T THINK HE MEANS YOU.
DAD... WHY DO YOU KEEP RUBBING YOUR EYES?
AND WHY YOU NAKED?

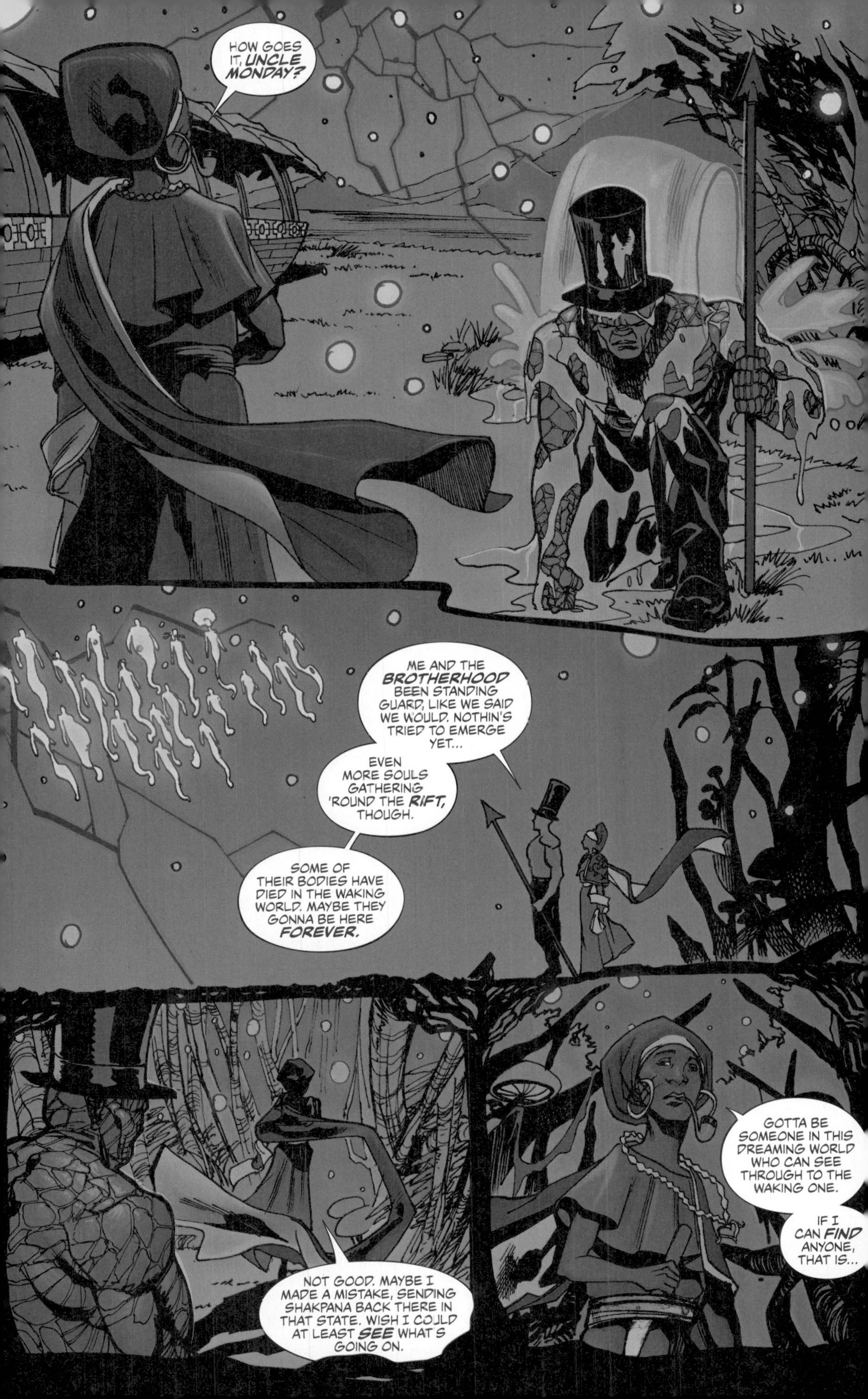
HOW GOES IT, UNCLE MONDAY?
ME AND THE BROTHERHOOD BEEN STANDING GUARD, LIKE WE SAID WE WOULD. NOTHIN'S TRIED TO EMERGE YET...
EVEN MORE SOULS GATHERING 'ROUND THE RIFT, THOUGH.
SOME OF THEIR BODIES HAVE DIED IN THE WAKING WORLD. MAYBE THEY GONNA BE HERE FOREVER.
NOT GOOD. MAYBE I MADE A MISTAKE, SENDING SHAKPANA BACK THERE IN THAT STATE. WISH I COULD AT LEAST SEE WHAT'S GOING ON.
GOTTA BE SOMEONE IN THIS DREAMING WORLD WHO CAN SEE THROUGH TO THE WAKING ONE.
IF I CAN FIND ANYONE, THAT IS...

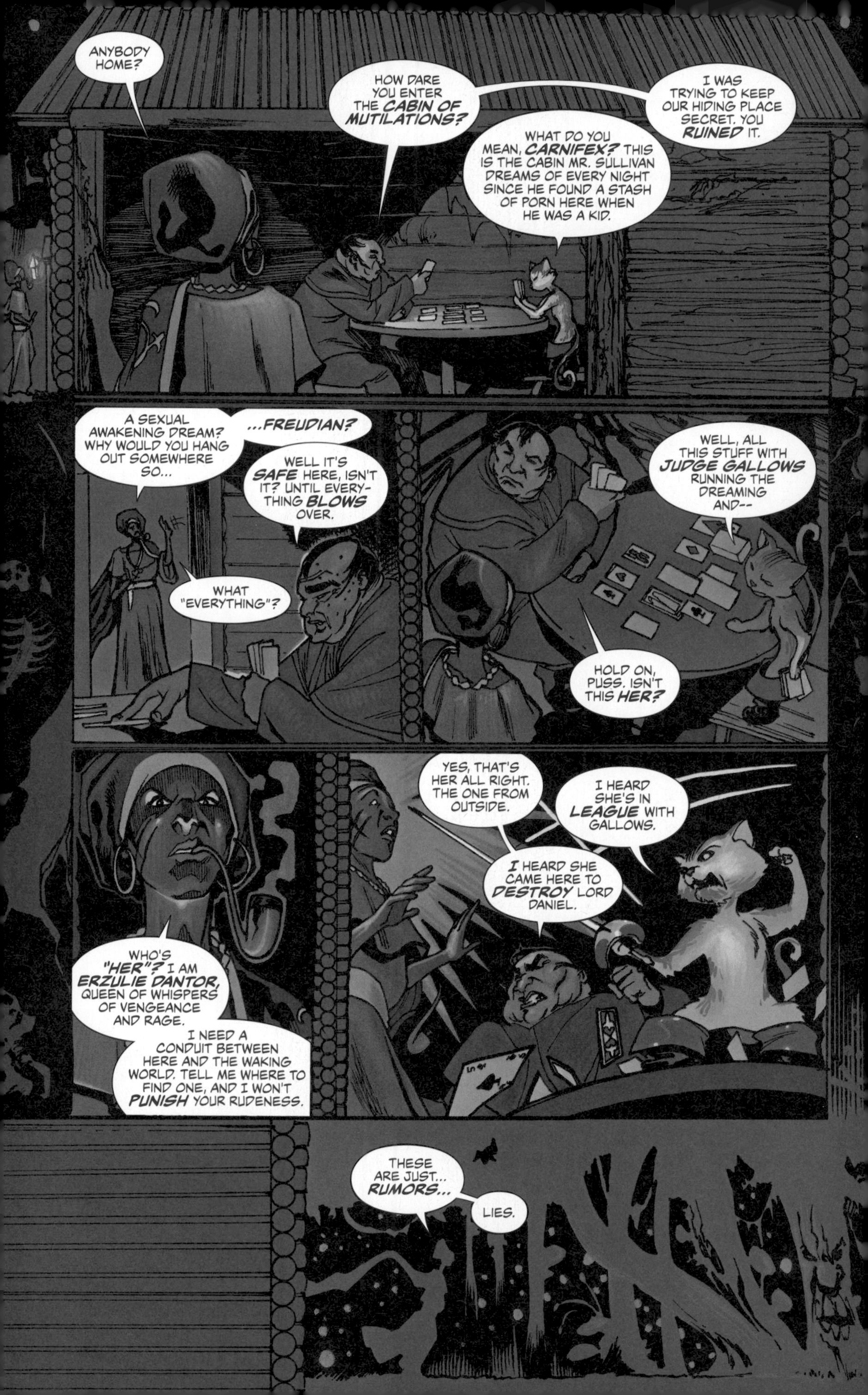

ANYBODY HOME?
HOW DARE YOU ENTER THE CABIN OF MUTILATIONS?
I WAS TRYING TO KEEP OUR HIDING PLACE SECRET. YOU RUINED IT.
WHAT DO YOU MEAN, CARNIFEX? THIS IS THE CABIN MR. SULLIVAN DREAMS OF EVERY NIGHT SINCE HE FOUND A STASH OF PORN HERE WHEN HE WAS A KID.
A SEXUAL AWAKENING DREAM? WHY WOULD YOU HANG OUT SOMEWHERE SO...
...FREUDIAN?
WELL IT'S SAFE HERE, ISN'T IT? UNTIL EVERY-THING BLOWS OVER.
WHAT "EVERYTHING"?
WELL, ALL THIS STUFF WITH JUDGE GALLOWS RUNNING THE DREAMING AND--
HOLD ON, PUSS. ISN'T THIS HER?
WHO'S "HER"? I AM ERZULIE DANTOR, QUEEN OF WHISPERS OF VENGEANCE AND RAGE.
I NEED A CONDUIT BETWEEN HERE AND THE WAKING WORLD. TELL ME WHERE TO FIND ONE, AND I WON'T PUNISH YOUR RUDENESS.
YES, THAT'S HER ALL RIGHT. THE ONE FROM OUTSIDE.
I HEARD SHE'S IN LEAGUE WITH GALLOWS.
I HEARD SHE CAME HERE TO DESTROY LORD DANIEL.
THESE ARE JUST... RUMORS...
LIES.

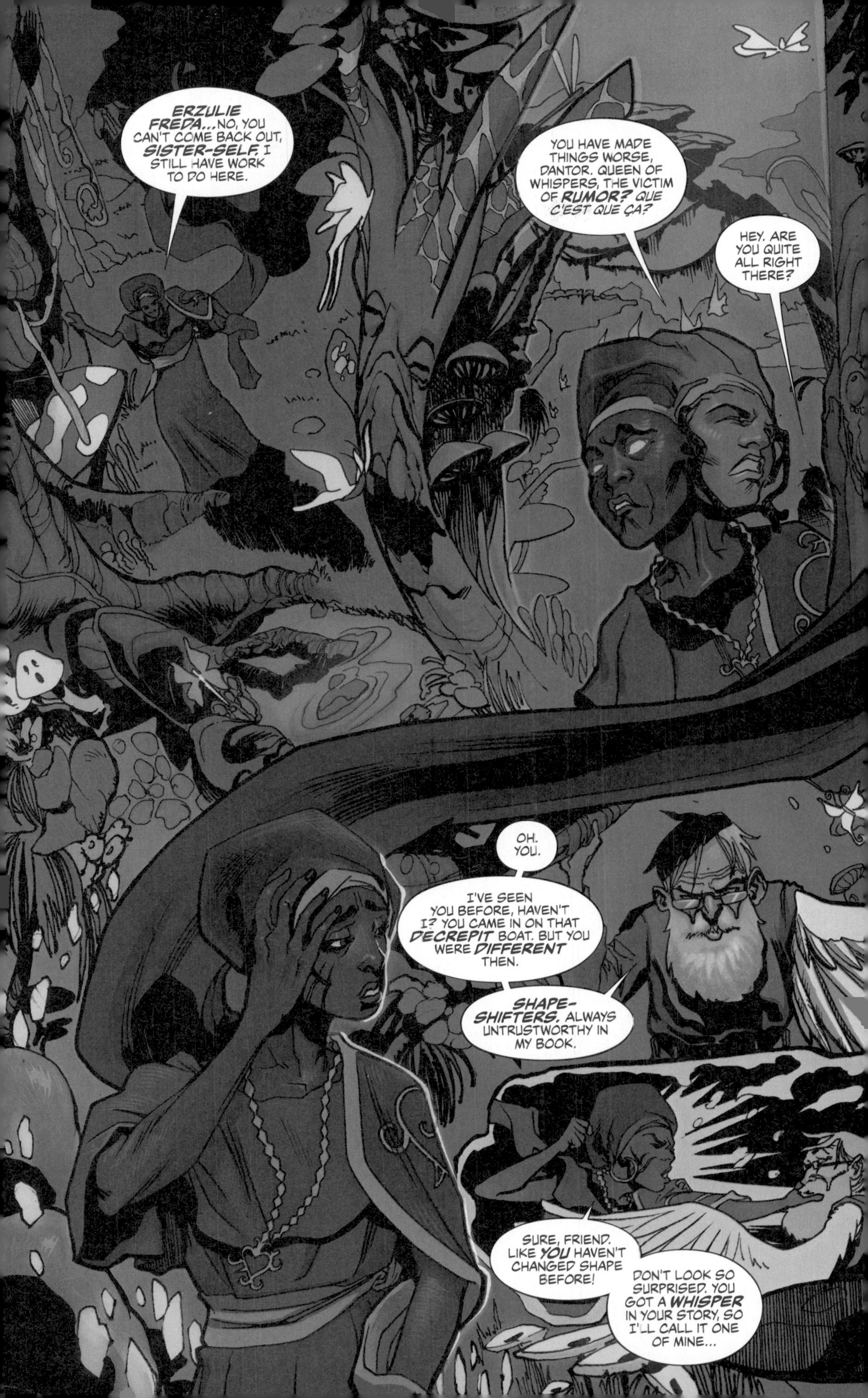
ERZULIE FREDA... NO, YOU CAN'T COME BACK OUT, SISTER-SELF. I STILL HAVE WORK TO DO HERE.
YOU HAVE MADE THINGS WORSE, DANTOR. QUEEN OF WHISPERS, THE VICTIM OF RUMOR? QUE C'EST QUE ÇA?
HEY. ARE YOU QUITE ALL RIGHT THERE?
OH. YOU.
I'VE SEEN YOU BEFORE, HAVEN'T I? YOU CAME IN ON THAT DECREPIT BOAT. BUT YOU WERE DIFFERENT THEN.
SHAPE-SHIFTERS. ALWAYS UNTRUSTWORTHY IN MY BOOK.
SURE, FRIEND. LIKE YOU HAVEN'T CHANGED SHAPE BEFORE!
DON'T LOOK SO SURPRISED. YOU GOT A WHISPER IN YOUR STORY, SO I'LL CALL IT ONE OF MINE...

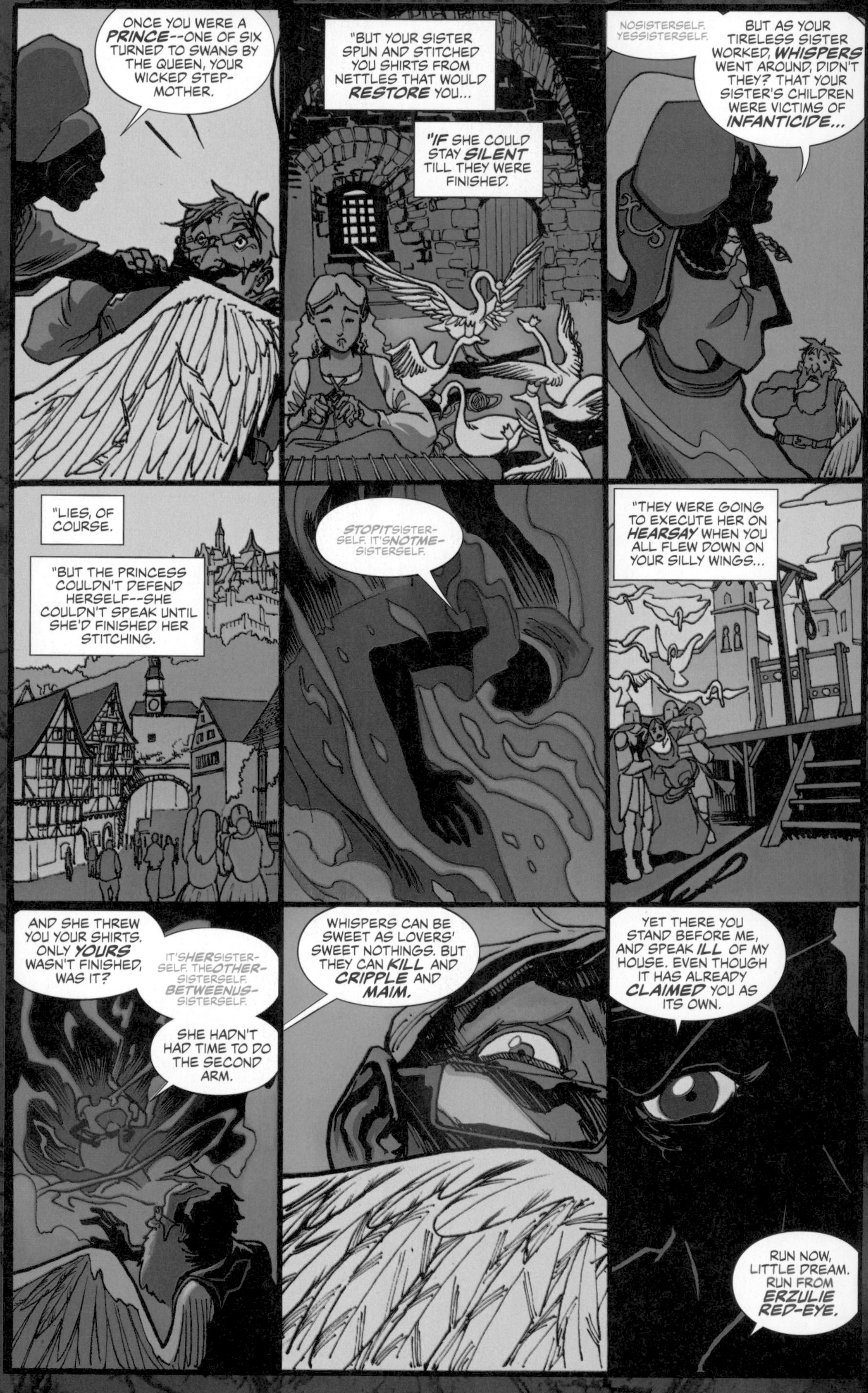

ONCE YOU WERE A PRINCE--ONE OF SIX TURNED TO SWANS BY THE QUEEN, YOUR WICKED STEP-MOTHER.
"BUT YOUR SISTER SPUN AND STITCHED YOU SHIRTS FROM NETTLES THAT WOULD RESTORE YOU...
"IF SHE COULD STAY SILENT TILL THEY WERE FINISHED.
NOSISTERSELF. YESSISTERSELF.
BUT AS YOUR TIRELESS SISTER WORKED, WHISPERS WENT AROUND, DIDN'T THEY? THAT YOUR SISTER'S CHILDREN WERE VICTIMS OF INFANTICIDE...
"LIES, OF COURSE.
"BUT THE PRINCESS COULDN'T DEFEND HERSELF--SHE COULDN'T SPEAK UNTIL SHE'D FINISHED HER STITCHING.
STOPITSISTER-SELF. IT'SNOTME-SISTERSELF.
"THEY WERE GOING TO EXECUTE HER ON HEARSAY WHEN YOU ALL FLEW DOWN ON YOUR SILLY WINGS...
AND SHE THREW YOU YOUR SHIRTS. ONLY YOURS WASN'T FINISHED, WAS IT?
IT'SHERSISTER-SELF. THEOTHER-SISTERSELF. BETWEENUS-SISTERSELF.
SHE HADN'T HAD TIME TO DO THE SECOND ARM.
WHISPERS CAN BE SWEET AS LOVERS' SWEET NOTHINGS. BUT THEY CAN KILL AND CRIPPLE AND MAIM.
YET THERE YOU STAND BEFORE ME, AND SPEAK ILL OF MY HOUSE. EVEN THOUGH IT HAS ALREADY CLAIMED YOU AS ITS OWN.
RUN NOW, LITTLE DREAM. RUN FROM ERZULIE RED-EYE.

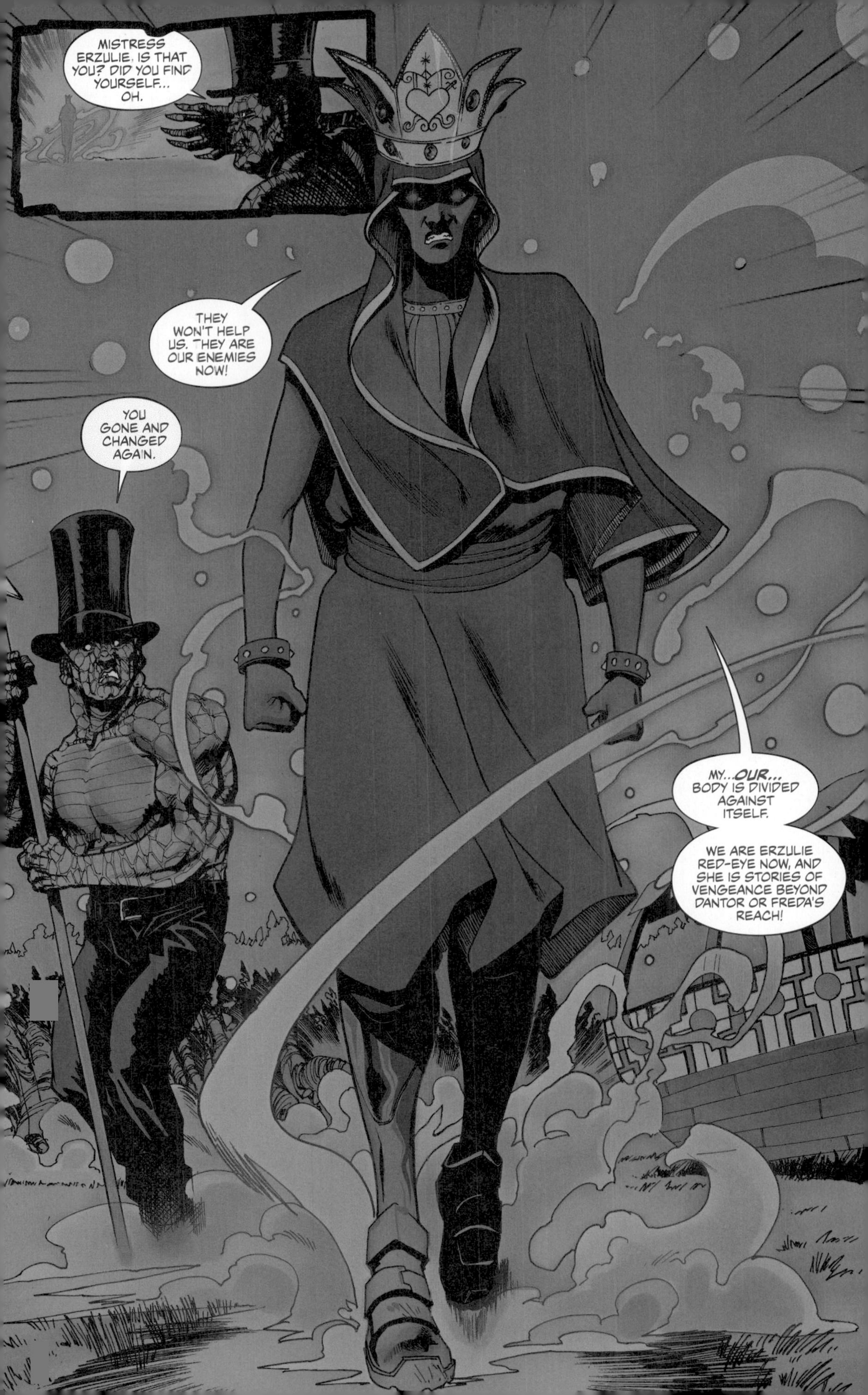
MISTRESS ERZULIE, IS THAT YOU? DID YOU FIND YOURSELF... OH.
THEY WON'T HELP US. THEY ARE OUR ENEMIES NOW!
YOU GONE AND CHANGED AGAIN.
MY...OUR... BODY IS DIVIDED AGAINST ITSELF.
WE ARE ERZULIE RED-EYE NOW, AND SHE IS STORIES OF VENGEANCE BEYOND DANTOR OR FREDA'S REACH!

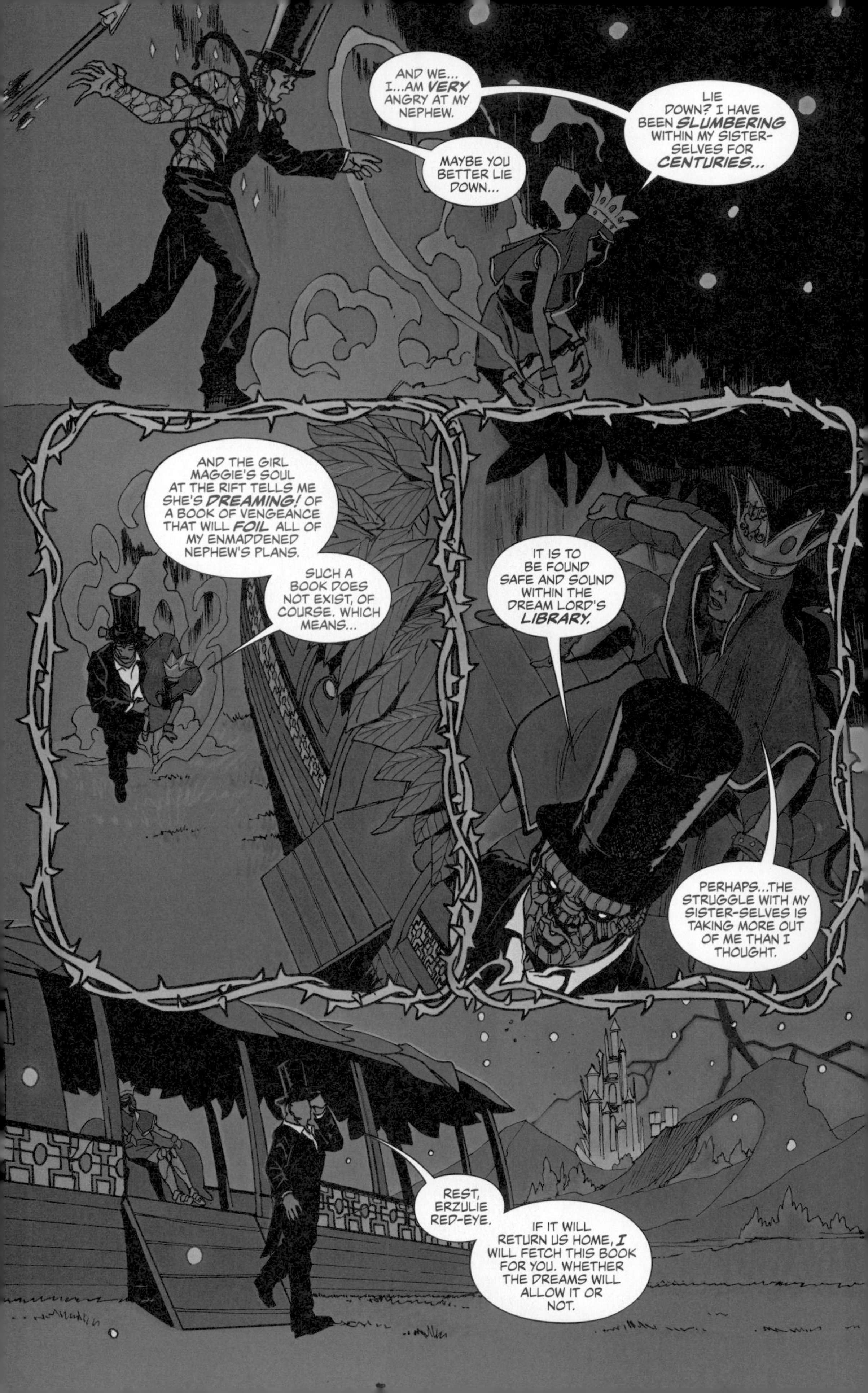
AND WE... I...AM VERY ANGRY AT MY NEPHEW.
MAYBE YOU BETTER LIE DOWN...
LIE DOWN? I HAVE BEEN SLUMBERING WITHIN MY SISTER-SELVES FOR CENTURIES...
AND THE GIRL MAGGIE'S SOUL AT THE RIFT TELLS ME SHE'S DREAMING! OF A BOOK OF VENGEANCE THAT WILL FOIL ALL OF MY ENMADDENED NEPHEW'S PLANS.
SUCH A BOOK DOES NOT EXIST, OF COURSE. WHICH MEANS...
IT IS TO BE FOUND SAFE AND SOUND WITHIN THE DREAM LORD'S LIBRARY.
PERHAPS...THE STRUGGLE WITH MY SISTER-SELVES IS TAKING MORE OUT OF ME THAN I THOUGHT.
REST, ERZULIE RED-EYE.
IF IT WILL RETURN US HOME, I WILL FETCH THIS BOOK FOR YOU. WHETHER THE DREAMS WILL ALLOW IT OR NOT.

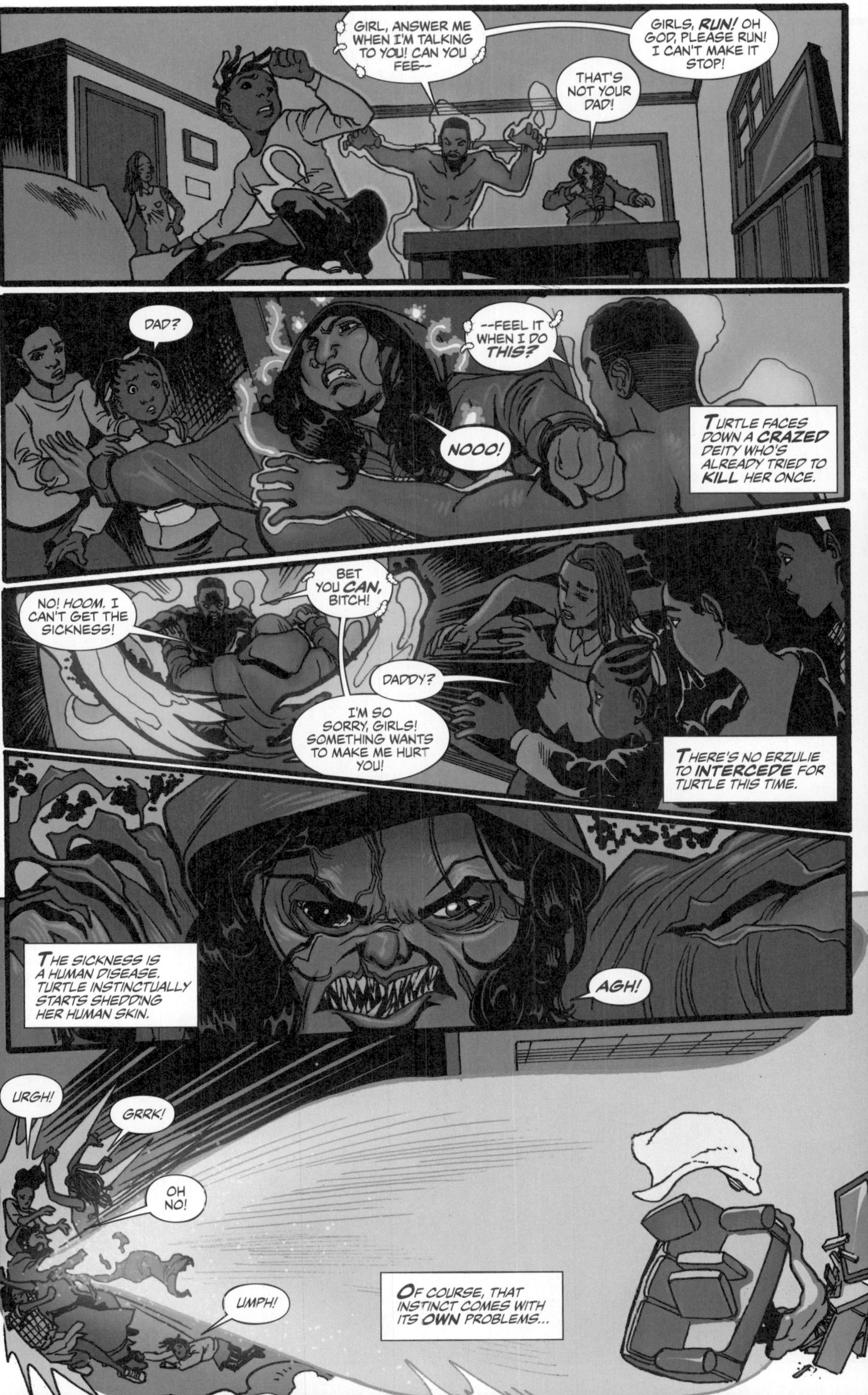
GIRL, ANSWER ME WHEN I'M TALKING TO YOU! CAN YOU FEE--
GIRLS, RUN! OH GOD, PLEASE RUN! I CAN'T MAKE IT STOP!
THAT'S NOT YOUR DAD!
DAD?
--FEEL IT WHEN I DO THIS?
NOOO!
TURTLE FACES DOWN A CRAZED DEITY WHO'S ALREADY TRIED TO KILL HER ONCE.
NO! HOOM. I CAN'T GET THE SICKNESS!
BET YOU CAN, BITCH!
DADDY?
I'M SO SORRY, GIRLS! SOMETHING WANTS TO MAKE ME HURT YOU!
THERE'S NO ERZULIE TO INTERCEDE FOR TURTLE THIS TIME.
THE SICKNESS IS A HUMAN DISEASE. TURTLE INSTINCTUALLY STARTS SHEDDING HER HUMAN SKIN.
AGH!
URGH!
GRRK!
OH NO!
UMPH!
OF COURSE, THAT INSTINCT COMES WITH ITS OWN PROBLEMS...

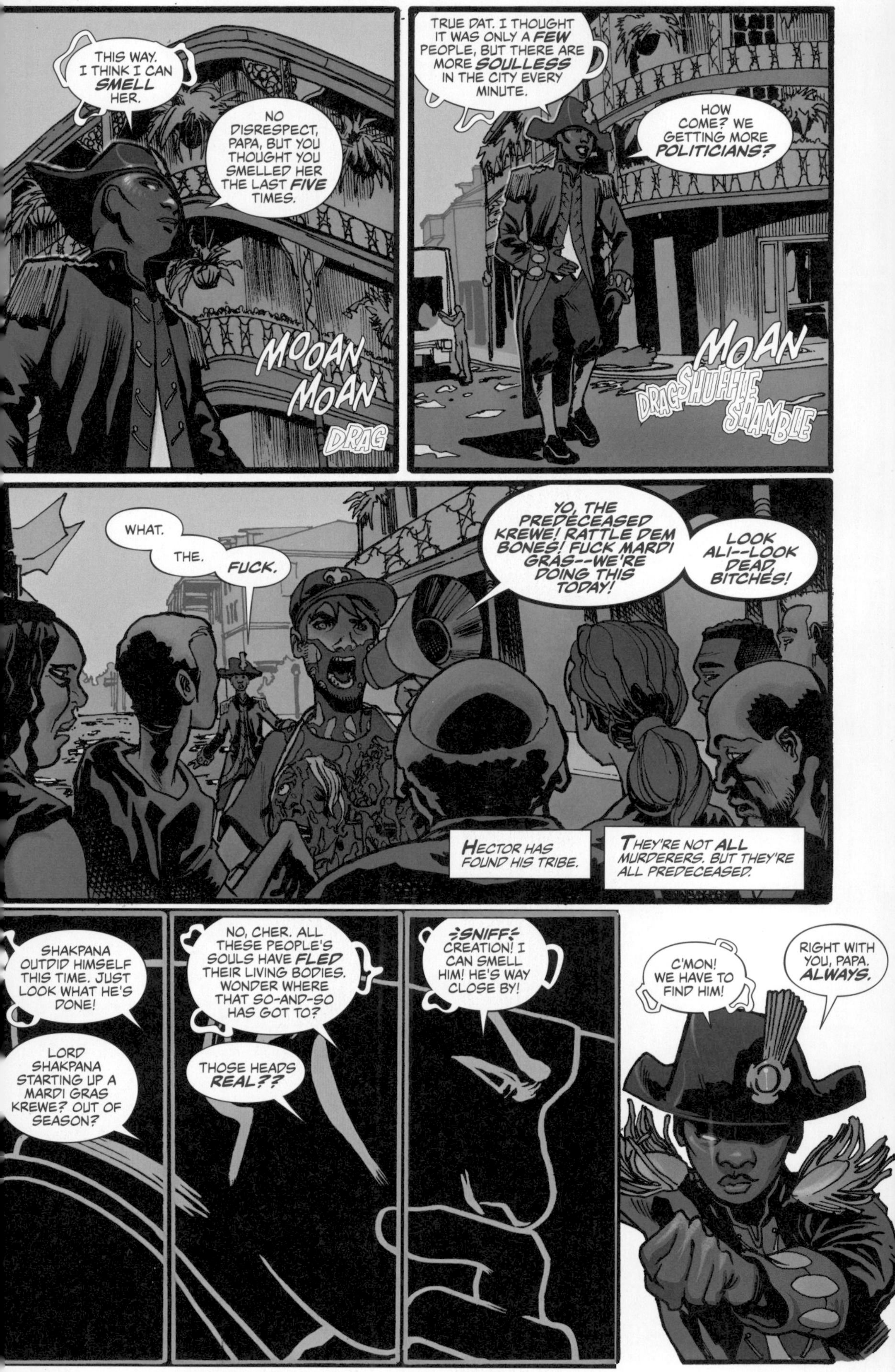

THIS WAY. I THINK I CAN SMELL HER.
NO DISRESPECT, PAPA, BUT YOU THOUGHT YOU SMELLED HER THE LAST FIVE TIMES.
MOOAN
MOAN
DRAG
TRUE DAT. I THOUGHT IT WAS ONLY A FEW PEOPLE, BUT THERE ARE MORE SOULLESS IN THE CITY EVERY MINUTE.
HOW COME? WE GETTING MORE POLITICIANS?
MOAN
DRAG SHUFFLE SHAMBLE
WHAT.
THE.
FUCK.
YO, THE PREDECEASED KREWE! RATTLE DEM BONES! FUCK MARDI GRAS--WE'RE DOING THIS TODAY!
LOOK ALI--LOOK DEAD BITCHES!
HECTOR HAS FOUND HIS TRIBE.
THEY'RE NOT ALL MURDERERS. BUT THEY'RE ALL PREDECEASED.
SHAKPANA OUTDID HIMSELF THIS TIME. JUST LOOK WHAT HE'S DONE!
LORD SHAKPANA STARTING UP A MARDI GRAS KREWE? OUT OF SEASON?
NO, CHER. ALL THESE PEOPLE'S SOULS HAVE FLED THEIR LIVING BODIES. WONDER WHERE THAT SO-AND-SO HAS GOT TO?
THOSE HEADS REAL??
SNIFF CREATION! I CAN SMELL HIM! HE'S WAY CLOSE BY!
C'MON! WE HAVE TO FIND HIM!
RIGHT WITH YOU, PAPA. ALWAYS.

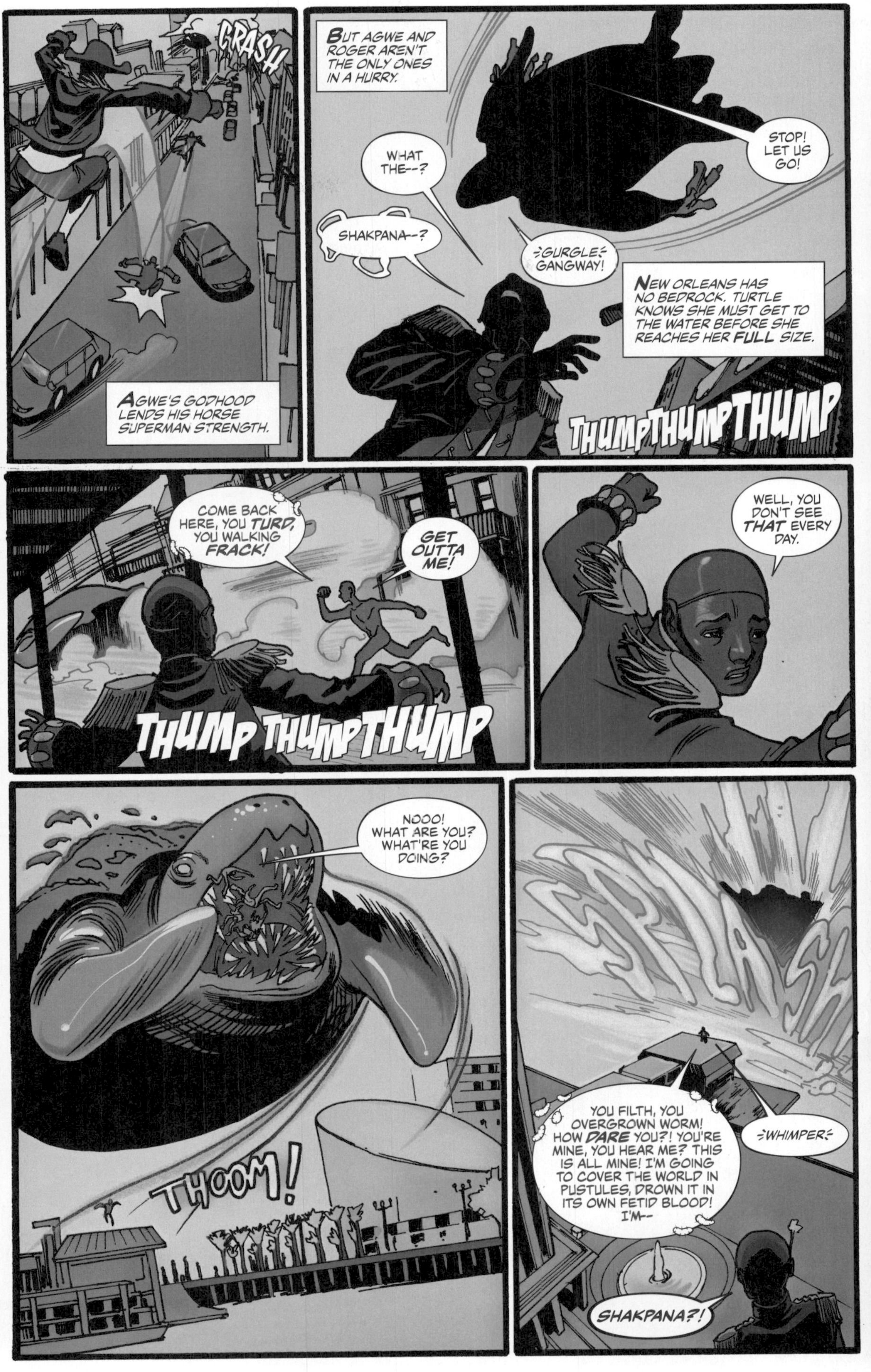
CRASH
AGWE'S GODHOOD LENDS HIS HORSE SUPERMAN STRENGTH.
BUT AGWE AND ROGER AREN'T THE ONLY ONES IN A HURRY.
STOP! LET US GO!
WHAT THE--?
SHAKPANA--?
=GURGLE= GANGWAY!
NEW ORLEANS HAS NO BEDROCK. TURTLE KNOWS SHE MUST GET TO THE WATER BEFORE SHE REACHES HER FULL SIZE.
THUMPTHUMPTHUMP
COME BACK HERE, YOU TURD, YOU WALKING FRACK!
GET OUTTA ME!
THUMP THUMPTHUMP
WELL, YOU DON'T SEE THAT EVERY DAY.
NOOO! WHAT ARE YOU? WHAT'RE YOU DOING?
THOOM!
SPLASH
YOU FILTH, YOU OVERGROWN WORM! HOW DARE YOU?! YOU'RE MINE, YOU HEAR ME? THIS IS ALL MINE! I'M GOING TO COVER THE WORLD IN PUSTULES, DROWN IT IN ITS OWN FETID BLOOD! I'M--
=WHIMPER=
SHAKPANA?!

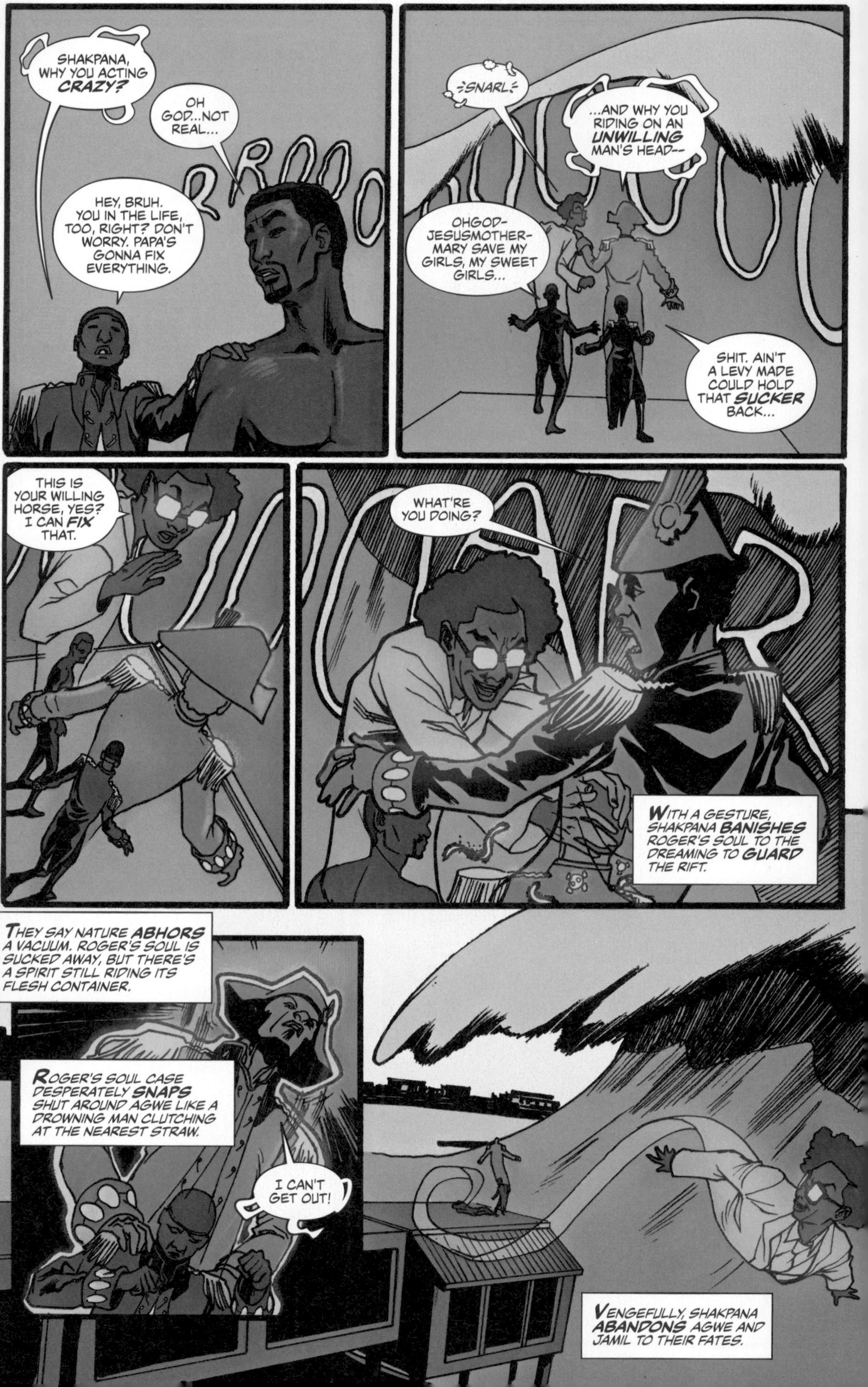
SHAKPANA, WHY YOU ACTING CRAZY?
OH GOD...NOT REAL...
RROOO
HEY, BRUH. YOU IN THE LIFE, TOO, RIGHT? DON'T WORRY. PAPA'S GONNA FIX EVERYTHING.
SNARL
...AND WHY YOU RIDING ON AN UNWILLING MAN'S HEAD--
OHGOD-JESUSMOTHER-MARY SAVE MY GIRLS, MY SWEET GIRLS...
SHIT. AIN'T A LEVY MADE COULD HOLD THAT SUCKER BACK...
THIS IS YOUR WILLING HORSE, YES? I CAN FIX THAT.
WHAT'RE YOU DOING?
WITH A GESTURE, SHAKPANA BANISHES ROGER'S SOUL TO THE DREAMING TO GUARD THE RIFT.
THEY SAY NATURE ABHORS A VACUUM. ROGER'S SOUL IS SUCKED AWAY, BUT THERE'S A SPIRIT STILL RIDING ITS FLESH CONTAINER.
ROGER'S SOUL CASE DESPERATELY SNAPS SHUT AROUND AGWE LIKE A DROWNING MAN CLUTCHING AT THE NEAREST STRAW.
I CAN'T GET OUT!
VENGEFULLY, SHAKPANA ABANDONS AGWE AND JAMIL TO THEIR FATES.

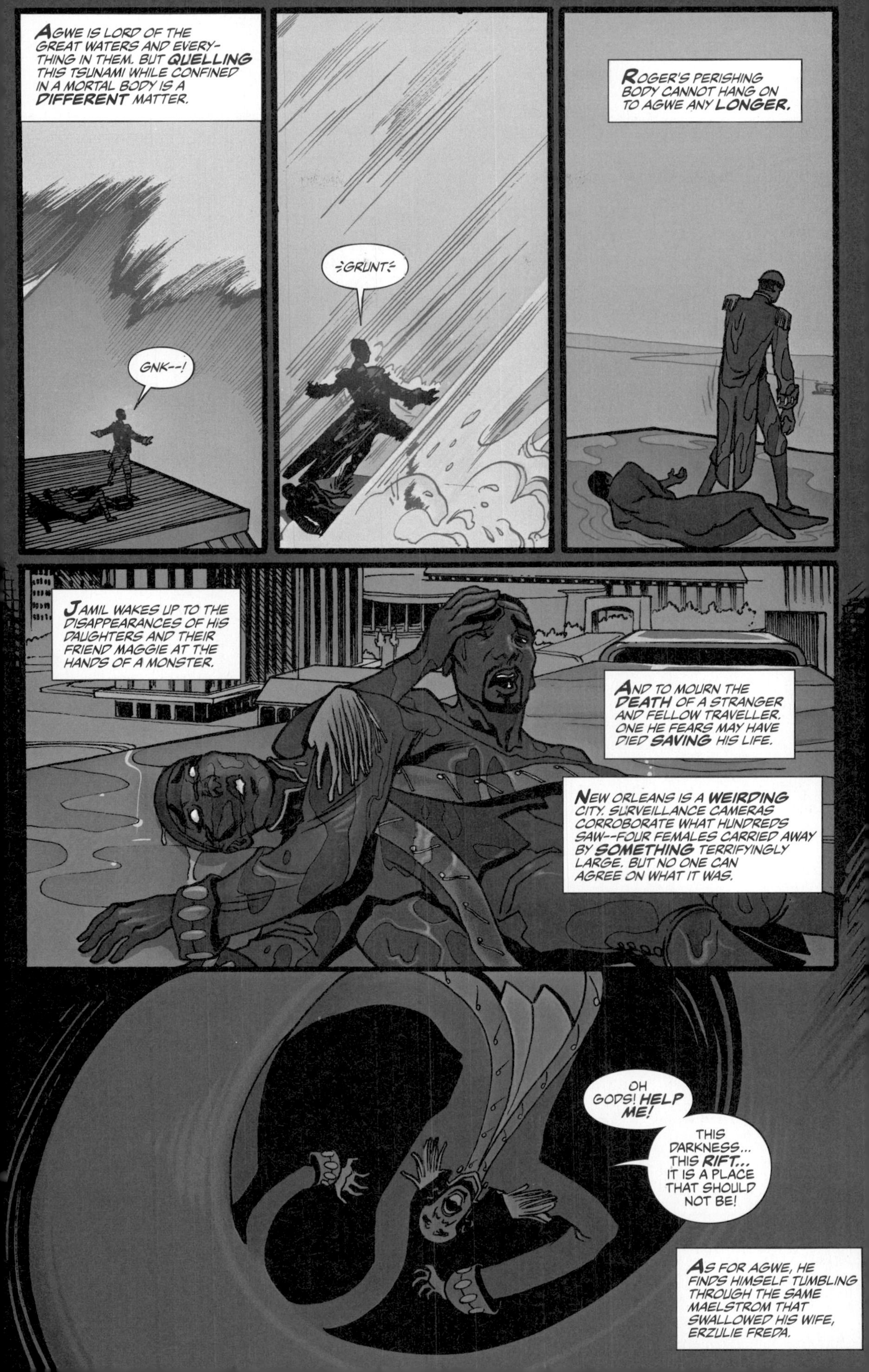
AGWE IS LORD OF THE GREAT WATERS AND EVERY-THING IN THEM. BUT QUELLING THIS TSUNAMI WHILE CONFINED IN A MORTAL BODY IS A DIFFERENT MATTER.
GNK--!
GRUNT
ROGER'S PERISHING BODY CANNOT HANG ON TO AGWE ANY LONGER.
JAMIL WAKES UP TO THE DISAPPEARANCES OF HIS DAUGHTERS AND THEIR FRIEND MAGGIE AT THE HANDS OF A MONSTER.
AND TO MOURN THE DEATH OF A STRANGER AND FELLOW TRAVELLER. ONE HE FEARS MAY HAVE DIED SAVING HIS LIFE.
NEW ORLEANS IS A WEIRDING CITY. SURVEILLANCE CAMERAS CORROBORATE WHAT HUNDREDS SAW--FOUR FEMALES CARRIED AWAY BY SOMETHING TERRIFYINGLY LARGE. BUT NO ONE CAN AGREE ON WHAT IT WAS.
OH GODS! HELP ME!
THIS DARKNESS... THIS RIFT... IT IS A PLACE THAT SHOULD NOT BE!
AS FOR AGWE, HE FINDS HIMSELF TUMBLING THROUGH THE SAME MAELSTROM THAT SWALLOWED HIS WIFE, ERZULIE FREDA.

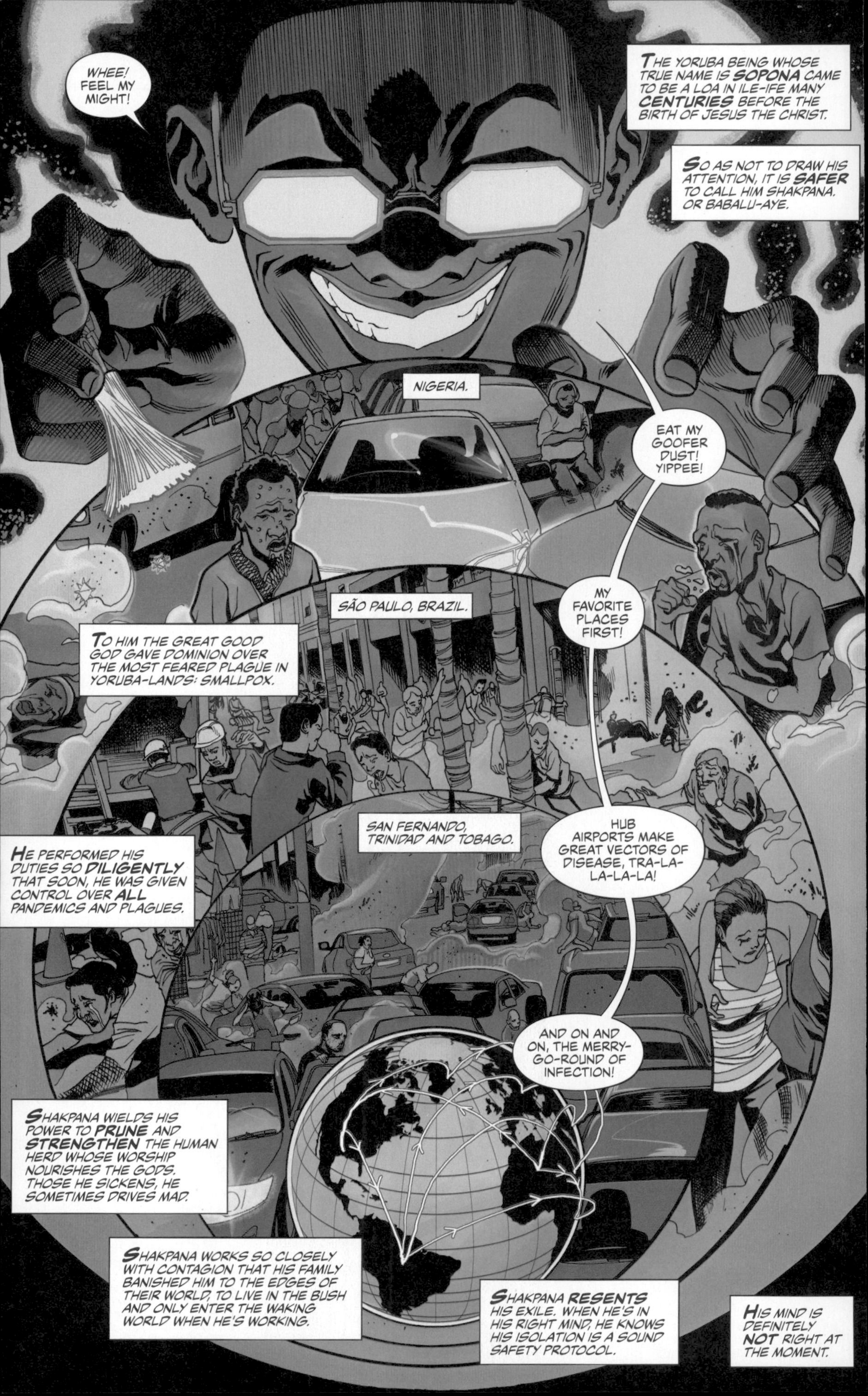
WHEE! FEEL MY MIGHT!
THE YORUBA BEING WHOSE TRUE NAME IS SOPONA CAME TO BE A LOA IN ILE-IFE MANY CENTURIES BEFORE THE BIRTH OF JESUS THE CHRIST.
SO AS NOT TO DRAW HIS ATTENTION, IT IS SAFER TO CALL HIM SHAKPANA. OR BABALU-AYE.
NIGERIA.
EAT MY GOOFER DUST! YIPPEE!
SÃO PAULO, BRAZIL.
MY FAVORITE PLACES FIRST!
TO HIM THE GREAT GOOD GOD GAVE DOMINION OVER THE MOST FEARED PLAGUE IN YORUBA-LANDS: SMALLPOX.
SAN FERNANDO, TRINIDAD AND TOBAGO.
HUB AIRPORTS MAKE GREAT VECTORS OF DISEASE, TRA-LA-LA-LA-LA!
HE PERFORMED HIS DUTIES SO DILIGENTLY THAT SOON, HE WAS GIVEN CONTROL OVER ALL PANDEMICS AND PLAGUES.
AND ON AND ON, THE MERRY-GO-ROUND OF INFECTION!
SHAKPANA WIELDS HIS POWER TO PRUNE AND STRENGTHEN THE HUMAN HERD WHOSE WORSHIP NOURISHES THE GODS. THOSE HE SICKENS, HE SOMETIMES DRIVES MAD.
SHAKPANA WORKS SO CLOSELY WITH CONTAGION THAT HIS FAMILY BANISHED HIM TO THE EDGES OF THEIR WORLD, TO LIVE IN THE BUSH AND ONLY ENTER THE WAKING WORLD WHEN HE'S WORKING.
SHAKPANA RESENTS HIS EXILE. WHEN HE'S IN HIS RIGHT MIND, HE KNOWS HIS ISOLATION IS A SOUND SAFETY PROTOCOL.
HIS MIND IS DEFINITELY NOT RIGHT AT THE MOMENT.

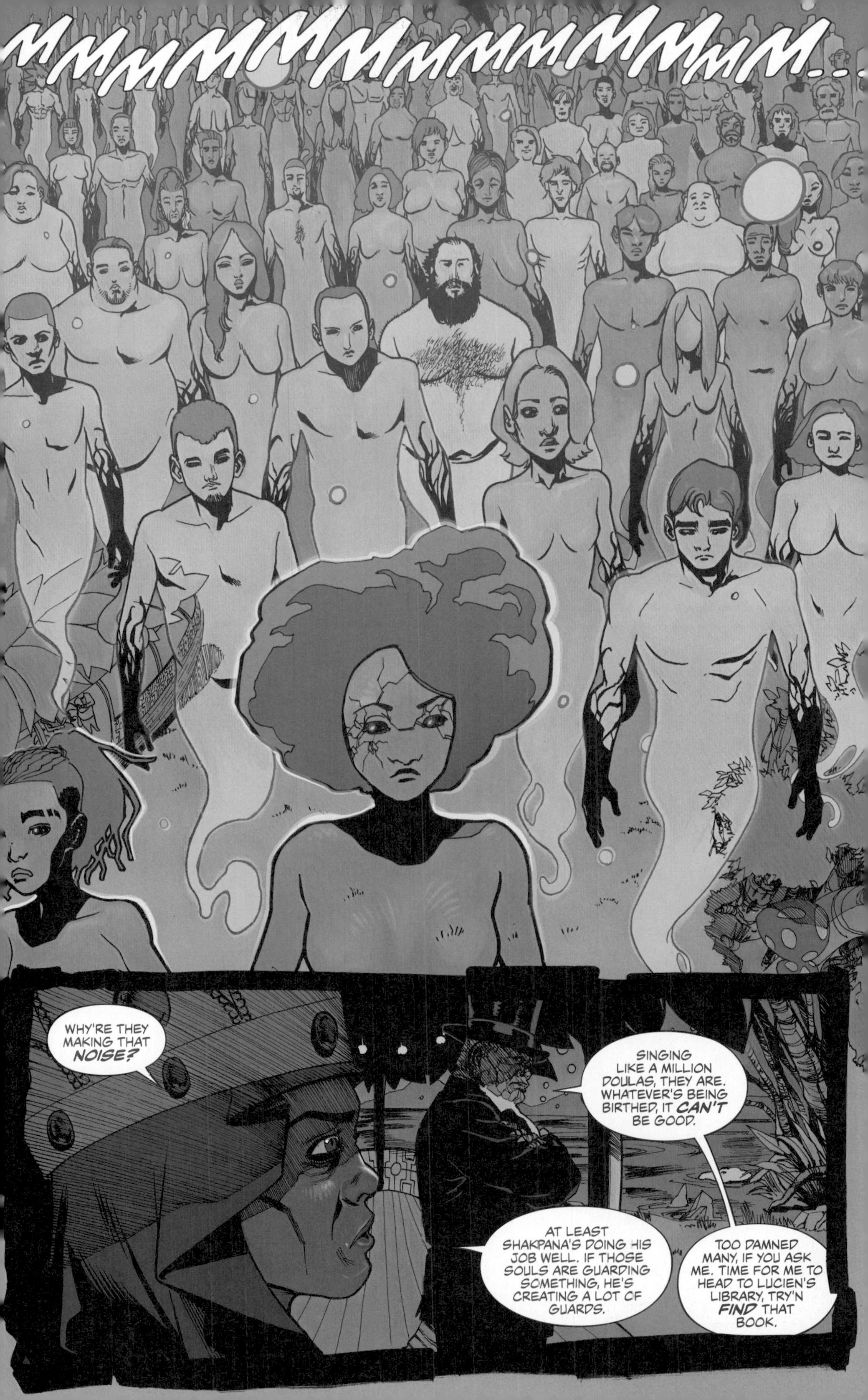
MMMMMMMMMMMMMMM...
WHY'RE THEY MAKING THAT NOISE?
SINGING LIKE A MILLION DOULAS, THEY ARE. WHATEVER'S BEING BIRTHED, IT CAN'T BE GOOD.
AT LEAST SHAKPANA'S DOING HIS JOB WELL. IF THOSE SOULS ARE GUARDING SOMETHING, HE'S CREATING A LOT OF GUARDS.
TOO DAMNED MANY, IF YOU ASK ME. TIME FOR ME TO HEAD TO LUCIEN'S LIBRARY, TRY'N FIND THAT BOOK.

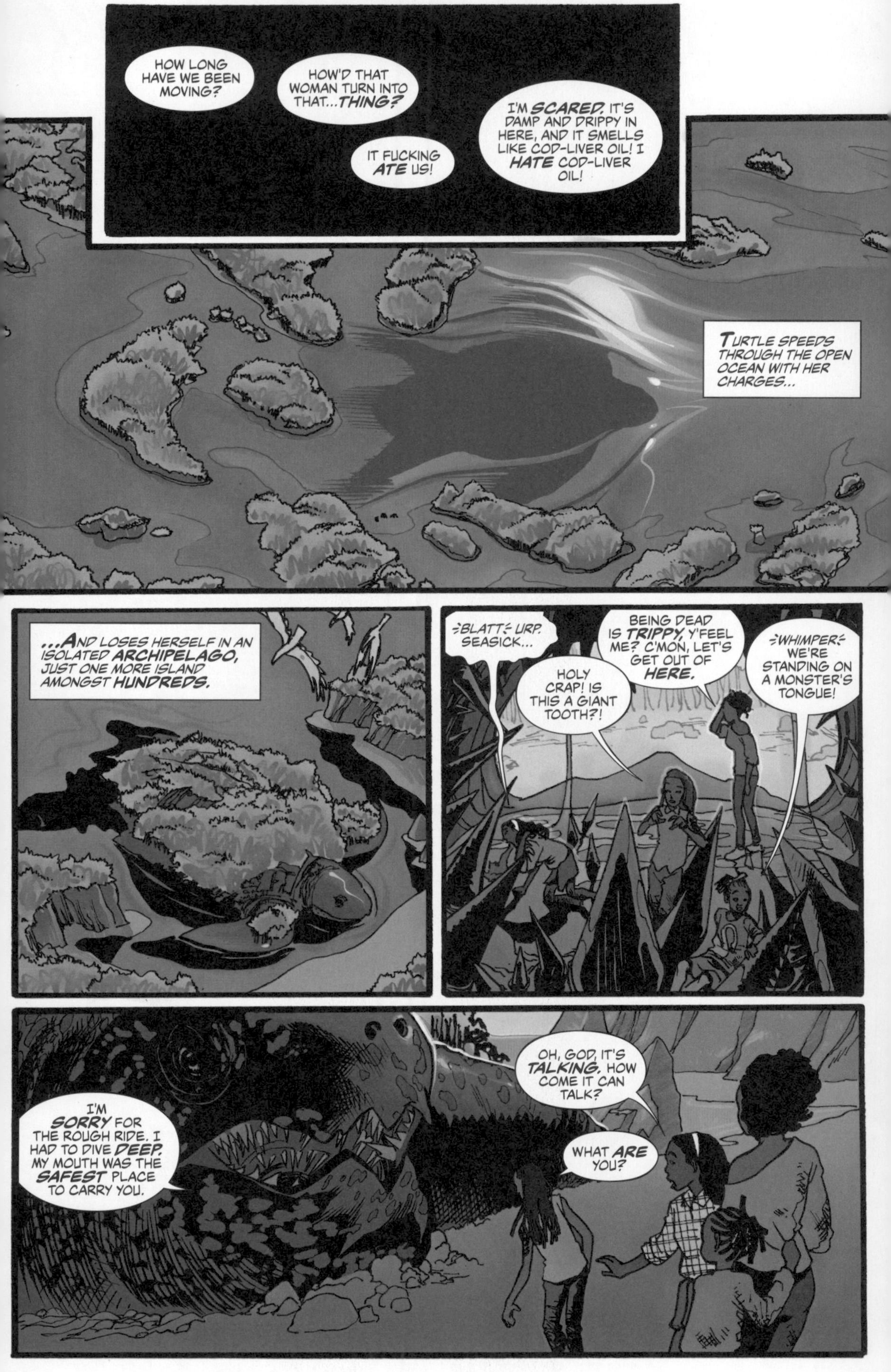
HOW LONG HAVE WE BEEN MOVING?
HOW'D THAT WOMAN TURN INTO THAT...THING?
IT FUCKING ATE US!
I'M SCARED. IT'S DAMP AND DRIPPY IN HERE, AND IT SMELLS LIKE COD-LIVER OIL! I HATE COD-LIVER OIL!
TURTLE SPEEDS THROUGH THE OPEN OCEAN WITH HER CHARGES...
...AND LOSES HERSELF IN AN ISOLATED ARCHIPELAGO, JUST ONE MORE ISLAND AMONGST HUNDREDS.
=BLATT= URP. SEASICK...
HOLY CRAP! IS THIS A GIANT TOOTH?!
BEING DEAD IS TRIPPY, Y'FEEL ME? C'MON, LET'S GET OUT OF HERE.
=WHIMPER= WE'RE STANDING ON A MONSTER'S TONGUE!
OH, GOD, IT'S TALKING. HOW COME IT CAN TALK?
I'M SORRY FOR THE ROUGH RIDE. I HAD TO DIVE DEEP. MY MOUTH WAS THE SAFEST PLACE TO CARRY YOU.
WHAT ARE YOU?

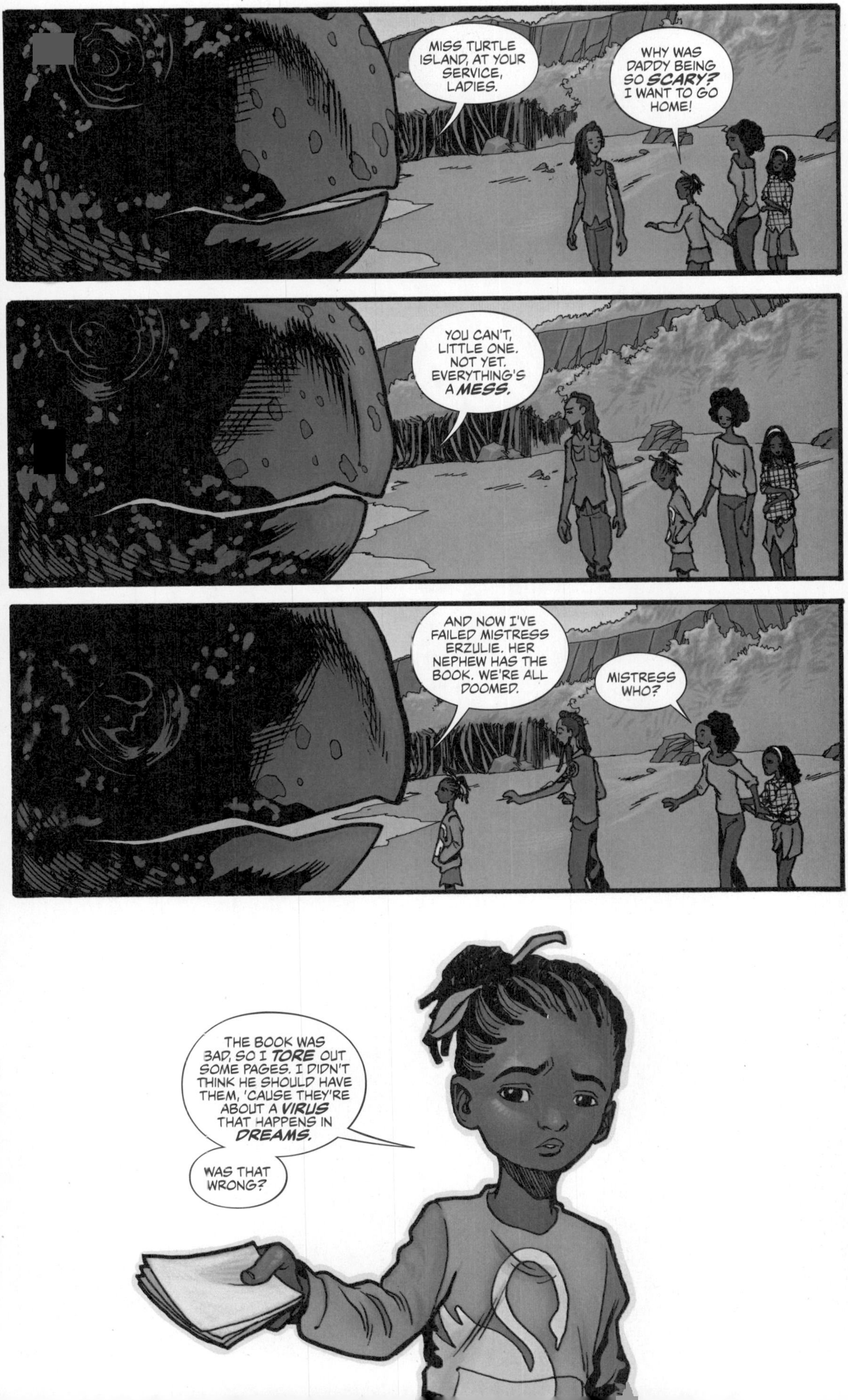
MISS TURTLE ISLAND, AT YOUR SERVICE, LADIES.
WHY WAS DADDY BEING SO SCARY? I WANT TO GO HOME!
YOU CAN'T, LITTLE ONE. NOT YET. EVERYTHING'S A MESS.
AND NOW I'VE FAILED MISTRESS ERZULIE. HER NEPHEW HAS THE BOOK. WE'RE ALL DOOMED.
MISTRESS WHO?
THE BOOK WAS BAD, SO I TORE OUT SOME PAGES. I DIDN'T THINK HE SHOULD HAVE THEM, 'CAUSE THEY'RE ABOUT A VIRUS THAT HAPPENS IN DREAMS.
WAS THAT WRONG?

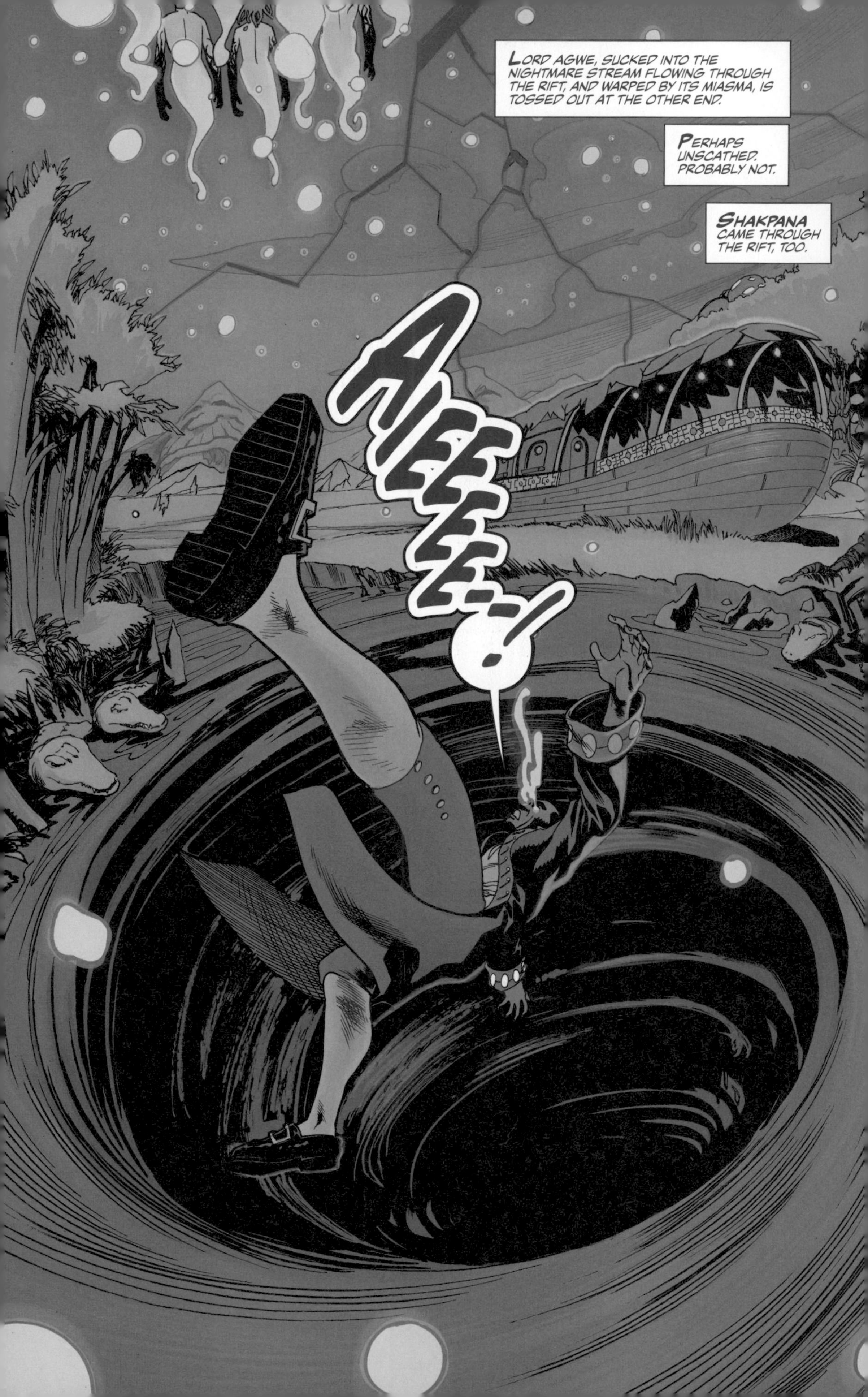
LORD AGWE, SUCKED INTO THE NIGHTMARE STREAM FLOWING THROUGH THE RIFT, AND WARPED BY ITS MIASMA, IS TOSSED OUT AT THE OTHER END.
PERHAPS UNSCATHED. PROBABLY NOT.
SHAKPANA CAME THROUGH THE RIFT, TOO.
AIEEEE--!

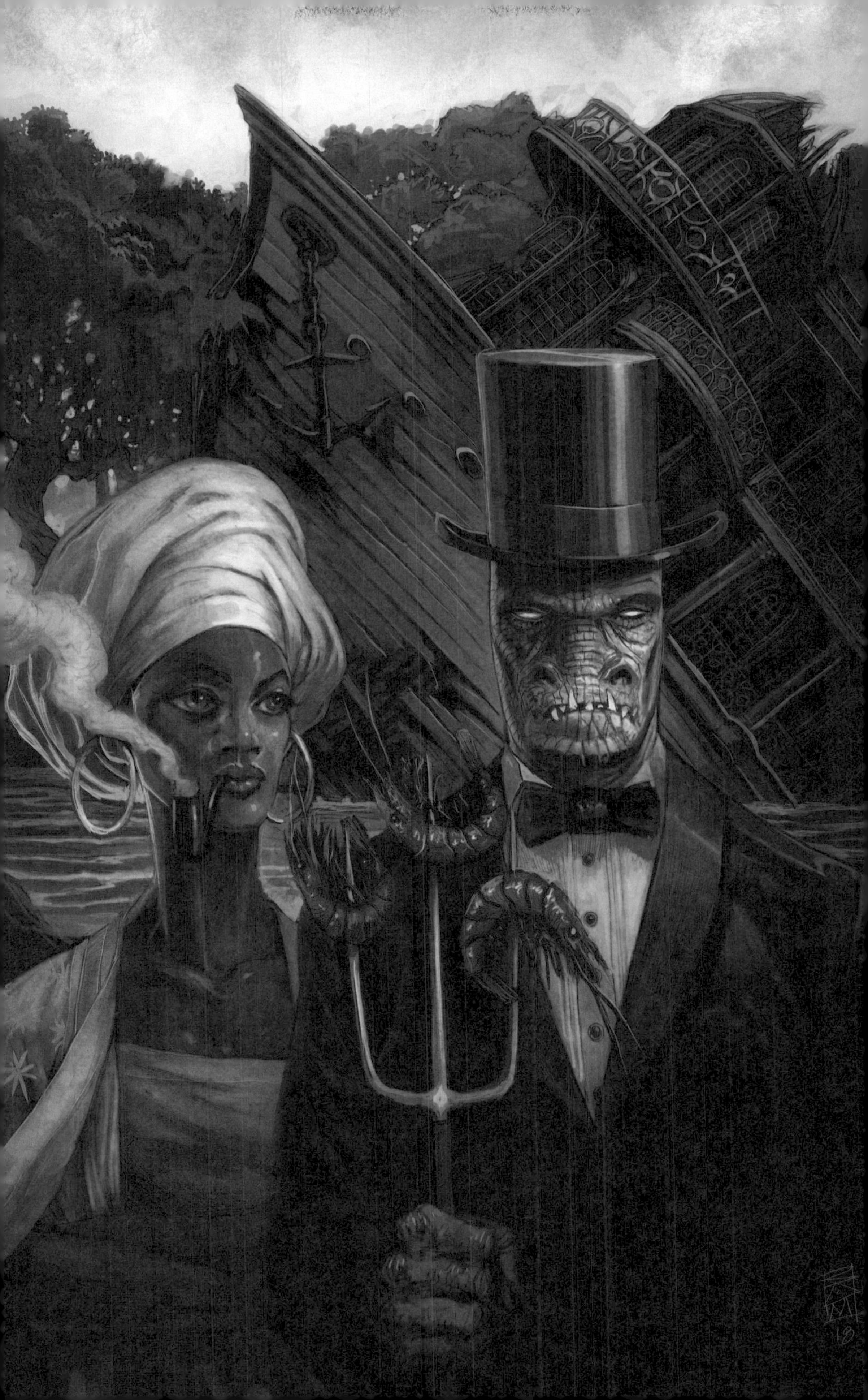

HOUSE OF WHISPERS

Open the Unusual Door

WRITTEN BY
Nalo Hopkinson
and *Dan Watters*

ILLUSTRATED BY
Dominike "DOMO" Stanton

COLORS BY
John Rauch

LETTERS BY
AndWorld Design

COVER ART BY
Sean Andrew Murray

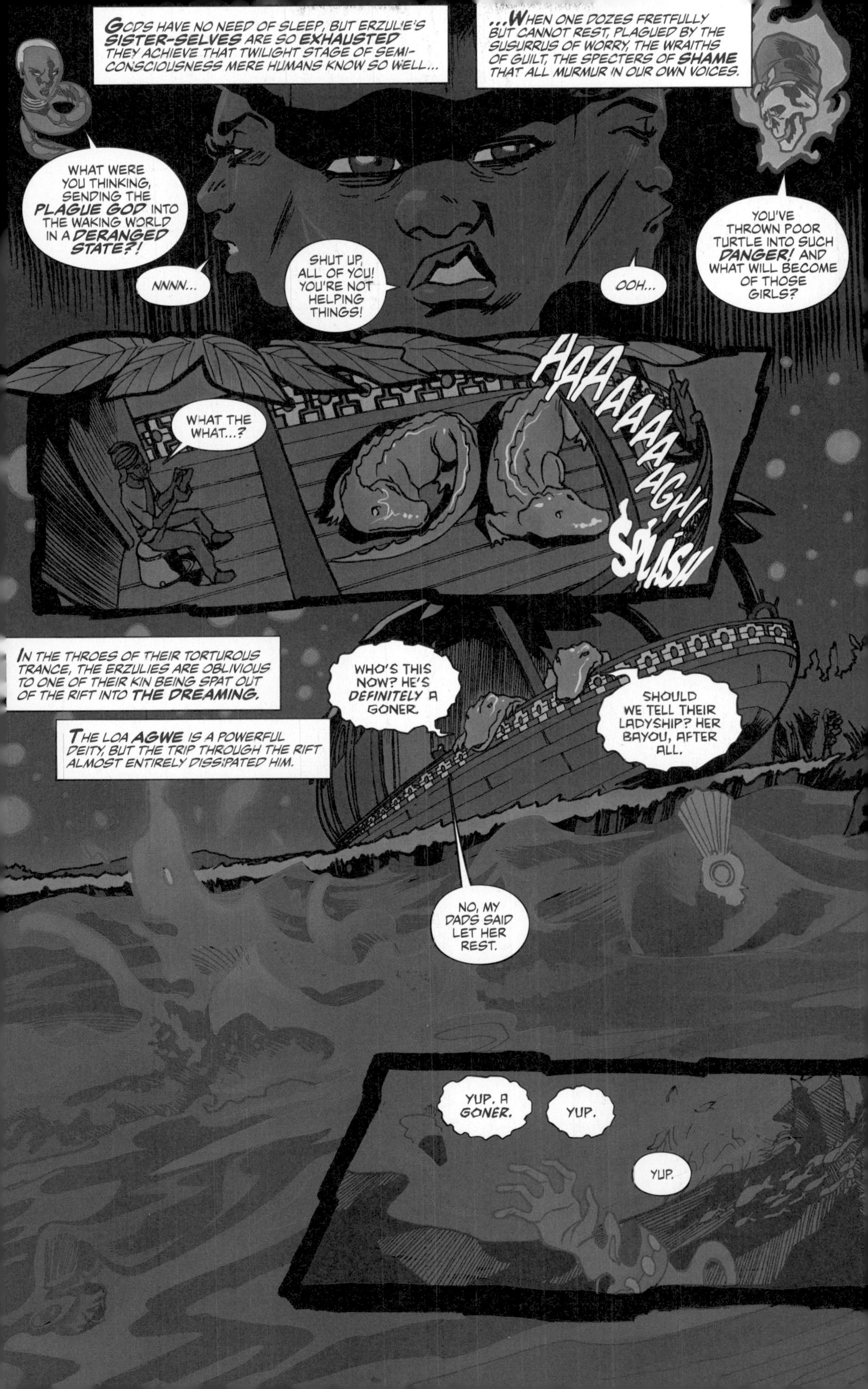
GODS HAVE NO NEED OF SLEEP, BUT ERZULIE'S SISTER-SELVES ARE SO EXHAUSTED THEY ACHIEVE THAT TWILIGHT STAGE OF SEMI-CONSCIOUSNESS MERE HUMANS KNOW SO WELL...
...WHEN ONE DOZES FRETFULLY BUT CANNOT REST, PLAGUED BY THE SUSURRUS OF WORRY, THE WRAITHS OF GUILT, THE SPECTERS OF SHAME THAT ALL MURMUR IN OUR OWN VOICES.
WHAT WERE YOU THINKING, SENDING THE PLAGUE GOD INTO THE WAKING WORLD IN A DERANGED STATE?!
YOU'VE THROWN POOR TURTLE INTO SUCH DANGER! AND WHAT WILL BECOME OF THOSE GIRLS?
NNNN...
SHUT UP, ALL OF YOU! YOU'RE NOT HELPING THINGS!
OOH...
HAAAAAAAAGH!
WHAT THE WHAT...?
SPLASH
IN THE THROES OF THEIR TORTUROUS TRANCE, THE ERZULIES ARE OBLIVIOUS TO ONE OF THEIR KIN BEING SPAT OUT OF THE RIFT INTO THE DREAMING.
THE LOA AGWE IS A POWERFUL DEITY, BUT THE TRIP THROUGH THE RIFT ALMOST ENTIRELY DISSIPATED HIM.
WHO'S THIS NOW? HE'S DEFINITELY A GONER.
SHOULD WE TELL THEIR LADYSHIP? HER BAYOU, AFTER ALL.
NO, MY DADS SAID LET HER REST.
YUP. A GONER.
YUP.
YUP.

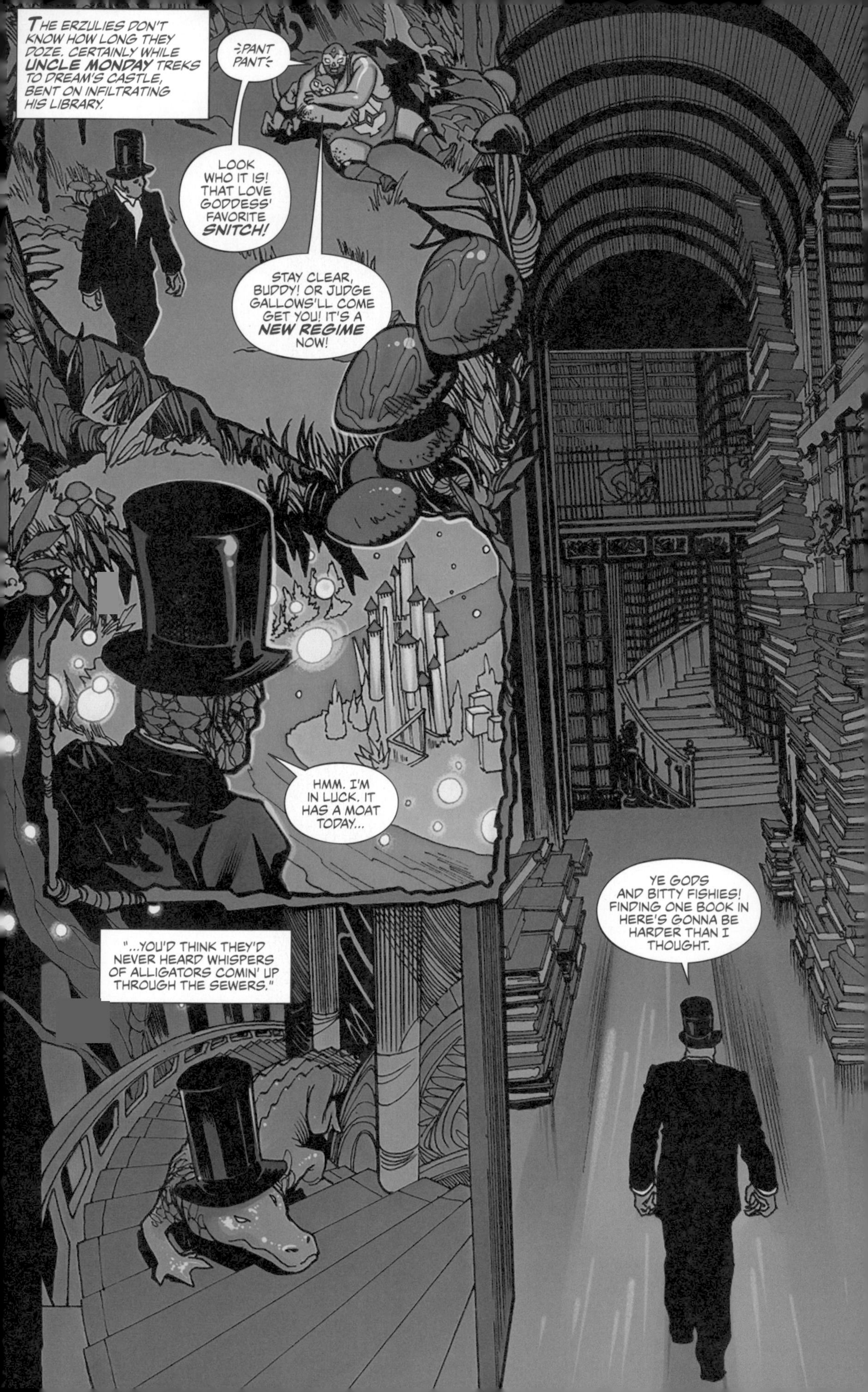
THE ERZULIES DON'T KNOW HOW LONG THEY DOZE. CERTAINLY WHILE UNCLE MONDAY TREKS TO DREAM'S CASTLE, BENT ON INFILTRATING HIS LIBRARY.
PANT PANT
LOOK WHO IT IS! THAT LOVE GODDESS' FAVORITE SNITCH!
STAY CLEAR, BUDDY! OR JUDGE GALLOWS'LL COME GET YOU! IT'S A NEW REGIME NOW!
HMM. I'M IN LUCK. IT HAS A MOAT TODAY...
"...YOU'D THINK THEY'D NEVER HEARD WHISPERS OF ALLIGATORS COMIN' UP THROUGH THE SEWERS."
YE GODS AND BITTY FISHIES! FINDING ONE BOOK IN HERE'S GONNA BE HARDER THAN I THOUGHT.

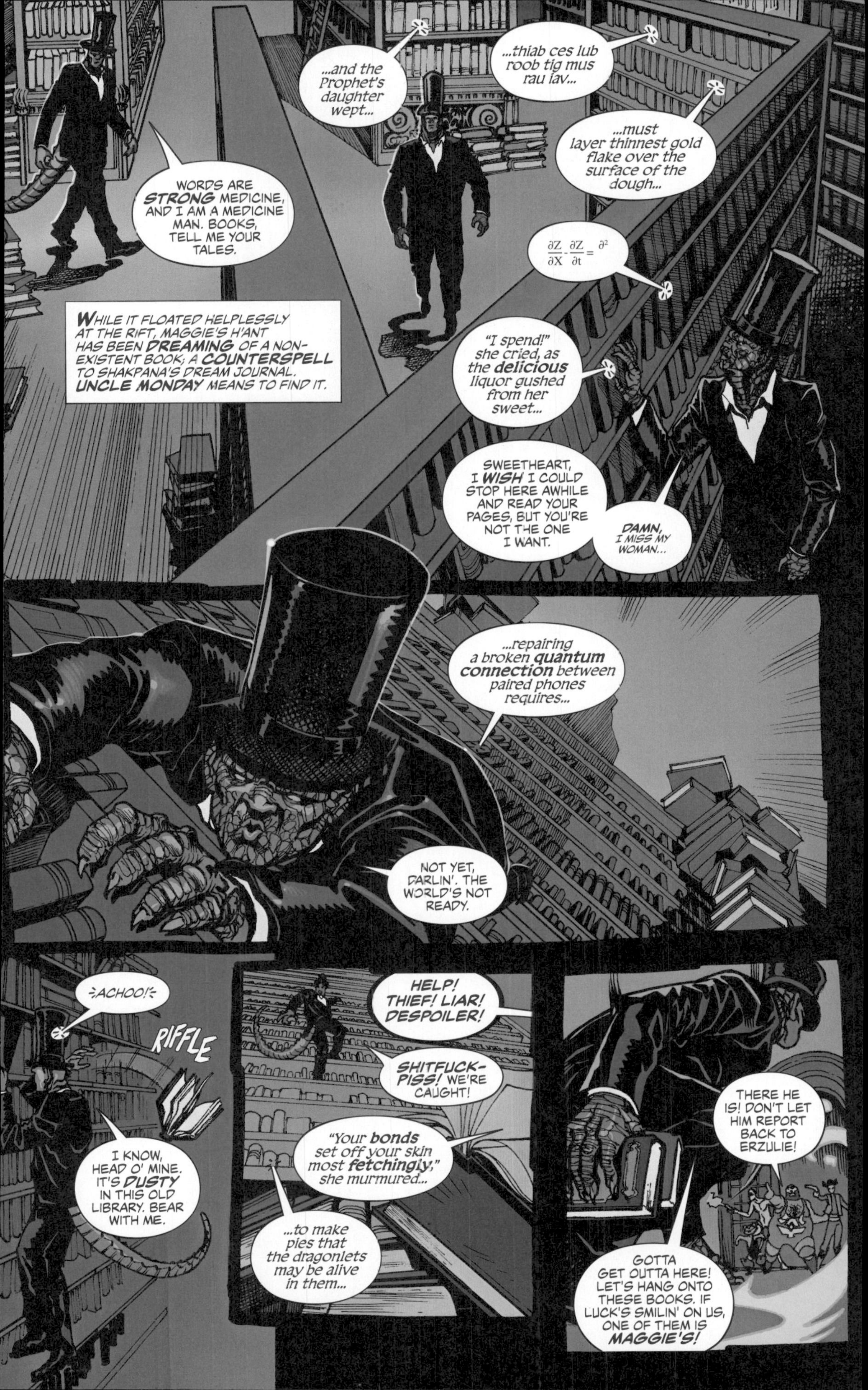

WORDS ARE STRONG MEDICINE, AND I AM A MEDICINE MAN. BOOKS, TELL ME YOUR TALES.
...and the Prophet's daughter wept...
...thiab ces lub roob tig mus rau iav...
...must layer thinnest gold flake over the surface of the dough...
$\frac{\partial Z}{\partial X} - \frac{\partial Z}{\partial t} = \partial^2$
WHILE IT FLOATED HELPLESSLY AT THE RIFT, MAGGIE'S H'ANT HAS BEEN DREAMING OF A NON-EXISTENT BOOK; A COUNTERSPELL TO SHAKPANA'S DREAM JOURNAL. UNCLE MONDAY MEANS TO FIND IT.
"I spend!" she cried, as the delicious liquor gushed from her sweet...
SWEETHEART, I WISH I COULD STOP HERE AWHILE AND READ YOUR PAGES, BUT YOU'RE NOT THE ONE I WANT.
DAMN, I MISS MY WOMAN...
...repairing a broken quantum connection between paired phones requires...
NOT YET, DARLIN'. THE WORLD'S NOT READY.
ACHOO!
RIFFLE
I KNOW, HEAD O' MINE. IT'S DUSTY IN THIS OLD LIBRARY. BEAR WITH ME.
HELP! THIEF! LIAR! DESPOILER!
SHITFUCK-PISS! WE'RE CAUGHT!
"Your bonds set off your skin most fetchingly," she murmured...
...to make pies that the dragonlets may be alive in them...
THERE HE IS! DON'T LET HIM REPORT BACK TO ERZULIE!
GOTTA GET OUTTA HERE! LET'S HANG ONTO THESE BOOKS. IF LUCK'S SMILIN' ON US, ONE OF THEM IS MAGGIE'S!

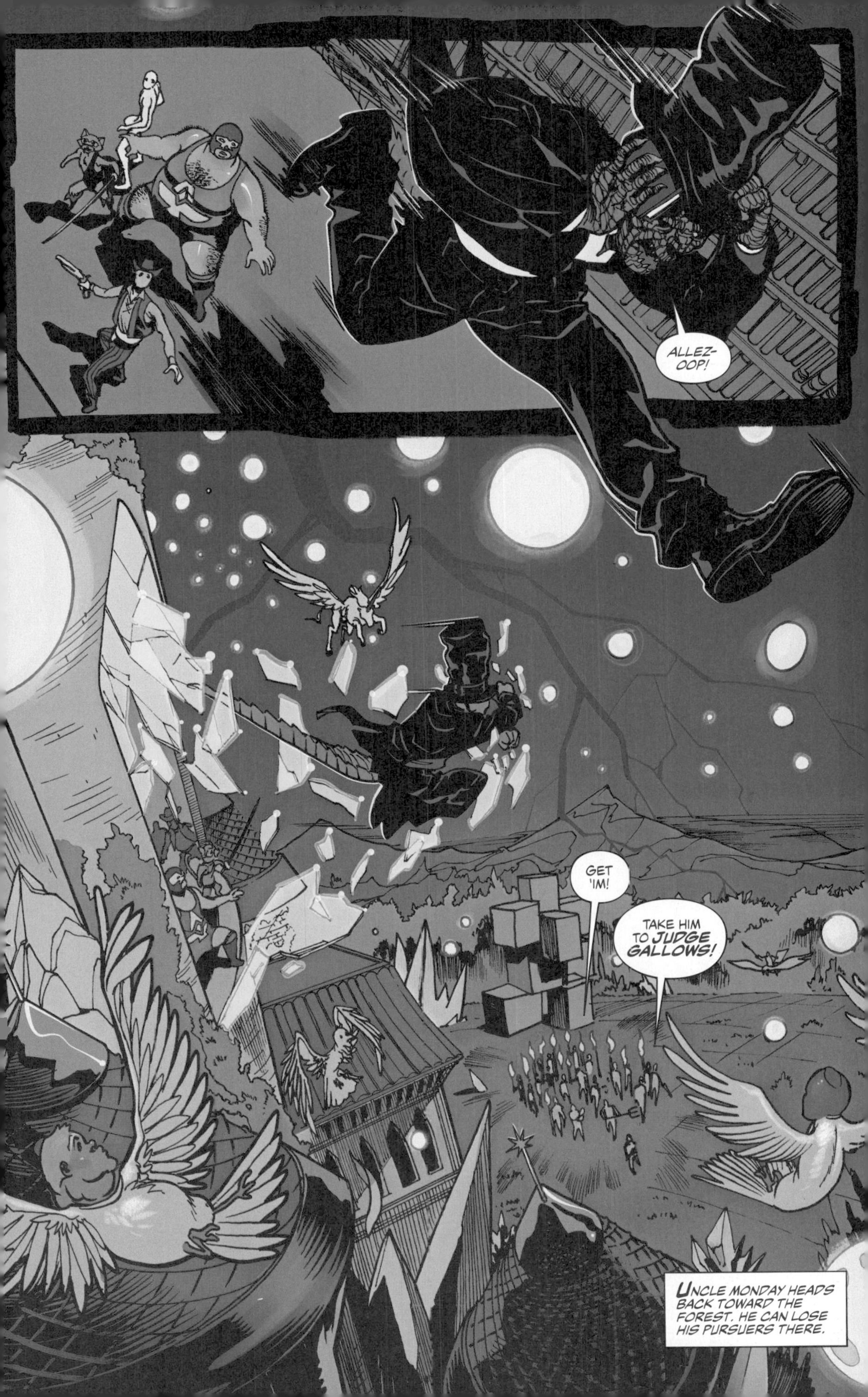

ALLEZ-OOP!
GET 'IM!
TAKE HIM TO JUDGE GALLOWS!
UNCLE MONDAY HEADS BACK TOWARD THE FOREST. HE CAN LOSE HIS PURSUERS THERE.

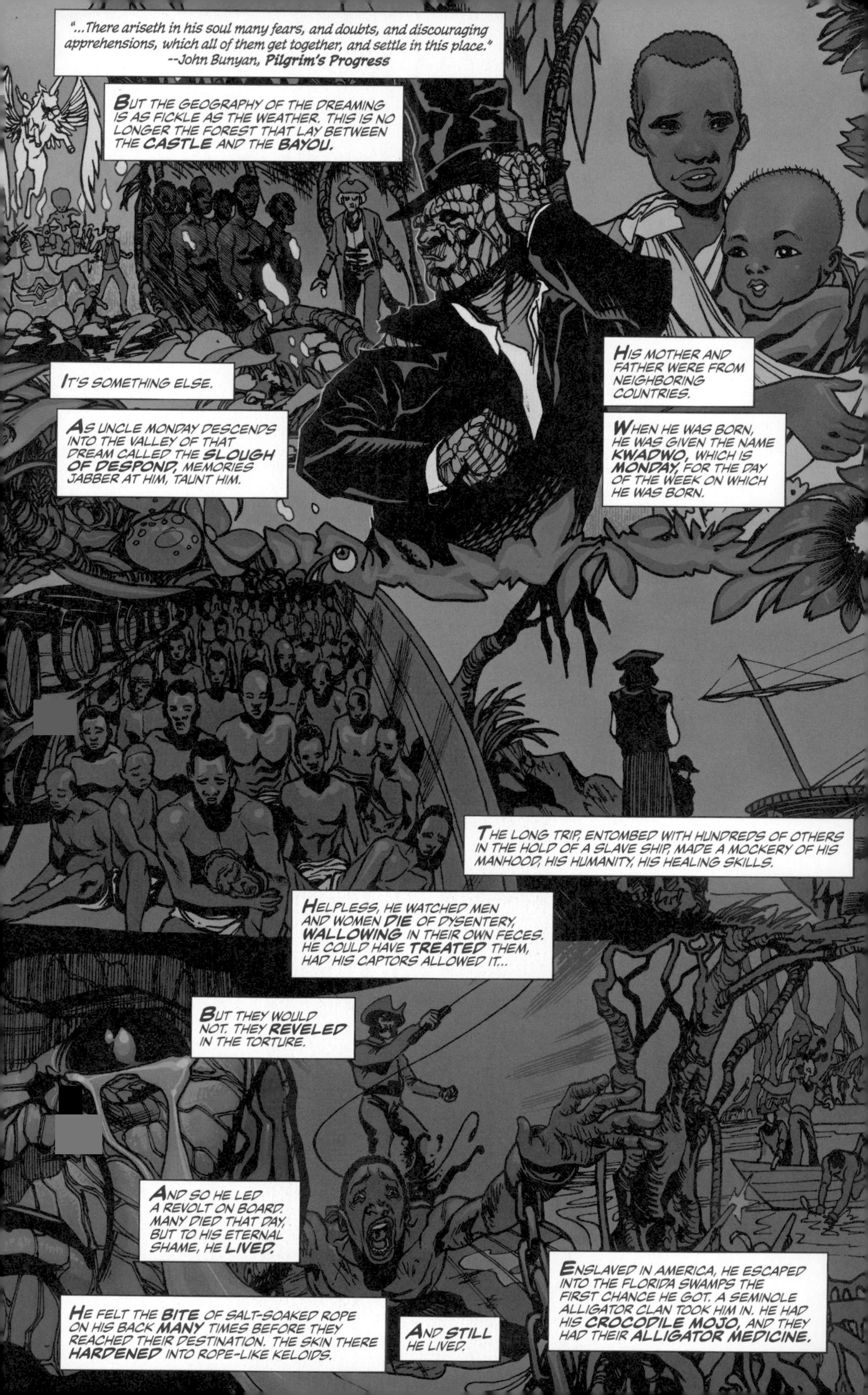
"...There ariseth in his soul many fears, and doubts, and discouraging apprehensions, which all of them get together, and settle in this place."
--John Bunyan, Pilgrim's Progress
BUT THE GEOGRAPHY OF THE DREAMING IS AS FICKLE AS THE WEATHER. THIS IS NO LONGER THE FOREST THAT LAY BETWEEN THE CASTLE AND THE BAYOU.
IT'S SOMETHING ELSE.
AS UNCLE MONDAY DESCENDS INTO THE VALLEY OF THAT DREAM CALLED THE SLOUGH OF DESPOND, MEMORIES JABBER AT HIM, TAUNT HIM.
HIS MOTHER AND FATHER WERE FROM NEIGHBORING COUNTRIES.
WHEN HE WAS BORN, HE WAS GIVEN THE NAME KWADWO, WHICH IS MONDAY, FOR THE DAY OF THE WEEK ON WHICH HE WAS BORN.
THE LONG TRIP, ENTOMBED WITH HUNDREDS OF OTHERS IN THE HOLD OF A SLAVE SHIP, MADE A MOCKERY OF HIS MANHOOD, HIS HUMANITY, HIS HEALING SKILLS.
HELPLESS, HE WATCHED MEN AND WOMEN DIE OF DYSENTERY, WALLOWING IN THEIR OWN FECES. HE COULD HAVE TREATED THEM, HAD HIS CAPTORS ALLOWED IT...
BUT THEY WOULD NOT. THEY REVELED IN THE TORTURE.
AND SO HE LED A REVOLT ON BOARD. MANY DIED THAT DAY, BUT TO HIS ETERNAL SHAME, HE LIVED.
HE FELT THE BITE OF SALT-SOAKED ROPE ON HIS BACK MANY TIMES BEFORE THEY REACHED THEIR DESTINATION. THE SKIN THERE HARDENED INTO ROPE-LIKE KELOIDS.
AND STILL HE LIVED.
ENSLAVED IN AMERICA, HE ESCAPED INTO THE FLORIDA SWAMPS THE FIRST CHANCE HE GOT. A SEMINOLE ALLIGATOR CLAN TOOK HIM IN. HE HAD HIS CROCODILE MOJO, AND THEY HAD THEIR ALLIGATOR MEDICINE.

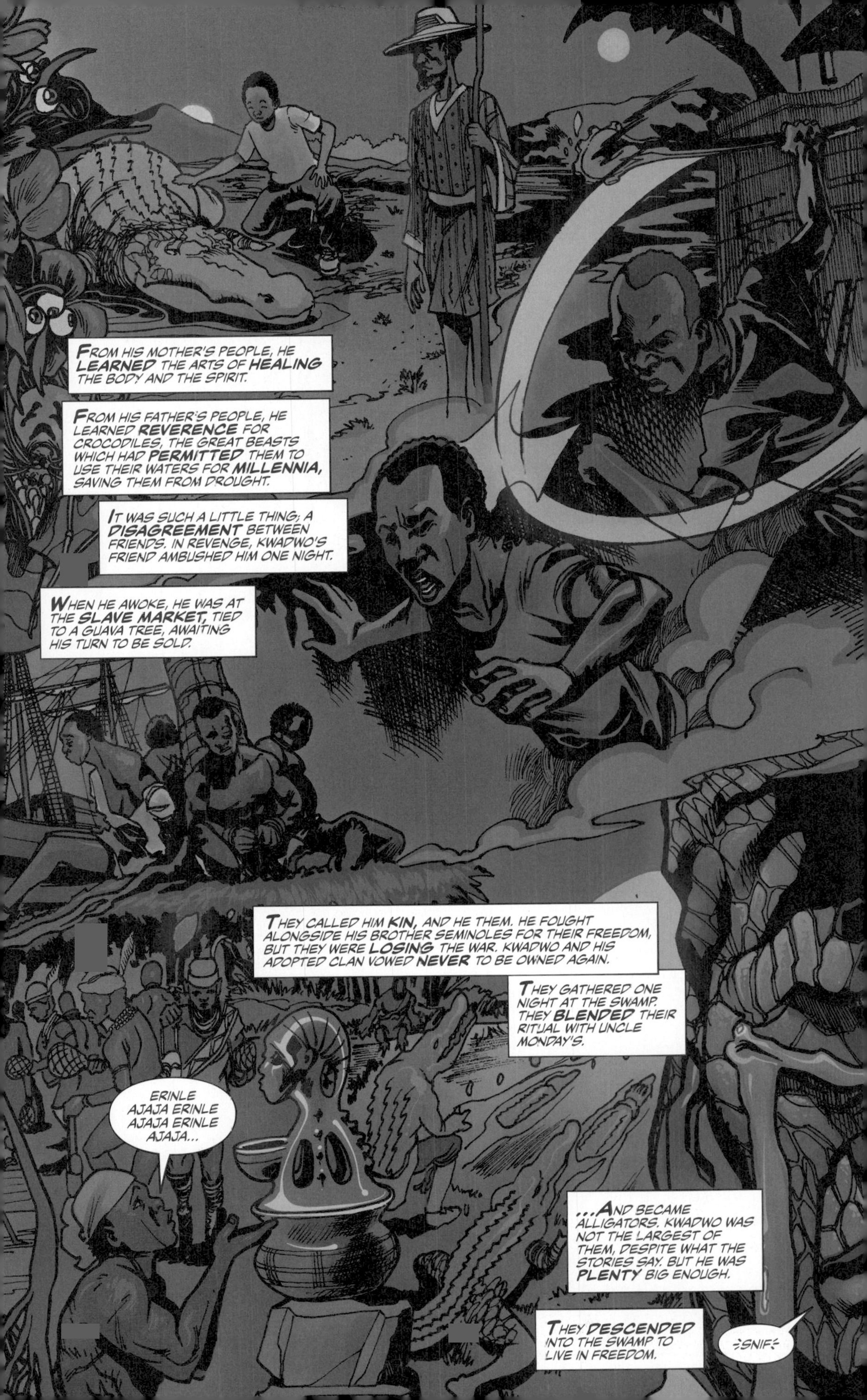
FROM HIS MOTHER'S PEOPLE, HE LEARNED THE ARTS OF HEALING THE BODY AND THE SPIRIT.
FROM HIS FATHER'S PEOPLE, HE LEARNED REVERENCE FOR CROCODILES, THE GREAT BEASTS WHICH HAD PERMITTED THEM TO USE THEIR WATERS FOR MILLENNIA, SAVING THEM FROM DROUGHT.
IT WAS SUCH A LITTLE THING; A DISAGREEMENT BETWEEN FRIENDS. IN REVENGE, KWADWO'S FRIEND AMBUSHED HIM ONE NIGHT.
WHEN HE AWOKE, HE WAS AT THE SLAVE MARKET, TIED TO A GUAVA TREE, AWAITING HIS TURN TO BE SOLD.
THEY CALLED HIM KIN, AND HE THEM. HE FOUGHT ALONGSIDE HIS BROTHER SEMINOLES FOR THEIR FREEDOM, BUT THEY WERE LOSING THE WAR. KWADWO AND HIS ADOPTED CLAN VOWED NEVER TO BE OWNED AGAIN.
THEY GATHERED ONE NIGHT AT THE SWAMP. THEY BLENDED THEIR RITUAL WITH UNCLE MONDAY'S.
ERINLE AJAJA ERINLE AJAJA ERINLE AJAJA...
...AND BECAME ALLIGATORS. KWADWO WAS NOT THE LARGEST OF THEM, DESPITE WHAT THE STORIES SAY. BUT HE WAS PLENTY BIG ENOUGH.
THEY DESCENDED INTO THE SWAMP TO LIVE IN FREEDOM.
SNIF

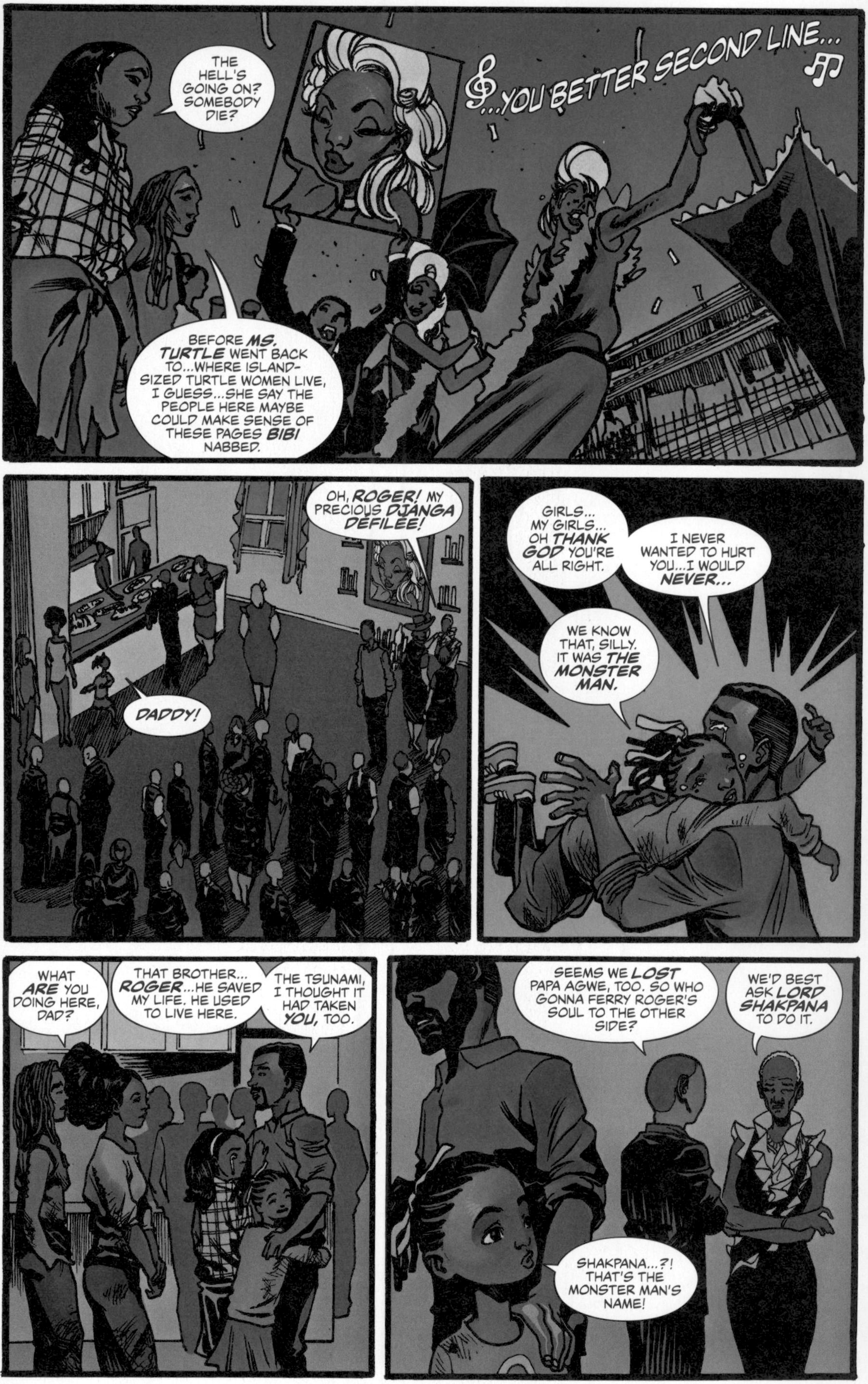
THE HELL'S GOING ON? SOMEBODY DIE?
...YOU BETTER SECOND LINE...
BEFORE MS. TURTLE WENT BACK TO...WHERE ISLAND-SIZED TURTLE WOMEN LIVE, I GUESS...SHE SAY THE PEOPLE HERE MAYBE COULD MAKE SENSE OF THESE PAGES BIBI NABBED.
OH, ROGER! MY PRECIOUS DJANGA DÉFILÉE!
DADDY!
GIRLS... MY GIRLS... OH THANK GOD YOU'RE ALL RIGHT.
I NEVER WANTED TO HURT YOU...I WOULD NEVER...
WE KNOW THAT, SILLY. IT WAS THE MONSTER MAN.
WHAT ARE YOU DOING HERE, DAD?
THAT BROTHER... ROGER...HE SAVED MY LIFE. HE USED TO LIVE HERE.
THE TSUNAMI, I THOUGHT IT HAD TAKEN YOU, TOO.
SEEMS WE LOST PAPA AGWE, TOO. SO WHO GONNA FERRY ROGER'S SOUL TO THE OTHER SIDE?
WE'D BEST ASK LORD SHAKPANA TO DO IT.
SHAKPANA...?! THAT'S THE MONSTER MAN'S NAME!

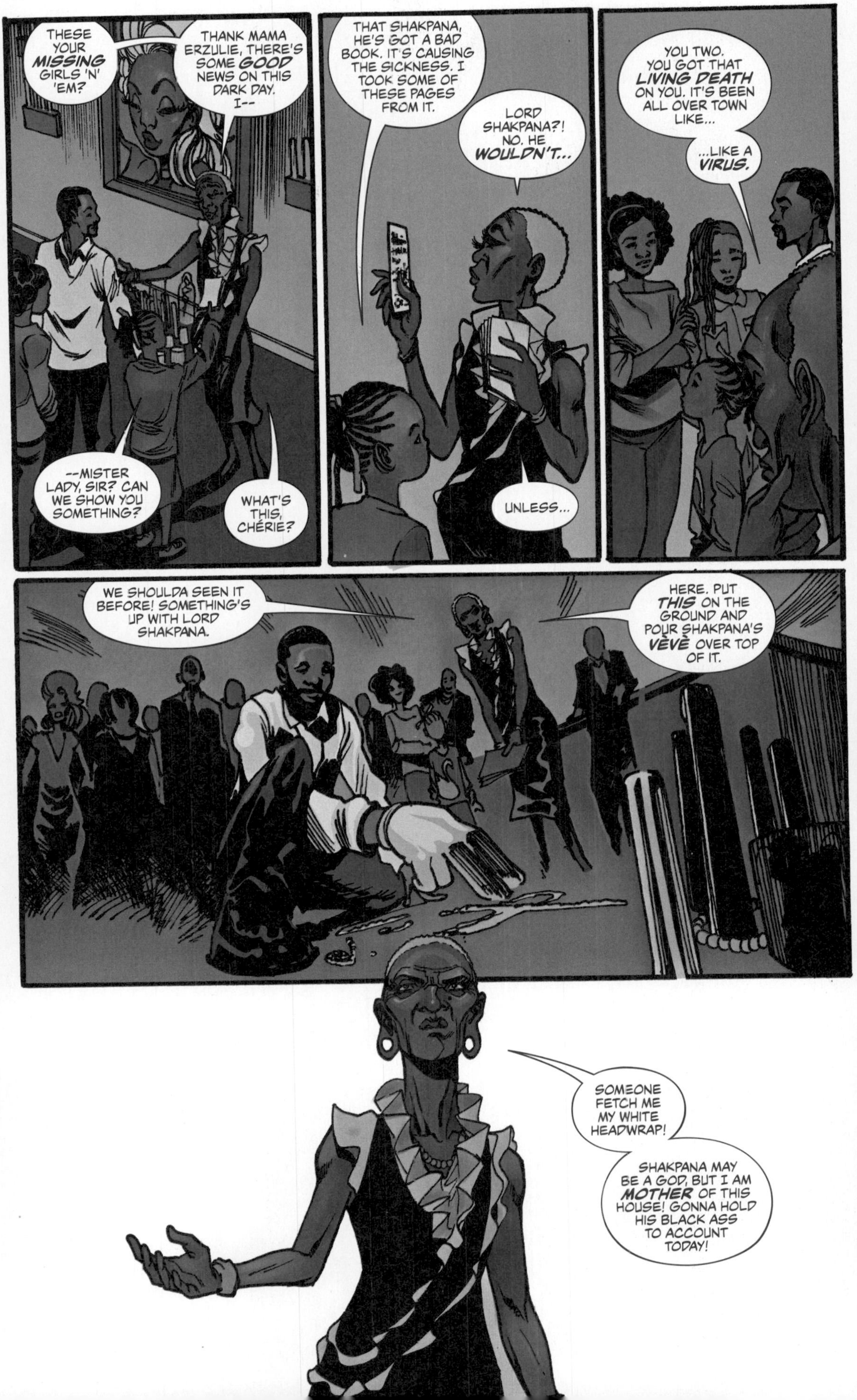

THESE YOUR MISSING GIRLS 'N' 'EM?
THANK MAMA ERZULIE, THERE'S SOME GOOD NEWS ON THIS DARK DAY. I--
--MISTER LADY, SIR? CAN WE SHOW YOU SOMETHING?
WHAT'S THIS, CHÉRIE?
THAT SHAKPANA, HE'S GOT A BAD BOOK. IT'S CAUSING THE SICKNESS. I TOOK SOME OF THESE PAGES FROM IT.
LORD SHAKPANA?! NO. HE WOULDN'T...
UNLESS...
YOU TWO. YOU GOT THAT LIVING DEATH ON YOU. IT'S BEEN ALL OVER TOWN LIKE...
...LIKE A VIRUS.
WE SHOULDA SEEN IT BEFORE! SOMETHING'S UP WITH LORD SHAKPANA.
HERE. PUT THIS ON THE GROUND AND POUR SHAKPANA'S VÈVÈ OVER TOP OF IT.
SOMEONE FETCH ME MY WHITE HEADWRAP!
SHAKPANA MAY BE A GOD, BUT I AM MOTHER OF THIS HOUSE! GONNA HOLD HIS BLACK ASS TO ACCOUNT TODAY!

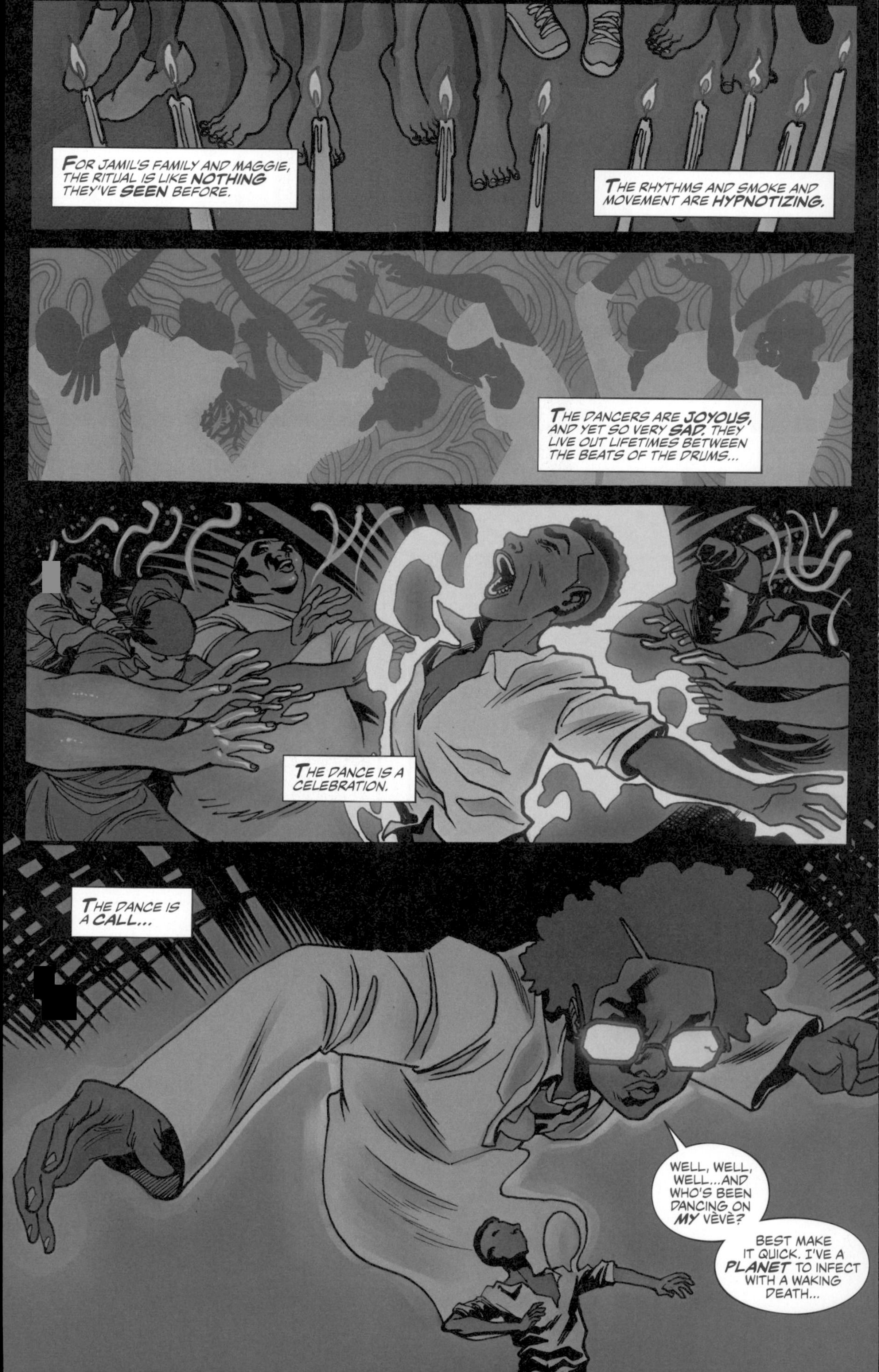
FOR JAMIL'S FAMILY AND MAGGIE, THE RITUAL IS LIKE NOTHING THEY'VE SEEN BEFORE.
THE RHYTHMS AND SMOKE AND MOVEMENT ARE HYPNOTIZING.
THE DANCERS ARE JOYOUS, AND YET SO VERY SAD. THEY LIVE OUT LIFETIMES BETWEEN THE BEATS OF THE DRUMS...
THE DANCE IS A CELEBRATION.
THE DANCE IS A CALL...
WELL, WELL, WELL...AND WHO'S BEEN DANCING ON MY VÈVÈ?
BEST MAKE IT QUICK. I'VE A PLANET TO INFECT WITH A WAKING DEATH...

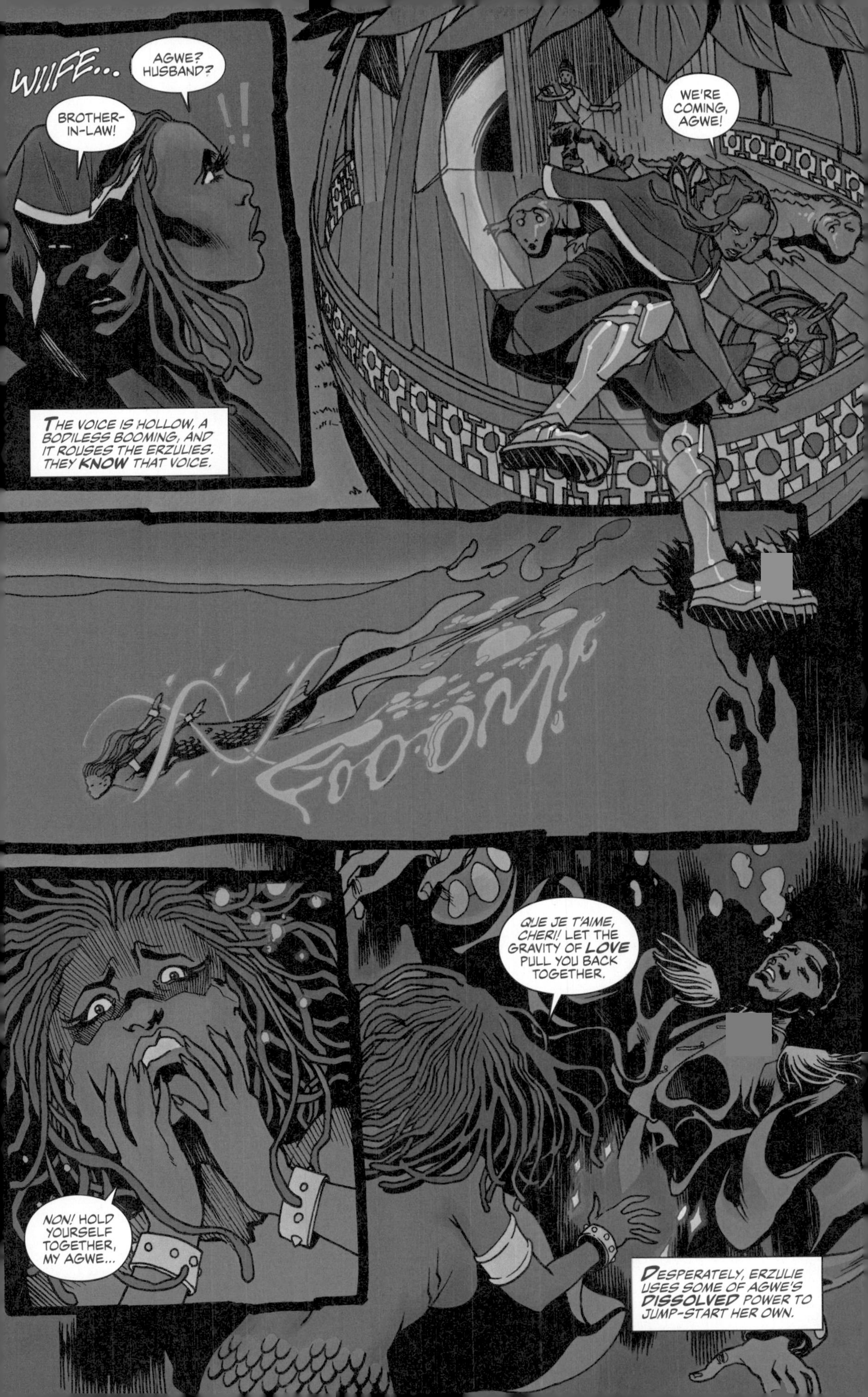
WIIFE...
AGWE? HUSBAND?
BROTHER-IN-LAW!
THE VOICE IS HOLLOW, A BODILESS BOOMING, AND IT ROUSES THE ERZULIES. THEY KNOW THAT VOICE.
WE'RE COMING, AGWE!
FOO-OOM!
NON! HOLD YOURSELF TOGETHER, MY AGWE...
QUE JE T'AIME, CHERI! LET THE GRAVITY OF LOVE PULL YOU BACK TOGETHER.
DESPERATELY, ERZULIE USES SOME OF AGWE'S DISSOLVED POWER TO JUMP-START HER OWN.

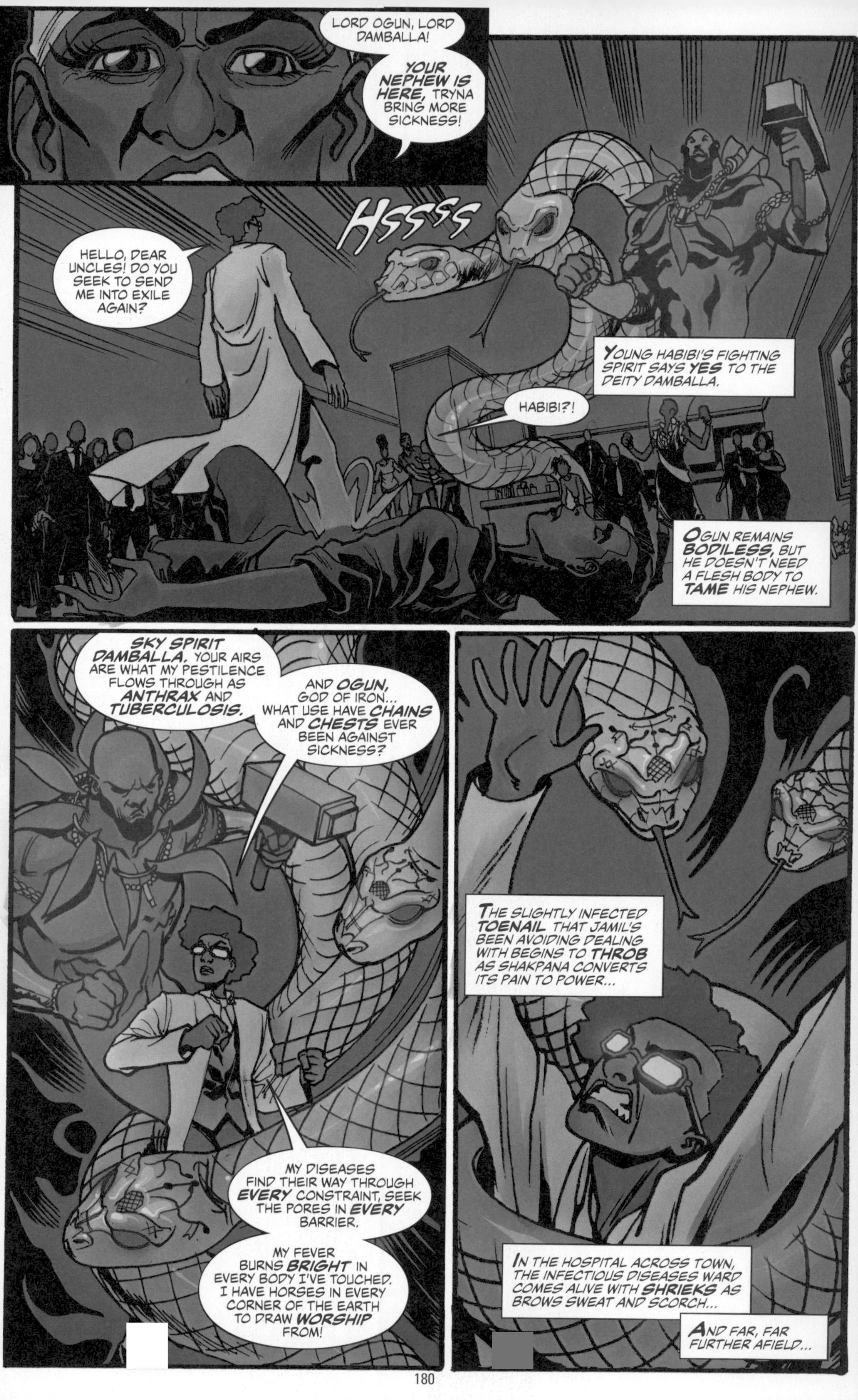
LORD OGUN, LORD DAMBALLA!
YOUR NEPHEW IS HERE, TRYNA BRING MORE SICKNESS!
HSSSS
HELLO, DEAR UNCLES! DO YOU SEEK TO SEND ME INTO EXILE AGAIN?
YOUNG HABIBI'S FIGHTING SPIRIT SAYS YES TO THE DEITY DAMBALLA.
HABIBI?!
OGUN REMAINS BODILESS, BUT HE DOESN'T NEED A FLESH BODY TO TAME HIS NEPHEW.
SKY SPIRIT DAMBALLA, YOUR AIRS ARE WHAT MY PESTILENCE FLOWS THROUGH AS ANTHRAX AND TUBERCULOSIS.
AND OGUN, GOD OF IRON... WHAT USE HAVE CHAINS AND CHESTS EVER BEEN AGAINST SICKNESS?
MY DISEASES FIND THEIR WAY THROUGH EVERY CONSTRAINT, SEEK THE PORES IN EVERY BARRIER.
MY FEVER BURNS BRIGHT IN EVERY BODY I'VE TOUCHED. I HAVE HORSES IN EVERY CORNER OF THE EARTH TO DRAW WORSHIP FROM!
THE SLIGHTLY INFECTED TOENAIL THAT JAMIL'S BEEN AVOIDING DEALING WITH BEGINS TO THROB AS SHAKPANA CONVERTS ITS PAIN TO POWER...
IN THE HOSPITAL ACROSS TOWN, THE INFECTIOUS DISEASES WARD COMES ALIVE WITH SHRIEKS AS BROWS SWEAT AND SCORCH...
AND FAR, FAR FURTHER AFIELD...

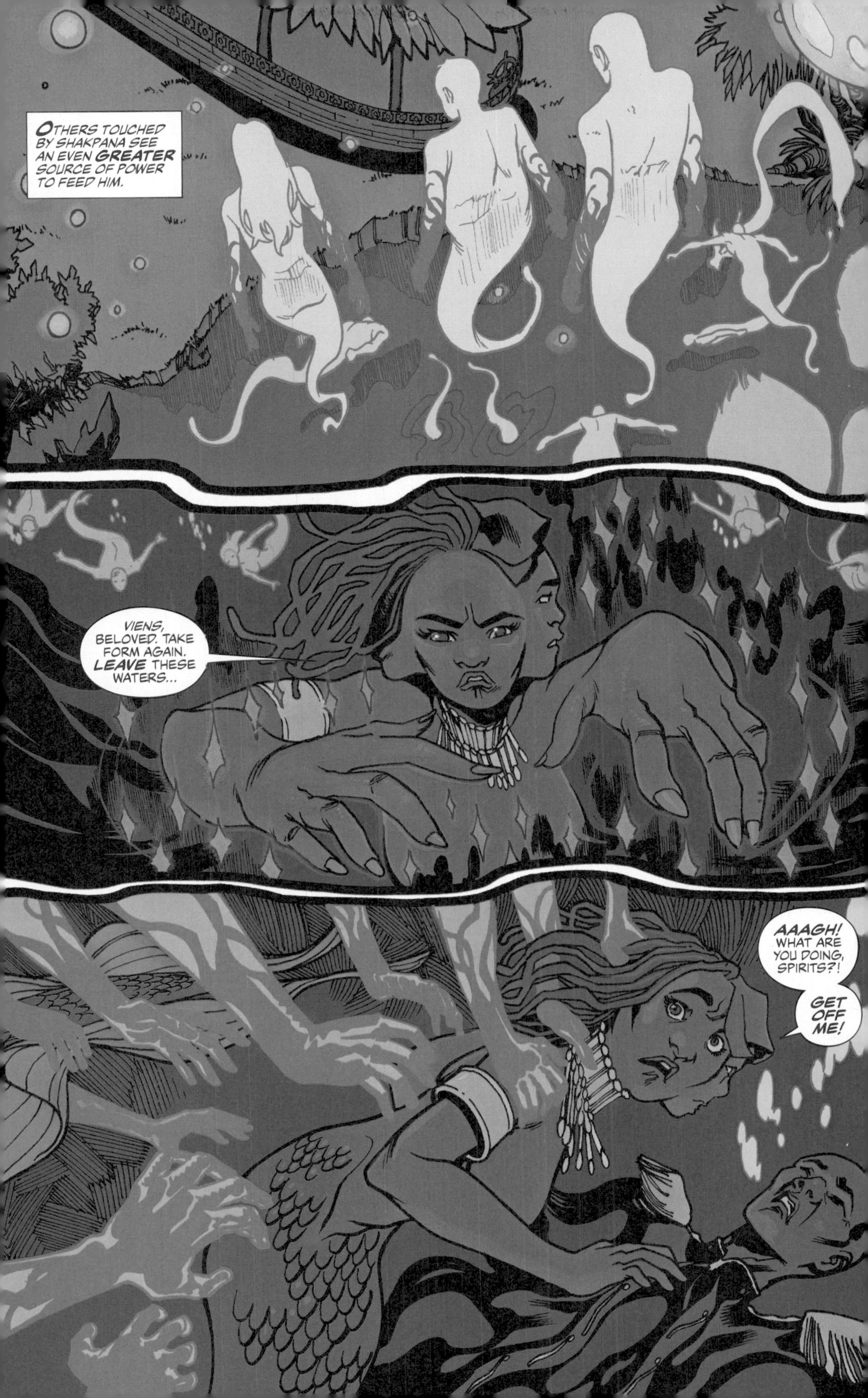
OTHERS TOUCHED BY SHAKPANA SEE AN EVEN GREATER SOURCE OF POWER TO FEED HIM.
VIENS, BELOVED. TAKE FORM AGAIN. LEAVE THESE WATERS...
AAAGH! WHAT ARE YOU DOING, SPIRITS?!
GET OFF ME!

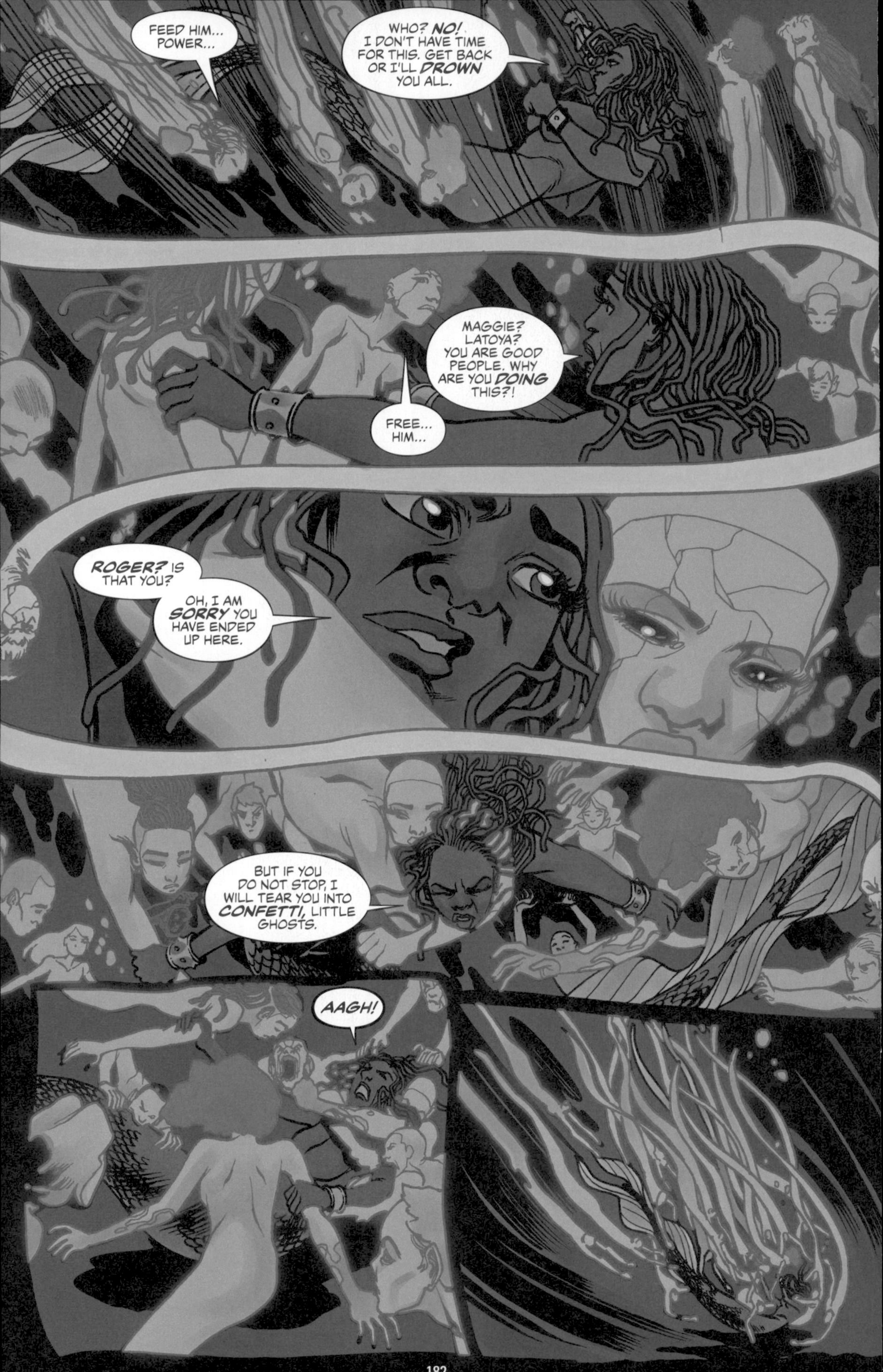
FEED HIM... POWER...
WHO? NO! I DON'T HAVE TIME FOR THIS. GET BACK OR I'LL DROWN YOU ALL.
MAGGIE? LATOYA? YOU ARE GOOD PEOPLE. WHY ARE YOU DOING THIS?!
FREE... HIM...
ROGER? IS THAT YOU?
OH, I AM SORRY YOU HAVE ENDED UP HERE.
BUT IF YOU DO NOT STOP, I WILL TEAR YOU INTO CONFETTI, LITTLE GHOSTS.
AAGH!

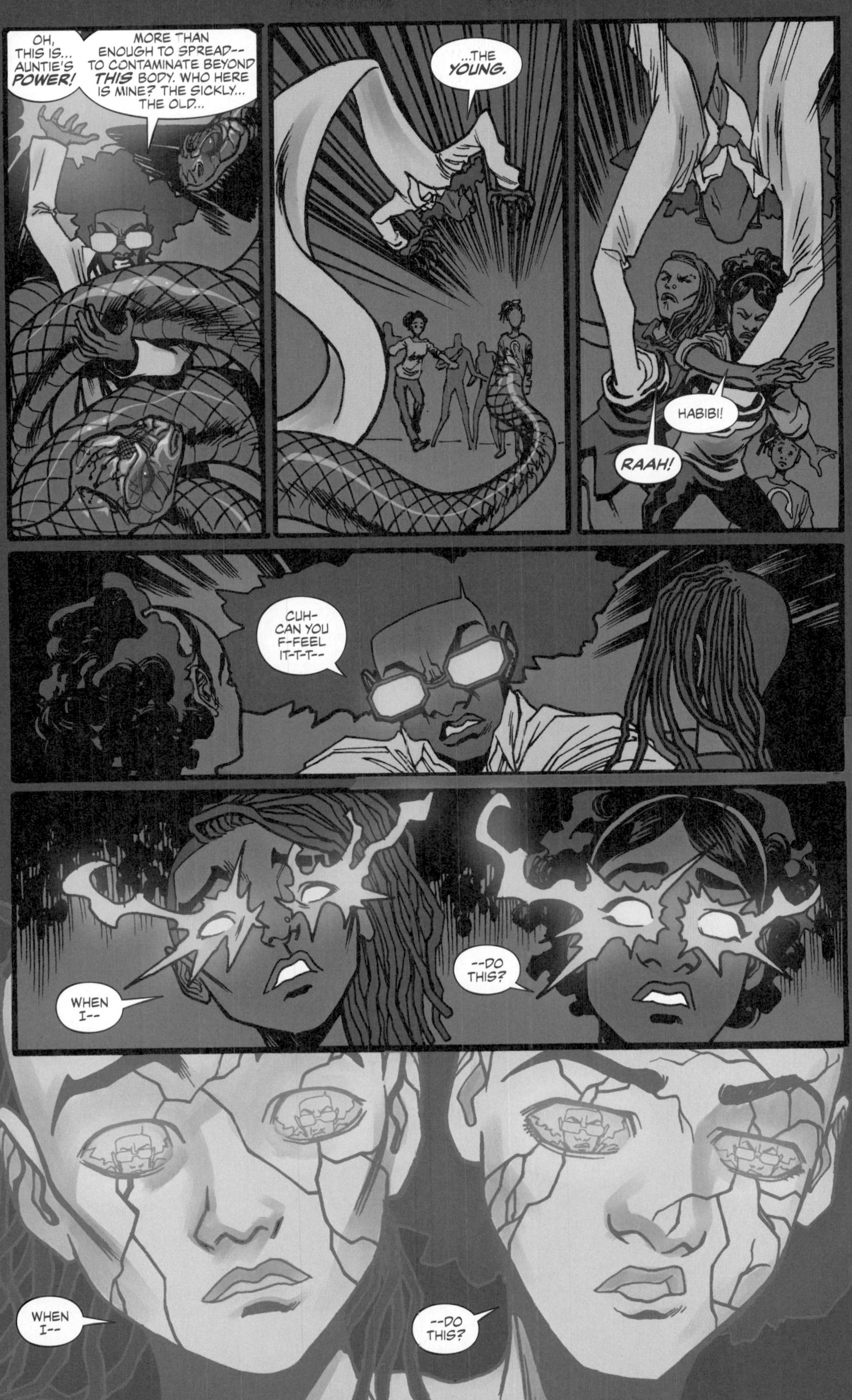
OH, THIS IS... AUNTIE'S POWER!
MORE THAN ENOUGH TO SPREAD-- TO CONTAMINATE BEYOND THIS BODY. WHO HERE IS MINE? THE SICKLY... THE OLD...
...THE YOUNG.
HABIBI!
RAAH!
CUH- CAN YOU F-FEEL IT-T-T--
WHEN I--
--DO THIS?
WHEN I--
--DO THIS?

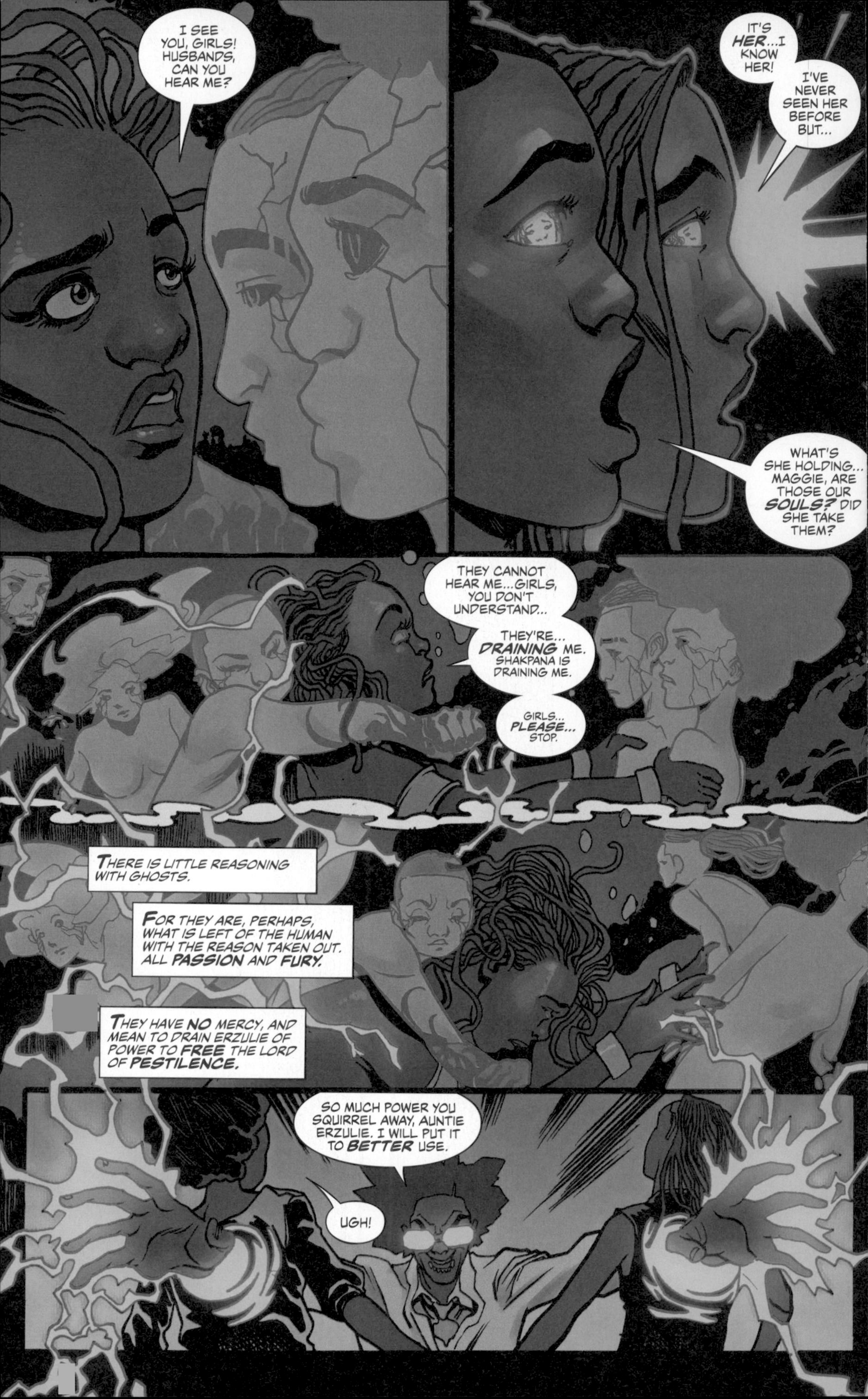
I SEE YOU, GIRLS! HUSBANDS, CAN YOU HEAR ME?
IT'S HER...I KNOW HER!
I'VE NEVER SEEN HER BEFORE BUT...
WHAT'S SHE HOLDING... MAGGIE, ARE THOSE OUR SOULS? DID SHE TAKE THEM?
THEY CANNOT HEAR ME...GIRLS, YOU DON'T UNDERSTAND...
THEY'RE... DRAINING ME. SHAKPANA IS DRAINING ME.
GIRLS... PLEASE... STOP.
THERE IS LITTLE REASONING WITH GHOSTS.
FOR THEY ARE, PERHAPS, WHAT IS LEFT OF THE HUMAN WITH THE REASON TAKEN OUT. ALL PASSION AND FURY.
THEY HAVE NO MERCY, AND MEAN TO DRAIN ERZULIE OF POWER TO FREE THE LORD OF PESTILENCE.
SO MUCH POWER YOU SQUIRREL AWAY, AUNTIE ERZULIE. I WILL PUT IT TO BETTER USE.
UGH!

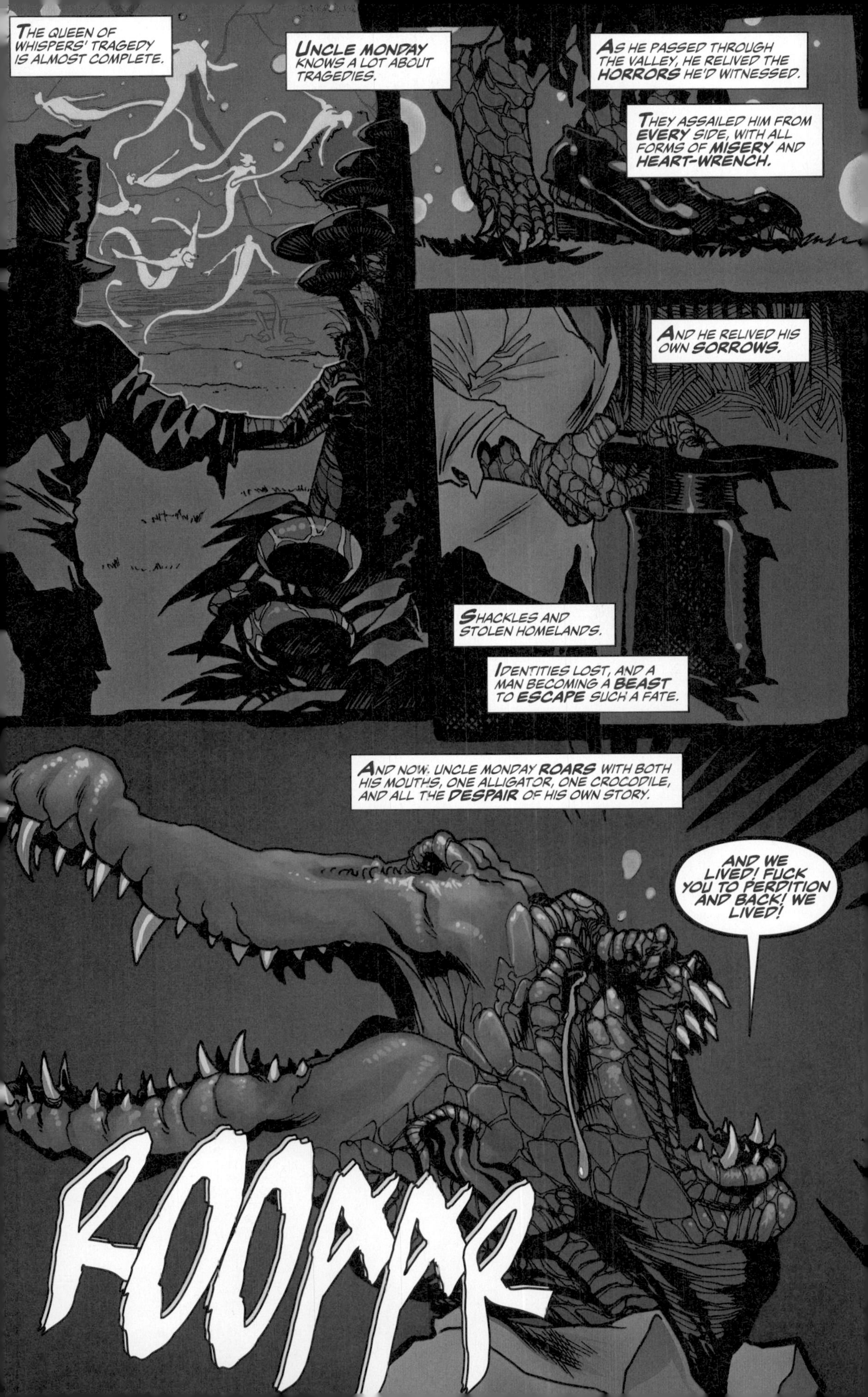
THE QUEEN OF WHISPERS' TRAGEDY IS ALMOST COMPLETE.
UNCLE MONDAY KNOWS A LOT ABOUT TRAGEDIES.
AS HE PASSED THROUGH THE VALLEY, HE RELIVED THE HORRORS HE'D WITNESSED.
THEY ASSAILED HIM FROM EVERY SIDE, WITH ALL FORMS OF MISERY AND HEART-WRENCH.
AND HE RELIVED HIS OWN SORROWS.
SHACKLES AND STOLEN HOMELANDS.
IDENTITIES LOST, AND A MAN BECOMING A BEAST TO ESCAPE SUCH A FATE.
AND NOW: UNCLE MONDAY ROARS WITH BOTH HIS MOUTHS, ONE ALLIGATOR, ONE CROCODILE, AND ALL THE DESPAIR OF HIS OWN STORY.
AND WE LIVED! FUCK YOU TO PERDITION AND BACK! WE LIVED!
ROOAAR

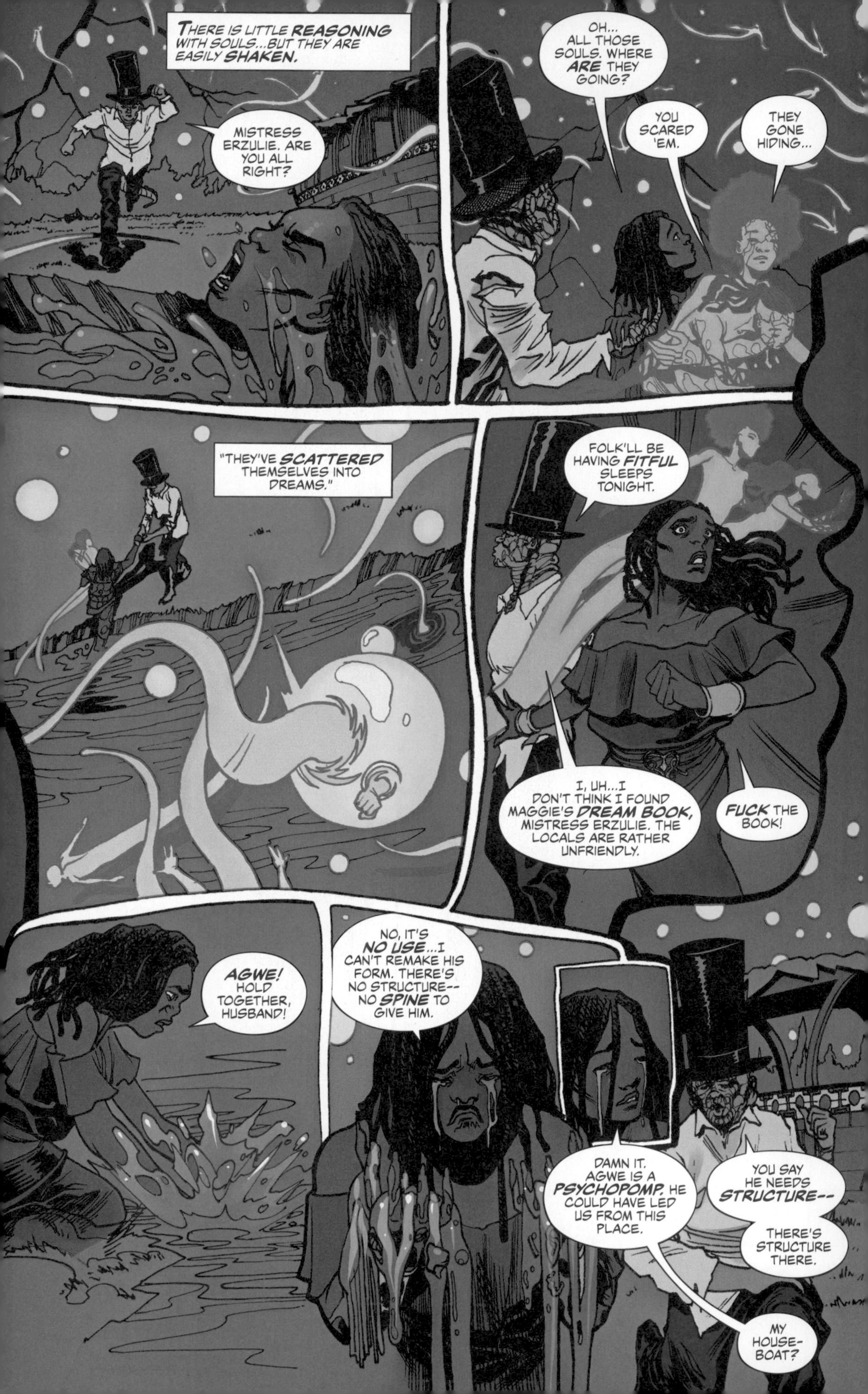
THERE IS LITTLE REASONING WITH SOULS...BUT THEY ARE EASILY SHAKEN.
MISTRESS ERZULIE. ARE YOU ALL RIGHT?
OH... ALL THOSE SOULS. WHERE ARE THEY GOING?
YOU SCARED 'EM.
THEY GONE HIDING...
"THEY'VE SCATTERED THEMSELVES INTO DREAMS."
FOLK'LL BE HAVING FITFUL SLEEPS TONIGHT.
I, UH...I DON'T THINK I FOUND MAGGIE'S DREAM BOOK, MISTRESS ERZULIE. THE LOCALS ARE RATHER UNFRIENDLY.
FUCK THE BOOK!
AGWE! HOLD TOGETHER, HUSBAND!
NO, IT'S NO USE...I CAN'T REMAKE HIS FORM. THERE'S NO STRUCTURE-- NO SPINE TO GIVE HIM.
DAMN IT. AGWE IS A PSYCHOPOMP. HE COULD HAVE LED US FROM THIS PLACE.
YOU SAY HE NEEDS STRUCTURE--
THERE'S STRUCTURE THERE.
MY HOUSE-BOAT?

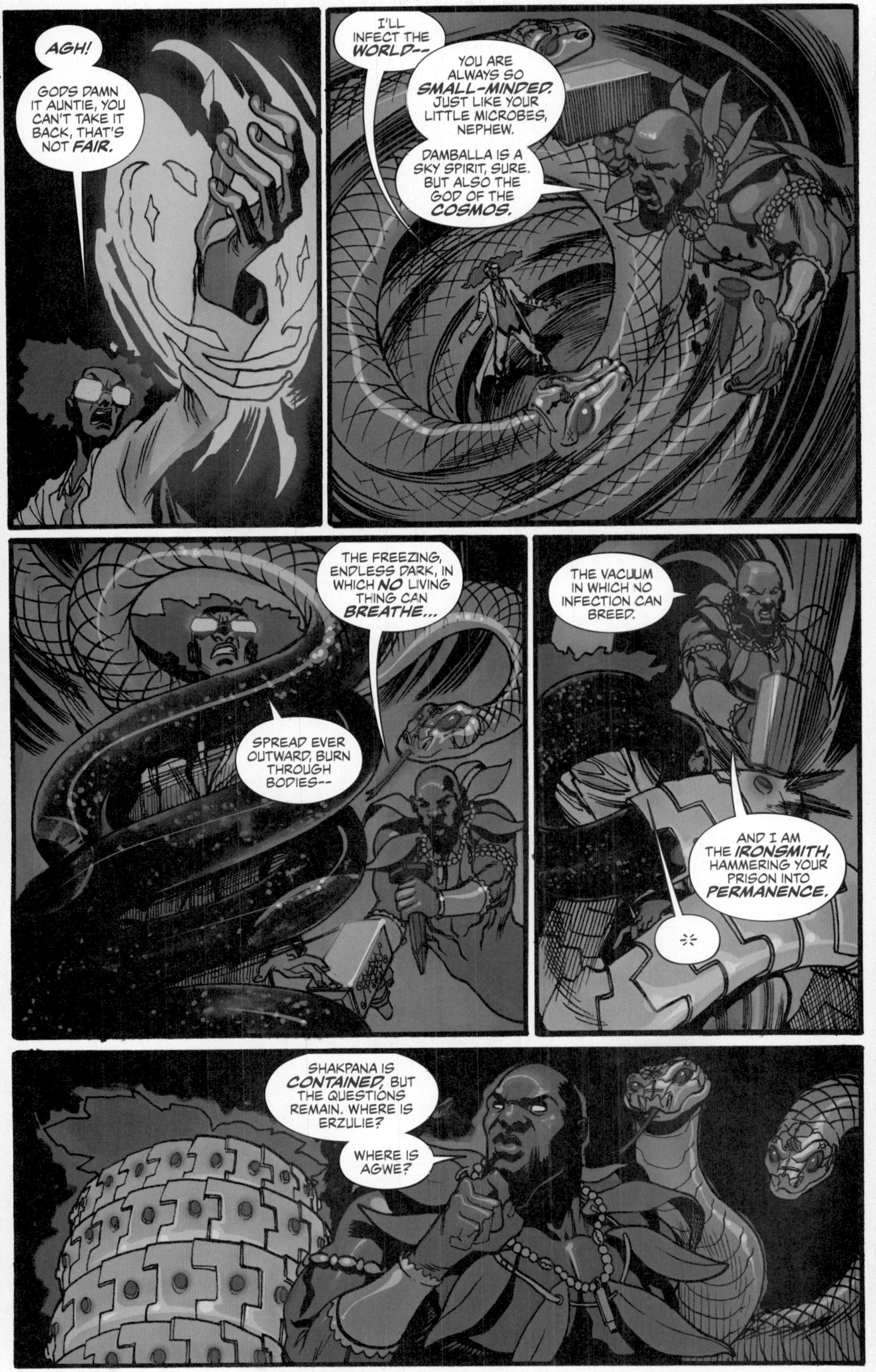
AGH!
GODS DAMN IT AUNTIE, YOU CAN'T TAKE IT BACK, THAT'S NOT FAIR.
I'LL INFECT THE WORLD--
YOU ARE ALWAYS SO SMALL-MINDED. JUST LIKE YOUR LITTLE MICROBES, NEPHEW.
DAMBALLA IS A SKY SPIRIT, SURE. BUT ALSO THE GOD OF THE COSMOS.
THE FREEZING, ENDLESS DARK, IN WHICH NO LIVING THING CAN BREATHE...
SPREAD EVER OUTWARD, BURN THROUGH BODIES--
THE VACUUM IN WHICH NO INFECTION CAN BREED.
AND I AM THE IRONSMITH, HAMMERING YOUR PRISON INTO PERMANENCE.
SHAKPANA IS CONTAINED, BUT THE QUESTIONS REMAIN. WHERE IS ERZULIE?
WHERE IS AGWE?

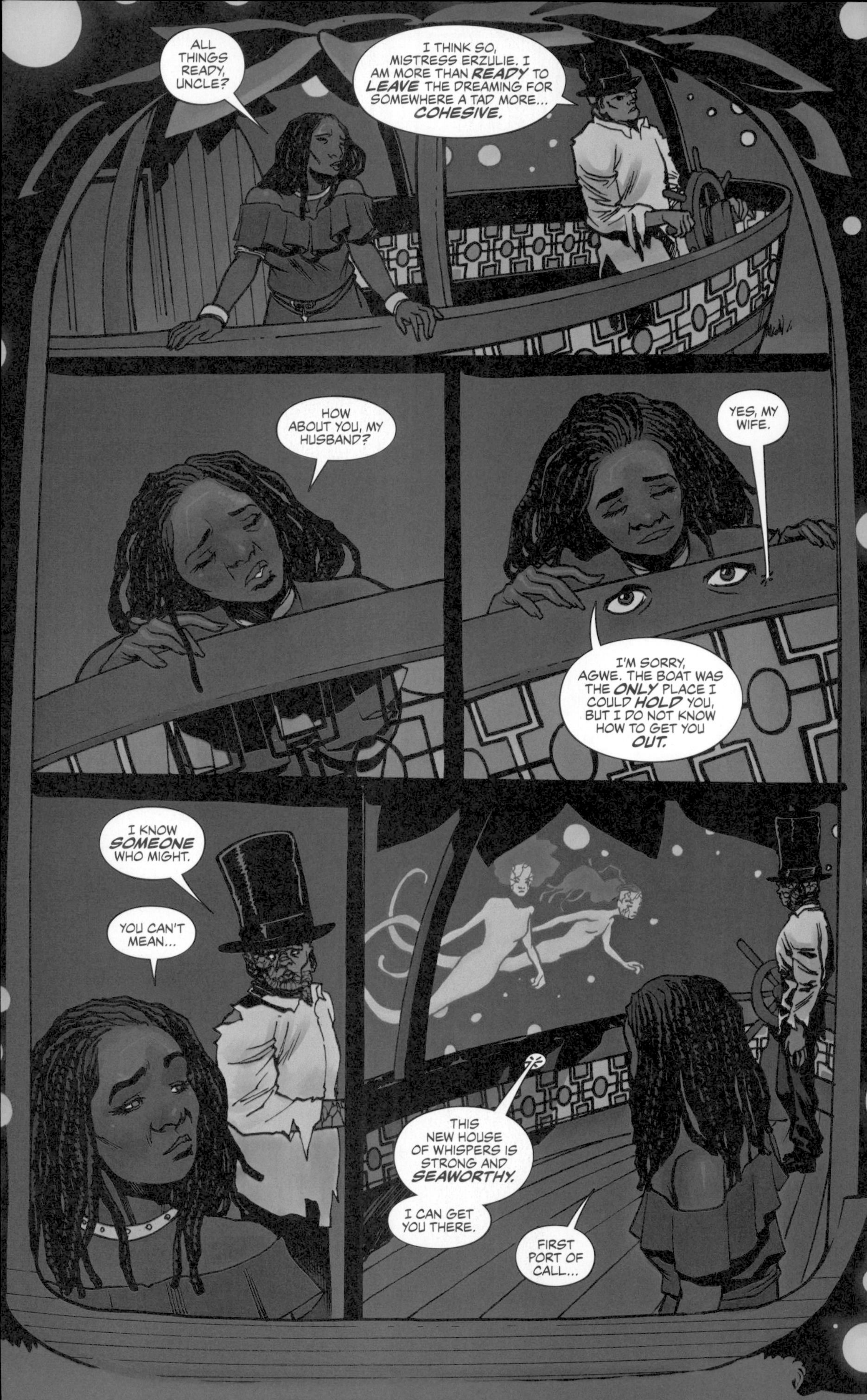
ALL THINGS READY, UNCLE?
I THINK SO, MISTRESS ERZULIE. I AM MORE THAN READY TO LEAVE THE DREAMING FOR SOMEWHERE A TAD MORE... COHESIVE.
HOW ABOUT YOU, MY HUSBAND?
YES, MY WIFE.
I'M SORRY, AGWE. THE BOAT WAS THE ONLY PLACE I COULD HOLD YOU, BUT I DO NOT KNOW HOW TO GET YOU OUT.
I KNOW SOMEONE WHO MIGHT.
YOU CAN'T MEAN...
THIS NEW HOUSE OF WHISPERS IS STRONG AND SEAWORTHY.
I CAN GET YOU THERE.
FIRST PORT OF CALL...

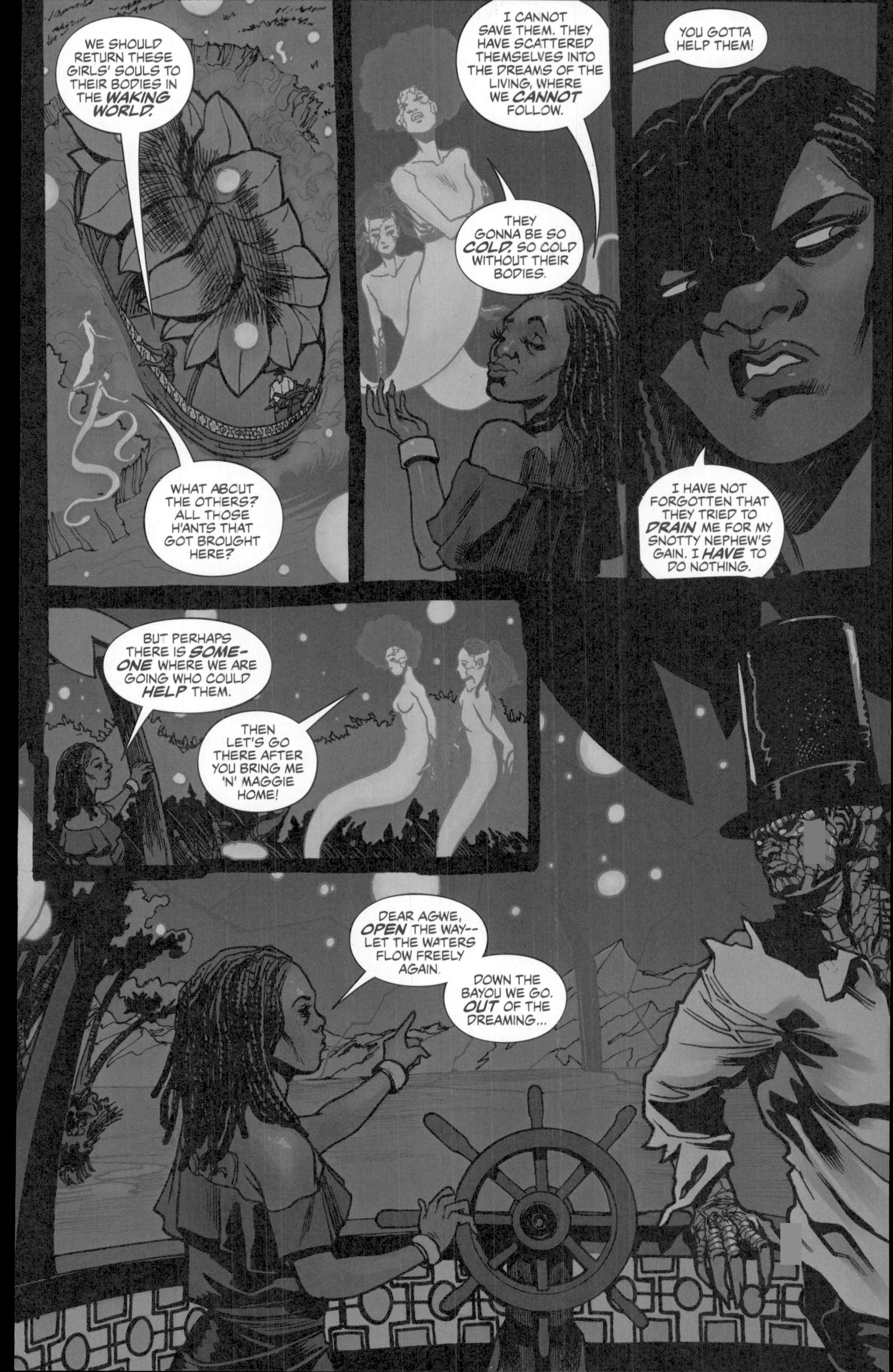
WE SHOULD RETURN THESE GIRLS' SOULS TO THEIR BODIES IN THE WAKING WORLD.
WHAT ABOUT THE OTHERS? ALL THOSE H'ANTS THAT GOT BROUGHT HERE?
I CANNOT SAVE THEM. THEY HAVE SCATTERED THEMSELVES INTO THE DREAMS OF THE LIVING, WHERE WE CANNOT FOLLOW.
THEY GONNA BE SO COLD, SO COLD WITHOUT THEIR BODIES.
YOU GOTTA HELP THEM!
I HAVE NOT FORGOTTEN THAT THEY TRIED TO DRAIN ME FOR MY SNOTTY NEPHEW'S GAIN. I HAVE TO DO NOTHING.
BUT PERHAPS THERE IS SOME-ONE WHERE WE ARE GOING WHO COULD HELP THEM.
THEN LET'S GO THERE AFTER YOU BRING ME 'N' MAGGIE HOME!
DEAR AGWE, OPEN THE WAY-- LET THE WATERS FLOW FREELY AGAIN.
DOWN THE BAYOU WE GO. OUT OF THE DREAMING...

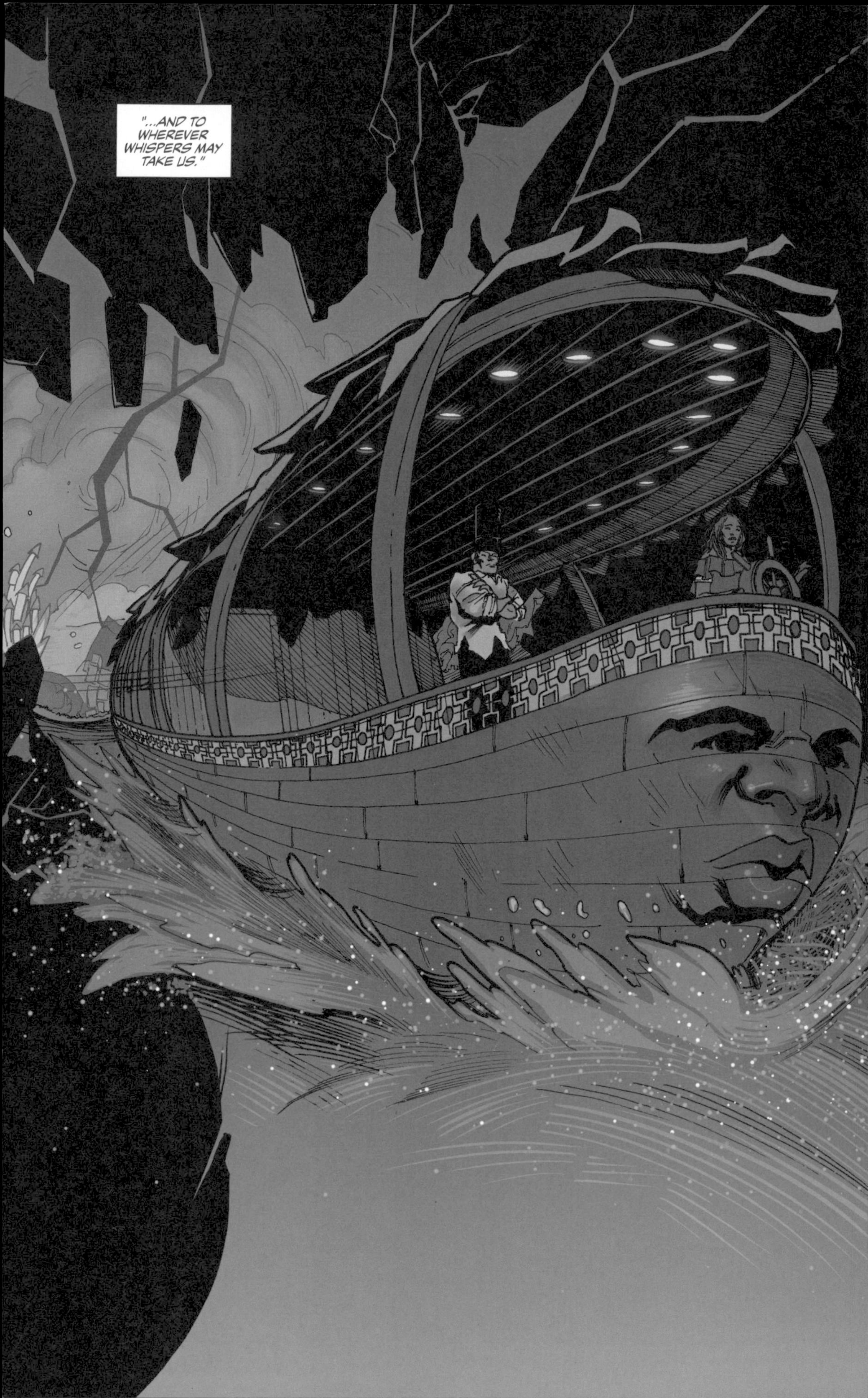
"...AND TO WHEREVER WHISPERS MAY TAKE US."

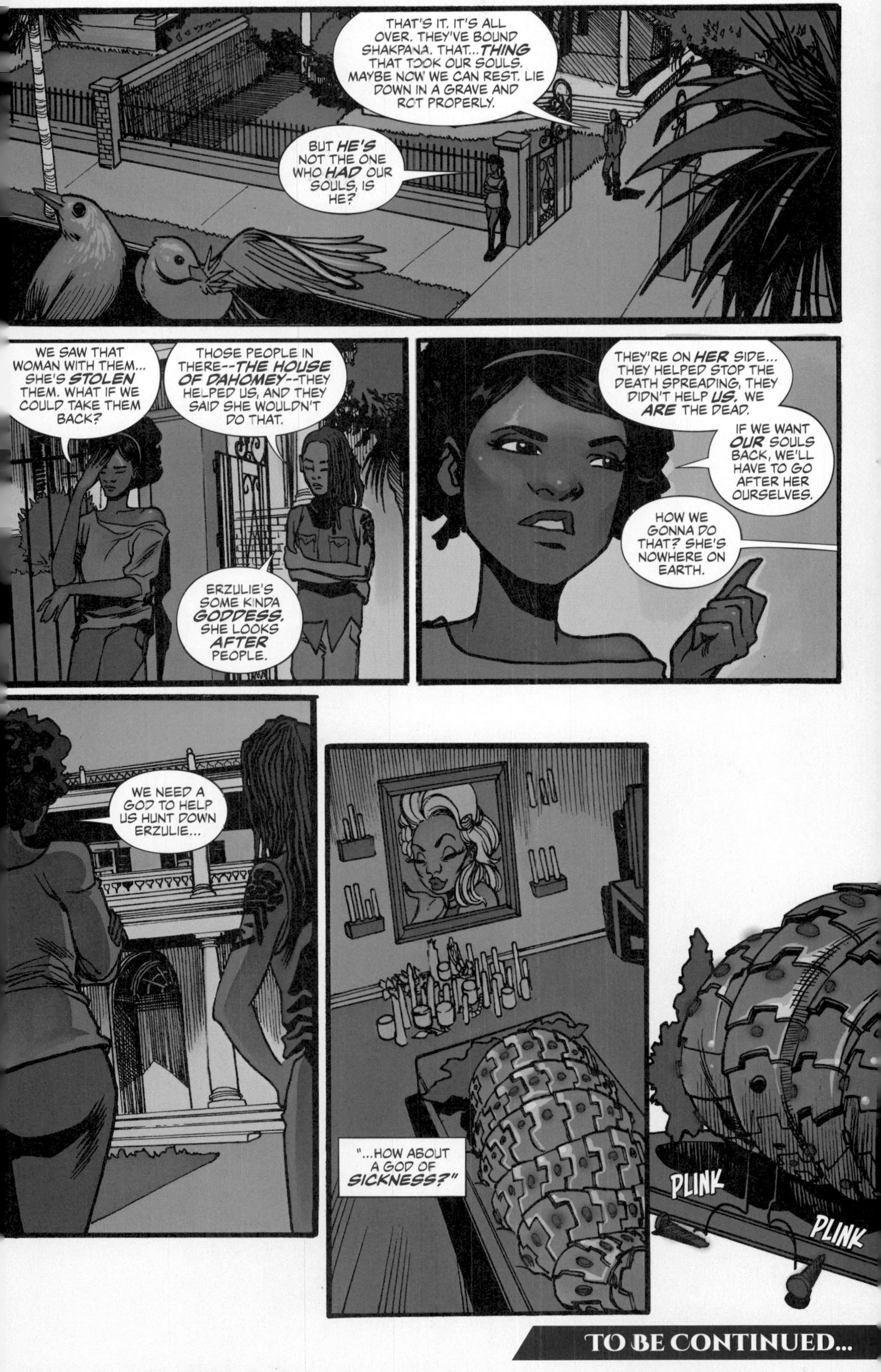
THAT'S IT. IT'S ALL OVER. THEY'VE BOUND SHAKPANA. THAT...THING THAT TOOK OUR SOULS. MAYBE NOW WE CAN REST. LIE DOWN IN A GRAVE AND ROT PROPERLY.
BUT HE'S NOT THE ONE WHO HAD OUR SOULS, IS HE?
WE SAW THAT WOMAN WITH THEM... SHE'S STOLEN THEM. WHAT IF WE COULD TAKE THEM BACK?
THOSE PEOPLE IN THERE--THE HOUSE OF DAHOMEY--THEY HELPED US, AND THEY SAID SHE WOULDN'T DO THAT.
ERZULIE'S SOME KINDA GODDESS. SHE LOOKS AFTER PEOPLE.
THEY'RE ON HER SIDE... THEY HELPED STOP THE DEATH SPREADING, THEY DIDN'T HELP US. WE ARE THE DEAD.
IF WE WANT OUR SOULS BACK, WE'LL HAVE TO GO AFTER HER OURSELVES.
HOW WE GONNA DO THAT? SHE'S NOWHERE ON EARTH.
WE NEED A GOD TO HELP US HUNT DOWN ERZULIE...
"...HOW ABOUT A GOD OF SICKNESS?"
PLINK
PLINK
TO BE CONTINUED...

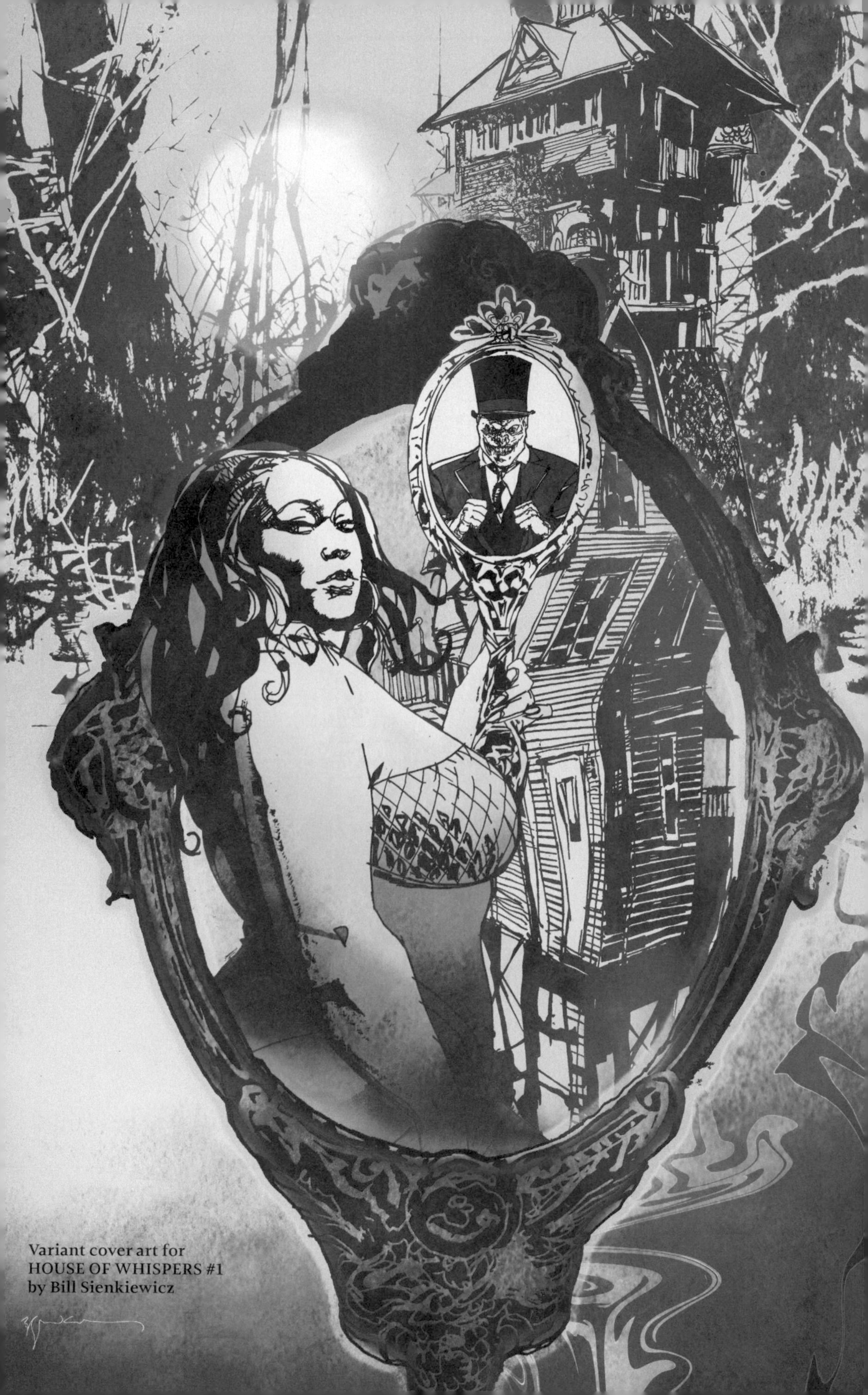

Variant cover art for
HOUSE OF WHISPERS #1
by Bill Sienkiewicz

DOMINIKE "DOMO" STANTON SKETCHBOOK

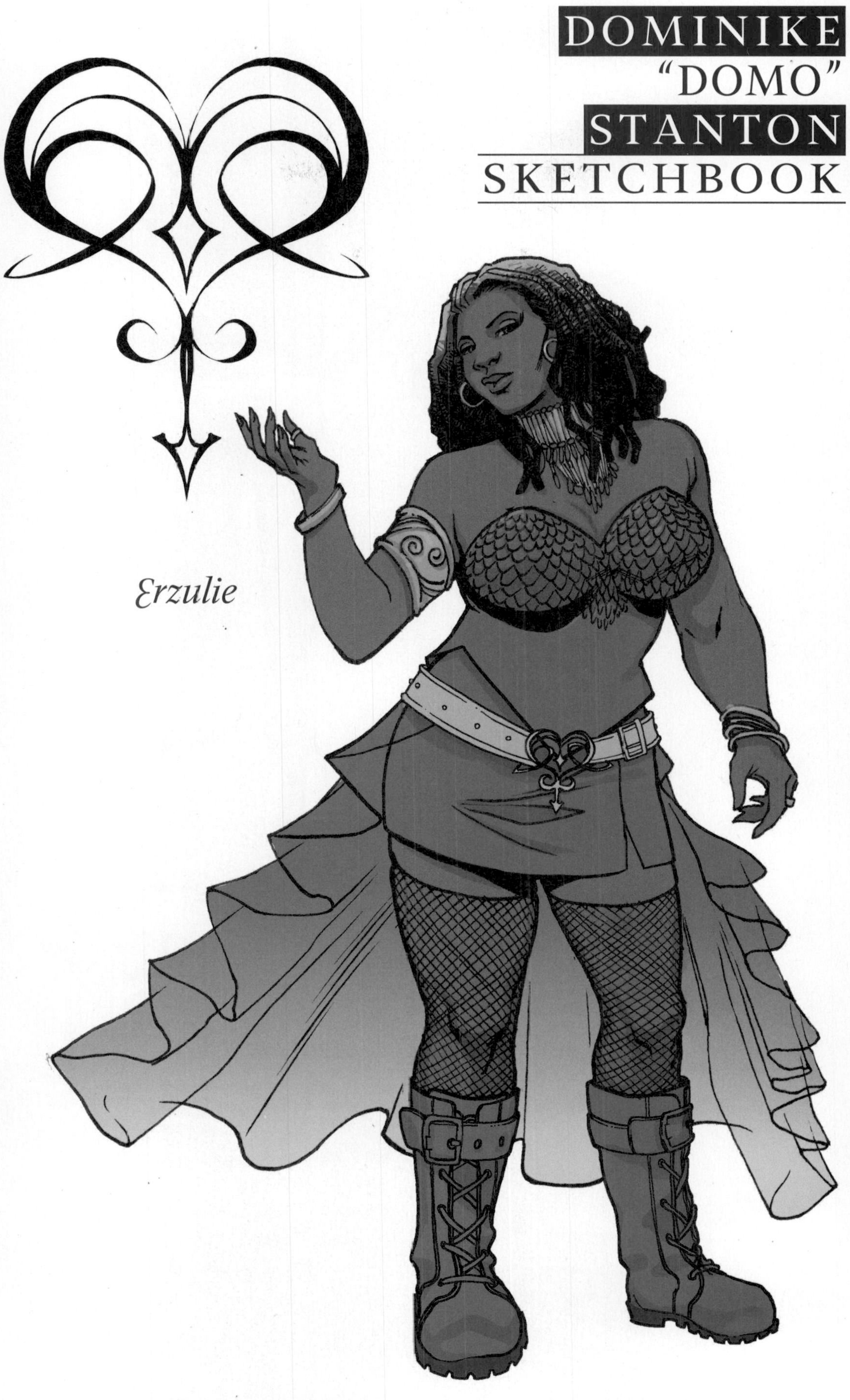

Erzulie

Habibi

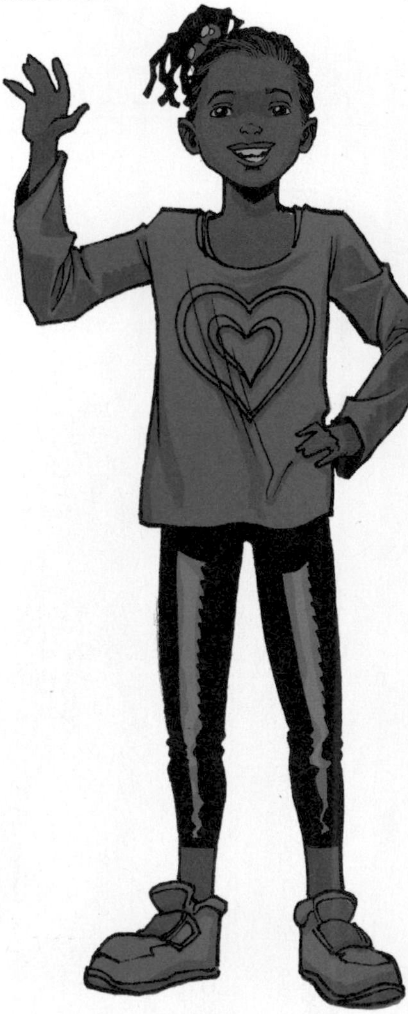

Lumi

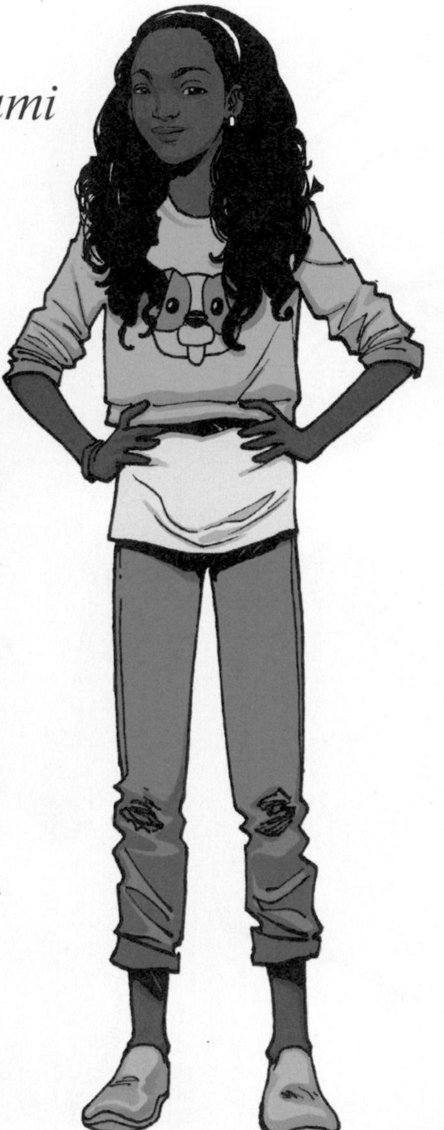

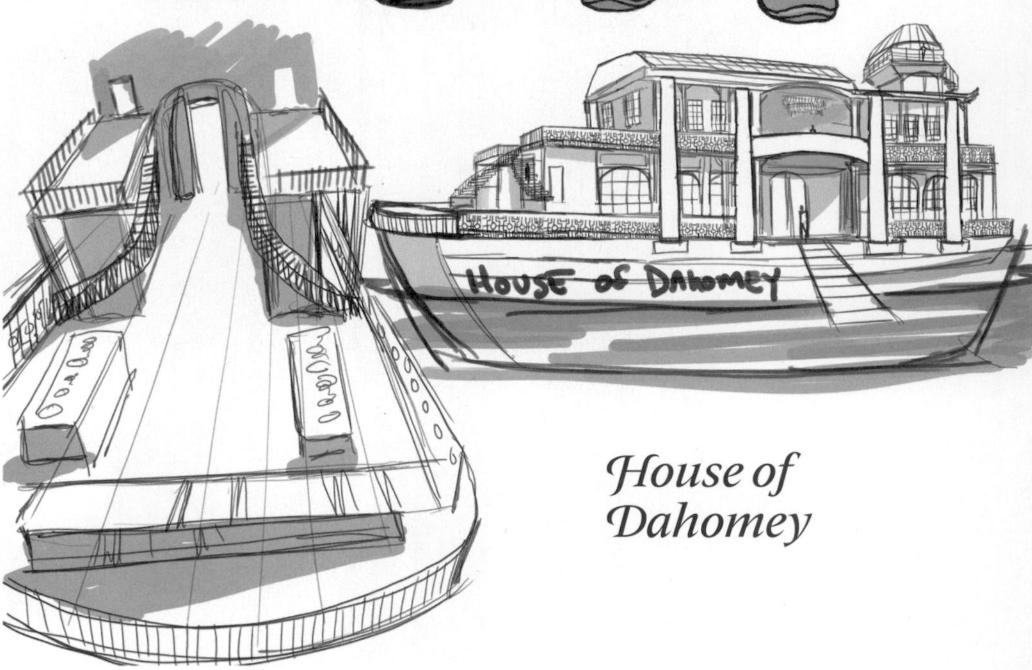
HOUSE of DAHOMEY

House of Dahomey

Latoya

Maggie

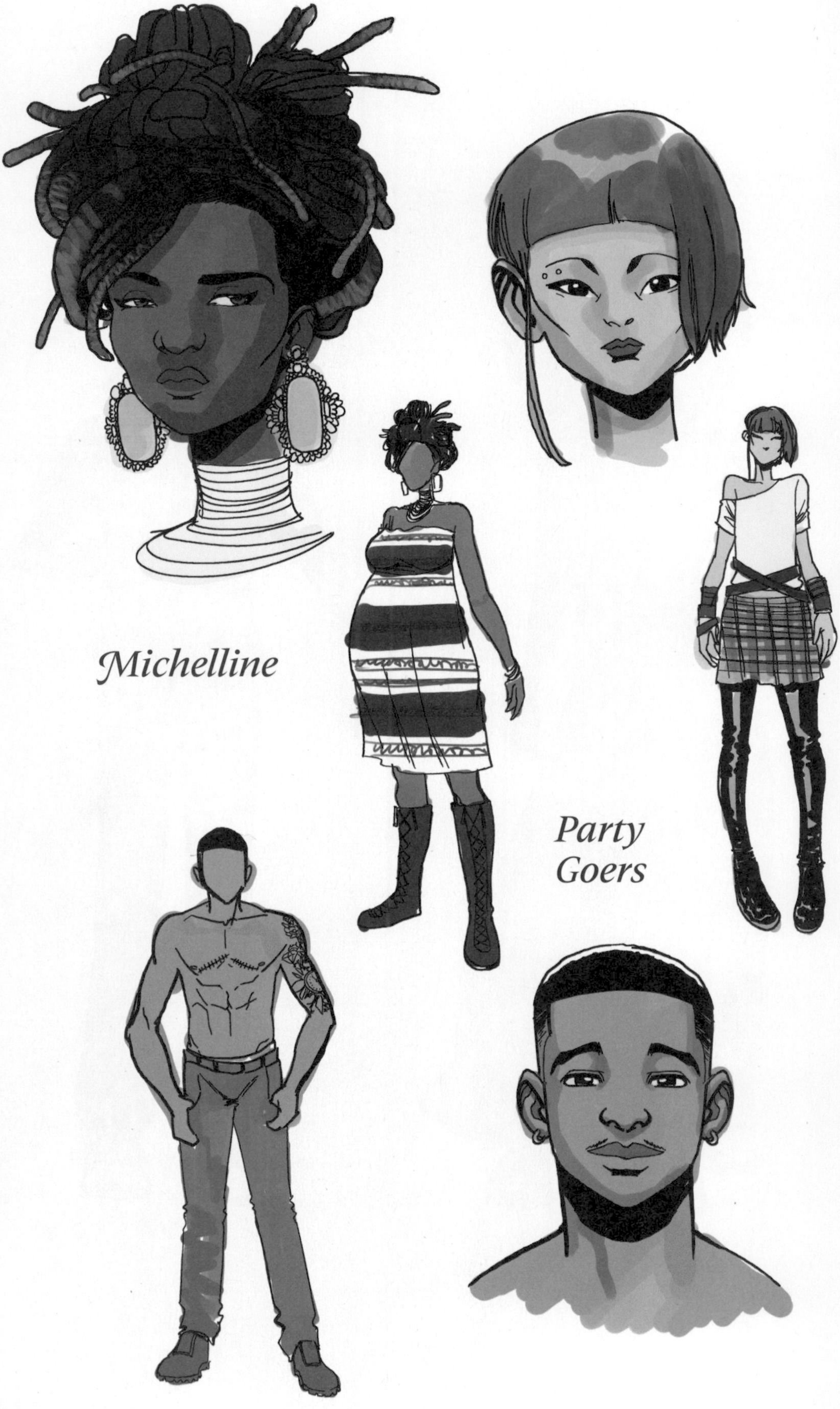
Michelline
Party Goers

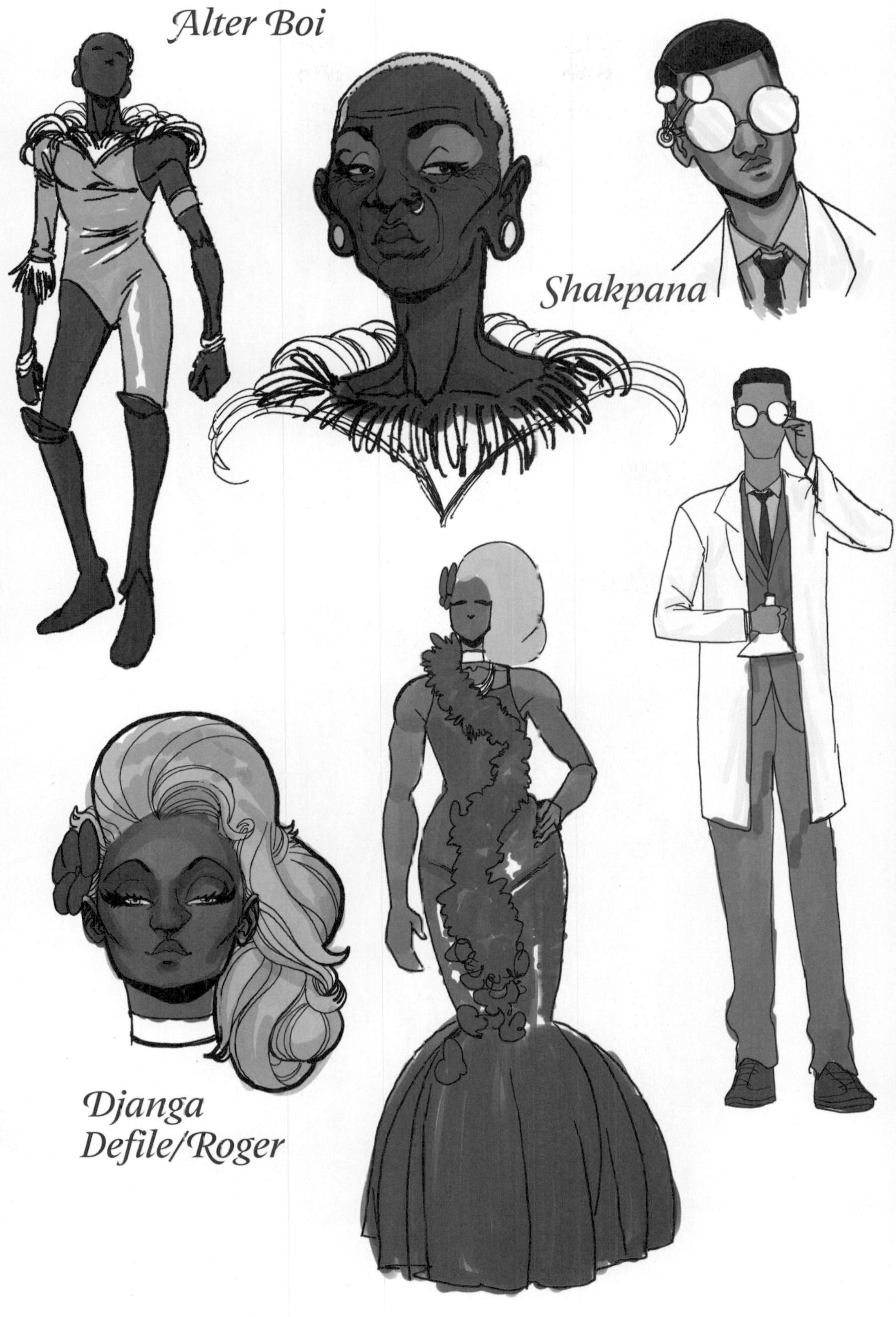
Alter Boi
Shakpana
Djanga
Defile/Roger

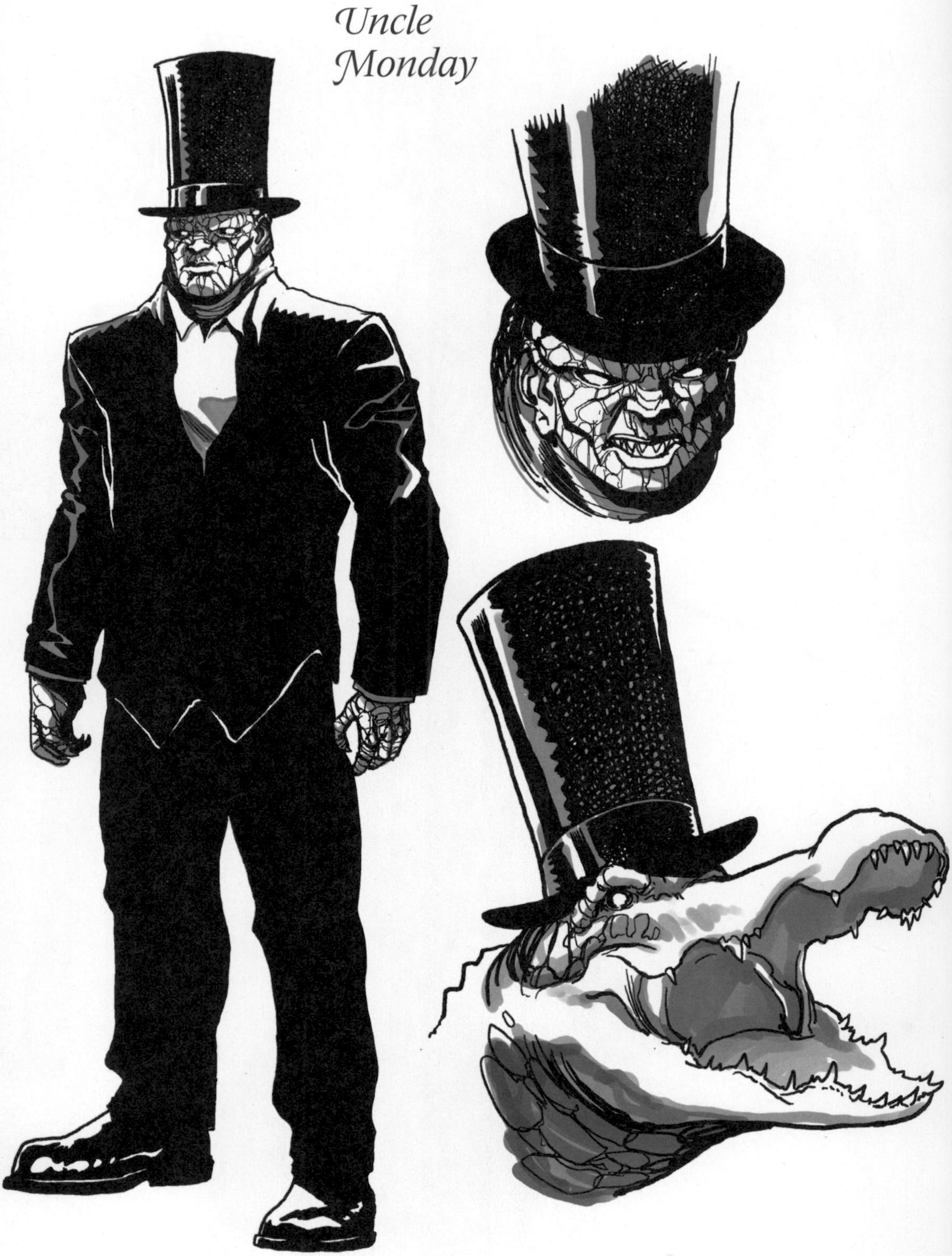
Uncle
Monday

ADDITIONAL UNCLE MONDAY CHARACTER STUDIES BY JOHN JENNINGS

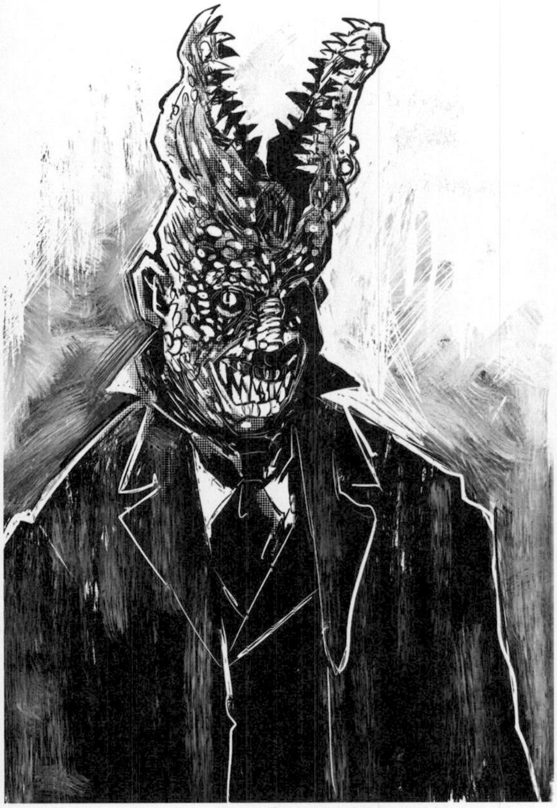

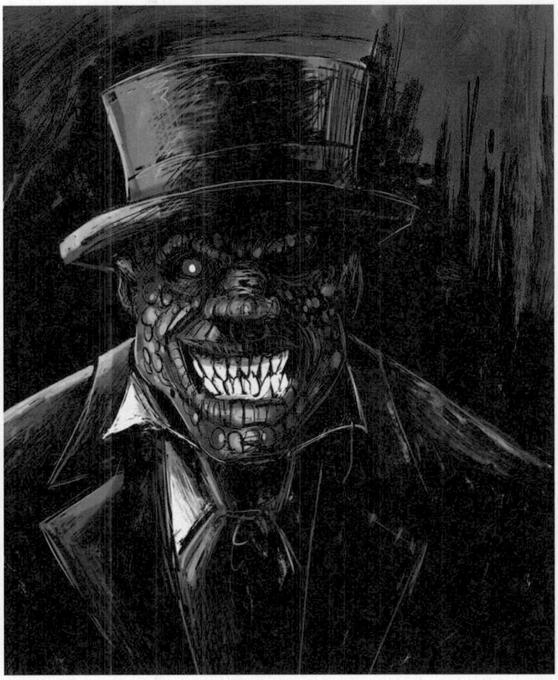

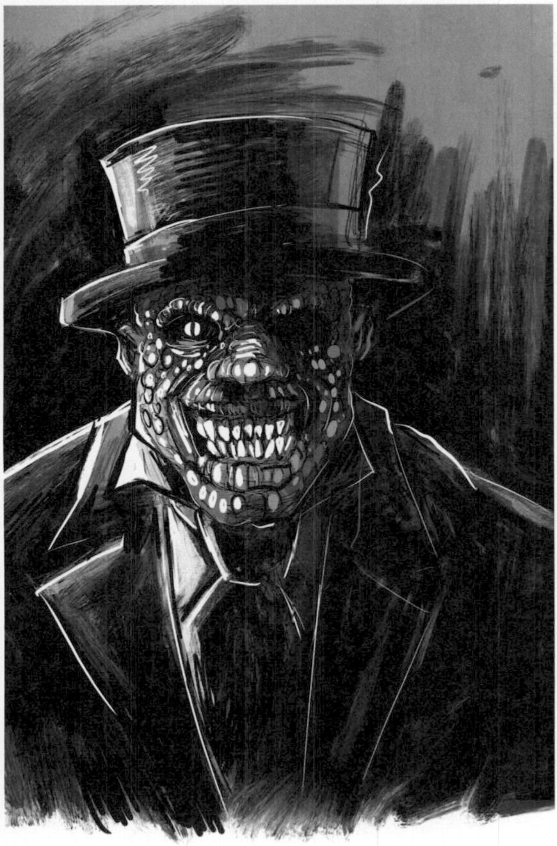

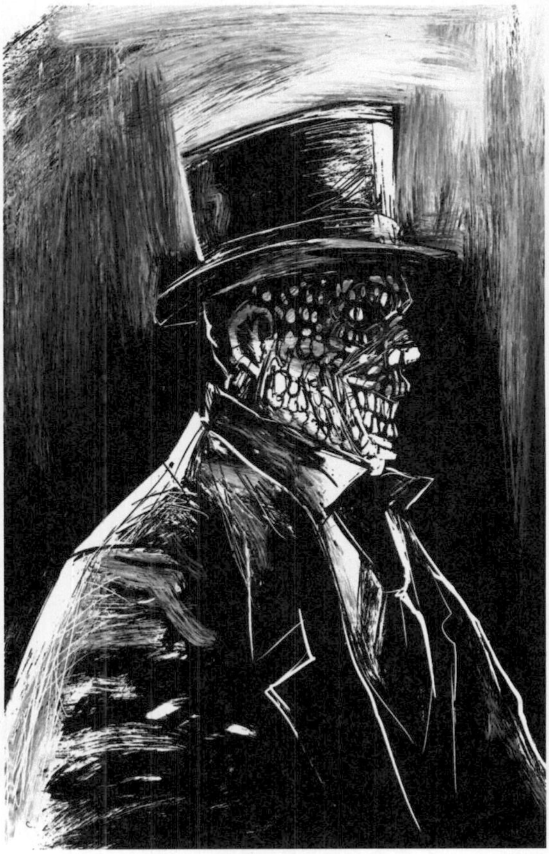

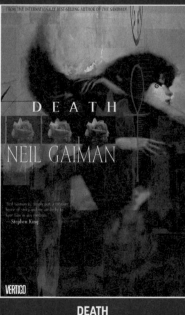